(continued . . .)

Also by Whitey Herzog

WHITE RAT (1987)

You're Missin' a Great Game

*From Casey to Ozzie, the
Magic of Baseball and How to
Get It Back*

Whitey Herzog

and Jonathan Pitts

BERKLEY BOOKS, NEW YORK

YOU'RE MISSIN' A GREAT GAME

A Berkley Book / published by arrangement with
Simon & Schuster, Inc.

PRINTING HISTORY
Simon & Schuster hardcover edition published in 1999
Berkley edition / March 2000

For information address:
Simon & Schuster, Inc.,
Rockefeller Center, 1230 Avenue of the Americas,
New York, New York 10020.

The Penguin Putnam Inc. World Wide Web site address is
http://www.penguinputnam.com

ISBN: 0-425-17475-1

BERKLEY®
Berkley Books are published by
The Berkley Publishing Group, a division of Penguin Putnam Inc.,
375 Hudson Street, New York, New York 10014.
BERKLEY and the "B" design
are trademarks belonging to Penguin Putnam Inc.

PRINTED IN THE UNITED STATES OF AMERICA

11   10   9   8   7   6   5   4   3   2

• Acknowledgments •

The authors wish to thank Steve Weinberg, for the constant encouragement that breathed life into this project; our wonderful agent, Faith Hamlin, who helped energize, sharpen, and dress this up for the folks in the Big City; the McIntyre Committee at the University of Missouri School of Journalism; Frank Scatoni, for his suggestions and logistical support; and our editor, Jeff Neuman, whose clarity amid adversity far exceeds that of his beloved Red Sox.

Heartfelt thanks, too, to Dawn Klingensmith, a perfect-pitch editor who should never work this cheap again; to Shelly Ossana, for her tolerance for ambiguity; to Mary Lou Herzog and to the entire Pitts family; and to Gary Smith and Bob Costas, exemplars of humane writing whose generosity of spirit, we hope, are a small part of this book.

And finally, with affection to Pearl Millner, the greatest Cardinal fan we know. She was really there, doing that snake dance downtown, when her Redbirds won the World Series in 1926. And she never stopped listening.

—JONATHAN M. PITTS

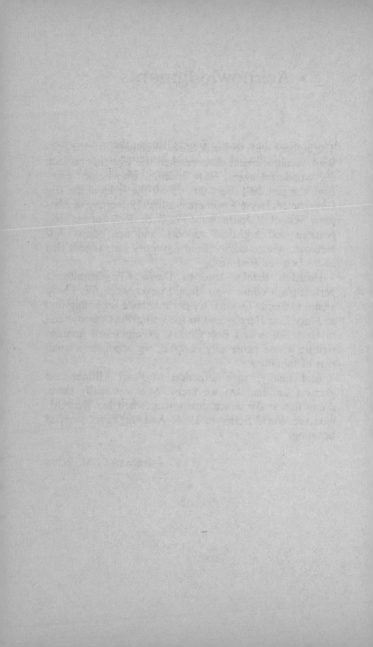

Behind every half-decent baseball man, there's a better one who took the risk of writing his name in the lineup for the first time. The fans don't get to see that first leap of faith, but it goes straight to the heart of the game.

This book is dedicated to the people who took that risk for me. To Vern Hoscheit and Harry Craft, who were like fathers to me in my early days with the Yankees. To Casey. To Lee MacPhail, Hank Peters, and Bing Devine, great baseball men who decided they saw talent in me, gave me a chance to shine, and showed me what real leadership means. To Joe McDonald, who was always my closest workin' buddy in baseball. And finally, to two great Americans, Gussie Busch and Gene Autry, who not only had the foresight to oppose salary arbitration, but whose genius for work and passion for the game will always resound through my life. And, I hope, through the Pastime's.

—WHITEY HERZOG
December 1998

• Contents •

Straighten It Out

If you came to my house in south St. Louis County, grabbed a beer out of my Anheuser-Busch refrigerator—it looks just like a six-foot can of Budweiser—and sat down for a cold one, you'd notice something in my den that I enjoy a hell of a lot more than beer. I've saved a good wool baseball cap from every big-league organization I ever worked for. They're hanging on pegs, all in a row, right across the top of my bar. The room is filled with stuff I love being around—black-and-white and color photos, plaques and pennants, drawings and lithographs, even uniforms I wore in my forty-plus-year career. Right on that wood-panelled wall is a picture of me with Casey Stengel—the first mentor I had in the big leagues, and the best—sitting on a Honda motorcycle. Casey scribbled something on there about me looking like Evel Knievel hurdling a canyon, but he spelled it 'hurtle;' the Perfesser never was too good with English. Above those glass doors is a shot of me in a rowboat with Jack Buck, the Hall of Fame broadcaster, spoofing *Jaws* in a Budweiser commercial everybody had a great time making. Everyone's on display here, from Ted Williams to Nolan Ryan to Harry Caray. It's a hell of a tour.

If there's anything I like most, it's the caps. There are, if you can believe it, ten of them.

By the time you finish hurtling through these reflections, you'll know what all those caps are, and there might even be one or two more before I'm through. They stand for a long life spent in a wonderful game—

traveling all over America, living in big cities and back-water towns, getting to know some of the damnedest people you could ever meet (including some of the craziest), matching wits with the best in the world at what you do year after year. They also stand for the different hats I've worn in the game—as a player, a scout, a coach, a development man, a manager, a general manager, and a front-office guy. Talk about ways to find out what you're made of; the game's been that to me and then some, and I don't give a damn if you're a CEO or a car mechanic, you can't ask much more of your profession than that.

I'll be honest with you: A lot of things about the big-league scene today make me want to throw up. (I've turned down so many managing offers since I retired in 1994 I can't keep track of them all. Most would have made me the highest-paid manager in the history of the major leagues—which is what I was when I left the St. Louis Cardinals in 1990—and top dollar for managers is three times what it was then.) But that doesn't change what a privilege it's been. I grew up a southern Illinois kid, worshipping that world from a long ways off—a New Athens wiseacre who skipped school to hitchhike to games in St. Louis and see some of the best talent in the major leagues. Times would change in ways I could have never seen coming, and I ended up making more money than Williams, DiMaggio or Musial probably ever dreamed of. Sitting here with a cool drink—I'm favoring Lite lately; I'm slimming down—a glance at those caps makes the hops and barley taste just that much sweeter.

Now, when I was first wearing that blue cap of the Kansas City Royals, I had an outfielder on my spring roster named Willie Wilson. If you're a baseball fan, you've heard of him: rangy kid, good speed, stole a lot of bases. Hit for a high average when I managed him. Willie is a good person, but when I first saw him in our rookie camp, he had himself a big problem: He thought he was a power hitter. He had size—he was 6-2, 6-3, weighed about 190—but I *still* don't understand what in the hell told him he had home-run pop in his bat. Even in the minors he hadn't gone deep much; the fly balls he hit just gave the outfielders a long way to run before the catch. Well, I watched Willie hit a few times, and it didn't take Connie Mack to figure out that swinging for the fences wasn't going to be *his* ticket to the Hall of Fame. He might hit his 12 homers, but the rest of the time he was going to make himself an out, kill our rallies, and put the Kansas City fans in a coma.

What Willie did have, though, was speed, and a home ballpark that favored speed. Royals Stadium—now called Kauffman Stadium or "the K," for my ex-boss, the late Royals owner Ewing Kauffman—had big dimensions, which made it even harder to hit the ball out, and fake turf that turned ground balls into states of emergency. With the wheels he had, if Willie'd just learn to switch-hit, beat the ball into the ground, and take off running, he'd be on base more often than Babe Ruth ate hot dogs. Now, even today, most *good* baseball people don't recognize what an edge it gives you just to get your guys on base, let alone speedsters like Willie. He doesn't *have* to hit home runs; just having him on base jacks up the odds you're going to score runs, and that raises the odds you'll win games. Then it becomes like compound interest: Game in and game out your edge adds up, and before you can say Jackie Robinson, you find your ass at the top of the standings.

One day in spring training I'd had enough, and I put it to him plain. I said, "Hey, man, do you want to play in Fort Myers all your life, or do you want to make it to the major leagues?" He looked a little put-upon, and I said, "I'll let you make that choice, but I'm gonna have Chuck Hiller in the cage tomorrow morning at eight o'clock"—Chuck was going to be his batting coach—"and if you want to learn to switch-hit, be here. If not, I don't give a damn." Let him try his Hank Aaron impersonation in Triple-A. I had a big-league team to run.

Boy, he didn't like that. Smoke was coming out of his ears. But next day, eight o'clock sharp, here comes Willie. He sets to work on grounders. A year later, his average jumps about a hundred points. Willie won a batting title, stole 83 bases one year, and led the league in hits and runs for an American League champion. The Royals played hard, heads-up ball, the kind I enjoy and that fans have always paid good money to see. They set Kansas City attendance records five years running. *That's* baseball like it oughta be.

I learned something important in Kansas City: Never finish second. We finished three games out in 1979, first time I hadn't won a division title in four years there, and just as I expected, old Ewing sacked my ass the minute the season was over. Well, a couple of years later, Willie figured he'd try the home-run thing again. It didn't work out too good. His run totals dropped, his hit totals fell, and he was never the same player. A manager's job is to look at the assets he's got, evaluate them, and get the most mileage out of them he can. In dealing with players, you have to ask yourself what each guy does best. Can this guy hit for power? Does that one have a good arm? You look at what each person does well and doesn't do well, then put him in situations that maximize his abilities. Don't ask him to do what he isn't good at; let him succeed with the talents he's got. He deserves that! It makes him feel a part of the team, it's good for the ballclub, it gets your different parts working together. It's also how you end up with a pennant in your back pocket and another year on your contract.

I'm leading things off with Willie because he reminds me of what's happening in baseball today. The game's had some good luck the last couple of years, like Mark McGwire's home-run chase with Sammy Sosa, which really has drawn a lot of fans and sparked interest. But it still has big problems—bigger than it has any idea. You and I could sit here all day and bullshit about what they are and how to fix them. We all know what some of them are. But I'm telling you, a lot of the biggest problems, baseball ain't even *talked* about yet. Not too far down the line, that's going to cost us in a very, very big way.

The reason major-league baseball is so hard for me to watch today, and the reason some fans have had a hard time figuring out whether they still enjoy it or not, is simple. It's like Willie. It's a singles hitter trying to go deep every time up. I've never seen such uniformly horseshit baseball, such a lack of understanding of how to play the game or run it. I can't stand looking at it any more than I could stand there and watch Willie fly out to the warning track day after day. A singles hitter trying to go deep is not only going to fail at what you already *knew* he couldn't do, he's also going to forget how to do what he's actually *good* at. A lot of what's passing for baseball today is about as fun to watch as Willie popping up with a runner on third.

My whole career tells me that people love baseball, when they do love it, because it shows them a good, fair test of ingenuity and skill. What made it satisfying up until fifteen or twenty years ago was that it was the fairest test in all of sports. Every team played the same schedule; after 154 or 162 games, when your ballclub finished on top and played in the World Series, you *knew* you had one of the two best teams. Fans knew it, too. When they saw the October Classic, they knew how much the clubs had gone through to get there. Those teams had put all their baseball knowhow together and used their resources the best. A whole year's worth of big leaguers fighting for victories and jobs had weeded out everybody that hadn't. The rules put excellence at center stage.

Over the past ten or twenty years, that's changed. The rules on the *field* haven't changed much; if you'd gone to a game forty years ago and came to one now, you'd still know what was going on, something you can't say for some other big-time sports. But the situation *off* the field has changed so drastically that it's affected every other facet of the game. And three very, very big things have gone wrong.

First, if Willie Wilson were playing today, he wouldn't have to listen to Whitey Herzog. He could try to stuff my ass in a clubhouse trash can and he'd still be making $4 million a year in the big leagues. That's how many more teams there are now, how many more jobs, how much less talent there is relative to demand. Second, only two teams used to get to the big dance at the end, but so many clubs get in the playoffs now that the fans don't know whether they're seeing the best. In some divisions, you can barely top .500 and you'll win; someday we'll have a division champ with a losing record. When I managed the Cardinals against the Minnesota Twins all the way back in the 1987 World Series, Minnesota had the *fifth*-best record in the American League. They won the Western Division, but four ballclubs in the East—all playing the same schedule as the Twins—had more victories. I said so in the papers at the time, and they gave me so much hell you'd have thought I shot the pope. All you had to do was look at the standings; I was just saying it like it is! What did it tell fans that not only did Minnesota get *in* the Series, but proceeded to kick our ass around that lunatic Homerdome, where you can't see a pop fly or hear it come off the bat? Excellence got whiffed. It's only gotten worse since.

Third, everybody in the big leagues today knows, before a single pitch is thrown, that the teams in the smaller markets—the Kansas Citys, Oaklands, Pittsburghs, and Montreals—have no chance of competing for a pennant anymore. It ain't going to happen. The fans know it, the writers know it, the players know it. Those teams' budgets—which only two years ago ranged from the Pirates' $9 million to maybe $20 million—can't get them enough quality big leaguers to be competitive. What's worse, the rules we have in place prevent those teams from improving themselves and getting back in the hunt. How the Pirates, A's and Expos do on the field, even if they play to the absolute best of their abilities, *makes no difference*. And the Atlanta Braves, with their $65 or $70 million payroll? They can play lousy baseball day in and day out (as I have seen them do) and *still* win their division by eight to ten games. It doesn't matter if your scouts are sharp or stupid, if your manager is Humpty Dumpty or the second coming of John McGraw. Brains, hustle, and good, sharp play—those don't matter. One thing matters and one thing only: *money*.

Don't believe me? Take a look at the last few World Series. Going back six or seven years now, I've never seen so many baserunning mistakes, botched throws, and mental screwups in my life. The showcase of the sport looks like eighteen monkeys making love to a football. If this is the best our game has to offer, why am I changing the channel to the NBA? And if the rules don't change, we'll never see a team in the big show again whose payroll isn't in the top five. That really came to pass in 1996, when the Braves ($65 million) and Yankees ($60 million) bought themselves a party. A year later the Florida (Blockbuster) Marlins got to play the big-budget Cleveland Indians. Both years, same thing: four-hour games, horseshit throws, teams kicking the ball all over the field. Somebody lost; that's all *that* proved.

Baseball's rules today don't promote what's best about the game: the fairness and integrity that give every team a chance to win if they use their abilities right. If there's no incentive to show the game respect, why should anybody? Would you? Good play is a lost art. Nobody's saying that or writing it anyplace, but I'm telling you, *that's* the biggest story in the sport. And unless we make some basic changes soon, it's going to get worse.

Things do look better than they did five years ago. In towns like Cleveland and Baltimore, where they have nice ballparks that respect the game's history, and where they can afford to pay for teams that are going to win, it's good. Players like Piazza, Griffey, McGwire, and Chipper Jones would have been standouts in any era. But you know what? I'm still thinking of that scene in the movie *Titanic:* The boat's clipped the iceberg, but nobody really knows it yet. The band's still playing, the chandeliers are up, the drinks are flowing. The man who built the ship checks the hull and tells everybody they're going to sink. They laugh it off. And before they know what hit 'em, they're all swimming in the North Atlantic.

I still see Willie Wilson sometimes, at banquets and reunions and so forth and, do you know, after all these years, that crazy sumbuck is still mad at me? God almighty, people are funny. He would never have made it to the big leagues his way! Well, if nobody talks to Willie now—I mean if we let baseball stay the way it is—it's going to keep swinging for the fences, popping up, killing rallies, and looking like hell. With a good manager, the game can be straightened out. But we have to get together, face the facts, and act before it's too late.

My profession is never going to solve its problems by shaking the ballparks with rock 'n' roll, juicing the ball, and bringing the fences in. All the 15–13 scores in the world ain't going to do it, and neither will letting every damn team with a winning record into the postseason. Beyond all the home-run hoopla we've been seeing, something else is going on: Lots of good fans are losing interest in the big leagues because it's a great game being played lousy—and managed even worse.

Baseball still teaches the same things it always did, when we're smart enough to know the game and manage it right. I say, let's stop handing today's Willie Wilsons millions a year for fouling up their swings, misunderstanding the sport, and driving away the fans. Let's get some of the money out of it and some of the brains back in. Let's motivate people to excel. Let's get the National Pastime back.

I'm not wearing any of those caps anymore, at least for now. For the past few years, I've made do with a khaki fishing hat, but I've seen the game through its biggest changes and from every possible angle. I'm like the good third-base coach on a close play: He knows the game, he can see all the action in front of him, he's in the right place to wave that runner home or hold him up. I can see how the parts all fit. There are other guys out there, too, baseball men who know a line drive from a luxury box, and maybe they'll join the conversation. If the genius lawyers and salesmen and tax collectors running the game now want to listen, they can. If not, let 'em enjoy their swim. It's gonna be cold.

A lot of players, parents, and fans across America have yelled the title of this book at the men in blue. "Hey, ump!" they'll holler, "You're missin' a great game back there!" Well, baseball itself is a little near-sighted right now, and there ain't any harm in riding it some. Maybe we can be the bench jockeys.

So have a beer, if you like, as we talk about what really makes this game the National Pastime. Meet everybody from Casey to the Splendid Splinter, from Tom Seaver to Ozzie Smith. Try on a few caps and see if they fit. Just do me a favor: When we're done, hang 'em back up on the wall. It's too much fun remembering how they got there in the first place.

Part One

Baseball Like It Oughta Be

• 1 •
Tra-la-la

I'll never forget the first spring training game in
1956, my rookie year. I had come up through the New
York Yankee organization, and we were about to play
the Dodgers in an exhibition down in St. Petersburg,
Florida. Mickey Mantle got sick before the ballgame,
and our manager, Casey Stengel, never one to do things
the hard way, decided not to change the whole lineup
around. He just crossed out Mickey's name and wrote
mine in the third spot: H-E-R-Z-O-G. Now, I had no
more business hitting third for the great New York Yankees than the hot-dog vendor in Section C, but I wasn't
going to pull Mr. Stengel aside and say, "I don't know
if I'm ready, Sir." He was a legend. The Yankees were
a legend. It was one of those times you just sharpen up
your spikes, take your best shot, and live with the consequences.

Well, Carl Erskine was pitching for the Dodgers that
day, and he was known throughout baseball for a breaking ball that swooped down on you like a falcon on a
chipmunk. In those days, they threw you the curve till
you proved you could hit it—which I can tell you flat-
out, I hadn't—so it didn't take a genius to know what
was coming down the pipe. My first time up, Carl broke
off a hammer on a 3–2 count—snapped the damn thing
right off—and I took it for strike three. Never even
moved the bat. Welcome to the big show.

Next time I come up, my ass is still a little red, and

3

this time the bases are loaded and the game's on the line. And I'm getting ready to leave the dugout, swinging my two bats a little bit, when Stengel summons me over to him. For some reason I still don't understand, Casey was always singling me out for special instruction, and I still had no idea what to make of it, or him. "Hey, Doctor, c'mere a second," he says. He grabs me by the flannel and looks me in the eye, and I look up into that wrinkled old mug of his, and he says, "Just go up there and tra-la-laaaahhhh."

I don't know if I've heard him right. I say, "What?" He says, "Doctor, just go up there and tra-la-laaahhhh." And he walks away.

Now I'm standing there, a major-league game between the Yankees and the Dodgers on the line, and I'm thinking, *What in the hell is this guy talkin' about? Am I in St. Pete or on Mars?* I mean, the wheels are spinning fast. I'm picturing myself going up to home plate and dancing a jig, but that image goes kind of blurry. The game won't wait for you to figure it all out. So I just take my bat up there and dig in, and I'm back to my own thoughts: *Bases loaded, okay, he got me with the hook last time. He's going to try to get ahead of me and spin me another one.* And sure enough, I get behind in the count, and I'm sitting on the curveball, and here comes a big banana, bending downward, and my eyes light up. I swing hard and clean, and I'm telling you, I clocked it—a line drive like I never hit before. A game-winner for sure.

Well, Charlie Neal's at second—I'm left-handed, and I pulled it—and he jumps up, spears the damn thing, and turns it into a double play. Inning's over!

In my game, a thin line divides the heroes from the screwups, and as I'm standing there in the batter's box, it ain't hard to figure out which side my ass is firmly planted on. I head back to the dugout, and there's Casey looking at me. He's got a little bit of a smile, almost like he's having himself one hell of a fine time, and he puts a big hand on my shoulder. I look into that creased-up face, and he says, "See what I told you, Doctor? Just tra-la-la." And he wanders off, shaking his head.

A great teacher leaves you to translate for yourself, and Casey, with that mumbo jumbo of his, sure fit that bill. At the moment, all I'm thinking about is that I damn near knocked in some runs and won the game, but now I've got this to chew on, too. As I'm trotting out to center field, still turning it over in my mind—maybe it was then, maybe later; it's hard to know—it comes to me. Sometimes it really is better just to go up there and relax. Swing easy, put it in play. It's what the big power hitters tell you: It's when they ain't *trying* for homers that the ball jumps out of the park. Just meet it and let something happen. *Tra-la-la*.

As time passed in my career, I realized Casey had left my mind full of nuggets like that: little ideas on fielding, hitting, approaches to baseball, every one of 'em essential to understanding it right and clean as a well-hit ball. It's still for bigger minds than mine to understand how a man can invent his own language, or why he might think to do it in the first place, but Casey did. And I finally figured out that spring that even though I had no idea what the hell he was talking about half the time, when Casey Stengel came up to me and started spewing that "Stengelese," he was offering me an education. I turned into a world-class translator, boy, and it's a good thing: If I hadn't been, my life would have turned out a whole lot different.

I first met Casey in 1955, when I came to the early camp with the Yankees that they used to call rookie school. I was a young centerfielder, and I was full of piss and vinegar and other nasty concoctions. The Yankees had given me a bigger signing bonus than they'd given that kid from Oklahoma, Mr. Mantle, and I figured that was about right. I had good speed and a strong bat, I knew the game, I was a hell of a handsome devil, and I knew I was bound to be a big-league ballplayer and a big shot or go broke trying. Yankee Stadium seemed like as good a place as any. Even though I grew up in a little Illinois town not forty miles from St. Louis—the heart of Cardinals territory—the Yanks had always been the team I dreamed about, the one I wanted to play for. I don't know if young players today have a clue how the very idea of Yankee Stadium, with its facade and monuments and history, used to mesmerize anybody who gave a damn about the game, but it did. That's me: only the best. Well, I'd taken the bus with a buddy of mine to Branson, Missouri in 1949—back then, they had a lot more trees than they had theaters—and, after a tryout there, signed a minor-league contract. I got to rookie school six years later.

My first impressions of Casey were like a lot of other people's. He looked like maybe he'd just combed the straw out of his hair. His ears were so damn big that if they'd had jumbo jets back then, he'd have slowed 'em to a crawl. So much doubletalk flowed out of his craw you weren't sure his parents had raised him in English. That, plus the fact he later happened to manage some of the most talented teams ever assembled, still has people in baseball thinking Casey was some clown who fell asleep on a turnip truck and woke up one day in the Hall of Fame. How was I supposed to realize I was looking at the most intelligent man I'd ever know?

Casey ran that camp like an old schoolmaster, hammering away at the sport's little details that, as I learned, make the difference between winning and losing games, between a good club and a great one. Like the best teachers, he gave you the big picture in little doses, and he was flashing 'em to you all the time, like a good catcher with his signs. If you were smart and gave it enough thought, you learned them all and eventually saw how they fit together. That's the same as saying you learned baseball. I became a good manager in my time, and I hope a pretty good baseball man, and I can tell you right now that what Casey taught that spring, I used my entire career. I still do.

It was amazing how he talked to you. You're heading out to hit: "Butcher-boy, butcher-boy," he'd say. You're thinking, "What?" Well, he wants you to fake a bunt and chop it on the ground, see? Get it through the infield and get on base. Surprise 'em a little. Nobody'd ever used that term before. Or you're standing on second base in practice, minding your own business, maybe thinking just how wonderful it is that you got there in the first place, and suddenly he's behind you: "You're important to me, young fella; you're half a run." One day he comes up to me, jabs me with a finger and says, "I'm gonna tell you one thing; never worry about gettin' fired, 'cause if you don't own the ballclub or die on the job, it's gonna happen." He was talking about managing. I don't know why he picked me to say that to—I was just a wiseass kid—but when I took up that line of work myself years later, I never forgot those words. First of all, they were a kind of history lesson: Connie Mack had managed the Philadelphia Athletics for fifty years, a record that's going to stand forever. Why? The man owned the team. His job evaluations were pretty good. But more than that, Casey was right: You only control so much in this game, so why worry about it? Remembering that frees up your mind so you can do your job the right way.

Casey invented the whole idea of rookie school, just as he was the guy who invented the fall instructional leagues we have today. The Yankees would take their top prospects down to Florida for two weeks before the major-league camp opened, then invite some of them to stay on at the big camp. Rookie school. I'll never forget my first time there.

On the first day, Casey stood in front of us, leaning on a fungo bat, and explained what he tried to do as manager. He said it like this: "Mr. Lopez has a team over there in Cleveland that's pretty good"—he was talking about Al Lopez, the Indians' manager, and they had a damn good team—"and he's got them good pitchers over there, and I know they're gonna win 92 games. And I think about it, and I've got Mr. Raschi, Mr. Reynolds, and Mr. Page"—he meant Vic Raschi, Allie Reynolds, and Joe Page, three of his outstanding pitchers—"and I think that we can win 92 games. And now I've gotta figure out how I can win three more. And so I'm gonna hit this ball against that wall, and I'm going to teach you how to get it off the wall," and then how to do this and that other little thing that could win you those extra games. That's what he taught; he always said the other guy's team had the ability to win 92 games, and *we've* got the ability, so we've got to try and win three more. That was the approach he took.

And Casey broke it down into the hundred little things that would make the difference. He was going to have his team get from third to home faster than the other team by getting a better jump off third base. He was going to teach you how to take the proper lead off the bases—not "the right way" or "the wrong way," but the Stengel way, the way he wanted it done—so you'd have that little edge. He kept drilling you on those things and drilling you till you could practically do them in your sleep. Once I began coaching and managing, I kept passing them along to my own players, to everybody from the youngest rookie-league bushwhackers to the George Bretts, Ozzie Smiths, and Vince Colemans of the world. To this day, if I went by the park to watch my grandkids play and the coach asked me to help with their baserunning, I would show them Casey's way, how Casey wanted it done.

What he was showing you was that baseball, when it's played right, is made up of a lot of smaller plays, and each one gives you an edge if you work at it. It's also a game of large samples: Over 154 or 162 games, the little things accumulate and pile up and turn into big ones. That's the game's most essential fact. It's a game of percentages, and any way you can tilt the wheel your way a little, you do. Casey tilted it one degree here, another one there, till the ball just seemed to roll the Yankees' way and you looked up in August and saw New York right where they always seemed to be, at the top of the standings looking down. Writers and fans hardly ever notice these little things, and you hardly ever hear anybody mention 'em, but they decide championships. No good club ever won a thing without 'em.

Take baserunning. Today, people think of it in terms of stolen bases alone, but that's bull, and Casey understood that. He was passionate on the subject to the point of being a nut, and he taught it better than anybody I ever saw. Thinking ahead was part of it. He told you to check out the defense before you came to bat; instead of looking at the girls in the stands when you were on deck—something ballplayers have always been tempted to do—look at the outfielders. The leftfielder, for example. Does he throw left-handed? If he does, you've got an edge. If you hit it right down the line, you know he has to turn his back to the diamond to pick it up. To throw to second, he has to turn back around and come across his body with the ball. That gives you a little extra time, and it means if you hustle a little bit, you can turn a single into a double. Same thing if the rightfielder is right-handed. Play in and play out, the Yankees made hay out of situations like that. They could run the bases like nobody else—not *steal* bases, *run* 'em—and it added up to runs, and runs added up to leads, and leads added up to those three extra wins Casey wanted.

On defense, too, the little things counted. Say the Indians have a guy on first. Then let's say the next batter gets a base hit to right. Now: The rightfielder wants to come up throwing so he can hold that lead runner at second. That way, he'll keep a force play in effect. You or I would think in terms of which base to throw it to: Do I go to second or third? Well, Casey would say, "Never throw to the wrong base, keep the double play in order." But he took it a step further. On relay throws, he talked about which *side* of the fielder to throw it on. In his mind, it was easier for a fielder to move fifteen feet to his glove side (his left) than to move one foot to his right on a relay. That way, he could glove that ball out of the air, turn, and fire in one motion. But if it's to his throwing (right) side, he's got to reach across, catch it, and turn awkwardly across his body before he throws. A good runner takes advantage of that every time, and that might mean a run, an extended inning, a game. For the Yankees, Casey made it automatic: *Never throw to a shortstop or second baseman's right.* I'd never seen a manager take the time to explain it like that, and I never would again.

On the offensive side, Casey didn't just holler at you to score runs; he taught you how. During batting practice, after you'd hit, he made you stay on the bases when the next guy came up. He'd drill you on your jumps off the bag. As you know, when you're on third, if the batter puts it in the air, you can't leave till the ball is caught; on a grounder, you can take off right away. Casey pounded the difference into your head. On contact, you practiced your jump. Fly ball, *back*; ground ball, *go!* You did it again and again till you got so damn good at it you could watch the flight of the ball from the pitcher's hand and know before the hitter swung if it'd be on the ground or not. In games, if Casey had the "go" threat on, you scored. Years later, Gene Mauch, one of my American League managing rivals, asked me, "How come your teams get from third to home faster than anybody I ever saw?" I told him, "We work at it." I never told him *how* we worked at it. It ain't my fault he never went to camp with Casey.

I ended up in a lot of camps with good managers— the Harry Crafts, the Charlie Dressens, the Paul Richards—and no one else ever broke the game down the way Casey did. When I think back, it was like learning physics: The field is ruled by properties you can't see, but those properties make everything happen that you *can* see. Only the best teachers know the laws and have the sense to make them clear to the young and the brainless. In Casey, I had an Einstein.

History tells us Casey won 1,905 ballgames, and that his Yankees won ten World Series championships in a twelve-year span. Nobody will ever do that again, not in this age of free agency and the draft. But the thing is, he's still never gotten his due. When George Weiss, the Yankee GM, first brought him in to replace Bucky Harris in 1949, everybody in New York and around baseball thought it was a joke. Here was this backwoods clown who'd managed for years in the big leagues—with the Boston Braves and Brooklyn Dodgers, truly terrible teams—and had a record so far below .500 nobody ever thought he'd see the light of day. A guy so bumbling he'd been exiled to Oakland for five years, where he managed in the Pacific Coast League in the prime of his career. Add the fact that he jabbered like some lunatic bumpkin who fell off a hay wagon, and the writers were laughing their asses off before he ever got to Yankee Stadium. They figured they'd get a real manager soon.

Well, don't believe everything you hear. Most people didn't know baseball then, just like they don't now, but Casey knew exactly what he was doing. For one thing, you should've seen the players he'd had with the Braves and Giants. I mean, you can't make chicken salad out of chicken shit; I don't care if you're the Galloping Gourmet. It reminds me of what happened to Jim Riggleman and the Cubs in '97, when they set a record by losing their first 14 games and never crawled out of that hole. I felt sorry for Riggleman. He kept putting Mel Rojas into games. They'd just gotten the guy from the Expos, big free-agent deal. I called him up and said, "Rig, I wouldn't put him in the game with a *five*-run lead! Oh, my—he's gonna get your ass fired!" He started laughing. I said, "I only called you 'cause I like you, but you keep putting him in there, you're gonna be looking for a job!" But if you've traded for a guy who's been a great relief pitcher, and if he goes bad, you say, "Well, we ain't going to win if he doesn't do the job we expected him to do." So you keep strapping him out there, and you keep losing, and the next thing you know, you're fired! The worst thing that can happen to a manager is if your closer goes in a slump. That gets you dumb in a hurry.

With Casey, his first couple years with New York, the talent he had was mediocre, yet he still found a way to win. Injuries *killed* them his first two seasons. DiMaggio missed a lot of games and had to be replaced—one year by a rookie from Joplin, Mantle, who was still plenty raw. In fact, the Yankees weren't favored to win the pennant in any of the first five years they went to the World Series under Stengel. Casey didn't always have the best damn team in that league.

All that time, from the early days on, Casey was learning. And he always knew the basic thing: Baseball is supposed to be a hell of a good time. That's smarter than you think. One day in Pittsburgh, the fans are booing him when he comes to the plate. So he takes some action. In a big sweeping motion, he bows at the waist and doffs his cap. Big deal, right? Well, you know what happens? A bird flies out. All of a sudden they're cheering and rolling in the aisles. They thought Casey was out of his mind. People say that story's a myth, but I *knew* the man, and I'm telling you, that's the truth. He was a showman, boy, a carnival barker; he knew if you kept 'em laughing, they'd forget how rotten your team was and keep coming to the ballpark. When you were around Casey Stengel, you had a good time or died trying.

Casey's father was a Kansas City dentist, and Casey himself went to dental school. That takes some skullwork. He was going to follow in dad's footsteps, in fact, but it's probably a good thing he didn't. I say that not only because Casey was a hell of a hitter and a ball-player, but because he knew that, in baseball anyway, you could *think* too much for your own good. One time when he was managing the Mets in '62—the worst team that ever played—his pitcher gave up a couple hits in a row, so they needed to get somebody up in the bullpen. Casey snatched up the phone and called down there, and everybody heard him holler, "Get Miller up!" Pitching coach said, "Okay." Well, as it happened, Casey had two pitchers on his staff named Miller. Both of 'em were *Bob* Miller, as a matter of fact: One was a right-hander, one a left-hander. A couple moments later, the phone was ringing. It was the coach. "Hey, Casey, which Miller you want?" You know what Stengel told him? Two words: "Surprise me!" Can you believe that? *Surprise* him. This sonofagun's in the Hall of Fame!

You'd think that kind of thing would cause chaos, but in baseball it can work. This game drops worries on you that can haunt you twenty-four hours a day—*What if I move my foot back a little? What did he throw me on 2-2 last week?*—and if you let them, they'll drive you up the wall. Like I told the Jack Clarks and Darrell Porters years later, squeeze the bat too hard, you get saw-dust. Having a laugh ain't a sidelight in baseball; it's essential. That's why so many good baseball people can tell a hell of a joke. They might change the details on you from one time to the next, but every time you hear that story, man, if it makes you laugh, it's true.

Stengel made that part of his life. He thrived on stay-ing up, talking with the writers till four in the morning night after night. I never saw anybody, even the legen-dary Mantle, who could drink like Casey; he was *strong*, that man. He'd keep 'em laughing and spewing their food and clapping him on the back all night. Like he said, "Give 'em your own story, 'cause if you don't, they're just gonna go ahead and make up their own, and what good'll that do ya?" Then he'd reel off some more whoppers. Then there was his other motto for dealing with the press: "When they ask you a question," he said, "answer it and just keep on talkin'. That way they can't ask you another one." He had a hell of a good time, but if you paid attention, you knew you were looking at a man who was running the show his way.

That was just part of handling the press. When I became a manager, I was like Casey: I really enjoyed the print media, the writers that followed us for the whole season. It was the TV people who pissed me off. They'd show up at the end of the year—guys we ain't seen all season—jamming microphones in my face while I'm trying to eat a ham sandwich, asking the dumbest damn questions: "How's the chemistry on the ballclub right now?" "Is this a do-or-die series?" Chemistry and do-or-die, my ass. Like Casey told me, the newspaper guy can edit out a well-timed "sonofabitch" whenever he wants, but you can't erase it from film. So maybe you let one slip: "I don't know how that fuckin' McGee does it, Ronnie, do you?" "Sonofabitch really got them out of a jam, didn't he?" Or what if they're filming me and I scratch myself in some disagreeable spot? Think they're going to show that on the eleven o'clock news? Most of the time, dealing with the press is a kick, but sometimes you have to train people to treat you right. Casey did.

Being dense was Casey's brand of genius. He had trouble with names: he'd call you doctor, or the fella from Cleveland, or No. 39 if that was on the back of your shirt, or whatever else stuck in his mind. That was all he could remember. Before one Opening Day with the Mets, he's in the clubhouse introducing his starting lineup, and he says, "I've got the guy from Philadelphia"—he was talking about the late Richie Ashburn, who'd played for the Phillies for years and is now in the Hall of Fame—"and I got the guy from Minnesota," and so on down the line till he gets to the bottom of the order. He arrives at the spot for his rightfielder, but he can't think of who it is. So he just keeps rambling on—

he'd just talk till something came to him; it was how he lubricated his brain—and everybody's bent over trying not to laugh, because they know damn well Casey just can't think of the guy's name.

There was a buzzer in the clubhouse that sounded when it was time to take the field. Finally it goes off, and it was like a bell to him. And it comes to him; that's the guy: *Gus Bell*. "And my starting rightfielder is Mr. Bell." Everybody's jaw dropped. Casey was so clueless the answers just dropped out of the sky.

No question Casey was a great manager, a great mind, the greatest spokesman baseball ever had; definitely the favorite manager of the writers everywhere. But I used to think he'd almost lose a few games on purpose just to keep the race close, so they'd draw more people. Once I saw him fall asleep on the bench. I was with the Senators. Whitey Ford was pitching, and he was sailing along with a 2–1 lead, and I swear Casey nodded off! We could see it from our dugout. Well, we got five straight hits and he still didn't have anybody warming up. Finally, Frank Crosetti woke his ass up, and he got somebody up in the bullpen. I think they beat us 18 out of 22 that year; that was one of the games we won.

Well, as I said, I still don't know why Casey singled me out as his bobo. After all, that field was full of great ballplayers: Mantle, Yogi Berra, Hank Bauer, Joe Collins, Johnny Mize. It was like a wing of the Hall of Fame. He just seemed to like me. Or maybe it was just that he'd had a third baseman, Buck Herzog, with the Giants a few years back, and was glad he could remember the damn name. Maybe he just realized I was listening to him; a good teacher does like to have a good student. I doubt if he realized I would be a manager someday, but since he always knew more than he let on—not to mention more than you did—who knows? All I know is that even after he shipped my ass to the Senators—"Have a good year over there and I'll get you back," he said, though neither of us held up our end of the bargain—Casey always saw fit, whenever the Yankees came to my hometown, to seek me out at the batting cage, stand me in front of him, and shoot the shit. Later on, when I was a Mets coach in the mid-sixties and he still was a consultant with the team, he'd even wander over when I was running minor-league camp, pull up a chair while I was hitting ground balls, and go on and on about this kid or that one. He'd keep me from doing my work! But I'll be damned if I was ever dumb enough to run him off the field. I never stopped picking his brain.

Well, I'll never forget the day in 1975, when Casey was eighty-five and retired, and he drove all the way down to Anaheim Stadium from his home in Glendale. That's about a ninety-minute drive. I was an Angels coach at the time, under Dick Williams, and Casey and I sat in the dugout for a couple of hours and slung the bull about Nolan Ryan, Bill Singer, Frank Tanana, and our other pitchers. Frankly, he didn't like some of 'em too good. We said goodbye.

A month later, he was dead. Baseball hasn't been the same since, and you know what? I haven't either.

Casey had the basics hard-wired into his brain: The game's fun; human beings play it; baseball is a craft; the better you do, the more fun you have, and vice versa. These are the ABC's of my game, and Casey Stengel lived 'em to the hilt every day. That's what made him the best ambassador baseball ever had. Too bad the game, with the billions running through it today, has forgotten every last one of them.

Screwed-up as the big-league scene has been over the last several years, that man might make a difference even today. It's hard to say. I *can* tell you that if you'd seen the Runnin' Redbirds—my Cardinal teams of the eighties—and didn't know any more about it, you'd be surprised as hell to learn the Perfesser was my mentor. After all, he ran the mighty Yankees, the swaggering sluggers every kid worshipped: Yogi, Mantle, Roger

Maris. They had thunder in those bats. My teams stole bases and couldn't hit the ball out in batting practice. His guys shattered home run records; mine tried to tie Roger's mark of 61 each year—as a *team*. But what people don't realize is that those New York teams, as many balls as they mashed off the Yankee Stadium facade, weren't primarily a home-run ballclub. They based their dynasty on being the best defensive team and best baserunning team in the league. Like all great clubs, Casey's Yanks understood something our game has just about forgotten: that baseball, more than anything else, is a game of intelligence, craft, and doing the little things right.

· 2 ·
The Hub Factor

There's a lot to learn in baseball, from hitting to throwing to running the bases right, but when I was still an active player, *my* Achilles' heel was a pitch that gave me nightmares: that big, slow, nasty curve. I'm sixty-seven years old, and I'll tell you something—I *still* see that thing in my sleep.

In the minors, it didn't matter that much. I was in the bushes for four years, starting in Macalester, Oklahoma, in 1952 and including a season at Triple-A Denver where I had some real good numbers in that mountain air where the ball didn't bend too much. At that level, very few pitchers can throw the curve for strikes anyway, especially if they're behind in the count. You didn't see a lot of curveballs on 2–0 or 3–1; guys who could throw those moved up. No, you knew you were going to get the heater, so you could sit back, wait for it, and fatten up. That's what I did in 1955, and even if the numbers were a little deceptive—I hit 22 home runs and led the league in RBIs through July—it made for a hell of a pinball game in the Rockies.

In the major leagues, man, it was different. Every guy had a slow curve he could throw for a strike whenever he wanted. You could see it at any time. If they saw you couldn't hit one, that was all you got from *anybody* till you showed you could handle it. You had to face it head-on and learn. When I look back now at the year I came up, I don't even know if I was ready for the ma-

18

jors; another year in Denver might have helped me stop
lunging at the ball, a bad habit I never totally got rid of.
But at the time, I had one big problem to think about: I
was an American Leaguer now, and pitchers like Whitey
Ford, Herb Score, and Ray Narleski were lurking out
there, making their money picking yokels like me apart.

All I can say is, thank God for good teachers.

I bet you've heard of Johnny Sain, the great righthander, and that famous rhyme: "Spahn and Sain and pray
for rain." In the late forties, the Boston Braves' staff was
so thin they had to rely on those two great pitchers to
carry 'em through the whole season. Well, by 1955,
John's career was coming to an end with the Kansas City
A's. A few years later, Harry Craft hired him as the A's
pitching coach, and I had just been traded from Washington to Kansas City—another one of those wonderful
breaks you have no control over, but that end up changing your life.

Mr. Sain, a curveball-throwing fool if there ever was
one, was also a hell of a good old Arkansas boy, and he
came up to me one day that spring and said, "I hear
you're having trouble with the slow curve." I allowed
as how there were rumors to that effect, and John said,
"Well, if you don't mind staying after practice, any day
that I've got a little bit left, I'd be glad to throw to you."
Man, did I oblige. That one exhibition season, John must
have kept me after practice fifteen times, and he threw
me nothing but curveballs—slow curves, biting curves,
curves in the dirt, changing speeds on curves. Once I'd
seen enough of the damn things, I began to get a feel
for 'em. I learned to lay back on that pitch, how to look
for it, how to rip it or take it to the opposite field. I
never had a better feeling than when I started stroking
them around the yard off old John Sain.

As far as the whole American League knew, I was
still differently abled in that area, so curveballs were all
I saw for the first couple of weeks that year. I had a hell
of a time. I started off the season 36 for 90—a .400

average—and was hitting some nasty line drives all over the ballpark. God almighty, it's a kick to shock people. I rode an 11-game hitting streak into Cleveland, which had a pitching staff that paralyzed the best hitters in the league, and I had to face their aces, Mike Garcia and Early Wynn and Bob Lemon. I'll be damned if I didn't get a hit in every one of those games. Well, pretty soon, the pitchers and managers were saying, "Hey, that son-ofabitch can *hit* that." They started pitching me different, mixing things up a little bit. That alone was a feat, forcing them to adjust to *my* ass for a change. But I became a better hitter.

When I broke into the majors, it was tough, boy—a different scene than today. It was the middle fifties, and we fought for jobs like mongrels over scraps of fat. Think about it. There were fifty-some minor leagues at the time, all feeding two major leagues. There were only sixteen big-league teams, about half what you have now. The New York Yankees alone had twenty-three farm clubs in their system; the Cardinals and the Dodgers had twenty-six apiece. Multiply it out: That's about 14,000 paid ballplayers all told, each and every one of them with his eye on the 400 or so jobs available in the major leagues. That's a one in thirty-three chance of ever digging into a big-league batter's box.

You didn't get there by accident. You worked your way up slow, building your game one piece at a time, proving a little more at each level. Ninety-five percent of the guys who played in the big leagues had been in the minors for five years or more. Boy, when I look back and remember guys I played against in the Texas League, the American Association and the International League who never got a chance to play in the big leagues, it's amazing. Eddie Knoblauch—the uncle of Chuck, who's currently the Yankees' second baseman—played for years and years in the Texas League, and he was a *hell* of a player. He'd be hauling down $3 or $4 million a year today. But if you did beat the odds and get a shot, you'd better not have any holes. If you did, they'd root it out, beat you black and blue with it and run your ass back to the minor leagues.

Myself, I didn't aim to find out firsthand. I felt like a star, and I planned to be one. I could hit some, and with power. I had a good arm; I could field. Most of all, I could run like hell. When I was still with the Yankees, I ran races against Mickey Mantle in the outfield—he was a buddy of mine—and always kept pace with him for sixty yards before he pulled away. Very few guys can say *that* with a straight face. Hell, *I'd* be making $2.5 million in the big leagues today—$4 million if I was in Denver.

But you know what? After that hitting streak, I never got the lightning back. I eventually realized that if I made it, it would be as a pinch-running, off-the-bench, platoon-type guy. It was tough to face, but I had to be realistic. And it changed my goal: I just wanted to hang on five years and get my major-league pension. Hell, it was a privilege just to *be* in the big leagues, let alone getting rich and making All-Star teams. That $250 a month for life—beginning at age fifty—sounded pretty damn fine to me.

Well, I got the pension. But if Johnny Sain hadn't stayed after school and slung me those Uncle Charlies, I never would have. I'd have never hung on for the eight years I did. I'd have never been around to scout for the A's. I'd have never run the Mets' minor-league system for seven years, never managed in the majors, never taken six Missouri teams into the playoffs and three to the World Series. I'd have never made half a million dollars a year. Ozzie Smith might still be a San Diego Padre. And nobody, including you, would be reading this book, because I'd never have written it.

There's a lot to like about baseball, but the media say very little about the part I like best. You hear about money, contracts, greedy owners, and selfish players; you hear people talk about baseball like it's a thing:

"baseball should do this, baseball should do that." But one fact ain't changed. Wherever you've got good baseball, good people are at the heart of it—good teachers. They might have different styles; they might know different skills. But they've been there, they've learned, they remember. Without 'em, there'd be no Pastime at all. We call them good baseball men.

Mr. Stengel was the best I ever knew. I could name a hundred others whose love for the game—and maybe even, God bless 'em, for the Rat—kept my run of luck alive. Great managers like Vern Hoschheit, my first skipper in the Yankee chain, and Casey. Great organization types like Hank Peters, the A's GM, and Bing Devine, the Mets' boss who made me his special assistant. Even players like George Brett, Bruce Sutter, and Ozzie, who made me the certified genius you used to read about in the newspapers. They all sharpened my brains and kept me up and running on the basepaths. Good baseball men—they change lives. They pass the game along.

Well, the good baseball man isn't just some old-timer hocking into a spittoon. He knows the craft of the game. He knows the little things you have to do right. He knows the time, the repetition, and the stubbornness it takes to work 'em into your muscle memory. He knows there's picking up grounders and fly balls, moving side to side, moving front and back; he knows there's throwing from all positions, hitting to right and left, setting your feet right, knowing the strike zone. He may never end up a big-time star like Johnny Sain; he might be like me, a marginal pro, or like Bing, who knocked around the sandlots of St. Louis and barely played his way into Class D. But he appreciates the star player; and the star appreciates him. They talk the same language. When he's done playing, the baseball man is drawn to others who crave his knowledge. He'll sit all day and bullshit with 'em. He'll tell stories. He'll pass along facts. He'd do it all for free. And he's as key to baseball as a Mark McGwire home run.

• • •

Hub Kittle was way past sixty, with a face as worn as an old Rawlings mitt, by the time he came to the Cardinals as my pitching coach. He'd spent four decades hitting fungoes, steering buses, sleeping in back seats, telling stories of the old days, and sharing the secrets of making a hitter look foolish with a thousand beanpole kids you and I never heard of He'd worked in Mexico, California, Texas, Maine. Name the place, Hub had been there. God bless guys like him. They *are* the game.

I'm sure you remember a certain pitcher I managed named Joaquin Andujar. He was a firecracker. Strong right-hander, wonderful major-league stuff, funny guy, but a crazed Dominican with a hair-trigger temper. I'd watched Joaquin—I called him Goombah—in his Astros days, and I always liked the way he threw, but I knew he was a few stitches shy of a baseball on certain points. For one thing, he didn't like to be taken out of games. He'd throw a fit, toss his glove and sulk for days if you gave him the hook. Wouldn't talk to anybody. "I'm pissed, I'm pissed," he'd say. My friend Bill Virdon, the Astros manager then, told me if the planets weren't lined up just the right way, he'd gripe and whine like a crybaby. He was always in the middle of some damn hornet's nest or other, with teammates or coaches or the clubhouse boy. But the Cards needed pitching in 1981, so we traded for him, gave him the ball, and kept our fingers crossed.

I don't know what I'd have done without Hub: He made Goombah look like a prize pupil. Joaquin just lit up around him. Every time you looked up, he was launching his arm around the old guy's neck, flashing a big smile and hollering, "My Daddy! This is my Daddy!" Hub might squirm or wince a little once in a while, but I know he enjoyed it. He was a hell of a tough bird, but Hub realized a guy like that needs to feel appreciated, to get a well-timed pat on the rear. Joaquin diversified your day, and Hub liked that. Maybe when you've washed as many buses, shagged as many fly balls and wiped as many noses as he had, it just seemed one more part of the job.

Hub's attitude was a big, big reason I got so many great ballgames out of the guy who called himself "one tough Dominican." Señor Jack, as Ozzie called him, won 20 games for me twice and 15 another time, started some of the biggest Cardinal games ever, and pitched in two World Series. But the key to a Hub Kittle is he doesn't give a damn if you're a postseason ace or some snot-nosed kid in the Texas League: He's going to teach you the game. I'd see him take an eighteen-year-old pitcher who couldn't throw 83 miles an hour off to the side, and ten minutes later, the guy's out on the rubber humming it 88, 89. I can't even tell you how he did it except to use those five magic words: He was a baseball man.

There were so many others. Clyde McCullough was a Cubs catcher for years who ended up coaching for me with the Mets. He'd been a terrible hitter—had a big hitch in his swing—but learned how to catch so well they kept him around for twenty years. It made him a hell of a coach.

Better still, Clyde could spew gas like a hillside full of cattle. I'd turn the catchers over to him during the Mets' instructional league, and every once in a while I'd sneak up on him and he'd be going on about Charley Root and Jack Chesbro and every other old-time sonof-agun they'd never heard of. He could put it *out* there; not a word of it was true! But I'd watch them kids, and their eyes would go as wide as the scoreboard clock, and Clyde would slip in some little thing about framing the plate, balancing your weight, or getting a good jump on a bunt. Don't confuse him with facts, man: He was *teaching*.

One day he was on the mound talking to the pitchers and catchers. I heard him say, "Boys, there's *eighteen* different ways you can balk!" Instead of laughing out loud, I sidled up from behind and listened a while. He went through about three before he went off on a tangent. "Hey Clyde," I hollered, "what the hell's the other fifteen?" Everybody cracked up, including him. He didn't know! But I didn't see many more balks that year. He could take a few kids for a half hour, never have them put on a mitt or a chest protector, and leave them all with something they could use on the field three days later.

Two others were George Kissell and Dave Ricketts. George was already a well-respected Cardinal coach when I ran the Mets' minor-league camps in the sixties, and since the teams shared facilities in St. Petersburg, I saw him at work time after time. I'm telling you, George Kissell could talk for fifteen minutes about a groundball. He'd really break it down. He'd talk about gauging the bounce. He'd talk about how to place your glove the right way. He'd talk about getting into position, surrounding the ball, stepping through it so you weren't moving to your right when you threw to first. With George it was repetition, repetition, repetition, the same basics over and over till they sank in. He helped me all ten years I ran the Cardinals, and I'll be damned if he *still* isn't working for them part-time. They sent John Mabry, their young outfielder, down to the Florida instructional league last year, to teach him to play third base. They hooked him up with Kissell. He's damn near eighty now, and he'll talk baseball till they cart him off the field.

Ricketts, my bullpen coach with the Cards, is still their roving catching instructor. Dave worked with Tom Pagnozzi deep in the minors and was high on Eli Marrero, St. Louis' new young catcher, long before the current regime came to town. But Dave's best quality is his teaching. He'll show you how to do something, watch you try it, then make comments and correct you as needed. He even taught Tony Pena, the All-Star catcher we got from the Pirates in 1986, a new stance. Partly to save wear and tear—the Pirates were horseshit then, so he was on the field a lot—Tony knelt on his right leg and extended the left one straight out on the ground. Naturally, he couldn't jump out of the box fast enough to get topped balls and bunts, so Dave taught him an upright stance. Tony was damn gracious about it, too, and he was a hell of a catcher for the St. Louis Cardinals.

One thing I got a kick out of, though: We got rid of Tony later on, and I turned on the TV one day and saw him playing for the Red Sox. There he was, right back on one knee, with the old dead log stretched out there, trapped behind the plate. I'd have bunted the hell out of him, and he'd've had it coming; he *knew* better by then. I'll tell you: Dave Ricketts is a baseball man. And I don't care if you're the best player in the game, you never stop needing those guys.

When people ask me about baseball and how it's changed, there's two parts to the answer: there's on the field and off the field. Between the lines, the sport hasn't changed much; off the field, it's changed in one principal way everybody knows about. It's about all anybody *talks* about—money.

Money's altered my life and my family's. Mary Lou and I lived in a trailer for five years, driving it from one baseball stop to the next and hauling our kids with us. I never made more than $18,000 a year as a player, which was what the Detroit Tigers paid me in 1963, my last season on the field. I was fine that way; I enjoyed that mobile home damn near as much as the nice brick house and pool we've got in St. Louis today. As long as I've got my rods and lures, a car to get around in, and maybe a satellite dish to pull down those late games from the coast, I'm one hell of a happy Rat.

But the changes in my lifetime have been amazing. My last year as manager, I made thirty times my Tigers' salary. I got a $72,000 check in the spring for licensing revenues alone—a long way from the $125 Topps used to pay us. Once I passed twenty years' service in the big leagues, I qualified for the maximum pension—which is now $112,000 a year, the same amount Lee Iaccocca makes and the highest the federal government allows. If I die, Mary Lou gets the same amount for life—full boat. Nobody has to remind me to thank Marvin Miller, the first players-union president, in my prayers.

But you and I both know the money can get too big. I don't blame the players for taking as much as they can get, but when you look at it, money can corrupt the exact thing that produced it. There's no doubt that's happened in my game. And one way to look at the corruption is to see what it's done to the most important guy in the game—the baseball man.

I'll put it to you like this: Let's say you're a nineteen- or twenty-year-old kid. You want to be a ballplayer. And you're standing in the baseline listening to one of them old guys talking his piece. He's waving his arms and bugging out his eyes and talking about the anatomy of a line drive. You're following, but you're half-daydreaming about the anatomy of some girl you saw at McDonald's. You're still wiping the Big Mac sauce off your face. You didn't Supersize your meal, so your stomach's grumbling, the sun is hot, and this guy's going on a little bit.

Well, all of a sudden another guy comes striding across the field. He's a snappy dresser: He's wearing a three-piece suit and loafers and a big smile, and he's toting an Italian briefcase. He sets up a card table right on the field, sits down, and opens it up. Next thing you know, he's holding up a stack of thousand-dollar bills, waving them in the air. He's giving 'em away. How long are you going to listen to Grandpa flapping his gums? By the time he's discussing your relay throws, you're on your way to the bank.

That's what's happening in baseball. The guy in Gucci is an agent. Your fame and fortune's in his brief-case. Nobody within a line drive of the big leagues hires the Hub Kittles anymore. Big-league players laugh at 'em. George Kissell would never get a major-league job. Except in the low minors, today's player just gets irritated. He gives away the chance to bullshit with some good old guys. He misses a lifetime of lore. And color, craft, and history go straight out the window.

Don't believe me? Look down on the field. Right in front of your eyes, you'll see the most under-reported story in sports: Big-league millionaires who wouldn't know the cutoff man if he shook 'em out of a deep sleep. All-Stars who can't bunt or throw to the right base. Outfielders who stroll to the ball and give away bases. When you watch big-league ball, you're seeing players who haven't learned the game right and who have no interest in learning it. The Hubs and Kissells are there, but nobody's paying attention. I've never seen such horseshit play, and it's a hard, hard thing to watch.

Two summers back, I severed my Achilles' tendon and was flat on my ass for two months. I couldn't golf, fish, or leave the house. I spent some time in front of the old split-screen, boy, and I must have seen more Cubs games than Jim Riggleman, their manager, and more Braves games than Bobby Cox. I was in some pain—them pills didn't always kick in right—but that was nothing next to what I felt when I saw *that* action. It was a horror show. Nobody had a bench; nobody had ten pitchers. There's so much Double-A talent you can't even say what big-league tools are anymore. Even the stars are afflicted. I'm a big fan of Ryne Sandberg, but one game he was on first when the next guy up hit a double-play grounder. Well, on a close play at second, Sandberg not only failed to knock that second baseman on his ass, he kind of roamed off toward right field like he was looking for a picnic site. Double play! Next hitter, Sammy Sosa, hits a home run. The Cubs end up losing 4–3. That one play was the difference, and no one ever mentioned it—no announcer, no writer, not once. The media, boy—I can't believe they're watching the same game I am.

And how about those Atlanta Braves? The National League team of the nineties? That doesn't say much for the damn nineties. I like their four starting pitchers as much as the next guy—and for $30 million, they'd better be likable. I'd pencil Chipper Jones or Andres Galarraga in my lineup any day of the week. Javy Lopez, the catcher, is a good ballplayer, and the centerfielder, Andruw Jones, is going to be great. But the rest of that team, as a baseball team, is so mediocre it's a joke. It's been that way the whole decade.

Atlanta will always win their division with that starting pitching. The thing is, I don't know why Cox takes 'em out with seven shutout innings and only eighty-five pitches thrown. I'm damned if I can figure out why he'd want to get to that bullpen of his. How many games has this cost Maddux over the years? He's got eighty-two pitches, they take him out. That really screws him up. I'd say, "Hey, man, you can't throw 100 pitches every fifth day? Are you kiddin' me?"

They say the Braves are good because they built from within. Really? Look at the pitching staff. Who'd they get from within? Tom Glavine. Smoltz is from the Tigers; they gave up Doyle Alexander to get him. Neagle, they got in the Pittsburgh fire sale. Maddux, they bought for $28 million from the Cubs. And they tried to draft Todd Van Poppel number one. He said he wouldn't go to a losing team, so they took Chipper Jones instead! He was their number-two ranked guy. Talk about the luck of the Irish! Van Poppel just signed with the Pirates last year. What is that, his fourth team? Fifth? His ERA's bigger than my hat size. Now that's building from within!

But I say, as far as fundamentals are concerned, there's no way you can compare these guys to Stengel's Yankees, or the Big Red Machine, the great Cincinnati Reds clubs of the seventies. The Atlanta Braves are what I'd politely call the best of a bad lot.

One night in '97, they're playing the Marlins at home.

It goes to extra innings: bases loaded, nobody out, the Braves' top pinch-hitter, Mike Mordecai, at the plate. For a good hitter, that's a slam dunk: He shortens his swing, puts the ball in play, and the man on third comes home. Braves win.

But what happens? Mordecai never touches the ball. Three strikes, right turn. Next guy up, same thing. They're swinging from their ass, trying to hit it out of the park! Hell, all you need's a run; you don't have to win by four! I turned to Mary Lou and said, "Mary, are these guys trying to *win*?" These things are so basic they aren't even worth talking about, yet the best team in baseball doesn't do 'em. The Braves were one of the worst teams that year at scoring runners from third with less than two out.

This stuff is so prevalent that I can't even watch the World Series these days without wanting to scream. I still hear people talk about the '91 Series between the Braves and the Twins. "That was a classic," they say; "so good for the game!" Well, it did go seven games, and the seventh was a 1–0 decision in extra innings. But seven times horseshit is still horseshit! With all the poor throws, missed cutoff men, and baserunning screwups, that was the single most atrocious Series, fundamentally speaking, I ever saw. And it ain't changed much since. I tried to watch the Marlins play the Indians in '97, and the media kept saying how nice it was the Series finally went seven games. I *tried* to watch; I really did. But the games went so long, the play was so sloppy, and it got so late every game, I had to shut it off. I've got a life to live, man! I played some tiddlywinks *that* October.

The thing is, I know this isn't the managers' fault. Jim Riggleman's a friend of mine, and I know he's a good strategist. Bobby Cox is a good baseball man, and I'm sure it's not his fault his hitters don't always do what they should. The coaches and the managers—from the Hub Kittles in the low minors on up through the big-league skippers—are *telling* 'em to shorten up with two strikes, hit behind the runner, hit the cutoff guy. The problem is, the modern player knows he doesn't have to listen.

Part of the trouble is just supply and demand. In 1952, Moose Skowron hit .337 with 38 homers for the Kansas City Blues, the Yanks' top farm team. He was Minor League Player of the Year, hands down. The next spring, New York didn't even invite him to their big-league camp. They had Joe Collins, Elston Howard, Johnny Mize, Hank Bauer—ballplayers up the ass. They didn't want Moose hitting 10 homers in camp and getting the writers in an uproar. Today, with thirty big-league teams and 750 spots, a kid hits .350 in *rookie league* and he's in the big camp next year. There ain't enough *talent*.

The union's a big influence, too. A modern player would die laughing if he knew what happened to Mantle in '57. He'd won the Triple Crown the year before, hitting .353 with 52 homers and 130 RBIs. It was one of the best years in the history of baseball. The next year, he didn't do it again—"slumping" to a .365 average, with 34 homers and 94 RBIs, while leading the league in walks and runs scored—so the Yankees tried to cut his salary! God almighty. Now, players get rewarded for seniority as much as performance. How long has a guy been in the league? How long has that guy on the other team been in the league? The GM ain't negotiating anymore; he's *comparing*. You can't cut him back to a three-year player's salary, that's for sure, even if he deserves it.

But the most important force in baseball right now is that Gucci boy—the agent. The managers, the coaches—the baseball men—aren't the key players today. The Hub Kittles are just sideline codgers, chewing Skoal and spitting juice on their shoes. It's not the Johnny Sains, the Bing Devines, the guys who can teach you a new pitch or do something in the front office you never knew about. It's the agents. The agents, of all people, are running baseball today, and that's the biggest difference of all.

If you could sit in on a contract talk, you'd know what I'm talking about. I was GM of the Cardinals and ran the show for the Angels in the early nineties, so I know how this goes. There you are, sitting in your office having a plug of Red Man. You've played the game, lived it and coached it, taught it all across North America your whole life. Across from you sits this guy in an Armani suit. His cologne smells awful nice, and he shakes your hand pretty firm, but he wouldn't know a line drive if it hit him in the head. And he's talking up a storm. "Whitney, you need some left-handed relief pitching." "Whitey, you need power hitting off the bench." God *almighty*, that used to burn my ass. Hey— even agents can be honest if they try. Tell me how much *money* you want; don't tell me what I need. I don't know how many times I had to call a player and say, "Your agent's in my office. Come drag his ass out of here right now." I bounced more than one of them SOBs, and it always brightened the scenery.

But the most important thing is, even though they're setting the agenda, even though they're setting the salaries for us, the agents don't know a thing about baseball. Mary Lou knows more baseball than most agents. And *they're* the ones teaching our players what's important in playing the game.

The agent is like the judge who rules in salary arbitration cases: All he knows is stats, not baseball. If a client's a position player, the agent knows three things: home runs, RBIs, and batting average. Those things he can count. The better numbers his player gets in those areas, the more money he's going to make. Seems like simple math, right?

Well, if you understand baseball at all you know how little those figures have to do with winning, playing interesting ball, or putting fans in the seats. I've known many a horseshit player who hit .290. Thirty homers don't mean much today, and they mean even less if they don't fit into an offensive scheme. Later on I'll talk more about why these numbers don't mean you're going to win. The agents don't have the first clue about that. The question *I'd* want to ask is, does the guy hustle? Does he get to the ballpark on time? Does he go to the plate with an idea? Does he go from first to third? Is he a good guy off the field?

Those factors add up to a winning player. When I was still on the field, owners brought them up in negotiations. If you didn't measure up, they could cut your pay or ship your ass out. Hell, one year my general manager tacked $5,000 onto my salary just because I played hard, and that was back when the owners *really* clutched their coins. When I was manager and GM for the Cardinals— when I wore both hats—*I* sure as hell brought that stuff up. Now, nobody cares. It isn't even mentioned.

And players know the score. They know what they're getting paid for, and it ain't fundamentals. You might even say we're paying players not to learn the right way. Say a manager is down 3–2 and calls for the hit-and-run. Well, under the system we have, the batter has an incentive to want *no part* of that play. Why? He knows he'll have to swing at that next pitch. The runner's taking off, and the batter's got to protect him. Maybe it won't be a pitch he likes. He might hit a weak grounder and make an out. His batting average drops three points. And he hears his agent's voice in his head: "Hell of a play, Fred. You just lost money on your next contract." Next time maybe Fred won't be so damned dumb.

When I was managing, I never had a problem getting guys to execute that play. My players were great at it, great at hitting behind the runner and moving him around. I stayed on their ass about it all the time. In batting practice, my hitters always had to take it to right field two out of seven swings. They did it over and over. It helped that I had many of my best Cardinal players as rookies: Tommy Herr, my second baseman; Terry

Pendleton, my third baseman, and Willie McGee, my centerfielder, got used to that play before they ever came up for arbitration. If they came up with a guy on second and no outs, it was automatic: They got the runner to third. That's good, fundamental baseball.

Nobody's playing it much. I see situations all the time that *clearly* call for the hit-and-run. It just doesn't happen. Sometimes the runner takes off like he should; the hitter ain't swinging. Sometimes *nothing* happens. Or with a runner on first and nobody out, the batter's trying to go deep. Well, is the manager giving up? When the batter fails to try, does the skipper get on his ass about it afterward, or does he just stop calling the play? I don't know. All I know is, the agents don't keep track of that stuff, it won't get a player more money, and I see it less and less every year.

The game still has great teachers, including some of my own ex-players. Jamie Quirk and Frank White—I had them with the Royals—know the game inside and out. They're good big-league coaches; they pass it along. Tommy Herr, who was never out of defensive position his whole time with me, has a fine mind for the game. He just wrote a good book on fundamentals, and he'd make a hell of a coach if he ever decided to leave his Pennsylvania hometown and come back to the pros. John Tudor, the smartest pitcher I ever managed, coached in the minors for four years. He could fill a book with what he knows—setting up the hitters, making adjustments, changing speeds by feel. They might be the next Hubs, Clydes, and Kissells.

But the thing is, will anyone be listening? A good teacher needs his students, and you can't solve the problem by raising your voice. The guys who need to hear you—you'll only turn 'em off that way. I can't even blame them much; they do what they're asked to do. In baseball, we need to set things up so they listen to the right folks again.

If we spot the problem, think hard, and adjust the

rules, we can get the balance back. When baseball men matter again, you'll make everybody rich in the ways that count. And you know what you're going to find? You still have a hell of a game.

· 3 ·
Diamonds in the Rough

Most days I'm out of bed reading a newspaper or two before Mary Lou gets up. I'll demolish 'em front to back: news, politics, sports, I like to keep up. And one morning two summers ago, before my coffee'd had a chance to percolate, my eye fell on a brief in the sports pages that took me back thirty-four years, to a ball field I'd nearly forgotten—and to a time, before the big dollars came in, when knowledge of the game made the biggest difference in the way things ran.

It was an obituary for a former big-league pitcher. The man had been murdered, at age fifty-four, in a convenience-store incident in Kansas City. I remembered him plain as a midday game. I'm the guy who gave Don O'Riley his shot at the major leagues.

I started scouting in 1964, for the Kansas City A's, the year after I quit playing. Casey was still with the Mets, but he always kept a big, grizzled ear to the ground as far as baseball in his hometown went. The Perfesser called one day with a heads-up on a kid who'd been in the joint, a skinny righthander with a good live arm. I made some calls, got hold of the O'Riley family, and gave Don directions to a field I knew in back of the Montgomery Ward building downtown.

Don was a shy sonofagun, but he had a pitcher's build, tall and lanky. As he aired it out, I got a good feeling. He had some juice, sizzled it into the mitt real nice. Hell, he was worth a crack. If it won't cost you too much, why not give a decent kid a chance? Don had had a rough life—he'd spent time in a juvenile facility for stealing, and his own dad, a North Kansas City policeman, had been the arresting officer. I can't tell you what went haywire exactly, but whatever it was, it had to be tough on the boy.

When I told Don I was interested, instead of jumping up and down, he started talking about his mom: She needed an ulcer operation, it cost $1,800, and they didn't have the money. So we fixed him up with a $2,000 bonus and a contract with the A's. *That* lit his eyes up. Mrs. O'Riley got her surgery, we got a prospect, Don got his chance, and everybody made out great. In my book, a hell of a deal.

Well, he never pitched in the majors for us—his career totals in the bigs were 47 innings, one win, one loss. Not what you'd call Bob Feller material. Our owner, old Charlie Finley, never liked Don much, but maybe he changed his tune when we lost the kid's contract to the Royals in the expansion draft: The old guy got $175,000 for him. That's right, an 870 percent return. *There's* a definition of good scouting: Start out with nothing but vigor and an old ball glove, end up with a pocketful of loot. And to think Charlie O. never said thanks.

I'm known around baseball as a good judge of talent. I can't sit here and tell you I deserve the label, but people around the game think I do, and it really got started that year I signed Don. I had a giant six-state territory—Missouri, Arkansas, Kansas, Oklahoma, Nebraska, and northern Texas—and worked it like a Show-Me mule on speed. I signed twelve ballplayers from that territory for a total of $125,000. Seven made big-league rosters inside of a year. A few—like pitcher Chuck Dobson—played parts in the three Oakland championships of the 1970s.

It was like hitting .400 as a rookie. I was the Freddie

Lynn, the Mark Fidrych of scouting, boy: first year, career year. Some guys beat the bushes for a lifetime and never flush out that much fowl.

I can't say just how I did it, but that doesn't stop people from asking. How can you tell a wannabe from the real McCoy? Even now, I hear that a lot. And the answer hasn't changed: It's hard to say. There's one scout who's famous for signing Stan Musial—as a pitcher. Well, if Ollie Van Eck's so damn smart, why didn't he sign Stan as a hitter? It's not as simple as it looks.

I got help from my buddies, Dodger scouts like Burt Wells, John Keenan, and Monty Basgall, who gave me more on-the-job training than any rival had to in the days when we were all competing for the same talent. Great, great guys. That was one thing.

But to answer right, you have to go back a ways further. Most of what I used in scouting, that year and all my years in the game, I'd learned in my hometown by the time I was twelve. It may seem like a long leap backward, but believe me: Behind every good baseball man, there's a kid with a bug up his britches.

The little burg of New Athens, Illinois, is fifteen miles south of Belleville, a few counties east of the Mississippi in the middle of the corn and the coal mines. I still get over there every few weeks to play pinochle, get the flattop levelled off or fish the old strip pits. Or I'll check in on my brother Butzy (it rhymes with Tootsie), who still lives in the little frame house we grew up in. In fact, if I took you over to New Athens, I could show you Whitey Herzog Field. It's at New Athens High, and they named it after me. They've had 167 straight sellouts at that ballpark. Of course, it only holds twelve people. The players' sisters and mothers go to the games. Even now, there aren't but about 2,000 people there, nearly all of 'em second- or third-generation German. Many speak the language, or at least English with an accent as heavy as potato salad—*yaaaahhh* instead of "yeah," that kind of thing. One of my best friends, Bill Schmidt, still gets out the *lederhosen* a few times a year and plays in an oom-pah band. If you heard him talk, you'd think he was a Dusseldorfer.

Even when I was growing up, and New Athens was thriving with industry—a foundry, two shoe factories, the Mound City brewery, and more—it was so small-town most outsiders wouldn't have looked at it twice. But it was a world of wonders for what it wasn't: There were no malls, no lighted ballparks, no video games, or VCRs. It was all neighbors and farmland, and whatever magic was going to happen, we had to make happen ourselves. You learn the most from what you do by hand.

That included baseball. If we wanted a diamond, we hacked it out of the rough. A farmer down the street had some pasture he wasn't using, so we mowed it and laid the lines down. If we wanted a game, we organized everybody—twenty, twenty-five kids most days—and got their asses on the field. From the minute school let out in the summer, we played all day every day: uptown against downtown, this block against that block. If the teams weren't even, we switched 'em around and played some more. Hell, I'd deliver the St. Louis papers all over New Athens, shoot the bull with the customers, and still be on the field before seven-thirty in the morning most days. By suppertime, I'd have pitched more innings— fifteen, sixteen in a row a lot of the time—and gotten more at-bats than my grandkids, in their organized leagues, get in a whole year. Chucking fastballs, running down flies: You name it, we did it, and we did it all-out. That's the way you learn the game.

I don't know if there are places like our New Athens now. Kids wait for life to come to them. If mom doesn't round them all up, herd 'em into the AstroVan and drive 'em to a fenced-off ballpark, there ain't a game. Kids have organized leagues and wear nice uniforms, but they play maybe one day a week. And the Little League coaches all have those pitch counters; after sixty throws, they go out to the mound and give Johnny the hook. They don't extend 'em; they baby 'em from the beginning. It's too much damn coaching, and the kids don't build up their arms. It's one of the main reasons we've got so many pus-arms today, right on up through the major leagues.

These coaches, boy, they're killing off our kids' love of the game. One day my oldest son was playing Little League ball. I flew in from Nashville, Tennessee, to see him play. Got off the plane, Mary Lou took me right to the ballpark. Bases loaded, 3–2 count, he takes strike three. So we're driving home afterward, and I don't want to butt in, but I figure I ought to say *something*. So I say, "You know, Dave, you gotta rip. You ain't going to get anywhere just taking." He says, "Dad, the coach had the 'take' sign on." Three and two, bases loaded, two outs, he puts the take sign on! Now that's a hell of a way to learn to play baseball. But that's what's happening in Little League today. Too much damn coaching, and they don't know jack.

Well, I was never a Fulbright Scholar, but even my homework taught me that with baseball, you could make things happen. If you came up to my study right now, I could show you the book that got me through grade school: *Greatest Baseball Heroes*. Hardback, a little frayed, pieces of string hanging off the binding—it's as broken in as my old Lew Fonseca mitt. Every time we had a book report due, I'd flip to the next chapter— Chief Bender, Lou Gehrig, John McGraw—and write that sonofagun up. None of my teachers ever said a word. By fifth grade, I'd worked through the whole Hall of Fame. One thing I learned early, boy: Baseball's an old game, but you can keep coming back to it for new material.

Since there was no TV, if I wanted to see big-league ball, I had to get cracking. I'd skip school and hitchhike to Sportsman's Park in St. Louis to see the Browns.

Well, let's be honest: I came to see the visiting teams, the *good* ones—the Yankees, the Indians. My principal would pull me aside next day and get a game report. "Newhouser was a little wild, sir," I'd say, or "Joe D. got himself three hits." Sonofagun was a baseball man! On game days, I'd get to the upper deck hours before anybody else, and when batting practice started, I'd scoop up every foul ball or home run, stuff it in a sack, and sell 'em all for a dollar each before I left the premises. Always got myself a nice bus ride home. Here I'd start off with nothing but ants in my pants and a passion for the game, and I'd come home rich, popular, and the talk of the town. Talk about baseball value!

Well, now that I've grown up a little bit, I can only repeat what I told you before: Good scouting ain't no *secret*. It's knowing you can ask a guy to throw more pitches than the coaches say now. It's knowing when you're looking at a player who loves the game and would play it for free; that's a guy who learns quick. You look for tools: Can he throw? Does he have good hands, decent speed, the right kind of body? One time the Mets flew me out to California to double-check a kid named Northbrook. They saw him as a power-hitting prospect. He was bulky all right, and when he made contact it went a ways, but I thought he was too thick in the shoulders to get around on the big-league fastball upstairs. We passed, the Orioles drafted him, and I heard he never got out of Single-A. If your man don't have the tools, catch the Greyhound home.

Beyond that, it's inexact. Every guy who makes it in baseball eventually realizes that, at each rung he climbs, he'll see problems he hasn't seen before. He was a stud in his hometown, but did he ever see thirty *other* kid superstars? That's rookie league: They're all like him. What about when the hard slider comes down and away? What'll he do the first time a pitcher with big-time heat sticks the bat up his ass? Will he crawl in a hole, or will he be a man and think about what happened? A real player looks himself in the mirror, trusts his coaches, and adjusts. He ain't too good to learn.

What you call that quality, I don't know, but whether you're Jerry Terrell or Joe DiMaggio—to name two guys who made every bit of their very different abilities—your true ballplayer has it. Maybe it's that look in his eye that clues you in, or the way he shakes your hand. When you talk to him, are you pouring Gatorade in a sieve, or does the glass fill up? Many a kid with big-time tools never got out of rookie league. I worked with a lot like that, and it can drive you battier than a Louisville Slugger. When I was with the Mets, I sat at my desk and released four number-one draft picks in one day; every one suffered from hardening of the earflaps. After my bosses finished their collective heart attack, I told 'em, "Look, if any of them guys ever gets to the big leagues, fire me, because I don't know what the hell I'm talking about." Never happened. My game's about people, so baseball judgment is partly personal.

They say it's tough giving guys their release, and they're not lying—especially at the lower levels, like in instructional league, because nine times out of ten you're really telling them to find a new profession. First time I ever made cuts, I made thirty-six in a day. Stayed awake all night the night before I did it, too. But if you're confident and your judgment's good, you're doing those guys a favor. Some players just don't have it, and it's your job to see it, make up your mind about it, and tell 'em to their faces. Very few ever argued with me. In fact, I got thank-you letters years after the fact. They'd say, "You know what? My wife and I are happy now. You were right. I'm glad I didn't waste five years being a baseball bum." Those letters felt good. As a baseball man, it may be the most important job you do.

When I broke in, you used your personal qualities as a scout, too: It was a must. There was no free-agent draft to regulate player acquisition, so the way things were, you had to use your initiative, make the tough calls, and stick your neck out. You had to look at a kid nobody else thought twice about and say, "Hey, I don't give a damn what other people are saying, that guy can be a hitter." There was no computerized national list for cross-referencing, no organized drafting sequence to take the pressure off, no fall-backs. If you saw something good, you had to have the nerve to write it down and mail it in.

I thrive in that kind of setting. If I tell my general manager "this kid's a great one," and I end up wrong— and that's happened a time or two—at least I've got my name in capital letters on that scouting report. Bing Devine, the great GM who hired me with the Mets, says that's what he liked most about my scouting: I was willing to state my opinion loud and clear. If I was wrong, he knew who to get on the blower. Give me accountability any day of the week. In fact, show me a good ballclub and I'll show you one that has it up and down the ladder.

You never knew what road that human element was going to take you down, and that was part of the fun. You followed your instincts. One place I ended up spending a lot of time that first year was Grand Island, Nebraska, the home of an outfielder I saw greatness in. Kid stood 6-4 weighed 200-plus pounds—fine-looking athlete, the picture of the All-American guy. I saw John Sanders play two games of legion ball, and with his smooth cut and physical ability, I told Hank Peters, "We ought to sign that sonofagun." Nobody was as high on him as me. As it happened, Bob Devaney, the legendary Cornhusker football coach, wanted Sanders as his quarterback, too, and in Nebraska, that's like the lottery office calling and saying they've got a ticket they want to give you. And remember, in those days, if you were a pro in one sport, you couldn't play college ball in another. If I got John Sanders to sign, he was kissing Big Red glory goodbye. I had to set the old White Rat charm to full wattage.

As the Sanders family found out, that can be blinding. I met John's folks—nice, nice Midwestern people—and learned what they liked to do, where they liked to eat. I took 'em out for steaks and applesauce; wined 'em and dined 'em. I saw everything in Grand Island but the island. We talked the attactions of baseball, the perils of the single-wing offense, all the future possibilities for their son. In those days, the personal element was paramount, and my lord, that made it a good time. In the end, the Sanders invited me to their house on graduation night—which is the first moment a kid becomes eligible—after the other scouts had left the state, so I got in the last, most fevered pitch of all. That was what you aimed for.

My campaign was a winner. I gave our boy a $25,000 bonus, his first car, and a chance for a life in the majors. John Sanders, big-time outfielder, was on his way.

Well, that car dropped a rod, so to speak. The A's sent him out to the minors for seasoning the next year, Boston snatched him off the waiver wire, and after that he never played an inning in Fenway or any other big-league park that I know of. I can't tell you what holes showed up in his game. I lost track of John after a while.

Funny thing is, you might say I went a little overboard on this kid. But I don't know if I'd buy that. For one thing, I found myself a world-class chophouse up there, Grisbach's Steakhouse, that's still one of the finest restaurants I've ever ate at. John ended up a colleague of old Bob Devaney after all: He got hired, eventually, as coach of the Cornhusker baseball team, a job he held for thirty-some years. There's many kinds of success in scouting. How many kids did he recruit to the game? How many swings did he straighten out? When the personal element is coin of the realm, you always end up rich.

Now, a scout is a little like a hitter. Even the best of them, the best of all time, fails seven times out of ten. As he's focusing on how to solve that next pitcher, he'd better find a way to get cozy with his failures, too. That's part of the game. And in scouting, even as you were looking for your next diamond in the rough, your detours and journeys off the beaten track could make for the best tall tales you ever got to tell.

I'll never forget when every team in baseball was hot for a powerhitting prospect in Asher, Oklahoma, a guy named Jack McClure. Every club in the world sent scouts down there on his graduation weekend. You talk about a feeding frenzy: The Yanks alone sent five guys; and Houston brought their manager, Harry Craft, their GM, and my good buddy Joe Frazier, a top scout, all for this one game. Well, the other team's pitcher couldn't bring it but 75 miles an hour, hardly pro-caliber stuff. The kid popped out three times. Hell, *I* couldn't tell if he could hit. But the Astros weren't worried. They swarmed his house, threw $75,000 at him—huge money for those days—and tore a few rotator cuffs patting themselves on the back.

You know what happened? Kid reports to Joe at Covington, Virginia in the Appalachian League, slams his bonus check in the bank, has a change of heart, drives home to marry his childhood sweetheart, and says the hell with baseball. He quits the game! Frazier and I still get a laugh out of it. Jack McClure might be driving a Peterbilt around Oklahoma City right now, and if he is, I'm sure he's a hell of a good trucker. God almighty, this game can spin your helmet around.

And the future Hall of Famers don't come with neon signs on 'em, either. Everyone knows that in the mid-sixties, when I was with the Mets, we had some of the livest arms ever assembled on a pitching staff: Gary Gentry, Jerry Koosman, Jon Matlack, Danny Frisella, Jim Bibby, Nolan Ryan—the list went on. All of 'em could bring it at least 96 mph. That was heavy artillery! But did you know Tom Seaver, who's probably the greatest Met legend of all time, was a guy we got out of a hat?

I was player-development director at the time, and our man on the West Coast, who saw Tom Terrific pitch for USC, didn't like the guy at all. "I've watched the son-ofagun for two years," the guy would say. "He don't throw hard enough!" The first club to sign Seaver was the Braves. The thing was, they *signed* him illegally: Southern Cal had already played their first game of the year when he put his name on the dotted line, and that made the contract null and void.

Well, the commissioner decided any team wanting to kick in the $40,000 the Braves had offered could put their name into a pot. And the only reason the Mets even did that was Bing Devine's gratitude to the customers. I remember him saying, "Look, we just drew 1,950,666 fans with a last-place team. How in the hell would it look if we didn't even kick in forty grand for this guy?" Only four teams were in the drawing—us, the Phillies, the Reds, and Cleveland. I don't care what anybody tells you, the best hitters need a blooper to drop in the gaps once in a while. Part of scouting is luck, and don't trust a soul who tells you different.

Even Nolan Ryan was the same. Today you think of him as the fire-balling Hall of Fame legend, the guy with the bionic arm, the man everybody in Texas wants to run for office. But when Nolan came out of high school, no one was very high on him. His prep coach down in Alvin, Texas, used him so often his arm was falling off, and by the time the big scouts got down there for a look, he'd be going half-speed. Our man in Texas, Red Murph, got so frustrated he couldn't see straight: He was seeing Ryan year 'round and knew how good he was. He'd call Bing, he'd call me, he'd call Bing's assistant, Bob Scheffing; he'd have called the towel boy in the locker room if that would've helped. "This kid can *throw!*" he'd say. "This kid can throw!" When we took Nolan in the eighth round, it was partly just to shut Red up.

And there's one wild pitch you can never count on:

Talent can bloom late in this game, especially pitching talent. Nolan's earliest outings, down in Marion, Virginia, promised nothing but a possible need for last rites. We didn't have a JUGS gun, but I *know* the sonofagun was over 100 mph; I never saw a pitcher with heat like that. But when they handed Nolan his howitzer at birth, they forgot to throw in the crosshairs. He had no idea— *no* idea—where that ball was going. Add in the dim lighting there, and a white building in centerfield that turned the ball into what looked like a snowflake in a blizzard, and you had a lot of eighteen-year-olds at the plate with their knees knocking. I thought he'd put somebody in a pine box.

Only maturity could straighten *that* out, but I watched Nolan the next spring, and it was not a promising sight. That kid had to be the laziest sonofagun I ever saw. He was like an old hound on the porch: Nolan Ryan wouldn't roll over to get in the shade. So how the hell could any of us realize he'd come to one big-league camp, see Tom Seaver's work habits, and have a conversion? Overnight, he became the hardest-working pitcher in our system, maybe the hardest-working I ever saw. For a quarter-century, Nolan Ryan never stopped applying himself.

You know the rest of that story. Nolan's a fine man, a gentleman, one of the best friends I have in baseball, and every bit the legend you read about. But anybody says he saw that coming is lying to your face.

On the other hand, sometimes you *do* see it coming, and it doesn't make a bit of difference. I saw a skinny, curly-haired righthander toward the end of 1964, a kid who pitched for Rollins College in Florida. Nobody'd thought much of him in the spring; he didn't throw hard enough. But he started coming on, and by the time I saw him win games in South Dakota, Kansas, and Wyoming that year, I said, *man*, he's good. Better-than-average fastball, a good, hard curveball, and he knew how to get hitters out. Finley had spent $75,000 to $100,000 already on pitchers like John Odom, Skip Lockwood, and Jim Hunter, and this guy was as good as any of them. I sat the kid down in a hotel room and said, "We want you. What'll it take to sign you?"

"Eighteen thousand dollars, a car, and four semesters of college," said Don Sutton.

I got Finley on the horn right then and there. I was halfway through my spiel when he cut me off. You know what he asked me? Not, "Whitey, how's his fastball?" or "How big is he?" That wasn't Finley. He wanted to know if Sutton had a nickname. That was his big kick that year: if you went by Blue Moon, Catfish, or Soprano, you were a hell of a player and you got rich. That damn Finley thought *he'd* built the A's, but he was nuttier than a June bug in July.

I covered the phone with my hand and said, "Don, ain't anybody ever called you *anything?*" No, he'd always been Don, he said. We came up empty.

I never got the money. My buddies with the Dodgers did. And 324 wins later—none of them with the Kansas City A's—Don Sutton told this exact story as they inducted him into the Baseball Hall of Fame.

A scout can never be totally ready for that high fastball called the human element. But he keeps it in mind his next time up, and it makes him sharper. He keeps finding ways to cover the plate. And like a Ted Williams or Tony Gwynn, he keeps his eye on the ball, sprays to all fields, and bunches his hits. He starts building his average. And for every O'Riley, McClure, or Sanders, he'll score a Dobson or a Sutton or a Joe Rudi—a clean base hit—and before you know it, he's helping you build a winning team.

That's less true now—a lot less. The role of scouting changed forever when baseball started the free-agent draft in 1965. We did it for the right reasons: to save money and even things out for everybody. It was the first time player procurement was regulated. If you finished last the year before, this year you picked first. Sounds fair, right?

Well, think about it: Let's say I'm a high-level Dodger scout, and I really like Joe Blow from Kokomo, a young first baseman. Our regional scout had him on the list for that territory, and I've gone there and double-checked him, and I agree. Well, if the Dodgers only pick twelfth, and the Phillies pick tenth and want Mr. Blow, too, it don't matter how many times I've gone to Indiana, talked to his folks, or seen him play: It's out of my hands. It's pure mathematics. With thirty teams in the big leagues, no matter how much I like that kid, I have a 3.3 percent chance of getting him.

To put it another way, my job ain't to get out there, rustle up prospects, use my brains, and go out and get 'em signed. It's to keep a *list*. Whoever is highest on it when the Dodgers' turn comes, that's the guy we get. The rest of our Top 50 list ends up someplace else. It's less about judgment, more about a long-shot roll of the dice. The risk and the personal element are gone.

As recently as twenty years back, if you wanted to know whose scouts were the best, it was simple: You checked the standings. The Pirates, Reds, Dodgers, and Cardinals in the National League, and the Yankees in the American, had savvy, innovative talent hunters all over the country. The Blue Jays became pioneers in Latin America and great at plucking guys off other team's rosters at just the right time. Those teams had good plans for keeping the best scouts, too. The Braves developed a pension system; the Cards offered Anheuser-Busch stock. However they did it, you could take it to the bank—if the scouts were good, they had an impact. The clubs excelled.

For a while there, that sure as hell included the A's. The year I joined them, 1964, Finley had made a huge profit in his insurance business—he'd come up with a plan for doctors—and he came barging into the office of Hank Peters, the farm director, one day. "Hank," he said, "I have to spend $900,000 by July 15, so let's sign some ballplayers." Finley was lucky; he had no idea that the big-league draft would begin the very next season. And Hank had wonderful scouts in place for him—not a lot of guys, but good ones: Tom Giordano on the East Coast, Clyde Kluttz in the Carolinas, Jack Sanford in Florida, Art Lilly on the West Coast. We fanned out all over the country. We signed Blue Moon Odom, Catfish, Skippy Lockwood, Joe Rudi, Dave Duncan, Rollie Fingers, Jim Nash. Then the next year, the first year of the draft, the ballclub was still so horseshit they got to draft first. They took Rick Monday, whom everybody liked, and Sal Bando a little later on. It was the core of the club that would win three World Series in Oakland.

Today, you could have a whole wing of Hall of Fame scouts working overtime and still have a rotten team. With the current rules, scouting doesn't mean anything. And when scouts are emasculated, so is baseball judgment. All those games in the New Athens pastures, the Ban Johnson leagues, the college and high school and Class D ballparks—they get wiped off the slate. And when knowhow and experience don't matter, when you play your major-league season and pick yourself a champion, what are you measuring? Does anybody give a damn?

Fans might be surprised to know how scouting works today. It ain't the cloak-and-dagger operation they might think, with each team hoarding information and competing with the others. That's as passé as knickers and the dead ball. Today's scout isn't even really scouting for his ballclub. First, he's scouting for player agents, who circle over his rankings like buzzards over roadkill possum. Those rankings are what the agent uses to calculate how much money to stick the ballclubs up for. And second, he's scouting for himself, looking out for number one. As far as my *team* goes, it doesn't make much difference if I know about Joe Blow in Indiana or not; we aren't going to get him. *But*. I've got a general manager scrutinizing me. He wants to make sure I'm earning my paycheck. So once the draft is over, and somebody else has Mr. Blow, I can at least say to my boss, "Hey, look, man, I had that guy high on my list." So I keep that list up. Forget classics like *Alibi Ike*; today, Ring Lardner would be writing *I Covered My Ass*.

With the stakes so low, scouts from different teams share their data. If I'm with the Dodgers and see some kid in West Podunk, and you're with the Cards and see another one in East Podunk, and we're buddies, I'll swap the name I got for the one you got. That way, we both score with our bosses. In the end, those players are items on a list that almost everybody has. They aren't guys with family troubles or money troubles or hitches in their swings; they're data bits in a computer. There isn't a scout in the world warming kids up behind Montgomery Ward, and that's a shame.

Now, with thirty rosters to fill, the hunt for talent is worldwide. The foreign-born ballplayer—the Australian player, the Korean player, the Venezuelan player—is hotter than a Juan Gonzalez line drive. Hell, the quality of pitching in Japan is better than ours right now—they throw harder overall, and they can thread a needle with their control—and you have to go to the Dominican to find kids who play the game as much and as hard as every kid in the U.S. did thirty years ago. But one more thing kicks scouting in the ass: Under the current rules, that foreign player isn't even governed by the free-agent draft. Anyone can buy his services at any time. And the monetary gap between rich and poor teams is so wide that the lesser teams don't have the budget to give some sixteen-year-old shortstop a $3 million bonus.

When I was running baseball operations for the Angels in the early nineties, we saw all this coming. We instituted the first worldwide scouting department—my ex-pitcher, Mr. Andujar, found me some good raw talent in the Dominican hills—but the Braves, Blue Jays, and Yankees came down and blew us out of the tub. Sure, it helps to have good scouts to find those players, but if you can't sign them, what's the use? Baseball's more about money than talent now. We shut the whole operation down.

And for a game based on the human element, here's one more ticket to the shithouse: Machines make a lot of decisions now. I'd like to toss all those Little League pitch counters on a bonfire. So a kid makes 100 throws; he ain't *pitching* for five days, for cryin' out loud—let him throw! And if it's not pitch counters or computers, it's radar guns. They wipe out the thinking process. If a guy can't flash ninety on the screen, nobody'll talk to him. Do you think we'd ever have heard of Eddie Lopat, John Tudor, or Tommy John if we went by numbers? How about Whitey Ford? Catfish Hunter, who became one of the greats, never threw but eighty-five miles an hour. Those guys couldn't break a pane of glass, but they thrilled the fans by showing the most fundamental thing about my game: There's more to it than brawn. Program *that* in your laptop.

Well, I'm not a sentimental guy, but when I opened my *St. Louis Post-Dispatch* that morning and saw Don O'Riley's name, I have to tell you something: My mind wandered a little bit. I found myself thinking of that year of scouting, of traveling all up and down mid-America with my best buddies, the scouts from the Dodgers and the A's. I thought of the little traveling society we had—rolling across the plains of Nebraska, the pastures of Oklahoma, through the heat, lightning, and thunderstorms of a Midwestern summer. I remembered looking high and low for one damn ballyard after another that not even the prospects' mothers could remember the names of, all for the sum of $7,500 a year, with a few expenses thrown in for laughs. I remembered pawing through two tons of dirt for a handful of diamonds, and how the ones we dug up really seemed to shine.

I sure was sorry to read about old Don O'Riley. That

story got me to thinking about the good old days—about that ballfield behind Monkey Wards, a young kid with a live arm and eyes that lit up, and his mama and his dad, and a lot of other wonderful things that died.

· 4 ·
Signatures

You almost have to shut your eyes to remember what the baseball world was like when I was a kid. They hadn't put a game on TV yet—that wouldn't happen till 1947, when the first World Series broadcast came out of Ebbets Field—so, whatever images you had of your big-league heroes, you formed from reading the newspaper or tuning in to a radio station fifty or 100 or 500 miles away. Cardinals announcer Harry Caray hollered the play-by-play into our living room, and sagas of the great Gashouse Gang teams of the 1940s, with Stan Musial, Marty Marion, and Enos Slaughter leading the charge, crackled over the radio.

When the mighty Yankees actually swung through the area, it was like the Ringling Brothers coming to town. You circled those dates on your calendar the day the schedule came out, and one way or another, you got yourself to the ballpark. Well, imagine how I felt one afternoon when I hitched to St. Louis, saw the great team kick the hell out of the Brownies again, and hung around the players' exit afterward to get a glimpse of my heroes. Right down the tunnel, looking sharp as Ty Cobb's cleats in a salt-and-pepper suit, walked none other than Joe DiMaggio.

Before I knew what I was doing, I said his name out loud—"Joe D.!"—and the Clipper actually heard me. He stopped, stepped aside for a minute, took my program and, right there under the Browns logo, signed his name.

It was like standing with a king. He gave it back, I stammered, "Thanks, Mr. D.," he nodded and headed off, and I've treasured that moment all my life.

Now I'm not a big memorabilia guy. I'm not like a lot of ex-jocks who have trophy rooms the size of my house. The whole collectors' industry mystifies me; I can't see paying $20 to stand in line for three hours and get some old third-stringer to write his name on my hat. I signed more than 2,300 big-league lineup cards in my day and only saved one. For some reason, I kept the card from Pete Rose's last game as a manager. (That's a funny story: We were playing the Reds and I went to home plate to hand in the lineup card, and he did, too. He said, "We're gonna beat your ass today," and I said, "You wanna bet?" He groaned and said, "Oh, don't say that!" I had managed 2,500-some games, I guess, up till that time, and I had never, ever saved a lineup card. After the game was over, I just threw them in the trash can. And yet I kept that one, the last lineup card Pete Rose ever wrote up. He was fired or suspended the next day. I don't know why I kept it; I have no idea.)

But come down to my den and you'll see a few things I've made a point of saving. I don't know how much money they'd bring, and I don't give a damn; I keep them because they have value to me. I really think about that word sometimes: Now that the big money has lumbered onto the scene and knocked everything on its ass, what does the baseball world really *value* anymore?

Baseball fans tend to be good-hearted, honest folks, and I really like most of the thousands I've met. My relationship with Missouri fans has been especially close: I'm a Midwesterner right to my jockstrap, and I think these people have a feel for the well-played, heads-up, no-bullshit baseball I brought to the Show-Me state. You ought to see St. Louis fans when I go out: If you and I drove to the bank or the grocery store right now, or ordered a grilled cheese and a glass of milk at any diner in town, three minutes wouldn't go by before some

stranger would come up, pump the hell out of my hand
and say, "Thanks for ten years of great baseball." It happens every day; they treat Mary Lou and me like kings.

Well, these are the people whose love for the game
put our three kids through college; they're just thousands
of old friends we've never met. If they ask nicely for an
autograph, I say, "Hand me a pen." It's a pleasure.

Most mornings I drive to Illinois and get out on the
water real early, and by the time I get back at 9:30, the
mail's on my desk. I'll dig in and go through it. Most
days I'll have a letter or two, postmarked Minnesota,
New Jersey, Florida, wherever—all over the U.S.—from
folks I've never heard of. I'll razor 'em open and shake
out a Whitey Herzog baseball card or two. Usually
they're photos from my time with the Cardinals or
maybe the Royals, and now and then my face'll even be
grinning out from an Orioles, Tigers, or Senators uniform. Most have a nice letter enclosed: "I've been a fan
for years, and my granddad is too," or "It's my son's
birthday, and he sure would be happy to add this to his
collection." I'll make sure I get the name spelled right,
sign it, seal it up, and send it off.

But what does it tell you when five or six of those
sumbitches fall out, all the exact same card? The writer
says, "Hey, we sure know a lot of Whitey fans up here
in Hoboken," or he tells me he's got a hell of an extended family up there in East Egg, with fifth cousins
and uncles and maybe the gardener and the family pet
thrown in, all of 'em Cardinal or Royal fans in dire need
of an autograph right away. After I'm done laughing, I
just slide 'em in the trash. These guys are selling my
name for cash, and I'm supposed to sit there all morning
and sign for 'em. Well, I've got stuff to do, man. How
dumb do they think I am?

Ballplayers get a bad rap for being aloof with the fans,
and a lot of them deserve it. If you're some screwball
kid who happens to be hauling down $2 million a year
for sliding around on a field, it's probably human nature

to figure you're a few rungs up the evolutionary ladder. Some players are magic with the fans, though—the George Bretts, the Ozzies, the Cal Ripkens—and God help my game if more guys with the generosity gene don't wander down the pike. I can't tell you how many times I've seen Ozzie stand in a line and sign for a thousand people, chat with every single one of them, never get irritated—even though I knew damn well he had someplace to go—and leave each and every one with the feeling that the greatest shortstop who ever lived was now their best buddy. That's magic for the game.

But man, has the climate ever changed. The average fan can't realize how much. I'll be out at the hardware store and some guy will step right in front of me, hand me a fistful of glossies and say, "Here, sign six of these, man." I had a guy collar me at a restaurant one time. He holds out seven ticket stubs—one from each game of the 1982 World Series, which my Cards won over Milwaukee—and unfolds 'em like a royal flush. If he'd said, "Would you sign these seven tickets? I really enjoyed that Series," or "I've got seven grandkids, do you mind signing?" I'd have said, "Sure, I'll be glad to." That's fine by me. But you know what this guy said? "Hey, sign these so I can make some money." Just like that! Well, what do you think DiMaggio would've said if I'd grabbed his arm back in the forties and hollered, "Hey, Joe, gimme half a dozen, I'm in hock!" I enjoy people, but I about knocked that SOB on his ass.

I could tell you horror stories. I don't believe in selling autographs, so I don't sign at card shows much now, but for a time I did. I'd go to the ones where they charge you one flat admission at the door. One day, I had people waiting for me in a two-block line, wanting to get their pennants, hats, and money clips signed. And this woman comes up—she's got twenty-five Cardinal pennants in her fist. I say, "Honey, there's a line out there! I'll sign two or three for you, but . . ." She frowns and says,

"What's the problem? My husband and I took a trip around the world with the money we've made off this." I about died laughing.

It's been this way for a while. In New York, outside the hotel we used to stay in, there's a stretch of sidewalk where there's always a few kids asking for autographs. So I sign a few. After a while, I notice it's the same kids, every day, every trip. And I start watching 'em. There's a guy off to the side, a grown-up in a leather jacket, slinking in the shadows looking as nonchalant as he can. Well, the minute you cross the "t" in "Whitey," this kid snatches the card, walks over there and hands it to the guy. He slips the kid five bucks and another card, and they start the whole charade again. The kids are making money, maybe to buy drugs; that sumbuck is stuffing his pockets with those cards and selling them at shows. He goes to Madison Square Garden and gets a lot of money for 'em. It's big business today! So before they decide every player is a money-grubbing jerk, fans ought to think about how much it's changed—in both directions.

Most of the stuff I keep ain't autographed, but it's got value because it reminds me of something in baseball I care about. Maybe it's a person I'm glad I know, a side-splitting joke I heard, or somebody who really made me think. Those are the things you remember. You look at a bat, a picture, or a signature like that, and it reminds you why you went through all this in the first place. Once in a while, if I'm showing guests through the den, I even realize I'm giving them a little tour of baseball history. I've seen more of that than most.

Over here along the wall of the spare bedroom, I keep something I may like best of all. Right after my best friend Roger Maris died in 1985—he was only fifty-one when lymphatic cancer killed him—his wife, Pat, a dear, dear friend of ours, gave us a plaster-cast image of Roger hitting his 61st homer in 1961. She called right after the funeral, where I was a pallbearer, and said she really wanted us to have it.

It shows a historic moment—you know the image, with Roger's shirt puffed out as he makes contact with that pitch—but a poignant one for me personally. It's interesting I'm writing this now, during the season Mark McGwire and Sammy Sosa are chasing that record. Mark's a worthy successor, a good hitter and a fine man, and Sosa has been gracious, too. But few people will ever know what Roger really went through that year. Here he was chasing a record synonymous with greatness. His mark stood thirty-seven years, longer than the Babe's did. And people are still mad he set it. What does it say about sports in this country that making history turned out to be one of the worst things that ever happened to a nice person like Roger?

He didn't give much of a damn about records, and he certainly didn't start the year with the idea of chasing the Babe, but the commissioner, Ford Frick, changed history when he dreamed up that crazy asterisk business. He said Roger had to hit 61 by the 154th game or any record would be tainted. Roger was a contrary sonofa-gun, bristly as his haircut, and did *that* ever set him off. He wanted it bad after that, and my Lord, did he ever focus. He learned to time that swing just right to jack those liners over the rightfield boards. As the pressure built up, he bore down. I don't know how in the hell he did it.

People fail to put this in its proper perspective today. Roger Maris was trying to beat the man who saved base-ball, and no one in America wanted him to do that. If anybody was going to do it, everybody wanted it to be their hero, Mickey Mantle. The New York writers wanted it to be Mantle; the fans wanted it to be Mantle. His teammates wanted it to be Mantle. Roger and Mickey complemented each other on that ballclub, spurred each other on, but the fact that everybody was rooting against Roger pushed him; it sharpened his mind. He later told me he didn't think the whole thing was worth the anguish, though. Is that a hell of a note? That whole year typified Roger's life in more ways than one.

For reasons that bring shame to baseball, this man who was one of the great players in history never got the credit he deserved. It wasn't just that he broke one of the great records in sports. It's not just that he won back-to-back AL Most Valuable Player awards, in '60 and '61, while playing on two of the best teams that were ever assembled. It's not just that he's the only two-time MVP since World War II who isn't in the Hall of Fame. What really fries me is people thinking Roger was some fluke who popped a few homers one year and disappeared. Fluke, my ass. Roger's all-around play was a living clinic in how to play the game.

The big debate you always hear is about Pete Rose: Should he be in the Hall of Fame or not? Well, let's leave aside those questions of character, gambling, and prison. I've asked a lot of people this question: If you could draft a twenty-two-year-old Pete Rose to start a baseball team or a twenty-two-year-old Roger Maris, which one would you take? Everyone I've ever asked has said, "Well, Roger." And I say, "Why ain't *he* in the Hall, then?" People talk about longevity, career average, stuff they know nothing about. Now, I'm not knocking Pete. He had to be persistent and play a hell of a long time to set that all-time hit record. If the game was 10–0 either way, he stayed in there. He always wanted to get that last at-bat. But as the Reds manager, he did get to write his own name in the lineup them last few years. And Pete was a singles hitter, below average defensively. He was not in the same league as Maris. *That's* the debate we should be having.

Roger brought *everything* to the table. He could run like a deer. He was the best baserunner on the Yankees. He knew defense and got to every ball, cut 'em off in the gaps. He played shallow, made you hit it over his head; when you did, he ran it down and brought it back in. I played with Maris and with Hall of Famer Al Kaline in Detroit, and I couldn't tell you which was the better defensive outfielder. Neither one ever missed a cutoff man. Kaline's arm was a rifle, but I never saw *anybody* who could bring it in like Roger—not Colavito, not Clemente, nobody. His throws from the corner would sizzle in like a rocket, hop in front of the fielder, and drop right in his glove, soft as a baby. Nobody ever ran on him.

I don't care if he never hit .300. Roger was a worrier, so he was susceptible to slumps; when he got cold, he couldn't hit his first-grade teacher. And he'd tail off at the end of the season. One year in Kansas City, he was hitting .340 and then went 9-for-96 to end the year. But how many players are hitting that high in September?

People also don't realize he was a victim of his own success. Roger was never a home run hitter, really. He was a hard line-drive hitter who could pull flyballs. Very few players can do that; it's very unusual. He could even pull outside pitches for flyballs. That served him well in Yankee Stadium, where they had that short porch in right and the club asked him to aim for the stands. It's the only reason he hit those 131 homers his first three years there, before he had to have the hand surgery that cost him his power. But if Roger had never left Kansas City—his favorite big-league town—I believe he would have hit .300. He'd have been that hell-bent, Brady Anderson-style player, the gung-ho athlete he was meant to be, and New York would have never rained all that abuse on his head.

Baseball writers pick Hall of Famers, and Roger ticked off a few I ain't going to name here. Roger didn't warm up to people; it wasn't his nature. He didn't like to bullshit, didn't go out and play the nightlife. Even before he went to New York, he was the type of guy who half-thought people were trying to take advantage of him. If he didn't know you, and you approached him on the street, said hello, and stuck out your hand, he could just about bite it off. And if he made up his mind about you or about anything, boy, that was *it*. Even about food! One year he decided he liked escargot, and that was what he ate for two months. Escargot for dinner, escargot for lunch, escargot for appetizers, the main course, and dessert. He ate escargot till he got tired of it, and then he stopped. He didn't care what the hell you thought.

But who ever said a ballplayer had to read Miss Manners? That stuff hasn't got a thing in the world to do with it. The writers who shunned Roger Maris ought to be ashamed of themselves. You should *never* let personal things interfere with what's right. The fact he ain't in the Hall of Fame is a crime.

In a way, Roger didn't give a damn. He just did what he set his mind to. When the Yankees traded him to St. Louis after the 1966 season, he didn't want to go, so I leaned on him some. Hell, Gussie Busch was dangling a beer distributorship, and those are gold mines if you run 'em right. He made up his mind to go, and he hit third for a club that won two more pennants and a World Series. And do you know that the winter after he set the record—and lost all that hair—he came back to Kansas City, where we both lived, and helped me build my family's first house by hand? I set in 18,000 bricks myself, and here was the great New York celebrity, the biggest star in baseball, traipsing over at seven-thirty in the morning in the cold to help me mix mortar in a trough. My family lived in that house, ten minutes from where I'd later manage the Royals, for twenty-seven years. Talk about cementing a friendship.

And they say he didn't love the game. Long after Roger retired, he'd come down to spring training with my teams, I'd give him a field, and he'd take my kids and his kids out there and throw them batting practice for hours. He loved the game, all right; it was New York he didn't like. The last time I ever talked to him was before game six of the '85 Series—one that would change *my* career. I'd heard of a new cancer treatment that Edward Bennett Williams, the owner of the Orioles, was using. Hank Peters had called to tell me about it. All Roger wanted to talk about was why my team was in a batting slump. "Your guys ain't hitting a thing," he said. "You can't score any runs!" Roger Maris was dying of cancer; within two months, he'd be gone. Yet all the man wanted to talk about was Pendleton, Ozzie, and Willie. You're telling me he didn't love baseball?

That plaque also reminds me that even after they plant you in the ground, you can keep on building. Roger's golf tournament in Fargo, North Dakota, where he grew up a schoolboy star, has raised millions for cancer research. He'd started it a long time before he got sick. When the lymphoma came back, Roger had to stop coming, but I'm there every June of the world. So are Yogi, Bobby Richardson, Tony Kubek, Moose Skowron, Hank Bauer, other ex-Yankees, and a lot of baseball fans. I get to trot out my Stengel impersonation, we shoot the bull and reminisce, and if the mosquitoes aren't biting too bad, everybody has a wonderful time.

Roger Maris. How can you not love a man who lifted the game? I don't care if they never put his plaque in Cooperstown: He's never coming down off *my* wall.

Over here, across the room, are two jerseys under glass: one from the Royals, another bearing my uniform number, 24, in bright Cardinals red. I don't just think of the double-knit they're made of, the miracle fabric that freed us all from the heat and suffering of them old wool flannels. I remember that I managed both big-league clubs in my adopted home state, which nobody's done before or since. But mostly, they take me back to 1985, when the two towns squared off in the first all-Missouri World Series since 1944, when the Cards beat the Brownies.

It was nice to feel at home in both places. But there

was nothing cozy about how the I-70 Series turned out. It'll always be part of White Rat lore.

Writers from both coasts took off before we ever got started. We'd knocked off the Mets during the season and the Dodgers in the playoffs, and there were no Yankees in sight, so as far as they were concerned, there wasn't going to *be* no World Series. Well, screw 'em; they missed one of the greatest Series ever. Had it not been for one horseshit call, the Cardinals would have won a best-of-seven championship in six while scoring only fourteen runs.

The pitching and defense were outstanding. Danny Cox, one of my starters and the toughest player I ever managed, would have been MVP. I'd have had one more scalp on the wall, and I might have gotten a charge out of beating the Royals, a team I'd parted with five years earlier on lousy terms.

But you saw the play.

Todd Worrell, my flame-throwing reliever, is in to close down Game 6. We're up three games to two, ready to finish 'em off. It's the ninth; we lead 2–1 and stand three outs away. We've ridden a six-month rollercoaster to get here. We'd lost our stopper, Bruce Sutter, and his team-record 45 saves in the off-season. I went to spring training with a bullpen in shambles. One writer picked me as the first manager to get fired. Yet we hadn't blown one lead in the eighth inning or later all year. My makeshift bullpen-by-committee has racked up 44 saves. Willie McGee has had an MVP year, hitting .353 We're on the brink of a second title in four years.

Well, their leadoff hitter, Jorge Orta, opens the last inning with a high chopper to the right side. Jack Clark, my first baseman, gloves it; Worrell covers the bag perfect. Clark tosses it to Todd. He stomps on the base. Orta's out by a long, long stride, and we have that all important first one down. But for no earthly reason anybody's ever figured out, Don Denkinger—a fine American League umpire, a man I've always respected, a guy

I even *like*—stands right there by the bag, in plain, Show-Me state view, sees the same play the rest of America saw, and waves that runner safe.

Now, most people don't realize that in baseball, the leadoff man is the most important hitter. A team that gets its first batter to first base scores a run in that inning between 50 and 60 percent of the time—in baseball, *huge* percentages. If that man makes an out, the odds drop to about 10 percent. In a one-run game in the ninth, that first man is big. In Game 6 of the World Series, he's huge. This was trouble and a half. I shot straight out onto the field.

I didn't know what the damn problem was. I could see from the dugout that the throw beat Orta by a full stride, so I knew *that* wasn't it. I thought maybe Worrell's foot came off the bag. So as the fans went into their I-70 uproar, I got in Denkinger's face and said, "Don, what's the deal? Did Todd miss the bag?" "No," he says, "the runner beat the throw." And I thought, *did I hear this sonofagun right?* He beat the *throw?*

I said, "Man, are you shittin' me? I *know* he didn't beat the throw; I could see that from the dugout. I thought maybe he missed the bag." "No, the runner beat it." "Damn, Donnie," I hollered, "I can call it from the dugout better than that!" And right there on the field, Denkinger gave me a look that told me everything.

It was a kind of helpless, "oh-well" shrug along with a pained little smile. Now, I know umpires, and he might as well have said it out loud: "Hey, Whitey, sorry; shoulda got it right, but that's baseball, huh?" Don Denkinger was telling me he knew he'd booted the call.

I stared at him. He knew he'd blown it, but I guess he was hoping it'd just even out and go away. We argued. He wouldn't back down. And with a strange, dark feeling, I headed back to the dugout, took a seat, and watched a scene unfold that will stay with me for the rest of my life.

You know what happened. Guys did things they

hadn't done all year. Darrell Porter, my catcher, missed a pitch for a passed ball. Clark misjudged a pop foul. We fell apart. The Royals scored two to win the game. We were so shocked about taking it up the rear we got stomped 11–0 the next day. My players lost a World Series they deserved to win.

What an ending: That one damn call might keep me out of the Hall of Fame, and Don Denkinger became famous for the gaffe that made the Royals champions.

In Missouri, we had Quantrill's Raiders and Wild Bill Anderson tearing up the ground all through the Civil War, but the fans' arguments over that call *still* make them psychopaths look tame. To the west, Royals fans: "The Cards should have shrugged it off and won!" To the east, Cardinal fans: "There wouldn't have been no self-destruction if not for that SOB ump!" The play went down as The Call, and you still see framed pictures of it in bars from Jeff City to Joplin.

What they're fighting about is a question as old as the game: What's more important, getting it correct, or following the idea that the ump's always right, no matter how far his head's gone up his ass?

Well, I've had fourteen years to think about this. And here's what I've decided: We blew game seven bad—I got kicked out, along with Mr. Andujar—but that wasn't the biggest chance we booted.

Let's go back to the field. I'm jawing with Denkinger. We're on national TV, 200 million people are watching, the call's on instant replay, and *everybody* can see the man is wrong. What would have happened if I'd said, "That's it, Don; I want to talk to the commissioner. Get him down here." And I'd have gotten Peter Ueberroth, who was right behind the Royals' dugout, down from his seat, and said, "Pete, let me ask you something. This game is 2–1. We should have a man out at first with nobody on, two outs from a championship. Instead, we got a runner on first with *nobody* out. The ump admits he missed the call. Everybody in the world knows he missed the call. And *you* know he missed the call. Now, if you don't change that, and that man ain't out, I'm giving you the game. I'm taking my team off the field."

What would have happened?

Pete would have said, "Whitey, we can't do that." And I'd have said, "The hell you can't. Then we ain't playing, because every sonofabitch in the world knows that guy is out. This is the World *Series*, man, let's get it *right!*" I'd have waved my hand from the dugout, my team would have jogged in and left the field, and 50,000 fans and announcers and reporters would've been running around raising all kinds of hell. I'd have been fined, suspended, maybe had my ass run out of baseball.

In other words, it would've been everything my game needed to kick it in the rear. If I had it to do over again, that's just the way I'd play it.

There was precedent. One century before, almost to the day, in Game 2 of a postseason series against the Chicago White Stockings, the Browns' manager, Charlie Comiskey, pulled his team to protest the umpiring. God knows what kind of calls *he* had to put up with. It caused a hell of a row, boy, and the series ended up being declared a 3–3–1 tie. Did *he* do right? Did he screw up?

The questions go to the heart of baseball. When should a bad call really be part of the game? When should it *not* be? If the ump blows one in June, you go out there, kick some dirt, cuss a little; and if the ump admits he booted it, hey—you've got half the season to make it up. But can you look me in the eye and tell me it'd be the same thing if you were two outs from the world's championship?

If I'd pulled the vanishing act, maybe we'd have instant replay in the World Series by now. Bad calls at the bases, and along the foul lines, can be fixed in two seconds with a look at video. You'd have to put some limits on it, but that's what we ought to do. Like I said, this is for the championship—let's get it *right*.

Well, I'm not God; I ain't even the commissioner. I'm

only an ex-manager. The thing is, only the Pastime could be fiendish enough to pick a guy like me, point its finger and say, "All right, buddy, you've got sixty seconds, 200 million people are watching, and I ain't asking you again: What's your answer?" It's that trick pitch you've never seen, coming in at 98 mph, and by the time you get set, *whap!* It's in the mitt. The hell of it is, once you've figured out what that pitch was, you may never see it again.

And then there's that lineup card. I guess it's got some value now that Pete Rose has all that notoriety to go with his fame. But don't put me in with those people who feel he got a raw deal. If Pete did bet on baseball, then I feel he got what he deserved. He won't admit he did it, and I doubt he ever will, but he probably did. He's a good baseball man. He loves the game. But he loves money, too. And he was making phone calls out of Riverfront Stadium, placing bets. It might have been a pay phone in the ballpark. Knowing Pete, it might even have been out of his office, going right through the switchboard!

Now, the average fan might say, what is wrong with betting on your team to win? What is *wrong* with Pete Rose betting on the Cincinnati Reds to win? After all, he's going to try to win, right? So why is that wrong? Well, let me tell you the kinds of things that could happen to a manager if he starts to bet on his own team.

No one that ever managed a baseball game could tell you whether they were going to win or lose. There are times when my fifth starter is gonna go against Randy Johnson and I have a good inkling we're gonna get our ass beat, but that's not usually the case. Now, let's say I bet a million dollars on Tuesday for my ballclub to win. And we lose. And then I bet $2 million on Wednesday, and we lose again. So now I'm down $3 million. Then I bet $3 million on Thursday for us to win. And we lose again. Now I'm down, boy. I've lost $6 million in three days.

And let's say the paper comes out the next day: "Herzog on Thin Ice; Chance He Might Be Fired." How am I gonna pay you if I get fired? That bookie wants his money and he wants it now. He calls me and says, "I want that money by Friday morning." He's gonna shoot my ass if I don't pay up.

What am I going to say? I say, "Look, hang with me; just bet the money on us to lose tomorrow." Next day, I screw my moves up. I let my starter stay in till he gets the stuffing kicked out of him. Or instead of using my best closer with a one-run lead, I put some rinky-dink guy in there. Or I go up and it's time to put my ace in to get the last outs, and I put somebody else in. Or I go an inning too long with another guy. Who's gonna second-guess me? We might still win that game that day, but I guarantee you, if I do that for a few days, we're gonna lose eventually. In the meantime, I'm telling the bookie, "Hang with me; if we win, keep doubling up. I'll get it done." That bookie would get his money within a few days.

I'm sure it didn't go that way with Pete, but that's the kind of thing that *could* happen. When you go into a big-league clubhouse next time, check out what's on the door: On a sign, right there, is that warning against gambling. Rape, robbery, murder, and gambling—that's how you can get in trouble in baseball. They aren't kidding. I don't give a damn *which* way you bet; you can't mess with gamblers.

Over there, above the sofa, is one of my favorite photos, a color shot of me with the smartest boss I ever had, the old eagle, Gussie Busch. It was taken right after we won the '82 Series. Gussie's looking sharp in a Cardinal red blazer, a scarlet cowboy hat and a black string tie, and he and I are having a laugh and a taste of the company product, chilled to perfection.

I'll tell you one reason I love that picture. It's not just that he and I were hard-headed, Braunschweiger-chomping Germans who knew each other like brothers. It's not just that great players like Ozzie, McGee, Sutter, and Lonnie Smith got their moment in the sun that night, or that I did, too. No, that Series gave me the best chance I ever had to think about what winning means.

The test of greatness is how often you keep your team in the hunt. Bud Grant, who lost three Super Bowls for the Minnesota Vikings, and Marv Levy, who lost four for the Buffalo Bills, had to be two of the greatest NFL coaches in history just to be in the position *not* to win. Hell, I'll never forget, right after we lost the '85 Series in Kansas City, one of the Anheuser-Busch people came up to me, put his hand on my shoulder and said, "We'll do better next year." *Better?* If you told a guy like that you'd take losing in Game 7 of the World Series any year of your life, he'd send out for a straitjacket.

In golf, when you're putting, you choose your line, stroke the ball, and hope that sonofagun rolls in. If it doesn't, you still know you did it the best you could. Now, I'm a very confident, optimistic person, but by 1982, I was starting to wonder. What happens if you keep on stroking it just right, putt after putt, and then one day you realize, *Hey, that sonofagun's* never *dropped in the hole?* What happens if you *become* Bud Grant?

All my life, I've been good enough to get my teams close. That was true when I was a kid, and it was truer still when I coached and managed. But the strangest things would happen once I got there. You'd have made money betting on Herzog teams over the long haul. But if you'd put your money on some horrible break happening at the last minute, you could've retired early.

It started when I was young. At New Athens High, a tiny school with less than 100 kids in it, our basketball players knew each other so well we almost never lost. Between halves, our coach always gave us the same pep talk: "Boys, remember—this half, shoot at the other basket!" That's all he had to say. My senior year we got to the state quarterfinals, knocking off school after school that were five times our size. But in our last regional game, we played in a gym with glass backboards. We'd never seen those. I was a good foul shooter, but I kept seeing those fans waving their arms through the glass. I missed all six of my free throws. We lost by a point.

Same thing with our baseball team. We went deep in the playoffs but had to play our final game under lights—something *else* we'd never seen. Out in center, I got blinded on a long flyball, it caromed into a cornfield, and we lost by a run.

It stalked me to Kansas City. I managed my ass off for the Royals for five years, and we played great ball there. All three times we won the division, we faced the rich, mighty Yankees in the ALCS. But one year, one of my starting players kicks two balls in the deciding game; I heard later he was up all night using drugs. Another year, a first-game injury to Amos Otis, one of my stars, forces me to shuffle my lineup. I move Al Cowens, my 6-2 rightfielder, to center, and replace him with 5-8 Hal McRae. Well, we're tied in Game 5, a trip to the World Series on the line, when New York's Chris Chambliss hits a fly deep to right center. It goes over McRae's glove—and the wall—by six inches. Cowens could have made that catch. Season over.

In 1985, not only did The Call stomp all over us, but the fastest ballplayer in history—our offensive catalyst that year, the base thief Vince Coleman—got run over by a two-mile-an-hour mechanical tarp before the Series began. Two years later, we played the Twins in the Series. Two guys, Clark and Terry Pendleton, accounted for most of our offensive production that year, but both went down with late-season injuries. We lost.

Fluke plays happen, and no good baseball man uses them as an excuse. But if your tombstone read "He came awful damn close," would *you* be satisfied? When Gussie and I hoisted those Buds and our trophy in this picture, it was a monkey off my back. I'm relieved I never had to face the biggest question of all.

Fifty-some years ago, Joe DiMaggio took the time to sign me that autograph. Twenty-five years after that, his playing days were over and he was a consultant for the Oakland A's. And he called me one day to offer me a job: He wanted me to be their manager.

I was tempted, boy. I'd coached most of those players myself, before the team moved away from Kansas City. I'd hit 'em grounders and fungoes and drilled 'em on fielding and hitting. I got half the pay the other coaches got and did twice the work. I'd driven 'em hard. I knew it was a hell of a group, and I knew they were going to win.

But I also knew that the A's owner, Charles O. Finley, was a meddler of the worst kind. He took credit where it wasn't due; he thought he knew the game. If you were his manager, he'd do everything but fill out your lineup card. Charlie was a good guy—he'd buy you a Scotch and soda any day of the week if he met you on a train—but if you worked for him, he thought he owned you. I turned the offer down.

Do I regret it? Those A's teams won three World Series in a row and went down in history as a dynasty. I might have been their Casey Stengel. But Charlie didn't understand something that Joe D. showed me just by the way he carried himself: That in this game, it's the people who count.

What do you value in baseball? Is it how much you win? Is it how famous you get, how they remember you, how much money you make? What kind of signature will you leave? Nowadays, it's hard to know what people think. But when the last inning is played, every man has to answer for himself.

· 5 ·
Ten Singles

I've always had a different idea about baseball assets than most people. Just ask the fans in St. Louis.

When I first came to the Cardinals in 1980, they had a bunch of veterans who were considered stars around the league and institutions in Missouri. They were sure as hell getting paid accordingly. We had the second-highest payroll in the big leagues and three of the top ten salaries in baseball. By the time a few months had gone by, I'd gotten rid of nearly all of them.

You should have heard the hullaballoo. People calling the sports-talk shows, saying, "Whitey's giving away too much!" "Who the hell is this guy, running off Ted Simmons?" "Handing over fourteen players and getting back eleven? Can't the sonofabitch count?" The same howling day after day after day. If it'd been legal, there'd have been a lynching. My ass would've been hanging from the Gateway Arch.

Ten years, three pennants, and a World Series championship later, the teams I put in their place had broken the Cardinal attendance record three times. We earned two other championships that got taken away. Our fan total passed the 3 million mark for the first time in the history of the franchise, then did it again. Downtown St. Louis was a sea of red on game days—shirts, foam cowboy hats, pennants, those crazy number-one pointing fingers, all mobbing the streets and swirling around inside the stadium. The Cardinals have been around for damn near a century, and we broke the club attendance record five times in ten years.

New York fans will argue with me—hell, New Yorkers, they think that if you don't live in their city you're just camping out—but we turned into the best, most talked-about National League team of the 1980s. Our fans saw great baseball moments, from Ozzie's backflipping magic to Vince Coleman's steals and Willie McGee's glovework in centerfield, where triples went to die. We went toe-to-toe with stronger, richer, deeper ballclubs like the Mets. McGee is back with the Cards and, even now, seventeen years after our last world title, every time he steps in the batter's box he gets a standing ovation. A hundred-some ovations a year—it's the damnedest thing I've ever seen.

I guess I wasn't as nuts as they thought.

Many, many more factors determine attendance than managing. Winning's the biggest. Players and ownership, the competition from other sports, and the regional economy do, too. I got my share of breaks in each of those areas. But one thing I'm proud of is putting a brand of ball on the field that jazzed up the fans and kept them coming. That was true at every stop, with the lone exception of Texas, where I only had one year to straighten out a panhandle-sized mess. Otherwise, the teams I managed drew 38 million fans—roughly the combined populations of New York, L.A., and Chicago, with a few Philadelphians thrown in to boo the rest of 'em. We broke ten club attendance records in those fifteen years, by far the highest percentage (.667) in the history of baseball. Sparky Anderson is in second place in that category, I hear, and he did it six times in twenty-five years (.240). To quote Casey, you could look it up.

The style we played is one you don't see much of today. Too many rules and trends work against it, including economics. When you do see it, it's only in spurts, and you're going to see less and less of it as time goes by if the rules don't change. Now, I know the

McGwire chase was great for attendance and kept the fans excited. Hell, I enjoyed it myself. But that ain't the only approach to baseball.

Writers used to call mine "Whiteyball," but I always thought that was crazy. It ain't a thing in the world but a style that goes back a hundred years in baseball history, to John McGraw's playing days with the old Baltimore Orioles before the turn of the century. (And it's no small factor that Casey Stengel played for John McGraw.) Hustle, scaring up runs, sliding hard—what McGraw called "scientific baseball"—goes to the heart of the game as the fans know it. And I should know; I'm a fan myself.

What happened in Kansas City and in St. Louis could happen all across the industry. It would be cost effective; it'd make sense. Baseball may be infatuated with homermania right now, but this game would be crazy not to look at what happened in my career, too. What we've got is a traveling circus with some great sideshow acts. But there's other ways to get crowds in the tent. If we woke up and used our brains, we could start a baseball renaissance that's rooted in the game itself.

I have some ideas how to do it. But before I get into all that, I want to tell you a story.

In the '84 offseason, we gave five guys to the Giants for a player who turned out to be one of the most important Cardinals in history. We'd have never won the 1985 and 1987 pennants without him. He was one of the scariest fastball hitters I ever saw. Some of his shots to the opposite field didn't just scatter the fans, they left the seats in splinters. There wasn't a pitcher in baseball that didn't fear Jack Clark.

Jack was a wonderful guy—we're still friends, and we'd do just about anything for each other—but he had some quirks. His talent for spending money, for one thing, was top-ten material. Jack made a million and a half a year, and he earned every penny he got, but he doled it out faster than his homers rattled off the score-board. One day, on his way to the ballpark, he pulled over on a whim, stopped at a car dealer, and bought two $90,000 Porsches. "One for me," he said, "and one for my wife!" He didn't save a lot, but he sure could get to the bank in a hurry.

He was also a big-time perfectionist. Jack wanted to win so bad he couldn't see straight. Sometimes that made him ride his teammates too much or say things that came out the wrong way. Sometimes it made him a better player. Mostly, it just wound him up too tight. Years ago, when Yogi asked, "How am I supposed to hit and think at the same time?" he might have been talking about Jack, who sometimes thought so much he forgot to swing.

Well, I'm known in the game as a rabid fisherman. When I'd talk to the writers before a World Series game and tell them I'd been out in the boat all that morning, they used to soil their britches, but I'd just laugh. When I *ain't* fishing, that's when you'd better call the men in the white coats. It gets me away from the phones and the agents, just clears out the cobwebs for me. Jack was the same way: A good day on the water would calm him down. That was where he could really hear you talk—about pitch counts, looking for the heater, laying off—and as often as not, it sent him on a tear.

One day, an old buddy of mine, Herb Fox, and I took Jack out on the back lake at Herbie's farm. It's a seventy-acre strip-mining pit, and the three of us were out in a fifteen-foot bass boat early in the morning. We caught a little bluegill and bass and talked some base-ball, some hunting, some fishing. It's a real pretty spot, nice and quiet with the sun rising up over the cattails.

Well, Jack must have had a fine day, because next afternoon at the ballpark, he comes up to me, all worked up, and tells me he's bought himself a new boat. I thought that was wonderful. "A new boat? I'll be damned, Jack. What kind you get?" I said.

"The number-one boat. It's a Ranger. A twenty-two-foot wide-body!"

"Twenty-two foot?! How big an engine?"

"It's 200 horse!"

Nobody on a strip pit ever needed that kind of power, so I'm already starting to laugh. "Two hundred horse? What the hell you gonna do with all that?" Jack looks at me with those killer black eyes and says, "I like speed."

God almighty: He likes speed! Well, I don't blame him; if you ever saw any of my ballclubs, you know I like it, too. But that still didn't tell me what he was going to do with a motor the size of Fenway Park.

Our next day off, Herbie and I are out on the lake again, sitting there in the calm waiting for some nibbles. I'm fishing topwater with my trusty White Rat lure; Herbie's going down deep. It's early in the morning, nice and quiet, the mist rising up silent and pretty like it does around dawn. Next thing you know, here comes Jack, with his wife and two kids and his new boat trailing behind his Chevy Suburban, right over the hill. I mean to tell you, that was a hell of a rig! They were making more racket than a sellout at the Homerdome. And Jack plops that monster in the water and fires up the engine, all 200 horse, and revs the hell out of it. I'm telling you, stuff was *flying*—water, weeds, old car tires, maybe even a few large-mouth too. He turned the lake over. Later on, when he's done, he backs the Suburban up to the edge, and the boat's so big he can't get the damn thing out of the water. It was a sight!

Well, no question about it: That boat was a beauty. But you have to ask yourself a question: How big a rig do you *need?* On Herbie's back lake, where a johnboat, two hooks, and a couple of a hours will fetch you a good lunch, all that extra juice is just going to stir up the neighbors and scare the fish away. Power's great, but without proportion, it won't help you a bit.

That's a perfect description of modern baseball.

• • •

In the wake of the '94 strike, I was like the fans—so disgusted with the players' union, the owners, the greed and the whole mess that I could barely stand to watch. I was tuning in to NBA games, women's golf, everything on the planet except postseason baseball. Well, what turned the owners pale—the Jerry Reinsdorfs, the Bud Seligs, and so on—was seeing people like me, fans of the game, boating, golfing, and going to the beach and happy as a clam about it. None of us *needed* the old National Pastime. We knew it, and they did, too.

Look what's happened since. Stadiums now are carnivals with ballfields attached. A kid can play Nintendo, catch a catapulted T-shirt, jackknife into a swimming pool, paint his face in the team colors, and get assaulted by rock'n'roll and never see a pitch. Why are owners called "the Lords of Baseball" when they obviously think the game's not interesting enough? I think they're wrong: Fans do still love the game. The problem is, they ain't seeing it much.

We really ought to rename the sport. It's not baseball now; it's Powerball. Sit in the bleachers today and you ought to wear a helmet. They say the ball ain't jacked up? Why does it bounce so high when I drop it on the ground? Throw in the smaller ballparks we have now, the incredible shrinking strike zone, and all the Double-A pitching we're seeing, which has been watered down by *more* expansion. And as McGwire said last year, baseball's a twelve-month job today; the players work out and stay in shape year 'round. Guys are a lot stronger now. So many factors have turned baseball into a home-run show.

It's causing a buzz, but let's look at what's happened. I talked to Stan Musial a while ago, and he said it right: "When I was playing, home-run hitters hit home runs." Today, *everybody* hits home runs. It used to be that if you were a home-run hitter, you hit 25; everybody else had less than 10. Now, a home-run hitter hits 55, 60,

70; a *non*-home-run hitter gets 25 or 30. Here's a stat for you: The year Ruth hit his 60 homers, only 334 were hit in the entire American League. He and Lou Gehrig had 107 between them. That's a third of the league total! The year Maris hit 61 homers, 1,400 left the yard. As I'm writing this, McGwire's about to break the record, and there will be around 2,500 in the National League. Mark would be a bona fide slugger in any era, but the elephants in this circus have stomped the old rules into the sod.

Baseball has always had pendulum swings between offense and defense. Look at the 1968 season, with that record number of shutouts, and the way we lowered the mound afterward. But home-run baseball is so prevalent now, the pendulum ain't ever going to go back unless we make some drastic changes. Yet, in the midst of all this racket, there's one question that nobody seems to ask: *Is this what we want?* In the long run, is this big-shot baseball good for the game? I've got a few views on that.

When I took over the Cardinals, they were a lot like the clubs of the nineties. Not that they hit a ton of homers, but they were a shiny, 200-horse engine churning up the lake. No defense, no running game, big numbers. The three top players—Garry Templeton, Ted Simmons, and Keith Hernandez—were making over $650,000 each, a king's ransom for 1980. Hell, I've lived in Missouri thirty-eight years; it's tough to *spend* that kind of money in the Show-Me state.

But you couldn't blame the brewery and old Gussie for raiding the vault for those three. Templeton, the shortstop, was the single most talented all-around player I'd seen since Mickey Mantle. He's still the only guy who ever got 100 hits from each side of the plate in a year, and he could run, field, and throw; the only thing he didn't have was power. Simmons, a .290 or .300 hitter every year, socked ropes all over the ballpark that made your jaw drop. Cha-Cha—that was Keith's nick-

name then—had been co-MVP of the National League
the year before; he was a fine hitter and hell of a first
baseman, one of the best ever to play the position.
George Hendrick, Tony Scott, and others kept the
Cardinals at the top of the NL in hitting with .280, .285
team averages year after year. We led the league in runs
scored in 1980. You'd think these guys could throw their
gloves on the field and win.

You'd think that if you didn't know baseball. If you
looked a little deeper—as the average fan and sports-
writer don't—you saw a team that played the game all
wrong. There was no identity, no strategy. They could
score, but it took them four hits to do it. It generally
takes at least three runs to win, but even *good* teams
can't count on 12 hits a day. You have to do more than
that. But nobody ran. Nobody went hard into second.
The defense was a floodgate.

When I traded Simmons and some other guys, man,
you'd have thought I'd traded Abe Lincoln and George
Washington. It was open rebellion! But the truth was,
even the fans didn't really like that team. The Cards
hadn't drawn 2 million since 1968. In spite of what you
hear now about St. Louis being a great baseball town,
tumbleweeds were blowing across the field in those
days. The city liked the football Cardinals better. The
fans who did show up went hoarse from booing. What
I'm trying to say is, it ain't that I took apart a team they
loved; I took apart a team they were *used* to. Even when
it's for the best—even when there ain't any choice—
people hate change.

Lucky for me, I didn't have to worry about it: I was
both GM and manager. With Gussie's blessing, I could
run off the stiffs and slackers and put together the ballclub I wanted. We rebuilt with the exact baseball assets
you don't see much of anymore. We picked up some
players nobody else wanted. We went after qualities that
ain't supposed to be worth two sacks of resin. We tight-
ened the defense, added role guys, and cut the payroll

30 percent. We had very few home-run hitters. And we ended up with a baseball revival.

I didn't want to screw around. When I set out to rebuild the Cards, I wanted to win. And when I say win, I mean win championships. To do it, I had two principles in mind.

First, in the modern game, with all its specialization, you had to have that great stopper in the bullpen. He comes in, gets you those last few outs—to me that meant five or six—and cuts 'em off at the knees. I'd learned that the hard way in my three playoff series against the Yankees. We played 'em tough each time but lost. Sparky Lyle, Goose Gossage, and the New Yorkers out-bullpenned me, and that was the end of *that* story.

Second, the National League had lots of big ballparks and fake turf. I called this "modern baseball geography," and to me, it changed the way you had to look at the game. To shrink a huge ballpark like Busch Stadium down to size, you needed good athletes with speed in the field. You also needed pitchers who threw strikes and let the other team make contact. Forget strikeouts. Their hitters wouldn't be able to put many over the wall, and your track stars could run down the balls that stayed in. Finally, since that turf is so fast, you wanted batters who hit the upper half of the baseball, smacked it on the ground, and took off. That would create new ways to get on base, stir up trouble, and score runs.

The right personnel at Busch wouldn't look like much. They wouldn't have to be big; they'd have to be smart. And if I was right, they'd be able to bring visitors to their knees.

At the Dallas winter meetings after the 1980 season, I put the plans in motion. First, we sent a young catcher we liked, Terry Kennedy, to the San Diego Padres, along with five guys I didn't need, for Rollie Fingers, probably the greatest reliever of all time. But that wasn't enough. The bullpen monster I really wanted was Bruce Sutter of the Cubs, and I kept on his trail. I offered them Keith Hernandez in a package deal, but the Cubs GM, Bob Kennedy, didn't want to take on that big salary. Instead, we had to offer a great-looking young hitter, Leon Durham, along with our slow-footed third baseman, Kenny Reitz. They bit. We had a bullpen for the ages.

For a few days, anyway. Now that I had Sutter, I could deal from strength. I packed Fingers along with Ted Simmons off to Milwaukee in a blockbuster deal that brought us David Green, a minor-league outfielder with world-class speed. Everybody saw him as the number-one prospect in the game. I have to laugh: He was so good, some of the Brewers executives damn near came to blows over giving him up.

But the track meet *really* started the next off-season. We sent two pitchers to Cleveland to get Lonnie Smith, who immediately stole 68 bases and hit .307 as our lead-off man. We traded for Ozzie Smith, who among his other talents may have been the most effective base stealer I ever managed. And our scouts noticed that the Yankees, after signing big Dave Winfield to a splashy free-agent contract, left a minor-league speedster named Willie McGee off their forty-man roster. We sent them a lefty we weren't using much, Bob Sykes, and brought Willie up that May. He was our centerfielder for the next nine years, and the best in the National League.

Those Cardinal teams usually hit fewer homers in batting practice than McGwire slugs in a season. But our runs-against dropped by more than 100. We cracked 200 steals in every one of the ten years I ran the team, a feat that will never be duplicated. It was anti-powerball—the John McGraw style, souped up for the AstroTurf era.

Within a year and a half, we won the World Series. That music you heard around Busch Stadium? It wasn't just "When You Say Bud"; it was cash registers ringing. Twenty-five million flooded through the turnstiles, scarfing up peanuts and Cracker Jack and raising hell. They woke up the whole downtown. They ate in the diners, they slept in the hotels, they drank in the taverns. Charlie Gitto, who runs one of the top restaurants downtown, still says they ought to name a day after me. "You guys did so much for business in the city," he says, "it's the least they could do." Instead of the big-engine baseball the fans *thought* they liked, we gave them the ten-horse kind they loved.

If my career proves one thing, it's that baseball fans ain't stupid. Even if they don't understand every wrinkle of the inside game, when they see it in front of them, they know it. And they respond. It's like the oil business, boy: Build your derrick in the right spot, you'll hit a gusher. All across America, that well runs deep.

My St. Louis teams will always be remembered as the "Runnin' Redbirds." We did run like a whirling dervish. Coleman, Tommy Herr, and Andy Van Slyke—youngsters we brought up through our farm system later on—only spun it around faster. Most days, I had five switch-hitters in the lineup, and we slapped 'em crazy. We really played the game different! That was some kind of baseball.

But most fans don't realize that even the basestealing we were known for wasn't really our foundation. That came in the form of a guy who couldn't get to first base any faster than I can. He wore big glasses, talked softer than a church mouse, missed the highlight reels, and rarely made a dent in those glamor categories you read about in *USA Today*. But if you want to learn about winning, money-making baseball, look no further than the man I got from Kansas City to squat behind the plate. Darrell Porter's style was the kind that turns chumps into champions—and takes a million fans and turns 'em into family.

You could see why St. Louis loved Teddy Simmons. He was a very visible citizen, raised a lot of money for charity, knew all the businesspeople, and the like. But more than that, he'd been the Cards' catcher for eleven years. Ted's .297 career average, 1,700-plus hits and nearly 1,000 RBIs had been the heart and soul of the offense. His numbers put him on a whole lot of top-ten lists. And you know what? If the National League had had the designated hitter, the man would have gone to his coffin a Cardinal.

But I don't usually see what others do in a player. That's just the way I am, and it was sure true in this case. Ted hit the ball like a sonofagun, but when I watched him play, I didn't see a motor that drove the Cardinals' boat. He was more like a leak in their hull. Ted Simmons, God bless him, was a fine person who played hard and cared about winning. But he had one major weakness as a ballplayer: poor arm strength. Unfortunately for the Cardinals organization, that one flaw was a bigger disaster than anybody around me seemed to realize. Ted's fluttery throws to second were enough to scuttle the Cards and keep the fans away. If you understand why, you know a boatload about the inside game of baseball.

Let's start with a basic fact: It's hard to score a run. Excepting homers, which are relatively infrequent, it takes planning. A runner gets on; the others have to find a way to push him around and get him in. Many games are decided by a single run, too. So it's just as important to stop the other guy from scoring a run as it is to get one home yourself. And your catcher is your most important guy in shutting chances down.

Let's say you're the Los Angeles Dodgers. It's the eighth inning of a big game, and you're behind 2–1. And let's say your leadoff man gets to first. Well, the next batter wants to move him over to second—into scoring position. Normally, that batter will lay a bunt down. He'll probably get thrown out at first himself, but he'll move that lead runner over. It's a sacrifice: He's swapped an out for a chance to score. The defensive team takes its pound of flesh, but with two outs left to go, the Dodgers have two shots at bringing that runner in.

We're in the big leagues now, and here's how it works among the best: What happens if the Dodgers can get that runner to second and not give up an out doing it? For example, what if that runner can just steal second? Then he'll be in scoring position with no outs. Then them boys in Dodger Blue have *three* cracks at driving him in. Baseball is a game of percentages, and big-league clubs always want that extra chance. If they get it, they're going to make some hay.

Busch Stadium made this problem even worse. In our park, just to cover the field, every manager used his fastest lineup anyway. That guy at first was bound to be a jackrabbit. Your catcher had better be on constant alert.

Well, in the major leagues, you don't give away critical odds for nothing—not and win, you don't. And Ted Simmons forked 'em over by the bushel.

Because Ted threw poorly to second, every team in the world knew they could swipe that base in the late innings. They knew that if they were behind, they'd eventually get their three shots to score. Hell, you always want to intimidate visitors on your home field, make 'em feel you've got the edge, but visitors to Busch always knew there was time to come back. It gave them confidence, kept 'em loose. I doubt five fans could have told you about this factor. Announcers never brought it up. It wouldn't show up in the *Post-Dispatch* box scores. But every manager worth his spikes was clued in. You'd be amazed—*amazed*—how many games that cost the St. Louis Cardinals.

Ted is a good test case for my beliefs about baseball. He did all the things that make a guy money. By the standards everybody still uses today, he was a star. But again: *Everybody doesn't know baseball.* Too many fans, media, and even baseball people get sidetracked by factors that just don't bear on the big picture. In the Simmons era, the Cards had never finished first.

So why extend it? At the winter meetings, I approached Harry Dalton, the Brewers' GM, and I said, "Hey, how'd you guys like to win the pennant next year?" When he allowed as how, yes, that would be a fine idea, I offered him Simmons, along with Pete Vuckovich, our best righthanded starter the past two years, and Rollie Fingers, for Green and three other guys. It may have triggered a brawl in their front office, but they couldn't pass it up. We made the trade.

I didn't know we'd actually face the Brewers (and beat them) in the Series the next fall. But one of the main reasons we got there was the guy I hired to take Ted's place.

St. Louis did not take to Darrell Porter at first. Maybe it was that five-year, $3.5 million free-agent deal I gave him. Maybe it was the drug problems he'd had, which were extensive and recent. Maybe it was the fact that, except for one big year with the Royals—a .291 average, 20 homers, and 112 RBIs in 1979—he hadn't rung up big numbers. Maybe they just didn't like a four-eyed ballplayer. All I know is, for a year and a half, they booed the hell out of the new cornerstone of the St. Louis Cardinals.

Well, to learn about what matters in baseball—not the ESPN or sports-column version—all you had to do was get to know Darrell. Behind the plate, he was smart, aggressive, tough as a boulder; in Kansas City, when he tagged you out, man, you saw constellations. As to the drug problem, the only reason fans knew about it was that he'd been man enough to face it, come forward, and seek help. Many guys in baseball did less in those days, including some on my own teams—one of whom, in my opinion, cost the Royals and their fans a trip to the World Series. Darrell Porter, as a man, always looked himself in the eye and did what he had to do to get better. That's a hell of a trait in a ballplayer.

It transferred to the field. The average fan doesn't realize how a .220 hitter can do more for you than a guy seventy points higher, but Darrell Porter was the best .220 hitter who ever lived. In spite of the glasses, he had a keen eye: His on-base percentage was around .380 for most of his career. That's the kind of discipline that keeps rallies going. It brings your big guns to the plate with runners on, giving *them* the chance to drive in runs. The media never mention that, but it's a crucial factor in working up an offense. McGee, Hendrick, Clark, and Herr were RBI stars at different times, but without Darrell's baseball knowledge, they'd have never had as many chances.

When Darrell did swing, he did it with a plan. He put the ball where it helped us. His outs went behind the runner, which allowed that runner to move up a base. His base hits, also behind the runner, would advance a guy two bases. On a Cardinal club that hit more chinkers and dying quails than you could shake a fungo at, that meant leaving our runners in a place they could score from. We got an awful lot of runs on infield squibbers that way, and many days that was the difference between winning and losing. Over the season, that piles up.

Darrell's strong throwing arm, good positioning, and quickness behind the plate shut down the leakage overnight. But he was also smart at handling pitchers, another of the catcher's jobs. Darrell knew the strengths of his staff. It would surprise you to know how many big-league catchers focus only on the hitter's weakness, asking pitchers to throw something they *cannot* throw, just so they'll stay away from a hitter's strength. But that's a fallacy: Big-league hitters can smack a horseshit pitch no matter where it's thrown. Darrell never asked a Dan Quisenberry, Dennis Leonard, or Bob Forsch to throw something he didn't know the man could get across for strikes. Hell, half the time, he didn't know if it was Babe Ruth or Oliver Twiddly batting. It didn't matter. A winning player knows a teammate's strengths; he works from strength. It's one reason why, in the eight years I managed Darrell Porter, I never called more than two pitches a game myself.

Finally, while I managed some of the greatest base stealers of all time—Vince Coleman stole 100-plus three years in a row, and you'll never see that done again—I'll be damned if the finest baserunner I ever managed wasn't Darrell Porter. He didn't steal, but he was a true Cardinal runner in the Enos Slaughter–, Red Schoendienst–, Stan Musial–type mold. He hustled, he thought ahead, he got good jumps; he cut the bases just right. If Darrell couldn't go from first to third on a ground-ball base hit, it couldn't be done. Such things wouldn't get him any money in today's game, and very few people realized he was doing them, but they made us all rich.

Darrell may have been off the fans' radar screen, but one thing they did know: The team was winning. They started showing up in droves. The media got jacked up. As we added speed and defense across the field, they fell in love with other heroes—McGee, Ozzie, Lonnie, Jack—and the Runnin' Redbirds consistently won more and finished higher in the standings than the so-called experts predicted. It's the nature of baseball that sometimes the guys who play it best are least visible to the naked eye. In Darrell's eight years with me, I won five division titles, two pennants, and a World Series. Not bad, boy. Those are stats I can get excited about.

My friend and fellow St. Louisan Bob Costas says St. Louis "remembered why it's the best baseball town in America" around this time. Give credit to the man in glasses and iron mask. Baseball, and baseball fans, would do themselves a big, big favor if they found a way to reward the Darrell Porter–type player. But they'd have to recognize him first. What he knows of the game brings us all to our feet.

Almost without exception, today's teams plan around the big blast. The goal is excitement. But the thing people don't realize is, even in a homer-happy era like ours, the long ball only happens a few times a game. The rest of the time, the players are mostly just standing around. Why? Well, if I'm on base, and that next guy up is liable to hit one into the next county, why the hell should I run? If I get thrown out stealing, that costs us a run. No sir, I'm going to sit on my ass for the team.

That's the exact attitude a real fan can't stand.

Hell, of all the fans I ever met, I think I'll remember one the most. This guy had seen my teams play in Kansas City and he'd seen them play in St. Louis. And he'd given it a lot of thought. After a Cardinals game one day, he came up to me and gave me the biggest compliment I've ever gotten in baseball. "Whitey," he said, "I don't care if you guys win or lose. They get their uniforms dirty. When your teams get ten singles, the fans are entertained." I never heard it said any better than that.

To me, it's simple: I have my teams play the way I live. I don't waste a minute. I'm up by six every morning, and I get more done by nine than most people I know get done in a day. I'm fishing, terracing the yard, painting the fence, talking on the radio—all this even though I'm 67 years old, the age where when you get up in the morning, what's supposed to be stiff is limber, and what's supposed to be limber is stiff. I'm planning what I'll do the next week, the next month. Friends talk about my energy, but it's just the way I keep my batteries charged. Life's a hell of a ride; why waste it in a parking space?

I crave movement in baseball, too. Game to game, pitch to pitch, you can always jab that beehive. Drop a bunt, charge a grounder, hit behind the runner. Knock the shortstop on his ass. Force something, man! The beauty of this game should be that you don't have to be born with a Nolan Ryan arm or a Big Mac swing. You don't have to be 6-8 or clean-and-jerk 400 pounds. You can be Darrell Porter and make things happen. And win.

I'll bet you've noticed how broadcasters like to go on and on about *signs* and *switches* and god knows what else. Well, I remember Jim Fregosi one time, when he was a player down in Texas; our Royals had had a fight with his Rangers, and afterwards, I ran into him in a bar. I heard him telling somebody he had our signs. Well, I didn't *have* signs! I had everybody on *go*, until I took it off. I just said, "You've got 'em read? I better get the coaches together. I'll have to change them tomorrow night!" And I laughed the whole way home. There's all kinds of ways to do it.

Take one of baseball's more interesting recent teams—the 1997 Pittsburgh Pirates. That was the year the Marlins won the World Series, then stripped themselves down like an old Chevy on cinderblocks, but Gene Lamont's Bucs were the story of that season. In an era of rich clubs and Little Orphan Annies, those guys stayed in the race with a $10 million payroll. That's a whole team making about what the Atlanta Braves paid one of their starting pitchers. As of June, Pittsburgh was still leading the National League Central, and fans all over the country were going nuts about it. Baseball ought to remember the four key words that explain why: America loves the underdog.

You don't have to be a Harvard egghead to figure out why, and again, it goes to the heart of the National Pastime.

This country was started from scratch. We built things from nothing, on brains, wits, and ants in our pants. Two centuries later, we still haven't forgotten that way of thinking. Baseball was dreamed up back then, and baseball keeps it alive.

Look at how it's played: out in the sunlight, where everybody can see. For the fans, there's time to argue every play till the cows come home. Nobody can hide. And the players look like you and me; they ain't mutants. John Kruk, David Wells, or Tony Gwynn could be poster boys for hot dogs and beer. Porter looked like my accountant. If Orel Hershiser mowed your lawn, you'd probably just give him a tip and go on with your day. Those are the guys the fans love. The key to baseball is, the regular Joe can use his smarts, work hard, and knock the bigger, richer guy on his ass.

When the Cards, with our ninety-seven-pound-weakling offense, went to the World Series three times in the 1980s and the mighty, big-budget Mets only went once, what really jacked up the fans? Crabby John Tudor outsmarting mighty Darryl Strawberry with a changeup. Ricky Horton, my chicken-wing lefthander, making the minimum salary but matching Doc Gooden pitch for pitch. Tommy Herr driving in more runs than Gary Carter some years. Sure, the Mets had a hell of a club and put it all together in 1986. But just as often, ten good singles can beat the towering home run. In baseball, the way it ought to be, the little blows can prevail.

Well, tell that to the '97 Pirates. The fact is, anybody that knows baseball realized they never had a chance. They played like hell, that's for sure, as good as they could. Their pitching was better than anyone expected, and they did the little things. It also takes a bad team at least till July to figure out how horseshit it is. That's when they all start catching up to you. Ten million dollars, a minor-league budget, only gets you minor-league talent. That shot was going to wear off.

The thing is, I ain't criticizing that team. It's the industry that's the problem. When a club like those Pirates hasn't got a prayer, baseball is in deeper trouble than it knows. If we don't use our brains and change the rules we have, you'll never see a '97 Pirates, a Darrell Porter, a ten-single offense, or the John McGraw style again. The game will lose the feel that connects it to its past and to the fans. And baseball will be just what America doesn't need—one more place where Goliath kicks the hell out of David, the big shots rule, and the underdog can never win.

· 6 ·

The Wizard

It's the ninth inning of Game 5 in the league championship series. The shortstop I call "Midget" seems a little fidgety. The Dodgers' massive righthander, Tom Niedenfuer, is glaring down from the mound. Fifty thousand fans in Cardinal red are buzzing like flies. We've lost the first two games in LA, evened the score here in St. Louis, and want to head back to California on top, not one loss away from the sudden end of a great season. Ozzie Smith—all 150 singles-hitting pounds of him—digs in left-handed, waggling his bat, as the pitcher everybody calls Buff (as in buffalo) rears back, winds up, and brings down some major-league heat.

Ozzie wheels like a lumberjack, fouls the pitch off, and drives himself into the ground like a corkscrew.

Hell, I'm thinking, *that* ain't Ozzie. Two outs, two runners on, 2–2 score—we need a base hit, not Babe Ruth. In the dugout, I'm wearing my usual stern look, but on the inside it was more like, *This guy's come to the plate 3,000-plus times lefthanded and never once hit a home run.* Even Jack Buck, the Cards' evenhanded announcer, makes a crabby remark on KMOX Radio, the voice of the Cardinals across Middle America— probably wondering, like all the rest of us, *What's with the Paul Bunyan routine?*

But 1985 has been a long, strange year. As I told you, we started off losing Bruce Sutter and his 45 saves in the off-season. That makes any genius manager 45 games dumber, and maybe it's why that writer said I'd be the first guy on the unemployment line. We came to camp with only one pitcher, Neil Allen, who had ever had a save in his life. We were picked to finish last. And my new number-two starter, John Tudor, didn't help my cause any; here I'd traded George Hendrick, my best power hitter the last four years, for him, to back up Andujar, and the sonofagun lost seven of his first eight decisions. It looked like a long season under the Gateway Arch.

But Tudor, who never threw a ball over 85 mph in his life, started working that now-you-see-it changeup of his, found his rhythm, and ran off 20 wins in his next 21, including 10 shutouts—one of the best stretches in Cardinal history. A second baseman with only 8 home runs, Tommy Herr, caught fire hitting in front of Jack Clark and drove in 110 runs. Down the stretch, he became the best clutch hitter I'd seen since George Brett. A minor-leaguer I didn't bring up till May, Vince Coleman, stole 110 bases and electrified our offense, not to mention all of baseball, with his arrogance and raw speed. With Jeff Lahti as my primary closer—he ended up with 19 saves—leading the way till I brought up Todd Worrell at the end of August, our bullpen never blew a save after the seventh inning, one of the best collective relief performances in the history of the game. And as Ozzie turned the shortstop position into his personal highlight reel, our fielders cut off lanes and gaps all over the field, throwing a big damp blanket on rallies all year.

The writers said we did it by running like rabbits, but mostly we seemed to just pull 'em out of our caps. We needed every puff of that magic to finish ahead of the mighty Mets—featuring Gooden, Darryl Strawberry, and my old friend Keith Hernandez—and make the playoffs. Which we did, by a margin of three games at the end of the year.

All of which only intensifies Ozzie's at-bat. Niedenfuer finally rears, wheels, and brings in another fastball. And as the Midget swings like a middleweight Mickey Mantle, and the ball takes off with a *crack*, climbs into the Missouri sky, and disappears over the rightfield wall, a ballpark full of maniacs do just what Jack Buck is hollering on the radio: "Go crazy, folks! Go crazy!" I guess all of us should have known, after 166 games of Cardinal abracadabra, that the Wizard might end up with the most amazing magic of all.

As Midget jumped and danced and waved his fist in the air, and galloped around the bases like a racehorse with jiggerbugs, all I could think was, he ain't had much practice on that home-run trot. Maybe that's why a hundred writers cracked up at my press conference a few minutes later. One guy with a very serious expression asked, "Whitey, are you surprised Ozzie hit one out left-handed?" "Hell, no," I said. "He's had 3,337 chances. He was due!"

Funny thing is, with Osborne Earl Smith, Jr., I wasn't too far wrong. Most fans appreciate Ozzie as one of the true gentlemen of this game, and one of the finest shortstops to ever break in a mitt—both of which are true. Many know he was even a harder worker than he was a natural talent—which, if you've seen him glide into the hole or catch one over the shoulder, you know is saying something. But hardly anybody realizes in how many ways Ozzie lived out the expression that today's Cardinals use as their slogan: "Baseball like it oughta be." Ozzie Smith used every resource available to him—talent, work, respect, hours of practice, imagination, and love of the game—to achieve what few in baseball can: doing the impossible, someplace on the field, day after day. As Casey might have said, for the Hall-of-Fame-type player, there's no such thing as luck. There's just the magic he's spent a lifetime getting ready for.

The Wizard turned out to be one of the most important people in my life and my career, and certainly in St. Louis Cardinal history, which makes it funny to remember how Number One's journey to his final baseball destination began. That moment took place at a weekday home game at Busch Stadium in 1981, in front of 13,000 horrified Ladies' Day fans who, if they'd heard of Ozzie Smith at all, probably thought he was an extra in a Judy Garland movie. That was when my shortstop at the time, Garry Templeton, pulled a stunt that was as far from Ozzie Smith, or anything he'd ever do, as a person can get.

I'd started to realize something was screwed up with the best player on my team (and maybe in baseball) a few weeks earlier. I was sitting in my office after the game one day when Garry sauntered in, plopped himself down and started spewing some foolishness I could not believe. "I don't want to play day games after night games anymore," he said. "I'm too tired." Now here's a kid with as much God-given ability as any player alive, the kind you see once or twice a generation: speed, arm strength, good bat, wonderful hands on grass *and* turf, everything in the world but home-run pop. I don't mind telling you that the first year I had him, Garry was the only guy I went to the winter meetings knowing I would not trade.

But here this kid has already told me he hates playing in Montreal, he don't like playing in the rain, he don't like batting against certain pitchers. Leave aside the fact that he's twenty-two years old, and I've got guys in their thirties, like George Hendrick, playing every day and never saying a word about it. I'm looking at a starting shortstop—a guy I'm paying $667,000 a year—who doesn't want to play half the damn games. I said, "What's the matter with you? You're *tired?* Get your damn rest!"

Those 1970s Cardinal teams were a shaggy-ass bunch and, like I've said, the St. Louis fans never did warm up to 'em much, but Templeton's antics pushed them over the edge. They could see he was dogging it on ground balls, pulling up short on the bases, and generally acting like he didn't give a damn about baseball or them and didn't care if they knew it. And in that Ladies Day game, he jogged to first when he should've been sprinting, and the crowd started booing up a storm, and at that moment, Garry turned to the fans, stuck his middle finger in the air, and grabbed the family jewels and gave 'em a good, hearty shake.

You couldn't keep me off the field. I went out and got him, dragged him into the dugout and would have done God knows what if a bunch of cooler-headed people hadn't intervened and pulled us apart. I'd never been so mad at a baseball player. After that, I didn't give a damn how much talent he had, it was only a matter of time before he was a former Cardinal shortstop.

It turned out to be a key moment in Cardinal history. I don't comment on social issues much, but I remember saying it at the time: Too many authority figures refuse to draw lines nowadays. "I'm drawing one right here," I said. There's a right way and a wrong way to act. Well, they don't call Missouri the Show-Me state for nothing. To Missourians, accountability is almost a religion, and I think this whole altercation was one reason they still treat me and Mary Lou like the second coming of Harry and Bess Truman. But even I had no idea that within a few months, I'd be making a trade that contained the extremes of big-time sports: Going out, a big-money star with a horseshit attitude and a lot of baggage; coming in, a player whose talent and passion for the game would stand for everything St. Louis fans would line up around the block to see. I can only hope there'd be room in today's industry for an Ozzie Smith, who showed the world for nearly twenty years that the road to greatness is always paved with class.

For Garry's sake and our game's, I wish he'd had half the natural spark and drive of an Ozzie Smith. There's no doubt in my mind his story would have ended in Cooperstown. But he did a wonderful backflip of his own. He went to San Diego to play for my old friend

Dick Williams, a great manager and baseball man, and in time, he really straightened himself out. He led the Padres' come-from-behind playoff win over the Cubs in 1984, when they went on to face Detroit in the World Series, and no team ever won a pennant without a hell of a shortstop. Garry and I talked some over the years, and I know that the player I had to trade—the guy I put on the disabled list as having a "chemical imbalance"— was never the real Garry. He'd had a tough life, boy. But Garry eventually became a coach, and the Anaheim Angels hired him in 1997 to manage in the minor leagues. He started out in Cedar Rapids, a wonderful middle-American town that couldn't be further from the Watts of Garry's boyhood. I'd love to talk to him some- time about how he'd handle situations like the one he put me in on that Ladies' Day in St. Louis.

But I wasn't thinking of history at the time: I needed myself a shortstop, and fast. Gussie'd had a five-word comment on the whole deal: "Get rid of the sonofa- bitch." He wanted to run Tempy off the next day, and he didn't care what we got in return, but that wasn't going to help us any. So I put Garry on the DL till everybody could cool down. The real problem was get- ting someone good enough to replace him.

Every scout drooled over Templeton's talent, but there had always been the off-the-field questions, and after this blowup, they'd all see me coming and look the other way. And to be honest with you, Ozzie was just one guy on my shopping list. I was interested in Rick Burleson of the Angels, Alan Trammell of the Tigers, the Cubs' Ivan DeJesus and even Jose Oquendo of the Mets, who I thought was the second-best fielding shortstop in the league, after Mr. Smith. But it was hard to get anything going, let alone go out and get a shortstop for the ages.

One reason Ozzie wasn't the only guy on my list was that he was considered a very poor hitter with no pros- pects of improving. That was everybody's scouting re- port. His lifetime average was in the .230s, and that was all singles: The only way he'd get a double was if he bounced one off the pitcher's skull. But Ozzie was such a glove wizard, and loved his native Southern California so much, that he was rooted deep as a desert cactus out there. It didn't seem like he'd ever budge.

As it happened, St. Louis baseball got help from a town it doesn't generally like too much—Hollywood. Ozzie's agent, Ed Gottlieb, had big, big ideas, maybe because most of his clients were stars in the movie business, where anything's possible if you put the right spin on it. Here it was 1980, when no player'd ever seen a $2 million deal in his dreams, and Ed Gottlieb strolled into the Padres' office, looked 'em straight in the eye, and asked for a five-year deal for $25 million. I don't know how he did it without laughing! The modern version of that might be a guy asking for $60 million a year. To this day, I don't know if he said it as a joke or if he saw what was coming in baseball.

Well, the agent's job is to rob the ballclub, so as far as I'm concerned, why shouldn't he just barge in there with a .38 and say, "Stick 'em up"? I still get a kick out of that. I wish I'd been there. But man, you talk about makin' people mad! The Kroc family, which owned McDonald's as well as the Padres, was not amused. They hated Ed Gottlieb more than they ever hated the Home of the Whoppers. Next thing I knew, a nervous Dick Williams and Jack McKeon, their GM, were approaching me at the winter meetings, doing everything but glancing over their shoulders and talking in a whisper. "Ozzie's really pissed 'em off," they said. "Are you still interested in him?" Well, hell *yes*, I was, and I said so. We agreed in principle—Garry Templeton for Ozzie Smith.

But old Gottlieb, God bless him, had made my job even tougher. Ozzie was only a three-year player at the time. And even though he was a weak hitter; even though nobody knew if he'd ever hit his weight; even though he was only on a one-year deal, he had something amazing in his contract: a no-trade clause. When Dick told me that, I about fell over. I said, "God almighty, he's got to be the only guy in the history of the world with a no-trade on a one-year contract! How in the hell did he get that?" They said he was such a poor hitter, nobody wanted him anyway. I can't tell you if that's the truth or not because I don't know. All I can tell you is, nothing about Ozzie was ever ordinary.

Not even trading for him. I couldn't just make a *deal* for the sonofagun; I had to fly out to Southern California, meet the man in person, look him in the eye, and persuade him to uproot his family, move from his warm and comfortable home state to the muggy Midwest, and become the next shortstop of a baseball team he probably knew next to nothing about. That's the only way he'd waive the no-trade and give us our middle infield back.

Well, to be honest with you, that turned out to be one of the things I remember best. It took me back to the good old days, like when I sat in the Sanders' living room in Nebraska, chatted up the parents and sold John on the finer points of the National Pastime. The stakes were higher now, but it was the same principle: Take a great idea, meet the player and his folks, know your plan and sell like a traveling preacher. And with the team I'd put together already, it *was* a hell of a plan. A great fielder like Ozzie, on the slick rug at Busch, was the last piece to the puzzle, the magnet who'd pull it all together. I didn't care if he hit .180: If he takes away 100 runs from the opposition, who cares if he ain't driving many in? The more I thought about it, the more I could see Ozzie in St. Louis, and as a part of that great tradition of Cardinal infielders: Rogers Hornsby, Red Schoendienst, Marty Marion. I was charged up and ready to go.

My family was visiting me for Christmas, but I cut the holiday short on December 26, 1981, and got on a plane to sunny San Diego. I had a whole day of meetings with Ozzie, his wife, Denise, and Mr. and Mrs. Gottlieb.

We talked baseball. We had cocktails. I told 'em about my vision for the Cardinals, past, present, and future. I got a feel for Ozzie Smith as a person and I liked what I learned: He'd studied every detail of my managing career, from Texas to St. Louis, so he and Ed knew I had the goods to deliver on my promise of building a winner. The steaks out there might not have been the equal of Grisbach's in Grand Island, but the company was outstanding. We all got along wonderfully—a great sign. By the time nine hours had passed, I'd offered Ozzie a one-year deal for $450,000 and my personal vow that if he didn't like me or St. Louis at the end of that season, I'd give him his outright release. They knew I was the real thing. None of us had a thing to lose.

When Ozzie flew to Missouri in mid-January, I kept my fingers crossed. The five-below-zero weather and howling winds couldn't have been much of a selling point, especially for a Southern California kid. But to his credit, Ozzie put that aside. He looked around town, met the players and saw where they lived, got a feel for a century of baseball tradition, and fell in love with the area. Ozzie became one of the last of a dying breed: a star player who makes a major choice based on personal factors like affection, a gut feeling, and a lot of trust. Ozzie always played the game with heart.

We all know Ozzie was an outstanding natural talent: The man's forty-five now, and if he were to swap his mike at *This Week in Baseball* for an old glove, he'd *still* be one of the top five shortstops in baseball. But the real challenge for a genius isn't to play well; he can do that in his sleep. It's to do it every day and to make himself better. It takes work: endless ground balls, endless batting practice, endless repetition. It takes the maturity to know, no matter what anybody gushes on TV or in the newspapers, that he ain't perfect. It takes listening to the coach inside who says, *I don't give a damn how many Gold Gloves you've got, or how they're all raving about you, you have to improve.* And day in and day out for fifteen years, Ozzie Smith took more responsibility for his God-given talent than any player, scrub or superstar, I've ever been around.

Ballplayers haven't got all day to make themselves better, so a lot of the time they have to ask themselves a question: "Am I going to practice my strengths, or am I going to work on the things I *can't* do?" That's a tougher question than you think, almost a test of his psychology. Many a big leaguer gives in to the temptation just to repeat what he's good at. Makes him feel like a star. And no fans would be the wiser. In Ozzie's case, that would've meant working with the glove. And I can tell you, he did practice hard in the field, but he also practiced smart. Wherever we were playing, he'd go out before batting practice, take grounders on both sides—a hundred to his backhand, a hundred to his forehand—and test the infield for bumps, bounces, and seams. He'd have somebody hit flares over his shoulder so he'd have to turn his back and flag 'em down, which is why Ozzie moved back as well as any shortstop who ever lived. He repeated plays over and over, the ones he could make and the ones he couldn't, till he could perform 'em on autopilot. His best never made the TV highlights: By the time he could do them in games, they looked easy. Ozzie's work bettered his strengths but also expanded what he could do.

We expected from the beginning to bat Ozzie eighth and plan around his below-average hitting. But, easy as it would have been, he never accepted that label. He just went to work. Dave Ricketts and Johnny Lewis, two outstanding coaches, drilled him on balance, plate coverage, staying level. Chuck Hiller got him to stay on top of the ball. I paid Ozzie a dollar every time he hit a grounder in a game; he paid me a dollar every time he popped up or struck out. I wanted him to scorch that rug, make 'em throw him out, and he got the message. I'd hand Midget his two or three dollars after the game, he'd smile and slide it in his wallet, and we'd be all set.

Halfway through his first season, when I was down $300 and counting, he was gentleman enough to call off the bet. But it was money well spent—an investment. A small part, maybe, of how Ozzie turned into a fine offensive player and one of the toughest strikeouts in baseball.

Those are outstanding traits for any number-eight or number-two hitter, to name the two slots he usually filled in the lineup. And by the mid-1980s, Ozzie's contributions at the plate were nearly the equal of his fielding. People still ask me how we made it to the World Series in 1987. That year, nobody on the Cardinals' staff won 12 games—the first and only time a pennant winner could ever say that, and it'll never happen again—and we lost half our offense when Clark and Pendleton went down with late-season injuries. But Ozzie stepped up to the plate. He took over the number-two spot full-time and turned it into an RBI slot: His 75 RBIs, his highest season total by far, kept us in the race. Ozzie always knew the big picture, what his team needed him to do at any given time, and found a way to do it. If he ever hit behind the runner, worked the count, or swung away, it was because the moment called for it. Smarts, class, and knowhow always increase your value, and Ozzie had 'em. He should have been MVP of the league that year.

That was even true of his base stealing. Ozzie Smith was not nearly as feared or as fast afoot as some of the other burners I had—Coleman or McGee, for example, who swiped a lot on speed, athleticism, and gall. Those three guys could steal 150, 200 bases a year among them, and they often did, but the guy who stole the most bases that meant winning baseball games was Ozzie. He'd steal late in a one-run game, in situations where we *had* to have someone in scoring position. Nobody keeps this kind of stat, but Ozzie's forty-some thefts a year often meant more to us than Vince's 100 did. He knew *how* to steal, but just as important, he knew *when* to.

A lot's been said about Ozzie in the field, and for my money, he's up there with the best ever. I played with Brooks Robinson in Baltimore, a guy who dove to his left so well at third base I still say he took two hits a game away from the opposition. Some great first basemen could dive well to their left, too. At short, Ozzie did the same thing: He made more diving plays to his left than any shortstop in history. That's partly because he *did* have showmanship to him—something fans all over North America appreciated—and wanted to get 'em buzzing about this sport. But Ozzie was also the first shortstop I ever saw who could dive to his right—backhand, into the hole—and *still* find a way to throw people out. He'd go airborne and horizontal, hit the turf, spring up with his hands like a jack-in-the-box, and be ready to fire. In baseball geometry, given the speed of the players and length of the baselines, that's a very, very difficult thing to do. Ozzie did it all the time.

But the thing very few people realize—and it may tell you more about Ozzie than anything else—is that as graceful as he always looked, number one was often in extreme pain. Small as he was, he took a hell of a beating out there: They'd go after him at second base, knock him ass over teakettle, bang him up good. He took more hits than an NFL cornerback. He'd twist his ankle, bang up his shoulder, get his shins raked. Next day, Midget might be whimpering around the locker room a little before the ballgame, but he was like an old hunting dog: I'd give him one or two aspirin, pat him on the back, and boy, he'd go out there and play like hell. You could not keep Ozzie Smith off the field. He was the toughest Cardinal I ever managed when it came to playing in pain.

The most serious injuries Ozzie had were to his shoulder. He came to St. Louis with what I call a "plus" arm, though it was never the gun a lot of shortstops have, especially the guys who play on turf. A shortstop's job involves *time*: He has to field the ball and get it to first in a certain span of time, and most of them aren't creative enough to realize you can save time in other ways than with a strong arm. Get to the ball faster; get it off quicker. Ozzie figured out early on you could save time those ways, too. But around 1985, his rotator cuff frayed right through. At that point, he lost whatever arm strength he had. Oz chose rehab over surgery, and worked his skinny behind off in the weight room. But he'd come to spring training and I'd see him throw and I'd think, "Here we go; he ain't gonna be able to play shortstop anymore." He simply could not go into the hole, plant his foot and fire.

But I'll be damned if he *still* didn't come up with an answer. Ozzie taught himself a new trick: going to his backhand, fielding the ball, and throwing it across his body *on the run*. My coaches didn't teach him that; *I* didn't teach him that. You wouldn't *think* to teach a guy that. Sometimes I'd shake my head and think, "How in the hell can he do that?" And for nine, ten years, Ozzie not only lived with pain on every single throw to first, he played shortstop in a fashion that I don't think anybody else has ever played it.

The key to Ozzie may be not so much his amazing natural ability, but the fact that he always found a way to do what he had to do. Maybe it wasn't an orthodox way; maybe it wasn't the way you'd teach a Little Leaguer to do it. And I still don't know if he'd make a great shortstop coach, because he did things in a way you probably couldn't pass on to ordinary people. But he always found a way that Ozzie Smith could do it. And till the day he quit in '96, he played the game's most important position as well as anybody in the history of baseball.

Few people got to see Ozzie practice, and nobody could look inside his head, so you might even say the public never got to know the best of Ozzie. That was true in other ways. It's tough for any manager to communicate with every player all the time—even a guy like me, who finds something to enjoy in almost every person I'm around. Ozzie always helped me in that area. If the situation called for it, I'd say, "Hey, Ozzie, see what Willie thinks about this," or "See if you can talk Terry into that." Smooth as a one-hop grounder, boy, he'd take care of it. Nobody ever saw half the things he did for our team or for me. That's why it was so funny when I read in the papers, in his last year with the Cardinals in '96, what a goddanged bad guy he is. They'd brought in Royce Clayton as his heir apparent, and I know that was a tricky situation for Royce, Ozzie, and Tony LaRussa. All of a sudden, Ozzie was supposed to have an attitude problem. Well, he wanted to compete! I don't give a damn what anybody says: There never was a better team player than Ozzie Smith.

That was even true when he thought I was full of it. Ozzie understood the game—one reason you never, ever saw him out of position on the field—and he was never afraid to get in my face when he thought he should. For example, I always rode poor Vince pretty hard. Like a lot of great athletes, Coleman was a hardheaded guy, and when I tried to teach him how to draw more walks, he'd get hot under the collar, and we'd go back and forth, and he'd end up sputtering, "Man, quit tryin' to take the bat out of my hands!" But we needed him on *base*, not in the top ten, so I kept the hard-line approach.

Well, one afternoon, Ozzie and Pendleton came in my office and asked if I wasn't being a little rough on Vince. "He's only a rookie, Rat," Ozzie said. "You're hurting his confidence talking to him like that." I heard them both out and considered their views. But in the end, I told 'em I really disagreed. Every player has different needs. I said, "If I don't do it this way, Vince Coleman won't ever become the ballplayer he's capable of being." After he left St. Louis to play left field for the Mets, his production fell way off, which supports my point. But

Ozzie didn't need the proof. He never brought it up again.

Maybe you can tell a champion by what he does when nobody's looking, but what Ozzie did in the open always elevated the sport, too. I've already told you about his class with the fans. Going back forty, fifty years, to the days of DiMaggio, Williams, and Aaron, I never saw a player as good with baseball's paying customers. It was like Beatlemania around him for fourteen years in St. Louis, yet I never saw him discourteous or crabby. He'd chat, listen, sign whatever was shoved in his face, and never stop till the last person in line was satisfied.

But Ozzie's popularity went beyond team loyalties. Long before his farewell tour of National League parks, he was the only player I ever saw who got standing ovations on the road. All they had to do was announce his name. It happened in San Diego; it happened in Cincinnati; it happened in New York, Pittsburgh, Chicago, wherever Number One took the field. Even though he'd been knifing their ballclubs in the back for ten, fifteen years, the fans knew the way he did it was bettering the game.

Maybe it was the smile. Maybe it was those crazy back flips he did to open our World Series games, which not only were punctuation marks for the way the Cards played baseball, but gave the fans an image of the joy at the heart of our game. You can sum up the magic the same way Casey might have if he'd ever seen the Wizard: *People came to see Ozzie Smith play baseball.*

Well, how much is *that* worth? If you made a graph of Ozzie's salaries, you'd see a chart of the transition in pay between the old and new eras. When we first got him, he made less than half a million a year—about what a mediocre rookie gets today. After he helped us win the World Series in his first full year, I made him the first million-dollar-a-year infielder. Once he'd proved he was one of baseball's most valuable commodities, he joined Mike Schmidt and Gary Carter—one in the Hall of Fame, the other on his way—as the only $2 million-a-year players. And his timing was good: The unions had been hammering Anheuser-Busch to hire more minorities and, in Mr. Smith, they had a fine citizen and role model. That didn't hurt his contract talks. By the time he quit, he was making $3 million a year and had lots of opportunities outside the game.

But it's funny, boy. Nobody quite understands *how* valuable Ozzie was. Nobody could have known this then, but if the Padres had given Ed Gottlieb and Ozzie that $25 million, they'd have had themselves a hell of a bargain. When I see the the guys who get $10 or $11 million a year today—the Gary Sheffields, the Albert Belles—regardless of whether they respect the game or the fans. . . . Well, it ain't worth getting mad over, so I grab my tackle box and head out for the lake. But Ozzie defined what this game will always need. He never got paid half what he was worth to Anheuser-Busch, to the St. Louis Cardinals or to baseball.

It didn't end great.

Tony LaRussa and his Redbirds were in a fix after 1995. Ozzie was forty-one, he'd been hurt the year before, and they needed shortstop insurance. Tony knew from his years in the Bay Area that Royce Clayton, who'd been a San Francisco Giant, was a hell of a fielder and a great athlete, so bringing him to St. Louis was a smart move. But it also opened a can of worms.

Ozzie had told me five years earlier that when he couldn't play shortstop, he wasn't going to play anymore. He wasn't going to go to the other side of the bag, to second, and get knocked out on the double-play and be crippled for life. I agree that he'd earned the right not to risk that. I can't second-guess Tony—I don't know the particulars—but I'd have handled that situation different. I'd have sat Clayton down and said, "Royce, you're my second baseman for now; when I want to rest Ozzie, you're going to be my shortstop." I don't think he'd have said no if you'd approached it like that. And Ozzie was their best shortstop anyway. In spite of his lesser range, the man knows *where* to play. That matters. He hit in the clutch all year. The Cardinals were 31–19 with Ozzie starting and only 56–55 with Royce in there. You could win with the man today. As for the heir apparent, Clayton is a Texas Ranger now.

The only thing bad I could ever say about Ozzie Smith is he would get me so damn mad when I'd go out to change pitchers. He'd be standing behind the mound, his arms folded, shaking his head in a big, over-blown show of disapproval. To Ozzie, when I took the pitcher out, it wasn't me taking control of the situation, getting good matchups and so on; it just meant the guy was sputtering and not finishing off his job. I was just out there cleaning up the mess. "Hey Midget," I'd say. "What the hell's the matter with you? I'm gonna bring in Dayley to pitch to the lefthander; he'll get him out. Then Worrell's coming in to get so-and-so, this is gonna happen, that's gonna happen—we're gonna win the game!" Ozzie didn't give a damn. "Same old stuff, Rat, every day," he'd say. Then he'd wander back to his po-sition, shaking his head in pity. Sometimes I wished Cox or Forschie or Magrane would throw a no-hitter just so I wouldn't have to listen to it anymore!

As much crap as the Midget gave out, I'm sorry he had to take a little bit toward the end. You know what's worse? I can't say for sure you'd even *have* a Wizard of Oz today. Would a guy hauling in $10 million risk his earning potential doing somersaults? Try to imagine Ozzie's acrobatics at $375 million Bank One Ballpark, with the swimming pool in the background, or the man working like a dog on grounders under some retractable roof. He wouldn't have to! If he did, it would be in *spite* of all that's happened in baseball, not because of it. If there's any less room for magicians like Number One today, that means you need to change baseball. And that's what the rest of this book is about. Change!

But for now, just think of that lunatic day in 1985, when Ozzie swung from the left side like Reggie Jackson, caught it on the sweet spot, and cracked one over the wall. That home run helped us shock the Dodgers and get to a World Series. We didn't win it, but hell, that wasn't the Wizard's fault. Crazy as he looked up there, wheeling his lumber with those 1-in-3,000 odds, I believe that sonofagun knew he could hit it out of the ballpark. The great ones always do.

• Part Two •

You've Got to Have a Plan

· 7 ·

Running Counts

It's opening day 1997, and Tony LaRussa's Cardinals are taking on the Montreal Expos. I haven't been to a game at Busch Stadium since the day I quit the Cards in 1990—I'd have so many people lining up for autographs, it'd raise the biggest rumpus you ever saw—but I do follow the Redbirds on my trusty, split-screen, satellite-dish TV at home, just like I do the other twenty-nine ballclubs around the major leagues. It's nothing—nothing in the bottom of the ninth, there's a cold wind gusting through the ballpark, and Tony sends his top pinch-hitter to the plate: thirty-seven-year-old Willie McGee.

Willie's been one of the wonderful stories in baseball the last few years, not to mention one of the most revealing. After I left the Cardinals, the ballclub let him go. As he drifted from Oakland to the Giants, then from Pawtucket to Boston, dragging an Achilles' injury behind him, his career seemed to be fading like a bloop single to right. But that was nothing new. Even when he was my star centerfielder—he won the batting title in 1985, for one thing, and was named the league's Most Valuable Player—few people outside St. Louis knew how good a player he was. Here was this shy, gangly kid, a preacher's boy from California, who never talked himself up, who hit more five-hoppers and rug-burners with that goofball swing than anybody I ever saw, and who rarely hit one out of the ballpark—well, I guess they figured the man hit .353 by accident.

Believe me, he didn't. Willie had speed and ability, but knowledge made his game a lot bigger than that. When the Cardinals brought him back as a spot starter in 1996, it didn't surprise me to see him spark those players to their first division title since I went off to catch bass.

St. Louis fans know the inside game as well as any in the country, and it's in their blood to love the underdog. Those are two reasons they went nuts over Willie the day I first brought him up from Louisville. The city's love affair has only grown in the seventeen years since, so much so that it borders on Show-Me insanity. Homers keep the turnstiles spinning, as Mr. McGwire keeps proving, but the Lords of Baseball forget something else at the heart of the game. Here's a guy who never hit fifteen dingers in his life, yet all he has to do today is tap the dirt off his spikes, and the best baseball town in America climbs to its feet and hollers itself silly. It's something to see. They're thanking Willie for years of heads-up, no-bull baseball.

Well, the Lords ain't the only ones not paying attention. Here it is thirty-two degrees, and Willie's been sitting for nine innings, and he digs in, and the cheering ain't even died down yet when the pitcher rears and wheels and brings it across the plate. Now, if you'd gone up to Willie a few seconds earlier and asked him, "Mr. McGee, what one pitch on planet Earth would you be happiest to see right now?", he'd have had a good answer. "Well, sir," he'd have said, "I've been freezing my ass off for three hours; I'm too cold to get around real quick, so I sure would appreciate a changeup." Then he might have smiled a little and added, "Oh, also, I'd sure like to hit it out of the park and get the game over with so all these good fans can get home. Could you leave it up high for me?" And sure enough, what should come wobbling across the dish—right on that first pitch—but a fat changeup right in his eyes?

As Willie belts it over the wall for the game-winning homer, and as the fans cheer like maniacs, spilling their Budweisers and pop—Wily Veteran Comes in to Save Day!—all I can think as he's touching the bases is, *God almighty, man! This is the big leagues? How can you throw Willie McGee a high changeup in that situation?* He's been sitting in the cold for three hours; challenge him! In baseball, where so many things can go wrong at any time, if you don't use your brains a little, you're in trouble. This pitcher didn't. Willie said, *thanks, I'll take it,* and won the game with one swing. In other words, he's a big-league player.

Television announcers dissect baseball today like it's nuclear physics. They spend four endless hours breaking it down: the ultrasecret signs, the inner thoughts of the managers, whether they've all got their caps on backwards or forwards. It's gotten so bad I don't know whether to bust out laughing or get up and turn the sound off. The truth is, none of that stuff matters.

Baseball, basically, is a simple game. There's a few essentials to know. They won't work every time, but if you apply them consistently, you'll cheat the law of averages and be successful in the long run. If you don't know them—or worse, if you know 'em but don't bother to use 'em—you can count on it: The law of averages, Murphy's Law, every law but Vern Law is going to kick your ass all over the lot. If you leave events to chance, you're going to have a short career. In baseball, *you've got to have a plan.*

You've gotta have a plan if you're trying to get a big-league hitter out. You've gotta have a plan if you're a hitter trying to get on base. You've gotta have a plan if you're managing a pitching staff, filling out a lineup card, planning out a budget, making trades, or orchestrating a draft. You've gotta have a plan to build a good big-league team or to change the rules that govern the sport. From field level in the dustiest, stickiest ballpark on earth, right up into the fanciest front-office suites of the majors, the ingredients of my game are essentially the same. Know them and use 'em or things ain't going to go the way you want. I'll say it one more time: You've got to have a plan.

That's a basic in life and in baseball, and a great place to see it at work is in the most basic battle in the game— the showdown between pitcher and hitter. Go into that battle without an idea, and you're going to take a licking. It's a law of the game and a good lesson to learn.

Ted Williams, one of the greatest hitters of all time, said years ago that hitting a baseball is the hardest thing to do in sports, and I still agree with him. God knows *I* never figured it out. Just think about it: That ball's nine inches in circumference, the bat ain't much bigger, and both are basically round. A big-league pitcher brings it to you from any number of angles, at any speed between 70 and 105 mph. You don't know where it's going, when he's going to release it, how hard it's coming, whether it'll move side to side or up and down, or how much it's going to move and when. You have less than a second to compute all this and make your swing. If you do make contact and keep it fair, somebody's liable to haul it in. It's no wonder the greatest of all time, including superhumans like Ted, fail seven times out of ten.

That's why good hitting, like anything worth doing in life, doesn't happen by accident. You're always unlikely to get a hit, but with a good idea, you can jack up your odds from unlikely to likely. There's information present in any situation a hitter can use to upgrade his chances, and if he's smart, he uses it. If not, he goes up there with his head empty, trusting to luck, the orbit of the planets, and his own awe-inspiring ability. In other words, he's happy to make an out.

I've told you how Ozzie recognized situations and what they asked of him. Willie was the same. *Good* player, Mr. McGee. I never had to coach him. I never gave Willie signs; all I'd do was write his name in the lineup and run his ass out there. He had speed and only middling power, so he hit the ball top to bottom to induce ground balls, especially on turf. He didn't waste his time trying to pull the ball; he smacked it where it was pitched, used the whole field. A switch-hitter, he was too weak from the left side to pull it so, in preparation for the times he'd have to shoot it to the right side to advance a runner, he made himself into a hell of a drag bunter. Each of those skills helps you win.

And, finally, if you were paying attention, Willie taught you something about conformity—namely, it generally ain't worth much. He swung like his feet were in two buckets; you'd never coach a kid to cut like that. But it was *his* swing, and he knew it and knew how to use it. I told my coaches if I ever caught them *talking* to Willie about that swing, I'd fire them on the spot. If you were half as smart as he was, you trusted him to do his thing.

Well, one reason I loved managing in St. Louis was that Cardinal baseball has always meant smart baseball. It's tradition. Today's Cards have some good, intelligent players, including Mr. McGwire, who's as smart as he is powerful, and Ray Lankford, who has matured the past two or three years to what I'd call a superstar level. But with all the small parks today, and the fences even moved way in at Busch, even the Cardinals are basically a home-run team like the rest of them now. Get a guy on base, wait for a long one. With Big Mac coming up, why risk running into an out? Why manufacture a run when one big swing's going to get you three? It ain't my favorite style, but I don't blame Walt Jocketty, their general manager, a bit: You have to adapt to your setting.

When I look at how some of the Cards approach their hitting now, I see how the pitcher-hitter confrontation has changed. The average final score does sound like it's from softball or the NFL. But I *still* wonder how many more runs some of these guys would get if they started using their brains a little. I don't see too much batting like it oughta be.

Two good examples are Royce Clayton and Delino DeShields. Royce was the Cards' shortstop for two and a half years before they traded him to Texas in '98, and DeShields is still their second baseman (though that could change any minute, knowing today's player market). These guys are good athletes, that's for sure. But I'm less convinced that they have much of an idea when they bat. Both like to be aggressive, maybe because they don't want to get behind in the count; if you fall behind, say 0–1 or 1–2, you have to be defensive and protect the plate instead of attacking the ball. But you have to be smart about it. Clayton, for one, hasn't been. That's why he struck out 109 times in '97—an acceptable number, *maybe*, for a power hitter who drives in runs, but way too many for a guy who's going to pout if he can't bat high in the order. You need your leadoff guy on first base, not making a right turn.

Aggressiveness is a plus, but aggressiveness without discipline is a ticket to the shithouse. And over and over, I see the same problem with these guys: In order to be aggressive, they swing at the first fastball they get. It doesn't seem to matter to them if it's in the strike zone or not; the first fastball they see, man, they're hackin'. Well, swing at a first fastball that's out of the strike zone, and not only can you not hit that ball hard, but if you miss it—which you will since it ain't in a good spot— you'll end up behind in the count, hitting at 0–1. That's what you were trying to avoid in the first place, so why do it? You have to use your brains a little.

And you know what? If you're a Clayton or a De-Shields—a nonpower hitter—you're going to have to know even more about hitting fastballs. That pitcher won't fear you much. He knows you won't hit it too far. So he'll bring you his heat, and you'd better let him know you're going to be selective about it. Don't give in and swing at *any* fastball; swing at the first fastball *strike*. Turn it your way. Be aggressive, but be smart.

Judging hitters, like many things in baseball, can be deceptive. Stats make some guys look better than they are. A lot of that type are what we call *mistake hitters*. Fred McGriff, who's now the first baseman for the Devil Rays, is one; Ron Gant, the Cards' leftfielder, is another. Instead of going up there with an idea, they're waiting for a cripple pitch—a hanging curve, a wobbly slider— that they can pound into orbit. They don't care where it is; if it's a mistake, they see it, react, and hit a rocket. The problem is, for good or bad, that leaves the pitcher in control of the situation.

They say McGriff is a fine person, but he's always been an overrated ballplayer. Here's a guy who hit thirty-plus homers for seven straight years, but in three of those years, he didn't even have 100 RBIs. That's not very good clutch hitting. Considering the players he's hit behind his whole career—guys like Tony Gwynn, Robby Alomar, Kenny Lofton, and Chipper Jones—he ought to drive in that many *every* year. I've proven that if you take a third-place hitter who can make contact, who doesn't hit into many double plays, and bat him behind decent hitters who can run, he can hit *ten* homers and still drive in 100. But Fred has holes in his swing that leave him vulnerable to good pitching. He's slow, he clogs up the bases, and he can be doubled up too easy. For all the good numbers he puts up, it's hard to believe he hasn't done better. That's why Fred's been on four teams in the last eight years.

As far as Gant goes, Ron had an awful year in 1997— he whiffed every third time up and, as Casey said, no-body ever got a raise for striking out—so maybe it ain't fair to look at that, but he's another one who has holes, sits on mistakes, and goes after the first fastball. He could improve on that. If he waited for the first fastball strike, that pitcher would come to him more. He'd see more pitches he liked. But he wants to wait for the ac-

cidental horseshit curveball and hammer it to East St.
Louis. He gets a few of those, and he knows what to do
with 'em, but is he in control of his at-bats?

So Gant and McGriff will finish most years with
good-looking numbers—90 RBIs, 30 to 35 homers. But
you can't say those numbers helped more than they hurt.
How many times did the guy strike out? How many of
those big numbers happened when your team needed
them? When the pitcher is determining what's going to
happen, not the hitter, how can you take the initiative?
I'll take the hitter who knows the situation and goes up
there with an idea—a Ray Lankford, a Tony Gwynn, a
Wally Joyner, a Mike Piazza—any day. With those
guys, you can go out and make something happen.

The good hitter also knows that the game situation dictates the way a pitcher's going to pitch him, and he uses
that to up his chances. He sifts through information. Is
it early in the game or late? That dictates how much of
a chance the pitcher might take. Are the bases empty,
or are there runners on? Same thing. How many outs
are there? Who's ahead in the game, and by how much?
Each situation rules out some possibilities you might
have to face.

Here's one example. Let's say that pitcher's strength
is his fastball. And let's further say you're a fastball
hitter. Well, he'll have to think twice about bringing the
heat. But if his team's ahead by three, and it's late in
the game, and you come to the plate with nobody on
base, you can't hurt him much no matter what you do.
So why should he screw around with his second-rate
junk? That's when he can make you hit *his* pitch. It's
not a risk to go with his best. If you're a good hitter,
you'll prepare for that number one and be ready. If not,
you're open to the whims of fate. And the next place your
bat goes, you ain't going to need your sunglasses to
see it.

Vince Coleman was one of my key offensive weapons, but he had trouble with a different idea. Vince was like Willie Wilson: He really never wanted to accept the type of hitter he was. Vince was critical to the Cardinals for his work on the bases, one of our key guys. He stole an unbelievable 400 in a four-year span—those are Hall of Fame–type numbers, and think of the wear-and-tear on his body—and his speed drove the other team's defense so batty they could never relax. His speed changed the complexion of our games.

The strengths he had, though, meant he should approach hitting differently from most players. I could never get through to Vince his exact role on the team, how to position his talents to help us best. That cost us games, cost him a ton of money in his career, and probably kept him from becoming the greatest leadoff man of all time.

Some hitters, when they get ahead in the count 2–0 or 3–1, you want them swinging away. Those are the guys with the sure bats. Vince's power was a different kind. We needed him on base so he could use his legs, and he was just as liable to get there with a walk as by swinging. Why risk making an out before you have to? Even if the pitcher fell behind him, say, 2–0, I'd flash him the "take" sign. He chafed at that; he wanted to be *macho* with the bat. But I'd say, "Vince, so what if it's a strike? Take it. You'll still be ahead 2–1, and you'll get the same pitch next time anyway! Give him a chance to walk you!" A walk for Vince was the same as a double, and that meant *runs*.

Jack Clark could pull a bullet. His strength, obviously, was his power. I could be blindfolded and tell when Jack was taking BP: He was the only guy I had who didn't sound like he was hittin' underwater. He'd crush 'em to right, right center, anywhere in the ballpark, and they'd look like they were departing the solar system. The man's power scared people, kept the defenses honest and kept our jackrabbits circling the bases.

But he was the damnedest guy to talk to about hitting.

For a guy who hit 340 home runs, Jack Clark might have been the worst guesser I ever saw. He terrified people as a fastball hitter, but he took the wrong message from that. He believed nobody—*nobody*—would ever throw him a fastball. So he never sat on his best pitch! Jack would stand there waiting for the curve, and while he was doing it, those pitchers would sneak heaters right by him—outside corner, inside corner, right down the pipe—that he could have hit to the moon and back. It'd make you so mad!

When Jack went down with his sprained ankle on September 7, 1987, he was in the middle of a historic year. Not only did he have 37 home runs and 93 RBIs at the time—Ruth-like numbers then—but he'd already walked 139 times and struck out 139 times. No hitter in baseball, not even the Babe, ever came to bat 300 times without touching the ball! Jack would have done that easy. Well, you have to take a lot of pitches to turn that feat. I know we'd have never won two pennants in three years without Jack Clark, and I love him like a brother, but the greatest fastball hitter of his era took more heaters for strikes than any player I've ever seen.

So you want to have an idea up there, that's for sure. But if it's the *wrong* idea, you're deeper in the swamp. My own career is an example of that. I already told you how I used to hitchhike to ballgames at Sportsman's Park as a kid. One of the main reasons I did it was so I could watch the great Stan the Man hit. I'd never seen anything like him. That stance looked like a question mark in trouble, but to me it was like poetry—all that awesome, coiled-up power, that wiggle and pose. I'd sit there with my mouth open. Honestly, the sight of Number Six at bat might have made me fall in love with the game more than anything else.

It also screwed me up big-time. I was a good high-school hitter, but once I saw him hit, I just had to change. I wanted to have my feet close together like Stan, boy, and as soon as I started doing that, I turned into a lunger at the plate. I can tell you flat-out I was never worth a damn as a hitter after that. What I didn't know then was that nobody on this planet could hit with that stance but Number Six himself. He and I are good friends now—hell, I'll even listen to him play "God Bless America" on that crazy harmonica he's got—and he always laughs when I tell people the truth: "Here's the sonofagun that ruined my career." But I'm just joking; I was the one who stopped doing what came naturally. I stopped using the idea that worked for the Rat.

Another all-time great who affected my career was Mr. Williams. When I was a player, one of the most amazing things you could do was watch Ted take batting practice for the Red Sox, and I never missed an opportunity. I played six years against him, and it's hard to find the right words to tell you just how good a hitter he was. Ted hit third in the Red Sox lineup, so Dom DiMaggio would take his four minutes' BP first, Johnny Pesky would take his, and then Williams would step in. Every player on the field—the Sox and whoever they were playing—would drop everything, flock around the cage, and watch the clinic he put on. I'd never seen anything like it in baseball. It was like McGwire's BP circus, only half a century earlier.

After he hit, Ted wouldn't go out on the bases like ordinary players; he'd just stand around and talk to you about hitting. The man was wacko on the subject. He really liked me, so we discussed it all the time. He spent a lot of time watching me hit and thought I had a wonderful swing. He'd go around telling people, "Watch that Herzog; he's got a great cut! He's gonna be a good one." It always baffled him that I didn't become as great a hitter as him.

Well, one reason I didn't was I listened to him too much. Every time Ted and I would talk about hitting, I'd jackknife into a three-week slump. It was like poison, boy—worse than if I'd never seen the guy. Ted taught the same thing as Musial: Not everybody can hit the same way.

Ted was a huge guy, much bigger and stronger than people realize—6-4, 220 pounds. He had better vision than some eagles I've known. He had the eyesight of one in 10 million people. He and Chuck Yeager had the two best sets of eyes in World War II; they didn't need radar when they flew them planes. Well, not only could Ted see enemy aircraft at two o'clock faster than anybody in the skies, he could pick up the seams on a 95-mph fastball. Those tools gave him a perspective nobody else had. For one thing, Ted Williams never minded falling behind in the count. That's why, to him, taking the first fastball was like a commandment. He was like a doctor taking your blood pressure: He had to gauge the speed of that ball. Well, that ain't true of most hitters, who get nervous if they fall behind 0–1. Ted didn't care. And after a certain point in his career, hell, Ted would take that next pitch, too. It didn't matter if it was right down central, pecker high; no umpire in baseball would call a strike on Ted Williams. He'd earned that kind of respect, but, hey: How many players can plan around that kind of edge?

The answer is, not many. That's why even though Ted may be the greatest hitter to ever wear spikes, he'll never go down as a Hall-of-Fame manager. His genius almost did in the Texas Rangers in 1972, the first year Bob Short, their owner, brought them from Washington, D.C., where they'd been the Senators. As a manager, Ted simply could not understand that most hitters, especially young ones, were nothing like him. And it screwed them up bad.

Ted's idea of offense was limited in the first place. He didn't like the running game; he was a sit-and-wait guy. Everything depended on base hits. And all he really liked doing was flopping his ass in the batting cage and watching his players swing. He'd tinker with that, critique 'em, yell at 'em. And even *that* didn't help 'em worth a damn. As a matter of fact, the greatest hitter alive turned 'em into one of the worst offenses in the major leagues.

I'll give an example. Ted had a strapping kid outfielder on the team, Jeff Burroughs, who had a lot of natural power. But Ted wouldn't leave him alone. He hammered away at the kid: *Take the first pitch! You can judge the speed that way!* But you had to know Jeff. He was a young guy, not very sure of himself, and batting 0–1 set his knees to clattering. He couldn't adjust, and right in keeping with an offense that got shut out 28 times, Jeff had a terrible year.

Ted talked me into taking that job for 1973 and went back to tarpon fishing. I couldn't save the Rangers, but I did see what was happening with Burroughs. I pulled him aside and said, "Listen, man, every time you swing at a strike, I'll pay you five bucks; every time you take a strike, you owe *me* five bucks." I don't know why ballplayers like taking money from the manager, but they do. And after about two months, Jeff got the idea: Swing the damn bat, man, you've got lightning in it!

Jeff ended up hitting 30 home runs and then the next year was named MVP of the league. We finished 37 games behind; I'm only a manager, not Moses. But I got that team running and forcing things. I offered the right idea for the players I had. And we never got shut out till our 81st game.

The key to offense is giving your team the most chances to score you possibly can. I don't care if you're playing at Busch Stadium or Fenway Park, there's twenty-seven outs in a game, and in that span, you're only going to get x number of opportunities. You'll have a certain number of guys get to first. How are you going to get 'em in? You don't just want to take advantage of every opportunity you get; you also want to make sure that, when you get them, you don't take them away from yourself. Here again, you've got to have a plan.

One major factor in offensive baseball is pitch count. Few fans know this, but a lot happens as a direct result of the pitcher's being ahead of the hitter or behind him. As an example, let's say Tom Glavine is pitching for Atlanta against the Dodgers. Eric Young of LA is on first base. There are no outs, and Bobby Bonilla is now at the plate. And let's say Glavine, uncharacteristically, gets wild and goes to three balls and a strike: a 3–1 count. Glavine doesn't want to give up a walk, so both Bonilla and Young, the baserunner, know Glavine's next pitch is going to be right around the plate. Bonilla's going to have a good crack at putting that ball in play.

This is called a *running count*, and it's one of the key situations in baseball. If the Dodgers' manager is on top of things, he's going to have Young take off running on that pitch. Why? Well, Bonilla's going to swing. That means he might hit a double-play grounder to the infield. If Young is running on the delivery, he'll get down to second faster, prevent that double play, and keep the inning going longer. More than that, if he wants to put the Braves even more on the defensive—always a good idea—he'll slide hard and knock the second baseman, Tony Graffanino, flat on his ass. Next time, master Tony's going to hurry that throw. And the Dodgers have taken charge of the game.

Now, there's no guarantee this is all going to happen. There *are* no guarantees. But your job as manager is to survey the situation and consider what's *likely* to happen. A running count is a situation you can exploit to be more aggressive than usual. If you're sharp, and the other guy's pitcher is struggling with his control, you can turn the pressure up that way, really commandeer the action. Over the long haul, you'll have more guys at second base, have rallies that last longer, and give yourself more opportunities to score. That's not everybody's style, but it's sure as hell mine. It's a winning one, and the fans can sense it from the stands.

I nearly took the Boston Red Sox managing job in

'97, and I'd have surprised some people this way. I'd
be aggressive on running counts even in a home-run
ballpark like Fenway. You'd have a tough time con-
vincing hitters in a small park that they've got to run on
3–2 counts; they're thinking "sit and wait." But the reason you run on 3–2 with less than two out is simple:
You want to break up the double play. Get down that
line and bust it up. Take an out away from the other
team if you can; give yourself more chances! But this is
something you have to *preach*. Even in St. Louis, home
of the Runnin' Redbirds, I had a hell of a time drilling
that into their heads. Before me, they were a one-base-
at-a-time team; they waited for base hits. They didn't
give a damn about double plays. Well, that's just like
saying you don't want to take advantage of every option
you've got. You don't want to bother. I'd send runners
on 3–2 that first year I was there, and instead of slamming that fielder at second, they'd wander out into right
field, humming a tune. I had to have meeting after meeting. These guys needed four hits to score a run, and
that's going to happen as often as the Cubbies leading
the race in September.

Well, everybody knows we became a running team in
St. Louis. We stole 200-plus bases nine out of ten years,
and just the threat of steals created hurried throws, nervous pitchers, mistakes all over the place. In his book
on managing, Bill James said this style changed baseball
more than any manager's has since the 1920s. And it
did have an impact. But more than exploiting our speed,
we were really planning around the fact that we lacked
power. We couldn't count on a two- or three-run homer
with our Punch-and-Judy hitters. We had to do what we
could to jack up the pressure, pile up runs however we
could. It took planning and coordination, but eventually
we got good at it, and that's the only way we could have
won.

I was lucky to have a team full of good guys who
trusted me, but it took time, boy, and I had to stay on

'em. Even smart people prefer a familiar idea that doesn't work to a new one that might. In my early St. Louis days, I'd say, "Boys, we have to run when we're five runs up; we have to run when we're five runs down. If we don't, we ain't gonna win!" It violated what they'd been taught about baseball. First, they were gentlemen and didn't want to show anybody up. Second, they were scared; if they stole a base in the sixth with a three- or four-run lead, they thought that pitcher'd stick one in their ear the next time up. And sometimes they were right. But you pay a price to win, and that was ours. They got the hang of it.

One game in 1987 really put that strategy to the test. We were at Busch Stadium playing Roger Craig's Giants, the team we ended up facing in the NLCS that year, and we had a good rivalry. Roger had a hell of a club, one with home-run power and good starting pitching. But we piled it on early. We were ahead 10–3 in the fifth, and Vince, who'd already stolen a base, took a purpose pitch on the arm and got a free pass. He decided to keep doing his thing. He swiped second. Then, on the next pitch, he swiped third. All hell broke loose. Roger stormed out of the dugout after me, both benches cleared, and we had a hell of a rhubarb, with players and coaches rolling all over the field, hollering and kicking and gouging. Roger was charged up, boy. "You're going to *run on me*, you SOB, when you're up by seven? You'd better tell them guys not to run!" he shouted. There's an unwritten rule in baseball that you don't run when you're far ahead; that's seen as showing the other team up.

Unwritten rule, my ass. People talk about the "book" in baseball. There ain't no damn book, and if there was, you'd rewrite it whenever you needed to. But Roger wasn't buying that. He didn't accept that the Cardinals had to steal their way onto the scoreboard. I said, "Roger, if that's the case, why don't we just give you fifteen outs, and you go ahead and hit, because if we *don't* run, we ain't gonna score!" If he'd promise me Jeffrey Leonard and Will Clark wouldn't hit any more homers, I'd be happy to call off the hounds.

He didn't take me up on it. And the game proved my point: At the end, Chris Brown, their power-hitting third baseman, came to bat with two runners on base. The score ended up 10–8 for us. They could have won with one swing! Roger never argued the point after that.

Stealing third is similar to that: Baseball people see it as rubbing it in. Both second and third are scoring position, so a lot of the time, getting to third is unnecessary for your purposes, a pointless risk. But with our team makeup, it was different. We stole third the way a good pitcher comes inside: hard, with a purpose, and whenever we needed to. And we often needed to.

Coleman was better at stealing third than anyone in history; he liked something about the pitcher's back being to him. He swiped third 26 times one year, which would probably be a record if anybody kept track. The year Lou Brock stole 114, I think he only stole third twice. We did it for a reason: Ozzie and Tommy Herr hit a lot of popgun flares to the outfield, so the fielders played 'em shallow. Well, if Vince was on second, and the leftfielder was only 180 feet deep, Ozzie's one-hop base hit to left wouldn't score anybody, not even Coleman. He'd score from third, but not from second. So with Herr or Ozzie at the plate, having Vince at second often meant nothing. In addition, let's say we had a man on third base with two out. Well, if the batter hit a typical Cardinals turf chopper, he was often quick enough to beat the throw to first base. If we had a man on third, that meant a *run*. And a run often meant a win.

These were bright ballplayers, guys with an *idea*— Ozzie, Herr, McGee, Pendleton, the whole group. They saw the big picture, and as far as stealing went, they figured out more on their own than my coaches or I ever taught them. Check the records: In all those years we stole 200 bases, we were never, in any season, thrown out eighty times. That's a hell of a percentage! And I'll bet you, if we were thrown out sixty-five, seventy times, thirty of those times were on hit-and-runs, when they weren't really stealing, or when it was a 3–2 count and an automatic running situation.

This all happened when other teams knew what was coming. They'd cheat, quick-pitch, do anything they could, but our guys were the damnedest base stealers you ever saw. Herr could steal you twenty or thirty and get thrown out only five times. Willie was very hesitant on the bases—he was fearful of making mistakes, and he didn't want to get thrown out—but he stole on sheer speed. Even Terry Pendleton, hardly our fastest runner, chipped in. Andy Van Slyke stole thirty-four one year, and he was a platoon player. Boldness is contagious. It was our way to win, and it helped us make the most of what we had.

The most amazing hitter I had those years might have been Tommy Herr. I can't think of a better example of how having a plan, a sense of the situation you're in, can help you succeed. If there was one guy I managed that I would want hitting for me in the stretch drive, in August and September, it'd be hard to pick between George Brett and Tommy. He didn't have much power, but he'd rope it to all fields, torch the lines, bleed it up the middle, even hit one out of the ballpark when you needed it. I don't know how he did that, but if he'd hit you ten homers a year, eight counted for something.

Tommy was one of those guys who never gave you any bullshit. When I first came to St. Louis, Ken Oberkfell, the regular second baseman, had a knee injury. Herr and Mike Ramsay were both here. I played Ramsay at short and Herr at second. When Obie finally came back—he had hit .300 the year before, so I had to put him in there—I called Tommy into the office and told him I was sending him to Springfield. He said, "Well, I'm glad I'm going to be playing every day." That's how he was. I said, "Well, the next time you come back, you'll stay." And the next spring I put him at second base and moved Obie to third.

Fundamentally, he was such a smart player. The whole time I managed him, he never screwed up a ground ball or a play that he should have made. He never made a mental mistake. And he played hurt. Tommy had two knee operations one year—two arthroscopic surgeries in spring training—and played Opening Day. That tells you something about a player's heart.

But his career year came in 1985. I found out I didn't have a third-place hitter I liked much, and I asked Tommy to take over the job. I sat him down in Montreal one day and said, "Listen, it's gonna take you a while to learn to hit third, but remember, Jack Clark is hitting behind you. On 2–0, 3–1, you're gonna see fastballs you can hit. They're not gonna walk you to pitch to Jack Clark." I could see he was listening. And in about ten, twelve days, he understood exactly how to exploit the situation. Knowing a fastball strike would arrive, he'd just wait; when it came, he'd smoke it. That year, Herr was a contact hitter with amazing numbers: 8 home runs, 110 RBIs. All because he had a plan.

Hitting's a tough business, but knowledge always makes the job easier. It hikes your odds and your confidence. Get those working together and you get base hits you never dreamed of. You take an average team and suddenly it's a scoring machine. You go on the attack. You win games. And you put a lot of happy fans in the seats.

The same holds true in every phase of baseball. Brains can mean extended innings, more runs, more fun; it can mean good trades, positive contract dealings, useful changes in the rules. The law is pretty simple: Leave your brains on the bench, and you're going to see a lot of fastballs sneak by on the outside corner; use them, and you might hit .300.

The damnedest thing of all, though, might be the way Mr. McGee, the darling of St. Louis, keeps fooling 'em.

Among the players, Willie's one of the most respected men in baseball by now. His teammates go to him for advice. They watch his work habits. They see that the game's about doing things right, not making the biggest splash. The Cardinal fans' love for Willie only shows how well they know the pastime.

But even they know there's a chink in the armor. Smart as Willie is, he never did learn to lay off the sinking curveball in the dirt. Get two strikes on him, and he's helpless. The man always chases that pitch, and when he does, you always think for a second he's some duffer on a public course shanking one out of bounds. It's ugly! I cannot figure out why they throw him a strike.

But they keep on doing it, and Willie keeps making 'em pay. As you read these words, he might *still* be circling the bases, winning ballgames for the Redbirds. Maybe the baseball gods are smiling on him.

· 8 ·
Mound Masters

When you think of the great pitchers, the fearsome hurlers of baseball, who comes to mind? Probably the Seavers, the Gibsons, the Randy Johnsons, the real mound monsters. They don't call Roger Clemens "Rocket," or Johnson "The Big Unit," for nothing. These guys look so big they can stand on the rubber and *hand* you the ball. Yet they're flaming it at you ninety-six miles an hour. They're the ones who make the tall tales, the legends, the ESPN highlights.

But what if a guy never had a fastball in his life? What if he wakes up one day and his arm's so sore he can't hardly lift it over his head? What if he's got the face of a kid who draws your cherry phosphates down at the corner drugstore? The Griffeys and Galarragas will pound him back to Peoria, right? And that's if he ever *got* to the big leagues. But again, the thing about this game is, a lack of size and strength don't always hold you back. In pitching, just like in hitting, you've *got* to have a plan, and brains can take you a hell of a long ways. In fact, they can bring you the best winning percentage in the history of a big-league franchise. I should know; I saw it happen myself.

Nobody I ever met defined the art of pitching better than an ornery lefthander from Massachussetts I got to manage for five years. Even when I think of the master craftsmen, like Whitey Ford, Steady Eddie Lopat, and Catfish Hunter—Hall of Fame types, all of 'em—

nobody ever did more with less than my favorite cranky Yankee, John Tudor. John won me 64 ballgames and only lost 27 between 1985 and 1990, a record that still leaves me shaking my head, considering the stuff he had. He's one of my favorite people in baseball, so I was damn proud a while back when he told a reporter, "Deep down, I'll always be a Cardinal." John's twelve years in the major leagues were proof that the soul of pitching ain't a bionic arm. It's having a good idea.

When I needed a number-two starter to follow Mr. Andujar, I looked to lefties who had done well at Fenway Park. With its crazy leftfield wall—so close to home plate you feel like you can touch it, and forty feet high—no southpaw could have survived there without brains and a plan. In our big stadium, we needed guys bright enough to keep the ball in the ballpark for our fielders to chase down, and Tudor had been over .500 for a five-year stretch in Boston—a sure sign of a guy with savvy. But when I traded George Hendrick to the Pirates for him in 1984, I had no idea I was getting a guy who'd get me to two World Series, pile up the best winning percentage (.703) in Cardinal history, and make jackasses out of the best hitters in baseball. John Tudor was the most amazing pitcher I ever saw.

He was crusty as a Maine lobster, and when he was crabbiest, I knew I was in for a hell of a day. Sometimes John would come in the dugout after warming up, sputtering and slamming the ball in his glove. "I ain't got shit, Rat, I got nothin'," he'd say in his clam-chowder accent. "We're up a creek, Rat." He'd wince, he'd cringe, he'd look like he sat on a tack. That's when I'd mark him down for a shutout. He seemed to have a theory: Expect too much and you'll get screwed. Well, when you can't crack eighty-five on the radar gun, maybe a foul mood and a chip on your shoulder are just the right ticket. They sure didn't hurt John.

A lot of pitchers get by with a below-average fastball. Most of 'em do it by mixing it in with breaking stuff.

That's more or less what Tudor did, too, though he walked a skinnier tightrope than that. He didn't want any right-handed hitters turning on his curveball, so he had a unique strategy: He never showed 'em one. That's right; in five years with the Cardinals, John Tudor never threw his curveball to a righthanded batter. That's 2,000-some hitters at least. If you don't play ball for a living, you might not understand how crazy that is. You've got to be a wrongheaded Missouri mule to do it, stubborn bordering on backwards. But once Tudor set his mind to something, he was like Fido with an old shoe: Yank on it all you want, you weren't getting it out of his mouth.

Breaking stuff wasn't his main attraction anyway. John lived off changeups, the pitches where you show your nerves by taking speed *off* the ball. There's a science to a good change, and very few pitchers know it. You show the hitter the exact same delivery you use for your fastball, yet it comes in just a shade slower. You slow it by changing your grip pressure, the number of fingers you squeeze with, the way you pull down on release. John was so accurate he could subtract two miles an hour, then one more, then put two or three back on a pitch later. He said he did it by "feel," though he had a hard time explaining what *that* meant. I do know he threw changeups off his changeups. It drove batters out of their minds.

You'd sit in the dugout and see the big sticks in the on-deck circle—Darryl Strawberry, Gary Carter, Bobby Bonilla—salivating at this guy's junk. You could read their minds: *I'm gonna hammer this slop to the next county*. They'd rush to the plate, get set for a certain pitch, and dig in. Then he'd stick it right where they weren't expecting it. Once they adjusted, he'd go back to the first location, with a little less giddy-up. He threw the ball smack out of his white shirt, too, so they couldn't get a good bead on it. The Barry Bondses and Ryne Sandbergs rarely got a good look or a good cut.

By the time John busted his low-80s fastball inside, it looked like a Dwight Gooden heater. Before they knew what hit 'em, they were on their way back to the dugout.

Today, it's a miracle if a guy has ten complete games in a season. In 1985, Tudor had 10 *shutouts*. One more and he'd have tied Sandy Koufax's all-time major-league record for left-handed pitchers. He should have, too: One night that September, in the middle of the pennant race, he baffled the Mets for nine innings at Busch Stadium and left with the score tied. But he was dueling one of their aces, Ron Darling, and we couldn't get him any runs, either. I brought in Kenny Dayley in the tenth, and he threw a pitch that Strawberry hit into the upper deck to win the ballgame. But Tudor still finished the year with 20 wins in his last 21 decisions and conjured us right into Game 7 of the World Series.

I've said a lot about setting up an offense, but 60 percent of a manager's job is really handling his pitching staff. Look at any ballfield. What's in the middle? The game revolves around what happens on the mound. And the manager sets the tone for how he wants his pitchers to pitch. He sets up their schedule, he moves 'em in and out of ballgames, he figures out when each guy will throw and to what batters. Like every part of the game, getting hitters out takes planning and knowledge. Leave too much to chance, you'll need a neck brace from watching balls disappear in the upper deck. Use your brains like Tudor, you'll steal a lot of pennants.

I know I can handle a pitching staff better than anybody else, but I didn't just roll out of bed that way. Every manager learns from hard knocks. I'll never forget one game during my first year of managing. My Rangers were playing the Tigers in Detroit; we were tied in the tenth, and Rusty Staub, a good veteran hitter, came to the plate with runners in scoring position. I had a choice to make: I could pitch to Staub or walk him and pitch to the next guy, Steve Kemp, a rookie who happened to be on a tear. I figured, why throw to the guy with the hot hand? I had my guy take his chances with Rusty. The old sonofagun bounced the damnedest seeing-eye dog through the middle of the infield and beat me. I said to myself, "You know what? I'll never do *that* again."

It gave me one rule I always lived by: When the game's on the line, look at salaries. If you have to pick between two guys to pitch to, and one's making $5 million while the other's getting $150,000, remember that second guy makes less for a reason. He ain't *done* it as many times. That matters! If they're both making $5 million, toss a coin; otherwise, pitch to the one with the skinnier wallet. Even Tudor might agree with me on that one; he was always a pretty frugal guy.

You work up a lot of theories about pitching over the years. The rule you never violate is the same as a doctor's: *Do No Harm.* It's harder to follow than you think. The arm was not designed to throw baseballs. Whether it's Nolan Ryan's supersonic right or Tommy John's cut-and-paste left, every time it does throw one, it gets injured. A starter rests three days between outings, and it ain't because he's sucking wind; his arm is healing from violence. That pattern—injure and heal, injure and heal—is like the heartbeat of a pitching schedule, and you'd better remember it. You have a ten- or eleven-man staff. If you don't guide it like a good traffic cop, you're going to cause pileups up and down the highway.

It takes some planning. Let's say Bobby Cox, the Braves' manager, looks up at a key point in the eighth inning. The game's on the line. He has to get Mark Grace out, so he needs a good lefty to face him—say his young reliever, John Rocker. Well, has he kept Rocker ready? It's a simple question, but it's basic to managing. Did Bobby look ahead to this point three or four innings back? Did he warm up the guy he needs now? If he's done his job, he can bring in the best he's got at the right time. If not, he either has to go to a lesser guy or jeopardize a precious asset: Rocker's arm.

It doesn't take a genius to look a few innings ahead, but you'd be surprised how many managers get caught with their pants around their ankles.

Planning from one game to the next gets a little trickier. Generally, there's two things in baseball that can get you fired: yesterday and tomorrow. You never know what reliever you'll need tomorrow, so the best thing is just to have depth on your staff. I always took ten guys that I had confidence in—not eleven or twelve, like the fad is now, but ten—and I used every one of 'em. If I didn't have confidence in a guy, I got *rid* of his ass. The guys I did keep knew I relied on them, which was good for morale, but more important, with ten good guys, I usually had enough arrows in my quiver to focus on *today*. The good skipper does his managing before the game starts. The guy you see out there *managing* is the one who's screwing up the arms.

You'd think any big-league manager would know certain basics, but it used to shock me watching some guys handle pitchers. Everybody knows arms are precious, especially now that they're worth half the national trust. But the moves I saw were unbelievable. Tommy Lasorda is a good, good friend of mine, and he deserves his status as a Hall of Fame manager. And speaking of having a plan, he and I had a good one. Gussie Busch had pulled me aside one day and said, "You're the best. I want you to make more than any manager in baseball." But Peter O'Malley, the Dodgers' owner, had said the same thing to Lasorda. So I signed a contract and called Tommy and said, "Tom, whatever we do, let's don't sign the same damn year! I'll sign this year and go ahead of you, you go ahead of me the next year, and we'll just keep it going." We did that four years in a row. Who needed an agent?

Well, the man won 1,600-some ballgames and two World Series, and that's no accident, but the fly in his ointment—and it baffled me, because Tommy was a pitcher himself—was that he never figured out how to handle a bullpen. He'd take a reliever and warm him up four or five times during a game and not use him; then he'd do the same thing the next day. The day after *that*, he'd put the guy in a game. He'd have nothing out there, and Tommy'd say, "Hell, you ain't pitched in two days, what's the matter with you?" Some managers think if a guy's not actually in a game, he's not pitching. But if he's tossing on the sidelines, man, he's getting hot. Over the years I dealt some of my pitchers to L.A.—Tudor, Worrell, Ricky Horton, Ken Dayley—and they always came back with the same report: Tommy was still messing up the pen.

A guy's only got so many innings in his arm. That's why I would never let Bruce Sutter or Todd Worrell or Lee Smith, my bullpen stoppers, warm up unless I knew that they were about to go in. If I didn't use them this inning, they'd pitch in the next one. I would never let them warm up without putting them in the game.

Pete Rose was like Tommy. Wonderful baseball man, but he was impaired when it came to handling pitchers. Here he had three worldclass relievers, Norm Charlton, Rob Murphy and Rob Dibble, all in the same pen. Two were lefties; Dibble, the righty, threw 100 miles an hour. With those three guys on your side, you shouldn't lose games after the sixth. Not too damn many. But Pete found a way.

He'd get Murphy up in the third; he'd warm him up in the fourth. Then he'd sit him down. He'd get Charlton up in the fifth. Sometimes I'd look down there, and he'd have both lefthanders going at the same time. Why would you warm 'em both up at once? You're only going to use one lefty or the other! Then, after he'd worked 'em out three or four times, Pete would put one in the game and be surprised he had no zip. "He can't be tired," he'd say. "He ain't pitched in three days!" Somebody counted how many times he warmed Murphy up one year, and it was over 200. I like Pete, boy—but I *loved* managing against him.

Hell, when you understand how to plan, even a lousy pitcher can be an asset. I used to have a guy I called my "spring closer." I'd use him in spring training; I'd take him on every bus trip. If we're a five-hour ride from home, and the game's tied in the ninth inning, I put him in in the last of the ninth. He'll get you home early! We wouldn't have to play extra innings and screw up my pitching staff for the next week. That's important!

Like I've said, I always want my offense to initiate the action, and it's the same with my pitchers. I want the other guys back on their heels. The best thing a pitcher can do along these lines is throw strikes. I don't give a damn if he strikes a guy out; a pitcher who's ahead is a pitcher who's in command. That's especially true early in the count, where you set the tone for the whole at-bat. It's something I always hammered into my pitchers: *Throw strikes*. People talk about the mastery of Greg Maddux, and I do like his control and movement. But what he does best is throw that first strike. Before the batter can dig in, he's down 0–1 and fighting for his life. I notice that when Maddux pitches against American League teams, he nibbles a little more and falls behind. He's not as confident or aggressive; he doesn't know the hitters. But like all good pitchers, when he can take the bull by the horns, he's tough to beat.

Pitching is really the flip side of offense. Remember what I said last chapter about running counts? A batter who's ahead in the count, say 2–1 or 3–1, has control. He knows the pitcher's got to come to him, give him something around the plate. And that control ripples through the whole offense. If there's a runner on base, he realizes he's safer running with the pitch. And if he *is* running, his team will hit into fewer double plays, force more fielding screwups, gain more bases, end up with more scoring chances.

A good manager knows all this and translates it into pitching. He pounds it into his pitchers: *Stay away from running counts*. Get ahead in the count and stay there.

If you were a manager and you convinced 'em to get ahead of every single hitter 0–1, create no running counts, and give up no walks, you'd win a hell of a lot more games than anybody expected, no matter *how* horseshit the rest of your team was. Nobody ever liked my starters in Kansas City much, but Paul Splittorff, Larry Gura, Dennis Leonard, and Andy Hassler—and others, like Steve Busby and Al Fitzmorris—made a hell of a staff because they came at you that way. They snuffed out chances the other teams never knew they had. The Florida Marlins could win if they did it that way.

Good pitching is a team thing. Just like in hitting, the individual glamor stats don't mean much. For instance, aggressive pitching doesn't always mean strikeout pitching. Ozzie Smith put this well: He loved playing behind Tudor because John always stayed around the plate, induced guys to hit grounders to the left side, and kept the Wizard busy and sharp. It kept McGee, Pendleton, and Coleman on their toes, too. Tudor knew it wasn't just him against the hitter, but him, his eight good fielders, and the whole big ballpark against the hitter. Batters knew if they stood there looking at pitches, they'd fall behind and go in the soup. They had to swing. That meant they had to try to beat our defense, and we covered that ballpark like a track team. I always said "make 'em earn every damn thing they get." Even in the field, the Cardinals seized the initiative. That's pitching.

The East Coast writers would see soft-tossers like Tudor, Horton, Perry, Kurt Kepshire and Dave LaPoint and scratch their heads. How in the hell could these guys have an ERA below the league average? My pitchers were smart enough to see the big picture. They'd throw strikes, get ahead, make 'em swing. Beyond that, we'd keep everybody ready and righty-lefty 'em to death. That's how we made up for the loss of Bruce Sutter's 45 saves when he went to Atlanta as a free agent. Our bullpen-by-committee got 44 and never gave up a lead

after the eighth inning till the sixth game of the World
Series. That's why pitchers like Steve Mura and Kurt
Kepshire could win games in the double figures for me,
then never win anything after they left the Cardinals. We
pooled our talents.

We worked together in another way. I had switch-
hitters up and down the lineup, and that gave me a big
edge. When the other team changed from a righty pitcher
to a lefty, I never had to pinch-hit for Ozzie, Willie,
Pendleton, Coleman or Herr. They'd just bat from the
other side. Well, my opponents didn't have that luxury.
If my starting pitcher was a righthander (for example,
Andujar), my first man out of the bullpen would always
be a lefty (say, Horton). That gave their hitters an opposite look, but it also made the other manager pinch
hit for some of his guys. It got players out of the game
early. By the late innings, I'd have a deep bench left,
he'd have nothing, and I'd have more cards to play to
close out my hand.

That's another foundation to building a staff: If three
of your five starting pitchers are lefthanders, you must
have three long relievers who are righthanders. Or for
three righty starters, have three lefty relievers. That way,
when your starter gets knocked out early, you can always bring in a guy who throws the opposite way and
make the other manager use up his bench. One of the
basic, indisputable tendencies of baseball is that a left-
handed pitcher is tougher against left-handed hitters; a
righty is tougher on a right-handed hitter. Managers juggle their lineups accordingly. That's why it amazes me
when some ballclubs don't keep it in mind when they
build a staff. The 1998 Cardinals had only one lefty,
Lance Painter, in the bullpen. That's big trouble, boy.
Once Tony LaRussa had used Painter, the other manager
had a green light to run every lefthanded hitter he had
out there. If the game goes twenty innings, he's liable
to have eight left-handed batters in the lineup, and there

ain't a thing Tony can do about it. Why in the world would you give away odds like that?

I don't believe in stereotypes or formulas in baseball, and I never used 'em. Every staff is different; every year is different. In 1985, injuries pushed me to use a four-man rotation, which I don't like as much, but we adjusted. You adapt to the material you've got at the time. But on game days, I strengthened my hand by following certain rules of my own.

For one thing, I kept every pitcher alert and ready. I had a rule with my relievers: I'd tell each one what his job was *every day*. For each and every game, I had two pitchers, my long men—one righty, one lefty—ready to replace the starter if he got in trouble in the first five innings. If my starter was a righty, say Danny Cox, I'd go to the lefty first; the righty became my sixth- and seventh-inning guy. If my starter was a lefty—Tudor, LaPoint—I'd do it the other way around. Then I'd designate two closers, a righty and a lefty. They were responsible for the eighth and ninth innings. I had a righty and a lefty ready for every segment of the game. I never had one pitcher who didn't like knowing his role, and it helped them all stay as sharp as a split-finger fastball.

You also plan for the unexpected. What if your starter gets in a jam early? You don't want to pull the trigger on him too soon, but you *do* want to warm up your long man just in case. Well, if I warmed up my long man— say, Horton or Billy Campbell—two times in the first five innings, but I ended up not having to use him, I'd tell him to head in the clubhouse, take a shower, change shirts, and relax. He was done. I *would* keep him on the bench in case of an emergency; if we went into extra innings, it could be a five-alarm fire, boy, and he'd come sliding down the pole. But basically, if I warmed you up twice and didn't use you, you had the rest of the day off.

You look ahead a few innings, too. I was known for my calm demeanor, on the bench, but every once in a while I'd get good and steamed, and I knew my pitchers had no clue what bug was up my backside. Let's say it's the sixth inning, we're playing Montreal, and the Expos are batting. It's two outs and nobody on. And my pitcher *walks* the next guy. Then the fourth batter makes an out to end the inning. No harm, right? Well, it's okay for *that* inning, but an inning or two later, one extra guy might get to the plate at the worst possible time. If I could see it was going to be Gary Carter or Andre Dawson, boy, that *really* fried me. The best place for the other team's weapons is on the bench.

I'd also talk specifically to my pitchers about coming situations. Let's say it was the fifth inning, my starter was Forsch, and he was tiring a little. I wanted to keep him in as long as I could, but I'd look ahead, too—a few batters, a few innings. I might say to Rick Horton, "Hey, if Keith Hernandez comes up with two on, you've got him; you're in there." Rick would get ready to face *that* guy in *that* situation. Every pitcher likes to prepare himself as specifically as possible, and if I stay on top of things, I'll know I've got the right guy ready for the turning point. I've thought it out ahead of time.

Now, that situation may never develop. Hernandez might come up with the bases empty, in which case it *isn't* a key moment. Then I'd leave Forsch in there and save Horton for later. On the other hand, the situation might happen, but Hernandez beats the odds and takes one down the line for two runs. Well, I don't give a damn: I still made the move that gave me the best chance. Big leaguers get paid to beat the odds, and when they do, you can't worry about it. That's the way Mr. Rawlings bounces.

Now many a manager, in the example I just gave, would have just left Forsch in to face Hernandez. Maybe he wants to give Forsch, after five or six strong innings, a better chance to get the victory. Or maybe his bullpen's tired and he wants to take off some strain. Now we get to another big question: When do you take your pitcher out?

Making that choice at the right time wins and loses a lot of ballgames, and you can't just go by the seat of your pants. Let's take this example. If that manager leaves Forsch in, he ain't thinking. Every ballgame only has so many pressure points where the game can bust open. When those do come, you'd better be ready with your best. You've only got a few bullets in your gun, and this is the time to spend one. If you don't, there might not be a win for Forsch to *get*. Win today, and to hell with the rest of it.

In changing pitchers, you also have to know your personnel. Anybody can watch a three-run homer sail over the boards and say, "Hey, that guy's lost it." But can you get him out *before* the damage happens? One pitch too late, you're as bad a manager as Joe Blow chomping hot dogs in the stands. Each pitcher has a danger point, a number of pitches or innings where he's liable to crack. You'd better know it so you can shut the gate with the hoss still in the barn. That's another move so good the fans won't know you made it—in other words, the right one.

Whether it's inning-to-inning or season-to-season, you do have to know your pitchers' mechanics. Bruce Sutter might be the most important pitcher I ever had, and he was sure as hell the best relief pitcher I ever saw. Sonofagun would come in with the bases loaded, fall behind 3–0, and *still* make 'em hit the ball, and most of time, them pitches weren't even strikes. Hell, Bruce won us a World Series in '82. And nobody knew his motion better than Mike Roarke, Bruce's guru and the Cardinals' pitching coach for a time.

His knowledge rubbed off on me. I knew Bruce had to come back behind his ear, then straight over the top, with his delivery. He threw that nasty split-finger pitch, which made the ball look like a rock skipping on water—tough to pick up, let alone hit—but it puts a violent torque on the arm. When you think of the guys who live by that pitch—the Mike Scotts of the Astros, the Sutters—how many had a couple of great years, then dropped off the map? Pitching's a dangerous living, boy, and you'd better use your head.

Well, one spring, Roarke and I were watching Sutter throw in West Palm Beach, and I saw he was coming kind of three-quarters, bringing the ball out to the side and across. I said, "Holy moly, Mike, he's all out of whack!" We got right on his ass about it, and he straightened it out—no harm, no foul. Bruce saved a lot of games for us; we saved him more arm damage than anybody knows.

You know what? If he'd stayed with the Cardinals, Bruce would have never gotten hurt. He'd have had guys like us watching him throw. Instead, he took Ted Turner's millions, went to Atlanta where nobody knew him like we did, and blew out his arm. I don't blame him for leaving; he wanted to stay with St. Louis, but our management jerked him around over some crazy no-trade stipulation nobody really cared about. Turner showed him the money.

But Ted didn't invest right. He had to pay Bruce even after he couldn't pitch anymore—that's why they call it a guaranteed contract—and Bruce is still laughing his way to the bank. But he never pitched good again. The main lesson is, the Braves just left too much to chance. If you don't have some plan about what you're doing, or one way or another, this game's going to kick you in the ass. And them spikes can be sharp.

When I was a kid playing ball, signing my first pro contract, and getting to the big leagues, you usually had four starters on your staff. Your bullpen consisted of the guys who weren't good enough to start. Your starter usually went nine anyway, so you only used those guys to mop up. You wanted complete games.

Has *that* ever changed. Specialization has made this a different sport. Today, not only is your bullpen more important, it's broken down into particular roles—middlemen, setup men, closers and the like. It's by far the biggest on-field change that happened during my career. And like I learned firsthand myself, there's one player who makes the biggest impact on winning or losing titles in modern baseball: the firebreathing monster who comes in at the end to shut the game down. The modern closer has changed the game, and he's changed the way I'll always think about building a staff.

My Royals in the late seventies came up against the Yankees three times in the playoffs. The League Championship Series was best-of-five then, and in '76 and '77 both, we took New York to the fifth and final game. One year we went to the ninth inning tied, the other year ahead by a run. But both years, the Yankees could bring on a great stopper at the end—Sparky Lyle, the great lefty. We had Mark Littell, a pretty good pitcher but just not on the same level. We couldn't counter. Not only that, but our organization decided never to *add* a good closer, even though some good ones were available. Ewing Kauffman and our GM, Joe Burke, had a no-free-agents policy. They said no player would ever make more money than George Brett; no pitcher would make more than Dennis Leonard. In the meantime, George Steinbrenner brought the coals to Newcastle: After '77, he went out and bought Goose Gossage, the scariest closer in baseball, to go with Lyle. Ewing and Burke stood pat, and we had even less of a chance.

Well, here's how I see it. In most games, you have twenty-seven outs to score your runs. Good closers cut those numbers. The Yankees hacked our chances from twenty-seven outs to twenty-one or even eighteen a game. Those guys were so good, if you wanted to score, you had to do it by the sixth or seventh because, after that, you were finished. That problem forced my hand as a manager. I had to make offensive moves earlier in the game than I wanted to. It changed everything. It cost me two or three trips to the World Series, and it made me look at modern pitching in a whole new light.

When I got to St. Louis, I made damn sure I got myself a top-flight closer. In fact, I went out and got myself the two best of all time. We had both Sutter and Rollie Fingers in the same pen for a couple of days! We traded Rollie before he ever pulled on the birds and bat, but the idea was set: I realized it was smarter to start building my staff at the back, with that one potent guy, and move forward from there. I'd get that guy who could shut the door the last two innings, cut the other guy's chances from twenty-seven to twenty-one, and hope my starters were good enough to get me through the sixth. That's why I never minded strapping adequate guys out there as starters—the Muras, the John Stupers, the Kepshires, and LaPoints. They were really just long relievers, setting up the Sutters, Worrells and Lee Smiths.

How do you tell a good stopper? He's got a hell of a fastball or one trick pitch. He might get his ass beat in the game today, but he'll go out there tomorrow like it never happened. A guy who can't make it as a closer gets a tight ass; he nibbles, he walks a guy next time. A good closer has a different makeup than other kinds of pitchers. He has to still have a lot of bulldog in him. He can also go hard for three innings without a second thought.

When I brought up Todd Worrell in 1985, he'd only been a reliever for two months. He'd been a starter at Louisville, and he lit up the radar guns. But the coaches there noticed that he started off throwing 93, 94 mph but dropped off to 85 by the third inning. Darold Knowles, Lee Thomas and I put our heads together and decided to try him at closer. Todd took to it like a catfish to water. I brought him up August 31, he pitched in the Series a month later, and it turned his life around. Ours, too.

Here's the deal in modern baseball. With these stopper

specialists on hand, if you have a chance to get one, you've gotta do it. Baseball's a game of percentages. A Worrell, a Sutter, a Gossage, or, nowadays, a Trevor Hoffman or a Billy Wagner will change the dynamics of your staff. He'll cut the other team's odds. And he'll do it before he even throws a pitch.

So pitching's not that different from hitting: Stock your arsenal; seize the initiative. Use every angle you can. But once you've done that, what do you do with what you've got? What if you have the right people but the wrong idea? Lord knows I see a lot of *that* today.

One bad idea is to train young pitchers to be closers from the get-go. I know a closer's important, but in the minor leagues you've first got to learn how to *pitch*. You do that more as a starter than as a reliever. You learn to pitch out of jams that way; you learn how to use your second pitch. We can always make someone a reliever later on if we need one, like we did with Worrell. It doesn't help a kid to make him a specialist too soon.

Another idea particularly drives me up the wall. It's become a stereotype, it doesn't work well most of the time, and I never hear anybody say a word about it. It's the so-called "one-inning closer." Tony LaRussa, a manager I do respect, started it in Oakland when he had Dennis Eckersley as his stopper. Tony made a hard-and-fast rule: He never pitched Eckersley more than one inning, and that inning was the ninth. It worked for the A's and it started a trend that hasn't stopped yet.

Well, every trend works best in a certain setting. Eckersley was a great control pitcher, and the strategy helped him focus—not to mention saving his arm. But the system worked because Tony had two good setup men, the righty Dave Nelson and the lefty Rick Honeycutt, who could hold leads in the seventh and eighth. By the time they handed Eck the ball, he was ahead. But what if those setup men, like most today, were horseshit? Would you *still* only ask Eck to get you three outs? I see so many ballgames lost in the eighth inning it makes me sick. The manager brings in a mediocre guy to hold a lead in the seventh or eighth, but he can't do it. What's the use of having a $5 million closer if he don't get any lead to protect? That's crazy!

If I was managing today, everybody in baseball would think I was nuts. I'd do a lot of things different. First of all, it's better to have your closer go two innings every other day than one inning every day. How do you know you're going to need him tomorrow? Start it in spring training; get him used to two-inning stints. Check it out: When Sutter pitched for me, he'd appear 65 times, but he'd get 100 innings pitched. Same for Worrell and Lee Smith. Today, a guy will have 65 appearances and go 55 innings. That's partly because of the agents, who push for more saves per inning pitched, but you're going to pay a guy $4 million and only get 55 innings? That's a joke. Why can't your closer come in with two outs and a runner on second in the eighth inning? If you've got an off-day the next day, why can't he come in in the seventh? I asked my stoppers to do that all the time. They never complained; they came in and got people out.

I'd even go one step further. Why do you have to be *ahead* to bring in your closer? If the score's tied in extra innings at home, you're *never* going to be ahead: As soon as you go ahead, the game's over. So you're going to leave him on the bench? If I'm at home and the score's tied after the ninth, I'll use my closer to keep us close till my bats can come in and win it. That's the goal, not beefing up some guy's save totals. Hell, I'm paying a lot for my pitchers. I'm going to get some value.

If you want to talk value, here's a stopper you never thought of: Nolan Ryan. He holds one of the greatest records in the history of baseball, and you never hear anybody talk about it. Nolan Ryan finished 78 games in a row in which he held the lead after the seventh inning. *Seventy-eight straight games.* Not only was Nolan the starter; he was his own closer, and he did not blow a save. That's three good years worth of saves. Nolan Ryan didn't *need* a closer. Talk about getting more for your money!

I've talked a lot about planning. But pitching's like anything else. You can do everything right and still end up in the crapper.

In the early eighties, the Dodgers were in great shape. They had a hell of a young closer, one of the best I ever saw. Historic stuff, outstanding makeup; Steve Howe would have been one of the greats of all time. And they had some young flamethrowers in the pen with him, including Dave Stewart—who's now in Toronto's front office—and Alejandro Pena. It was a wonderful young staff, but Howe developed a lot of personal problems. Were those Lasorda's fault?

For years after Howe self-destructed on drugs, they had a hell of a time trying to replace him. They rushed along Stewart, Pena, and other guys that weren't ready. They made a flurry of trades for lefty relief, all of which bombed. I'll never forget when I was managing the All-Star Game in Houston and Lasorda was one of my coaches. A photographer came up and said, "Hey, Tommy, how'd ya like to pose with all the ex-Dodger pitchers on the two rosters?" There were *nine* of them, all given away in trades! I don't blame Tommy for blowing a gasket. "What are you tryin' to do, make me look bad?" He ran the guy off! But it wasn't Tommy's fault one kid picked white powder over Dodger blue.

With the Cardinals, I was lucky enough to have more control than most. I had one main category of pitchers in my career: These Guys Will Get You Fired. No matter how in the hell they *threw*, they never *won*. Just check their won–lost percentage, from high school on up. They don't know how to do it! Pitching's so horseshit now, I *still* see some of them pitching in the big leagues. Two of 'em are on local TV all the time. It's desperate times!

But I was fortunate: I never had to use one. A lot of managers do, and there ain't much they can do about it.

As far as pitchers go, a good plan does go a long way, but I never said a guy has to be Neils Bohr to get people out. Sometimes it's just the opposite. I remember one day in 1981, it had to be 105 degrees in St. Louis—brutal weather. And on the old turf, they just laid the carpet on asphalt. If it was 105 on the street, it was 139 in the ballpark; they measured it. It was Bob Sykes's turn to pitch, and he was one of them lefthanded guys that seem like maybe they have dual citizenship—Earth and Mars. Bob's the guy we ended up trading for Willie McGee. You never knew what he was going to say to you or when, like he was five sheets under the wind in a typhoon.

Well, it was such a blast furnace that day, I thought, hell, if I don't mention the heat, Sykes won't figure out how bad it is, and I'll get three innings out of him. Then I could bring in Jim Kaat for three more and start trotting out my bullpen guys, one at a time, and hope nobody dropped dead.

I was a lot smarter than Sykes, but he's the one who threw a nine-inning shutout. Hendrick hit a homer in the tenth to win it, 1–0. I guarantee you, Bob had *no idea* how hot it was, and if he had, he'd have ended up a puddle of warm spit. Sometimes you have to empty your head to keep it on your shoulders. I almost hated to trade the guy.

I had other pitchers like him. Greg Mathews and Joe Magrane were roommates in '87, my lefthanded Intergalactic Twins. God almighty, they were funny; I think they spoke their own language, though I'm still not sure because I never understood what the hell they were talking about. Joe is articulate but from outer space, and Mathews—well, I'll just say he was the only pitcher I ever knew who *liked* to be operated on. One bad outing and *bam*, he was on the gurney. He wanted the latest surgery! Yet in the pennant race that year, they pitched both ends of one of the most important doubleheaders in Cardinal history.

We were two games up on New York with five to play. The Mets arrived in town a day early for a three-game series to end the year, and there they were—Gooden, Hernandez, Strawberry, Bob Ojeda—all in the ballpark to watch us against the Montreal Expos, a right-handed hitting team with power. All I had was the two lefties. We crossed our fingers. They threw a double shutout to clinch the pennant, and the Metropolitans choked on their popcorn.

But I still think of Mr. Tudor, pitching with the eye of a surgeon. We had to trade him to the Dodgers in 1988—his arm was sore, but Tommy still wanted him for the stretch drive—and he ended up missing most of 1989. He was miserable, boy. But I had a chance to get him back as a free agent for 1990, and I knew he was so smart he might find a way to help us. Well, what the hell did John Tudor do with his wounded wing and 78-mile-an-hour fastball but go 4–0 in April to win Pitcher of the Month, then proceed to finish 12–4?

John Tudor did more with less than any pitcher in the history of baseball. Sonofagun could've pitched right-handed and won, I believe.

When we got him back from the Dodgers, the Cards wanted to give him a two-year contract. Most people would've said "Where do I sign?" but Tudor was a different kettle of fish. He didn't even want to talk about it! With his bad arm, he only thought he'd go one more season, so the idea offended him. I had to laugh. I said, "John, they want to give you a two-year contract, *guaranteed*. Take it!" "Whitey, I'm only gonna pitch one more year." "Take the contract, John! You can still quit any time you like. You've earned it, with all the big games you've won for me." "No, I'm only gonna pitch one more year." It was like talking to a wall. And he'd bang the ball in his mitt, go out on the field, and loosen up.

He only pitched one more year, 1990. He never took the money. John Tudor turned down more than a million dollars because, in his mind, he wasn't going to earn every penny he got. Can you name a guy who'd do that today?

The ball can bounce funny in this sport, and you can think your way right into the ditch. But if a guy's got brains, a strong heart, and principles that ain't for sale, you can take it to the bank: He's going to pitch you some shutouts. I hope that's always true in my game.

· 9 ·

Running the Show

When I first joined the Cardinals, it was never a picnic scoring runs in Houston's Astrodome. The giant dimensions and dead, air-conditioned air were like a big blanket that smothered flyballs. And the pitchers they strapped out at you were a nightmare. Their 6-8 fire-balling righthander, James Rodney Richard, was just the beginning. Nolan Ryan was next, and then came Joe Niekro, the knuckleballing righthander who won 221 games in his career. Later they added Don Sutton. It was a hell of a mix of bullets and butterflies in south Texas, and you weren't going to score many runs. Prior to about 1985, we didn't.

But on one of my first trips there in Cardinal red, I saw one young pitcher I'd heard a lot about who intrigued me even more. Big, fearless righthander with a live fastball who came right at your hitters. Outstanding movement on his pitches. Looked damn good in them gold, orange and black jumpsuits, too, not to mention the sparkling gold chains. There was nobody quite like Joaquin (Goombah) Andujar.

Problem was, what I *had* heard set my antennas to twitching. Joaquin was already calling himself "one tough Dominican"—he said it like it was all one word—and from what I could see, he wasn't lying. But the word around baseball was he pissed and moaned all the time. He whined and pointed fingers. He hated his own manager with a passion and he made excuses when he screwed up. Great stuff, terrible head—the classic "is-he-really-worth-it?" type of ballplayer.

It was the manager part that surprised me. Their skipper at the time was one of my best friends in the world, Bill Virdon. Bill and I go back to my first days in the Yankee chain, when he was a smooth-swinging center-fielder, and we had our first professional tryouts together. We've been buddies for ages and stayed in touch over the years. He still lives in Springfield, Missouri, so we fish together even now, and I can tell you without a doubt that I've never known a kinder, more even-tempered human being in my life than Bill Virdon. So when their general manager, Al Rosen, called me one day wanting to get rid of Andujar—he wanted Tony Scott, one of our outfielders—I had to get Bill on the horn and find out what the hell was going on.

"Bill," I said, "I hear Andujar don't like you. I've never known a ballplayer not to like you. I've never known a *person* not to like you. What's the problem with this guy?"

He sighed a little, like he was already tired of the subject. "Whitey," he said, "I'll put it like this. The dumb sonofagun wants to pitch every day."

Well, everybody in the world knows pitchers don't pitch *every* day; not even Satchel Paige did that. I took it as a figure of speech. But before I could do that, Bill cut me off in midstream. "Listen, Rat, I'm not kidding you. I've got Ryan, I've got Vern Ruhle, I've got J. R. Richard, I've got Niekro. Andujar pitched one Thursday. We got rained out Friday and Saturday, so there weren't any games. And he comes into my office Sunday morning and starts raising hell. Says he feels fine, he's ready to go again. He's *ready!* The other four guys ain't even been out to the mound yet, and he thinks it's his turn!" Virdon tried to talk sense into him, Andujar flew into a conniption fit, they snapped at each other, and they'd been like oil and water ever since. "Whitey," said Bill, "I'm just telling you. This guy is out of his mind."

Well, I respect the hell out of Bill's opinion. He's a fine baseball man. And I'm not going to sit here and tell you I marked Andujar down as an aviation scientist. But how many ballplayers are? And you know what? My ears did perk up a little. Maybe I'm nuts, but I like a guy that wants the baseball. If a pitcher's biggest negative is he can't stand *not* pitching—well, I figure that's a problem I can live with. Maybe I can work out the details later. I told Houston I was interested, told Scott to pack his bags, and made the deal.

History shows it's a damn good thing. The '81 strike happened the day after I got Joaquin, so he didn't pitch for me for fifty-six days. But once we got up and zunning again, he went on a tear. He was 6–1 the rest of that season. Over the next five years, he pitched and won some of the biggest games in Cardinal history. He won 20 for me twice, won 68 in four and a half years, struck out 130 batters a season, and threw damn near 1,100 innings along the way. In both the years he won 20, he did it by the first week of August, so he *should've* won 30 both times. He got us to two World Series and helped us win one. We'd have never been the team we were without our OneToughDominican.

It wasn't hard to see how Andujar got on people's nerves: He was higher-strung than a tightrope walker. He'd steam through the clubhouse: "I'm pissed, Whitey, I'm pissed!" Sonofagun was *always* worked up about something. I almost never knew *why* he was pissed and mostly had no desire to find out. I'd say, "Pissed, huh, Goombah? Come on by my office at five o'clock, and we'll talk about it." "Okay, Whitey," he'd say, and he'd stomp off mumbling to himself *en espanol*.

Well, five o'clock would roll around, and I'd see him on his way out the door. I'd buttonhole him: "Hey Goombah, wanna talk?" He'd look at me like he barely knew who I was, think for a second, then remember. "Oh, no thanks, Skip," he'd say. "I'm not mad anymore!" And happy as a lark, he'd go home.

You'd see stuff like that and think, "Man, the wheel's still spinning, but the gerbil has died." But I'd figured it out right away: If I talked to Joaquin when he was mad, we'd have had fights. He was volatile; just getting *into* an argument with Joaquin was losing, and I'd be damned if I wanted to be short one happy pitcher when it counted most. If I just showed him I noticed, let him blow off steam and waited for him to cool down, we made a hell of a pair.

All Andujar wanted to do was go out on the mound and throw baseballs as hard as he could, and it's tough to fault a guy for that. But it's true he could take it a little far. Before we got him, he was well known for throwing tantrums when the manager came to take him out. He never thought he was done, and he'd storm off the field and have a three-day fit. But again, there was a simple solution: When he'd lost his stuff, I'd go to the hill, put my hand right on his shoulder, and say, "Hey, Goombah, great job. Gimme the ball, and I'll see you Tuesday." "Okay, Whitey," he'd say with a big smile. "See you Tuesday!" And he'd stride off to the showers looking like a proud son.

It wasn't logical. Joaquin already *knew* he was pitching Tuesday. He knew he'd pitched great; he *always* thought he pitched great. But he liked to hear me tell him when he was pitching again. He liked to hear me tell him how good he was. Gave him something positive to think about. And Tuesday night, he'd be ready to pitch for me, boy. He called me "Papa"—"Okay, Papa," he'd say. He rarely missed a start for me, and he and I never had any problems. Sometimes a guy's liability is really his strong point.

As Joaquin showed, there's more to managing than filling out the lineup card. You've got to be a good boss, just like you might be a good boss if you ran a corporation, a car dealership, or a furniture warehouse. Show people respect, be honest with them, and be ready to recognize what they do well, and you're most of the way to a good career. Baseball's a unique business, one where your assets are human beings with particular skills. One way to use them best is to like the people—a lot, if possible. The best thing I did for Joaquin was enjoy the hell out of him.

I love to fish a different hole every day, and one thing I appreciated was the way Andujar diversified my job. You could be winning, everyone's hitting, everything's running on all eight cylinders, and Joaquin would come in with something to stir up the pot. You were sitting on a time bomb every day; it could be anything. I enjoyed that, he knew it, and I think it made him want to do his best for me.

I had more than my share of the so-called problem guys in baseball—Alex Johnson and Rico Carty in Texas; Hernandez, Templeton, and David Green in St. Louis, and a lot more I could name if I wrote a longer book. I didn't succeed with all of 'em, but people did used to ask me how the hell I did so well with so many. My answer is simple: Be a good manager. It's like with any player: They need to respect you and respect your knowledge. They need to know you're going to be straight with them and never lie. Add that all together, and you've got an atmosphere of respect. You're showing they're worthy of a chance. Most ballplayers answer that challenge. Now, if you show that respect and they *still* screw up, get rid of 'em; they're usually no good to begin with. But most of the "problem" guys, I've found, ain't a thing in the world but decent people nobody's bothered to figure out yet.

One of my best hitters in the early years with the Cardinals—good team player, a guy with 20, 25 homers a year in his bat—was George Hendrick. He decided at one point not to talk to the media, which is why some writers called him "Silent George." That was his business. But the negative press he got from that had no relationship to the kind of person George was, the player I dealt with day-to-day. I'm not going to lie to you: Early in his career, George was no Barbie doll. He had a lot of problems not running balls out, jogging to flyballs in the outfield, that kind of stuff. So when I came to St. Louis, I got together with my old friend John McNamara, who was coaching for the Padres at the time. He had managed George in Cleveland, and I picked his brain in a lot of bull sessions. You wouldn't believe some of the stunts Hendrick pulled early in his career.

But you look at things in context. Here was a kid who grew up in Watts, the toughest area of Los Angeles. If you think that doesn't affect a guy, you're nuts. He was kind of a resentful person. When I was a double-check scout for the Mets, we had the number-two pick in the amateur draft in 1968, and Hendrick was far and away the best amateur in the nation that year, so I went out to watch him play one Sunday afternoon. Here he was performing in front of major-league scouts, and George wasn't even in uniform for the game: He had on a pair of Levis and a white T-shirt. He was a centerfielder, and there was no fence out there, and instead of coming in with his teammates in between innings, if he wasn't due to bat he'd just wander out and lay in the grass in deep centerfield, or out on the foul line, and take a nap. Who knows what the hell was going on in his head? That's the kind of personality you were dealing with.

But he was worth it. When a kid is as talented as George was, you owe it to him, and yourself, to try to change him. His career began in the A's system, and a lot of folks worked overtime with George. That's why I still say the most important person in any big-league organization is your rookie-league manager. He's not only a trainer and a bus driver and a father, he's *everything*. Those players don't know how to eat right; a lot of them have never been scolded, because their mommy and daddy don't want to get mad at 'em; they've never had a home-cooked meal because mom and pop have two jobs and couldn't find their way to the kitchen if you chased 'em with a food processor. A good rookie-

league manager turns boys into men. He can do more to shape your baseball resources than anybody else, including the player-development director and the big-league manager. Yet he'll never get paid enough, the fans will never hear of him, and it's just one more example of the old, true saying: "That's life."

By the time George got to the big leagues, he still made a habit of testing you, but you could work with him if you came at him right. When I hooked up with him in St. Louis, I just had to level with the man. All I wanted was for him to run the ball out. I said, "You want to get along with me, you just hustle and run the way you should, and you won't have any problems." He responded pretty good. For six weeks, he played wonderful. But all of a sudden, one day, he rounded first and stayed there when he should have gone on to second. And he got a sheepish look, crouched over and said to my first-base coach, "Uh-oh; I just got my ass in trouble." After the inning, I brought him in, sat him down, gave him an earful of what I thought, and fined him a few dollars. George didn't give me any bullshit; he just said, "I know, Skip, I know—it won't happen again." It didn't.

By 1981, George was a hell of a player and a wonderful person to be around. We became good friends: I took him and his boys fishing once in a while. By the time 1982 rolled around, and we brought some younger guys in to play around him, he had become kind of the elder statesman, and he really responded to that. George helped out those younger players, set a good example, and became one of the most respected players on my team. When I finally traded him to the Pirates in 1984, it was only out of baseball necessity.

I had a lot of players who were what you might call a little prickly. With Alex Johnson and Rico Carty in Texas, I had two good hitters, but I still can't tell you which in the hell was the worse leftfielder. I'd DH one and play the other in left, then switch it around the next day. That way I could hide one of 'em, and they never got tired. Then I found out I couldn't play Alex in the rain: He'd rust. The man had iron hands. So when it rained, I'd DH him. But terrible as his reputation was—I can't even remember how many times he got shipped from team to team—I had no trouble with Alex Johnson. He's a good person, a religious guy; his wife was a very nice woman. The main thing you had to know about him was, when he put the uniform on, he hated umpires. Loathed the *sight* of 'em. He thought every umpire's job was to take the bread right out of his mouth. He believed that; that's how fanatical a hitter he was. But like I told him, if he ran the ball out for me, I didn't give a damn about it, and once I levelled with him, he always did what I asked. I really liked Alex Johnson. Still do.

Amos Otis was an extremely talented player—good speed, Gold Glove outfielder, drove in 90 runs with 18 to 20 home runs a year for me in Kansas City. I'd worked with him in Instructional League in the late sixties, when we were both in the Mets organization, and I found out you couldn't say a good word to Amos Otis: If you said "Hey, great play" or "good hustle," he'd take the day off for the next two weeks and nosedive into a slump. Amos had a negative kind of personality; I'm not sure he liked himself that much. He looked for any excuse to take it easy on himself. But like I told every player I ever coached, it was my job to find a way to make every guy the best player he could be so he could make every dollar possible in his career. That's how I looked at my work when I was a player; I felt that was my duty to my family. So I pushed my players to do the same. I rode the hell out of Amos Otis. I ain't saying he enjoyed it, or even that I did, but he needed that to reach his potential. We did get his personality and skills to mesh—a guy has to *want* to use his tools. And for four and a half years, Amos was one of my best guys on a hell of a team.

Managing is actually the right name for the job: It

really means managing your resources, the way any manager does in any business. It means getting the most you can out of those resources in the time you have. You can accomplish that by knowledge of the game and strategy, by teaching skills, by the way you set up relationships and keep them going. Your good manager, by hook or by crook, takes the potential and the personalities and he translates the whole mess into W's in the standings. Some players call for more managing than others; everybody's different. And as long as you don't betray the bedrock principles you've got for *all* managing, it helps if you can tailor your approach to each guy.

Some players make it easy: You write their names in, and you know they're ready to go. I already told you Willie McGee was like that. So were Herr, Pendleton, Porter, and others. But one of the greatest pleasures of my career had to be managing George Brett in Kansas City.

Not only was George the best all-around player I ever managed, but his approach to the game was a study in getting the absolute most out of what you have. George was a young, popular single guy when I managed—the most eligibile bachelor in Kansas City—and that creates temptations very few kids can handle at that age. George needed a father more than he did a manager, and that's what I was for him. I taught him how to drink V.O. and how to not drink too much of it. We fished and hunted and did all kinds of stuff. It's one reason we're still good buddies today.

George was a hell-bent, throwback type of player who loved collisions, sliding, and getting himself covered in dirt and in trouble, so he was injured one place or another most of the time. I talked to him about that:In baseball, it ain't always so smart to go that hard. George thought through the consequences and faced 'em like a man. People don't know this about him, but he'd get keys from the stadium staff, get to the ballpark before anybody else—*anybody*, not just the players—and let himself in. He'd be in the trainer's room early in the morning, four or five hours before anybody else got there, and he'd sit in the whirlpool, tape himself, stretch—do whatever he had to to overcome his injuries and get ready for the next game. Even as a boy, George was a man as a ballplayer.

He's still a VP in the Royals organization, and he's been part of a group trying to buy the ballclub for years. For a while, he was even teamed up with Rush Limbaugh, the radio star; they're good friends from Rush's days in the PR office, when Rush was making $18,000 a year, not $30 million. Hell, George is one of the few players I could see working at any level of the game, and I'd work for him any day of the week and I hope he knows it. As a player, he took responsibility for every bit of his talent.

People talk about "psychology" in managing. That always makes me laugh. You didn't have to be Sigmund Freud to handle Brett. Or how about Willie McGee? You'd wind him up and send him out there: If you messed with McGee, you'd only be busting up what didn't need fixing. You'd talk to him before the game: "Hey, Willie, you comfortable?" "Yeah, Skip, I'm comfortable." "You relaxed?" "Yeah, I'm relaxed." "Need anything?" "No, no thanks, Skip." "What's your wife's name?" "Mrs. McGee." That's how you'd do it! With a fellow like Willie, *that's* psychology. I'd like a team full of 'em; I'd form a clinic, and they'd call me Sigmund Freud.

Maybe a manager sets a tone, but he's got only so much control over his fate. It's like the movie business: If the casting director's done his job, you're halfway to a blockbuster. After managing two teams where I didn't decide on personnel, I got lucky with Gussie Busch: He made me GM, too, and said, "Herzog, do what you gotta do." A lot of people thought I was power mad, but to me, it was just a chance to be held accountable. Hell, if

I'm going to get fired, I want it to be because of something *I* did. In Kansas City, off-the-field shenanigans played too big a part in how our team did. It had nothing to do with baseball! Old Gussie didn't make that mistake. He trusted me, got the hell out of the way, and gave me more power than anybody in baseball since Connie Mack—and Mr. McGillicuddy *owned* his club.

So I had a leg up: I put together a cast I could direct. I got guys I knew would listen, prepare themselves, carry out a game plan, and do it without whining. They also knew if they didn't toe the line, I could slam their ass on the first flight out of Lambert Field. That didn't happen much. Just about every last guy did what he could to be a hell of a big-league ballplayer. Ozzie and Tommy Herr studied every chart I ever posted on every opposing hitter; neither one was ever out of position the whole time I had 'em. Bob Forsch, the righthanded pitcher, never quite figured out how to punch 'em out in the World Series—he was better against hitters he knew—but you could count on him for a durable, solid 200-plus innings and 12–4 wins a year. Danny Cox battled his way through some of the biggest games in Cardinal history, usually when his arm was so sore he couldn't touch the top of his cap. Managing guys like that means getting them on your team in the first place.

Very few managers have much influence on their fates today. The GM's job is so complicated—bullshitting with agents around the clock and so on—and there's so much money tied up in it, most teams wouldn't even consider giving you both hats to wear. And they shouldn't. Managers also make a lot less than the players, and their contracts are shorter, so instead of being in command, they're as disposable as an old Bic lighter. And even in the best of times, you can be a hell of a manager and still finish last. What if your closer breaks down? What if you never had one in the first place? What if your best player ain't signed, and his heart ain't in it, or if he's going through a nasty divorce? Some of my best years of managing had the worst results.

Especially with all the lame-duck, little-fish teams we have now, a manager's job is more keeping it interesting than it is to win. You *know* you are not going to win in Minnesota or Montreal. Judging by the quilts they weave out of raggedy scraps, how can you not call Felipe Alou, the Expos' manager, and the Pirates' Gene Lamont two of the best in the game? Their payrolls are a third the size of the big-market teams, yet they keep their clubs in the hunt long enough not to be a laughingstock. It gives the organizations a fighting chance to survive. Jim Leyland did the same for years in Pittsburgh. He finally got his chance to work with a big-league payroll in Miami and won the World Series. But he had to feel like Custer at the last stand in '98 after they stripped the Marlins down to a Double-A clunker. Think that was what he expected when he moved down there?

No, nowadays, it's hard to separate a guy from the payroll he's got. If your ballclub has money and you've got any brains at all, you're going to win. Look at Joe Torre, for goodness' sakes. Joe is a good manager—I know that from managing against him when he ran the Braves in the early eighties—but he didn't look so good when he had a $24 million payroll in St. Louis. During those last, cost-cutting days of Anheuser-Busch, they were doing everything but pull up the carpets, and Joe got run out of town. But I've managed against a lot worse managers than him, I'll tell you that. He may not have seemed too smart in St. Louis, but look how smart a $70 million payroll makes you! If you're losing, they say, "He ain't doing anything!" But if you're winning 114 games and the World Series, they say, "He sure knows how to stay out of the way." That's how they talk about managing. (But I will say this: Joe Torre was the worst catcher I ever saw. The fans in the centerfield bleachers knew his number better than the ones behind home plate did!)

Tony LaRussa's another example. Tony's won everywhere he's been, and he's done well with what he's been given. But he has *always* had one of the biggest payrolls in the major leagues. What can you really tell from that?

Tony and Leyland are old friends. When Jim went to Florida, I heard people saying, "Yeah, Jim's good, but he doesn't have the record Tony has." Well, he never had the budget Tony had! No doubt about it—that's part of the equation.

I've learned a lot, good and bad, from watching other people manage. Some things, you can pick up from experience. Others you can't.

One of the fallacies you run across, when there's an opening for a manager, is when everybody looks to the minor leagues. If a guy's been down there a few years and won a lot, they say he's paid his dues; he knows how to win. It's his time. And sometimes that works out great. But life in the bushes, which is valuable in itself, won't teach you everything. A good big-league manager doesn't have to beat the path from Utica to Salt Lake first.

When I quit playing, I talked with Mary Lou, and we figured, hell, I might manage in the minors some day. I even got an offer to do that, in the Orioles' chain; Lee MacPhail asked me to run a Double-A club at Elmira, New York, before I got a different offer. I never expected to manage in the majors. You know how I found out I was cut out for it? By doing it. I got the chance even though I'd never managed before, and I took to it like a duck to an Illinois lake.

Part of it's just personality. Can you look a $5 million ballplayer in the eye and tell him what to do? A lot of times, when you bring a manager up that was in the minor leagues managing, he doesn't want to handle the stars. He doesn't want to face up to them. He likes all young people around him, because it's easy to manage young people; the toughest job is to handle that star, to make him contented, to get him to play the way you want him to play—where he's kind of the leader, so the young guys will follow him. Some guys who've managed ten years in the minors just don't want to handle that star. I've seen more players lose their jobs that way. The manager's new; he's got a little clout early. He says, "Hey, this guy won't do the job; he's overpaid." And now it's easy; you just say, "He's making too much money; he doesn't give a crap!" The team gets rid of the player, when the problem is the manager all along.

Another key job is dealing with the media. I've got a poem framed on the wall of my garage that reads, "Early to bed, early to rise; fish all day, and make up lies." I wouldn't call that my motto, since I do tell the truth, but it sure as hell helps if a manager has the gift of gab. Casey showed me that a good yarn keeps the writers occupied, spins the ball in your direction, and lets your team stay focused on playing the game. When I was coaching for the Mets, I got better copy than Stengel. Bing Devine tells me that Casey even worried about that, if you can believe it. It helps if you can tell a good story.

A lot of what I know, I got from a long list of managers I played for and watched up close. Some were good and some were horseshit. But every one had something to teach you if you kept your eyes peeled.

The best year of managing I ever saw was Don Zimmer with the Cubs in 1989. Zim's a great baseball man. For that one year, he could do no wrong. He tried everything, and everything he tried worked! He called the hit-and-run, he ran squeezes, he pitched out, he ran double-steals. He pitched guys on two, three days' rest. I saw the sonofagun calling for the hit-and-run with one out and the bases loaded. You talk about a way to get people killed! It was something. Ask the fans in Chicago; they ain't ever going to forget that summer. People say, "Don't you think he was just lucky?" It's like I always say: It's amazing how lucky you are when you're good.

One of the toughest jobs in baseball right now has to

be pitching coach of the Colorado Rockies: You've got to keep eleven guys positive about getting hitters out in that high-altitude launching pad. No matter what you do, there's going to be a lot of long balls. No lead is ever safe. Well, they've got the right guy in Frank Funk, one of the most optimistic human beings I've ever met. He reminds me of Charlie Dressen, who managed me on some awful ballclubs in Washington and Detroit. Charlie could look outside, see it coming down cats and dogs, and say, "Boys, it's 10 percent sunshine!" He kept you hopeful, and that let you swing a little easier.

I'm a little like that: I always believe I can win, and that's contagious with your players. If you know it, they know it, too. The only time I ever felt different was right before Game 7 in the I-70 Series. We'd had something taken away from us the night before, and we all had a sense of doom and gloom. I had a team meeting before the game, and that didn't change a damn thing. Afterward, I told some writers we were going to get our asses beat bad. And we did—11–0. That was my last team meeting.

People use terms like "baseball genius," but some kinds of intelligence are overrated. Paul Richards, who managed me in Baltimore in 1961, was an intellectual type. He was very aloof, and he really wanted everybody to think he was an Einstein. But he and Dressen would manage against each other, and they were so damn brilliant, they'd run out of ballplayers by the fifth inning. If you're going to be smart in baseball, you've got to understand when to make moves and when *not* to manage.

Here's an example. The toughest game to manage isn't the one-run game in the ninth inning. That might be hard for the fans to watch, but anybody can manage it. The hard one is where you're down by four runs in the middle of the game, say in the fourth or fifth. What do you do? You're close enough that you might still win; you're far enough behind that you can't count on it. Do you bring in your good pitcher to stop the bleeding? Your hitters might get you back in the game. But if they don't, you've screwed that pitcher up for the next game when you might need him. On the other hand, do you bring in your horseshit guy, run up the white flag, and save the star for tomorrow? Then you might be giving up a game you could've won. Toughest call there is.

The way Dick Williams managed posed a hell of a question. It had to do with how you use your personality. Dick was my teammate on the '62 Orioles, and he became one of the great managers in history. First, he won with the Boston Red Sox in Fenway; then, after I'd rejected the Oakland A's job, he took it before the 1971 season and dealt with a meddlesome owner, Charlie Finley, not to mention a crabby, contentious bunch of ballplayers, and won two straight World Series. He did a hell of a job with the Angels, too. I got to coach third for him in Anaheim in 1974, and boy, was he sharp: He always gave me the signs two pitches ahead. He stayed out in front of the guy in the other dugout. He used an up-tempo style with a lot of movement, and it really kept your batteries juiced. I loved coaching for Dick.

Dick's personal style was different. He was as nice a person away from the ballpark as you'd ever want to meet, but as a manager, he believed that if his players saw him as a nice person or a friend, it would screw up the team. They wouldn't play as hard for him. So he went out of his way to be abrupt, critical and distant. He made a conscious effort for his players not to like him. And mostly, they didn't. That was Dick's style, and obviously it worked for him.

I couldn't have handled my players like Dick did. I'm more of a people person; I tend to like my players. As long as they knew who was boss, as long as they respected my knowledge of the game when I put the uniform on, I didn't see any reason not to bring my personality into the situation. It's one of my resources; why shouldn't I use it?

I'd take a kid out hunting or bass fishing a lot of the time; that might get him settled and comfortable. I'd clean Jack Clark's fish for him, and I'd fillet his catch, and he'd have a good time and let go of his troubles at the plate for a while. Same was true with Darrell Porter. The problems Darrell had with controlled substances came from insecurities in himself. They made him so hypercompetitive on the field he couldn't think straight sometimes. Well, Darrell was also one of the finest fishermen I'd ever met. Wonderful instincts, a great feel for the sport. We spent a lot of hours out on the lake together. There's nothing better than getting out in a boat with your buddies, telling stories, shooting the breeze. The bond I had with Darrell really helped him play the game, I think, and he's one of the best friends I made in baseball.

I have to laugh. Darrell's a born-again Christian, and one day about a year ago, he was speaking at a prayer breakfast in Missouri, talking about how much our relationship had helped him. He compared me to Jesus Christ, for goodness sake! He said I had the ability to see what each person had to offer as an individual, that I put each guy in situations where he did best for the good of the whole group—something about how Jesus did that with his disciples. To me, that was less blasphemous than it was funny.

Well, I wasn't no savior as a manager. I was happy when Darrell found a religious purpose; it helped him answer some hard questions and got him through a lot of rough times. It also made him less aggressive at the plate, and by the time he got to St. Louis, that really showed. I saw this happening and I didn't say much, but one day he struck out four times on 14 pitches and never took the bat off his shoulder. Guys are going to get the collar once in a while, but man, there are *limits*.

"Darrell," I said, "what the hell are you thinking? Are you prepared? What are you waitin' for?" He gave me kind of a dreamy smile, shrugged, and said, "Oh well, the Lord will take care of it." I said, "Darrell, maybe the Lord knows all, but He ain't gonna get you any base hits. Swing the bat!" If we hadn't been friends, he might have crucified *me* with his Louisville Slugger.

On the personal front, a good teacher also knows nobody likes to get criticized all the time. Hell, in baseball, you can harp on guys constantly and always be right. That doesn't mean you should do it. I don't like to get criticized all the time; you don't like to get criticized all the time. I don't care if he's Ozzie Smith or the last guy on the bench, a player wants to be told how good he is. Pat him on the back when you really mean it. He'll play harder for you and make better decisions later on. Don't blow smoke up a guy's ass; if he's in a horrible slump, and you know he's really struggling and he's got to get out of it himself, stay out of his way till he works it out. Managing is building up, not just tearing down. A positive word can be good for everyone.

On the other hand, like I say, every word you speak has to be honest. If there's one rule you should never violate, it's Always Tell The Truth. I do that everywhere in my life anyway; hell, it's tough to remember a lie but, when you tell the truth, you don't have to worry about it. You'd be surprised how many managers lie to their players. Maybe a guy asks when he's going to be starting; the manager'll say, "sometime soon," or "just keep working at it, we'll see," when he knows perfectly well that ain't the case. Managers are just like anybody else: They might just be avoiding arguments or confrontations. Or maybe they're worried if they tell a guy he's a benchwarmer, he'll go negative and start causing problems. But players ain't stupid; they'll see the writing on the wall, and if you haven't been honest, you're *really* going to have problems. Tell a role player he's a role player; get it on the table. I never once had a player resent me for telling him the truth.

One of the recent coaches of the St. Louis Blues, Mike Keenan, was a good example of how *not* to do that stuff.

Instead of sitting down with a player and talking to him one-on-one, he'd go through the press. I never minded commenting on a ballplayer in the newspapers if it was positive; let 'em read about the good stuff. But a guy deserves to hear criticism to his face. Keenan, after hockey games, would have writers in his office and give 'em some incendiary quote about Brett Hull or Brendan Shanahan. They'd go to the player and get a response, and boy, the shit would start flyin'. That sends a terrible message. It's not good motivation, and it's no way to build something positive. Not to mention that it puts control in the hands of the writers, who have a different agenda than you do. A good coach or manager looks his players in the eye and runs the show himself.

The way you talk to players—now *there's* something that's changed. And for the better, in my book. I'll never forget one day in 1956 when I was playing for Charlie Dressen. Somebody screwed up on the field, and he wanted to make his point. He brought all twenty-five of us in the clubhouse and tore into us. "Listen, you bunch of ignorant, no-good hillbillies," he started, and he went on from there. Well, nobody said a word! Players weren't used to having rights then.

Call 'em hillbillies today, and they'll string your ass up from the nearest Universal machine. I don't care if you're managing St. Louis U. High, the Portland Sea Dogs, or the New York Yankees, players will not let you talk to them like that. They're more educated; they've been to college, they're in a union. They know how they ought to be treated. Just ask P. J. Carlesimo, the Golden State coach in the NBA, who got Latrell Sprewell's finger marks for a necktie. It's a bad idea to let the inmates run the asylum, but you need to address each person with respect. A good manager should be doing that anyway.

Ralph Houk was the best I ever saw at handling people. I got to play for him in Denver, in the American Association, and Ralph was a great manager because he knew how to keep twenty-four, twenty-five different personalities happy. That's harder than it looks. He let us know what he wanted us all to do, but he dealt with each of us on our own terms, too. He was the kind of guy you'd dive into a few outfield walls for. I did it myself, and I didn't think twice about it. I played some of my best ball for Mr. Houk, and I never forgot his example.

Whether a player was a star or a scrub, I always made sure he felt important. I levelled with each player when I had to, and I made sure he hustled. But I also tried to spend some time, even a minute or two, with each player every day. I wanted to know what was going on with his family, how his wife was if he was married, who was sick, and who was getting better. My players appreciated that. I'm good with names, too, because I *do* like people, and that helped. It meant something to Danny Cox that I remembered his wife, Nancy, when I saw her and said hello, or to Ozzie that I knew and liked his wife, Denise, and thought they had wonderful kids. I'm sure Willie McGee was glad I'd met his parents—good, religious people from the Oakland area—and gotten to know them a little bit.

Maybe what I learned best from Ralph Houk was how important *every* guy is. You can't win in baseball without an outstanding bench. A lot of the time, I spent more time with my twenty-fourth guy than I did with my stars. They *needed* your attention; the star already got plenty. Maybe I appreciated them because they were the kind of players I used to be. My lesser guys won me a lot of ballgames, and some of them are still my best friends.

But you'd better pick your bench right. You want good guys who are willing to sit, pinch-hit, and play roles, and who don't think they should be playing every day. I'm talking about guys like Dane Iorg, Mike Ramsay, Tito Landrum, Tom Lawless, Tom Nieto. They know they've got a job, but they ain't going to play unless somebody gets hurt. That sonofagun who thinks

he should be out there when you know he can't—
brother, that's when you get screwed.

But you have to remember another thing: Never keep
your bench around too long. Turn those guys over. If
you don't, they start thinking they're too important.
They want more money. When you're working within a
budget, you've got to try to turn half of them over every
year. That was my theory. I always did it that way.

Hell, managing's no different than the small-town life
I grew up with. Or the way I live now. I still drive over
to Waterloo, Illinois, just a few miles from New Athens,
every two weeks to get my flat-top razored up nice and
sharp. Only Gene (Hoagie) Hohnbaum really knows
how to do it right, so I've been going to his shop for
years now. I'll sit there with Hoagie and Vic Main, his
assistant, and the other customers, and we'll chew the
fat about which guy in town just retired or which one
damn well ought to start thinking about it, about who's
tearing 'em up in the Little Leagues or what old folks
are in the nursing home. I'll hear about my old buddies,
or who's raised $400 for the American Legion team at
a bake sale. It's life, and people are what that's about.

Sometimes that unruly kid in the family is the one you
like best, and ballclubs are no different. I wasn't the only
one who got a charge out of Joaquin Andujar. The players loved him as much as I did.

Ozzie still tells the damnedest stories. Like the day in
Montreal I came out to the mound to talk to Goombah
about pitching to Al Oliver. Ozzie's on the mound as
usual, with his arms folded, looking annoyed. Joaquin
wants to stay in there, of course, even though Oliver's
a good left-hand hitter. So I just say, "Look, man, I'll
leave you in, but be careful." Joaquin looks at me like
I've insulted his manhood. He frowns and points at his
chest. "He one tough hitter," he says. "Me one tough
pitcher!"

Before I can even put my foot in the dugout, the ball's

going over the left centerfield fence. And Ozzie comes to the mound laughing, slaps Goombah on the back and says, "Hey, Jack! You one tough pitcher; he one better hitter!"

When I'm speaking at banquets to raise money and such, fans always ask me about Joaquin. They want to know what he was really like. One night I was hosting a dinner in Collinsville, Illinois, for my youth foundation, and at the Q-&-A afterward, a guy stepped to the microphone and said, "Whitey, why in the world did you bring Andujar in to pitch in Game Seven?" He was talking about the last game of the I-70 Series.

Maybe I *was* asking for trouble a little. We were trailing 7–0 in the fourth, and tempers were frayed. Denkinger, who had stuck it in us the night before, happened to be the home-plate umpire, and we all knew he was ready to blow. But I needed a pitcher, and it so happened Goombah was the only healthy guy I had left. So I called down to the pen. "Hey Joaquin, you want to pitch?"

"Okay, Whitey," he said. "I got good stuff." Hell, he *always* had his good stuff, according to him. So I brought his ass in.

Well, Andujar threw one pitch. Denkinger called it a ball. And Goombah gestured with his hand up around his eyes, as if to say, "Was it high?" Denkinger went apeshit. He jumped out from behind the plate, stormed out there, and started picking an argument: "Hey, don't you try to show me up," that kind of stuff. So I went out there to mediate.

"Wait a minute, Don," I said. "All he's asking you is, *was the pitch high?* Nod your head yes or no, and get back to work! What the hell's the matter with you?" And he said something back, and I said something back, and pretty soon I hollered, "Well, if you'd done your damn job last night, we wouldn't be here!" I was right, but he still ran my ass out of the game.

About five minutes later, I'm sitting in the clubhouse minding my own business, having a nice cold Michelob, when who should come huffing and puffing in the door but Goombah himself. Denkinger threw him out too! That was the only time I ever had a beer with one of my pitchers before the game was over. Tasted pretty good, too, if I recall.

After that Series, I knew Joaquin was gone. Peter Ueberroth, who was commissioner, suspended him for the first five games of the next season, and the brewery made me trade him before the next season. It as a shame, in a way. We lost our Joaquin-in-the-Box and about nine surprises a day. But his high-wire act had worn pretty thin after five years. The funniest thing was Joaquin's agents, the Hendricks boys. They called me and said, "Are you going to pay our client while he's under suspension?" I could hardly keep a straight face. They had the nerve to ask that! I think it was Alan that called. I said, "Alan, I ain't even gonna give you an answer, because his ass is gonna be gone. I'm just waiting for the call from the brewery!" And sure enough, they called me about a week later. I didn't have to worry about it; we sent him to Oakland and turned the page.

Well, when you've got to ride the tiger in life, stay on his back as long as you can. If you asked me to rate my managing, I might say, "Hell, I rode a sabertooth for five years, got a lot of miles out of him, and never ended up inside till the end. I must have done something right."

Before the time bomb blew sky high, Andujar won us two pennants, made more friends than he could ever count, and never stopped wanting the ball. What more can you ask than that?

· 10 ·
Rocking the Boat

When I was a player for the Baltimore Orioles in 1962, I had some interesting teammates. Darrell Johnson, Dick Williams, and I were utility guys who were lucky to get to bat once a week. The manager, Paul Richards, was an intense, very distant guy to begin with: When he had to tell a player something, he didn't do it himself; he sent a coach down to the end of the bench. So most of the time, he barely acknowledged us. But we loved being in the big leagues, and the three of us made good use of our time on the pines. We always had a good time.

For one thing, we were the most ruthless bench jockeys in baseball: We'd watch the other team's guys, make fun of the way they looked or swung the bat, holler nicknames at 'em—the more creative the better—and yell everything we could think of all game long. That was our contribution. It was a good time, and we never, ever let up.

One day, in spring training, we were playing the Tigers, and Bill McKinley, the umpire, was behind the plate. We didn't stop at the usual, "Hey, ump! You're missing a great game!" Dick and I decided it was time for a historical reference. In honor of our assassinated twenty-fifth president, we started bellowing "They shot the wrong McKinley! They shot the wrong McKinley!" He didn't like that, and I ain't sure it helped us to bait the ump, but we did it anyway. We'd do the same thing with pitchers. Here I was a .240 hitter, and I'd come up to the plate my one time a week and wonder why in the hell I always ended up on my ass. They kept throwing at my head! I'd get up, adjust my cap, dust off my pants, and dig back in there. He'd still be out there fuming: "Call *me* names, you sonofabitch!" Anything for the team.

The three of us watched managers' moves like hawks, too. We talked situations and strategy all the time. And I guess it paid off. One day in 1966, I was coaching for the Mets and Kenny Boyer, the star third baseman, came up to me and said, "How the hell do you know so much baseball at your age?" I was thirty-five. I said, "Ken, you've been out on the field for twenty years; I've been watching. I damn well better know *something*." I'm just glad I got the chance to apply it. Dick, Darrell, and I all became big-league managers in our day, and I guess we've done all right.

Another guy who paid attention was Charlie Lau, our buddy and teammate. Charlie wasn't much of a hitter—a utility guy at best—but by the end of the next decade, he'd turned into the most talked-about hitting coach of his era. When I took over as Royals manager in 1975, I brought Charlie back from our minor-league system and made him our batting coach, and he did great with some players. George Brett, one of his many disciples, became a feared hitter under him. If only Charlie had soaked up as much about team spirit as he did the batting swing back in 1962, I'd have avoided one of the biggest controversies of my career.

Charlie's theories got you thinking. His main idea was that the front hand—the one on the bottom of your grip—drove the swing. You pulled the bat through the zone with that hand, almost creating a one-handed cut. The top hand was so insignificant you could let it come off the bat at a certain point. It seemed to work for Brett, and Hal McRae, my designated hitter, was a ferocious Lau supporter, though he was a good hitter before he ever came across Charlie. My feeling is it's hard to teach the same style to every batter. The Lau method promoted singles and doubles, but I saw some big, big men—the Al Cowens, the John Mayberrys—hit a lot more grubworms than I'd have liked. But I wasn't like Ted Williams: When Walt Hriniak, a Lau disciple, took over as hitting coach of the Red Sox one year, Ted stopped going to spring training. He couldn't stand to watch it! Overall, I saw Charlie as a plus.

My agenda was to win as many ballgames as possible. But what rubbed me raw was when I saw that Charlie had a different one. That was when I had to draw a line.

When he was batting, Brett had a habit of stepping out of the box and looking back into the dugout. He'd do it two, three times an at-bat, so often it would slow down the game sometimes. What he was doing was looking at Charlie, who was giving a signal to tell George whether they were going to pitch him inside or outside.

I've already told you baseball ain't astrophysics, but there's a few basics to look for. If George Brett, a left-handed hitter, gets an inside pitch, he's most likely going to pull it—take it to right. That means the shortstop is better off shading toward the second-base bag. If they pitch George outside, he's more likely to hit it away—to left—so the shortstop's better off edging to his right, toward third. Simple positioning. Now, the infielders face the catcher, so they can see his signs; they *know* where the pitch is supposed to go. Any batter can watch them and get an idea what's coming. It's common sense.

I watched this go on for months till finally one day I turned to Charlie and said, "Why the hell don't you just tell him to look at the shortstop? If he's playing close to second, they're gonna pitch him in; if he's playing straight up, they're gonna pitch him away. So he don't have to look in here all the time." That's all Charlie was doing: checking out where the shortstop was playing, and giving George that signal.

Charlie didn't want to explain that to Brett. I can't tell you *why* he didn't, but it sure looked to me like Charlie'd rather George believe he was a genius than have him learn something that would help the team. So George would come back to the dugout and say, "You were right; he pitched me in!" Well, *no shit*. George is a bright guy, and if you taught him anything useful he never forgot it. Charlie wasn't giving him the chance.

It was a hint of something that maybe went deeper. Charlie buddied up to the players, socialized and drank with them, and eventually he became like one of those teachers in school who mainly wants the students to like him. It got to where I'd post worksheets for my coaches and show up later to supervise, and Charlie would be off doing whatever the hell he felt like. He wouldn't be there! Well I don't give a damn if you're Mohandas Gandhi: If I'm your boss and I tell you to do something, you're going to do it. If you don't, you're going to face the consequences. It's the only way to run a team.

I don't mean to harp on Charlie; he worked hard overall, taught some players something, and basically was a good person. But the point is, the guy running the show had better have some bedrock beliefs, and he'd better enforce them. One of mine is simple: Winning comes first. Another is, the boss is the boss. When everybody ain't on the same page about those, you've got chaos. Charlie obviously wasn't working for me. If he wasn't working for me, he wasn't working for the Kansas City Royals. I told him to pack his bags.

Some people say my career was controversial. Bill James even wrote that controversy *defined* my career. I'd agree, up to a point. If people weren't helping the team—for *any* reason, from slumps to drugs to age to insubordination—I got rid of 'em. To me, that's simple. Hell, it ain't *my* job to figure out how people will react. If common sense shocks 'em, I say bring on the voltage.

Some people said I was jealous of Charlie, that I was afraid of his influence in the lockerroom and so on. What a load of bullshit. His firing did divide the team and cause a lot of friction, I'll admit that. But I couldn't help it. There can only be one boss; if you don't have that, you've got nothing. It was a no-brainer. I'd fire him again tomorrow.

In most ways, Kansas City was a great place to manage. After my Texas Rangers finished thirty-seven games back in my one year as manager—I did the best I could with a horrible pitching staff—I was lucky that Joe Burke, the Kansas City GM (and my ex-GM at Texas), came calling with another offer in 1975. It's one of my favorite towns in the world, and I already lived there. The Royals were only six years old, but they'd been a model for how to build a new franchise. They had developed outstanding young talent, including John Mayberry and Brett, who accounted for two runs a game between them. By the time I got there, that team was ready to blossom.

But as it turned out, things weren't all Show-Me state charm. That team was a place where doing things right got your ass in trouble.

One of my first moves was to bench a fan favorite, Cookie Rojas, the veteran second baseman. Kansas City fans had no idea how much range Cookie had lost in the field; fans don't know about stuff like that. But he was a major liability on defense. So here came a controversy. Jack McKeon, the outgoing manager, had kept a kid second baseman named Frank White on the bench. I had never seen a second baseman who could go in all four directions—forward, back, left, and right—like Frank. He had good hands, the vertical leap of a point guard, everything you want in an infielder. I gave him the job.

Well, all he did was immediately become half of the best keystone combination (with Freddie Patek) in the league. We won my first eight ballgames and never let up. We won 92 ballgames that year and cut seven games off mighty Oakland's lead in the AL West. Royals fans were seeing a second baseman who would go in the ballclub's Hall of Fame one day. And every time Frank White stepped on the field for a year and a half, they booed his ass off.

Hell, I didn't care. Like I've said, the fans don't always know baseball, and I don't manage by referendum. I want to *win*, and I'm going to do it whether they like it or not. The problem was, in that organization, the Cookie Rojas syndrome went up and down the ladder. We were winners, but when it came time to fish or cut bait, winning ballgames was not the top priority around there.

Here's an example. When I first came to town, there was rejoicing up and down the Paseo if the Royals drew a million fans a year. They never dreamed of drawing 2 million fans in a season, but I couldn't figure that out. I looked around and thought, "Hey, we're the westernmost ballclub this side of California. That's a lot of real estate." We had unrealized drawing power in six or seven states, from Nebraska to North Dakota and Colorado and back. I knew if we won and did it right, it would be a jackpot—and I knew we were going to win. So I worked myself a deal. I went to Burke and said, "If we draw 2 million fans, will you give me a $50,000 bonus?" He looked at me like I was out of my mind, shrugged, and said, "Sure." He wrote it in my contract and forgot all about it. I always had to fight Kauffman for a $10,000 raise anyway, even when we won the division, so I figured this was a good way to get compensated fairly. And if we did draw that many, fifty grand would be pocket change, and they ought to be happy to pay it. It's what I call enlightened self-interest.

Well, we did win. And I was right. Fans from the Ozark hills to the plains of Nebraska fell in love with the Royals. They drove in from Boulder and Laramie, from Kearney and Wichita and Broken Arrow, and we had ourselves a regional ballclub. And in 1977, when we staged the greatest September pennant drive in the history of baseball—we went 24–1 during one stretch that month—that was all it took to drive the attendance mark over 2.1 million. We won the division, had a hell of a team, and were so far in the black we needed flares to see.

The weird thing was how Mr. Kauffman reacted. Here we'd stomped the hell out of his team's attendance record, the Royals were the hottest ticket in town, and all he could think of to do was get steamed at the manager. He called me into the office one day, sat me down, looked me in the eye, and said the strangest thing: "You didn't draw all those people." He'd found out about my attendance clause.

Boy, was he ticked off. He cut me the check because he had no choice, but he'd have sooner handed the pennant to the Minnesota Twins. And from that point on, I knew that in that organization, ego trumped success on the field.

Getting credit seemed to be the big thing around there. Kauffman's wife, Muriel, was very conscious of bull like that. She never did understand why I was more popular in town than her husband. Here he was, a local businessman who'd bought the team and brought it to town, and now that the ballclub was winning—1976, my first full year, was their first championship—here came this wiseass manager with a brush-cut chatting up the press, cracking jokes, and soaking up the acclaim. You still hear stories about how she'd be driving around town, look up and see Whitey's grinning mug on billboards twenty-feet high, and start cussing a blue streak in her car. George Brett was the most beloved guy in town, and that was fine, but she thought Ewing ought to be second.

That kind of stuff drives me nuts. Any attention I got was attention for the ballclub. But she hated my guts for it, and it affected their judgment about the team.

How else can you explain the way the front office reacted the day I went to them with the toughest problem I had my whole time there? I'd found out, through sources I trusted, that four or five of our players were screwed up on drugs. Now, that isn't just a baseball problem; it's a legal one, too. Lots of people can get in trouble. So I set up a meeting with Burke and Kauffman and told them what I knew.

The most amazing thing happened: They started *arguing* with me. "You can't go around saying things like that," they said. "*Our* players aren't on drugs." I about fell over. "The hell they ain't," I said. "I can *tell* you who's on drugs." They didn't want to hear a word about their little darlings. They didn't listen to a word I said, and in the end, they kicked my ass right out of the office.

Well, all I can say is—too bad for them. What I told them was really just the tip of the iceberg. We all know today that this problem permeated baseball in the late seventies and early eighties, just like it did the rest of society. It turned into an embarrassment to the game and a fact of life for managers for a good ten years. You had to be realistic and deal with it. But honesty with that bunch was like a stick in a hornet's nest. That's a sure sign of an organization wandering down the wrong basepath. Worse than that, the problem never got faced. It nearly wrecked the team.

One outstanding player, and a person I liked, ended up with problems that cost us a key playoff game and, in my opinion, a chance at the World Series. I don't think he would argue the point. I asked management to get rid of him before the next season. They said they would, but they dragged their feet nearly into the next season. Their waffling divided the ballclub, and things got worse. By the time they finally did ship him out, the whole organization was tense. But I still had high hopes. I had brought a young kid, Clint Hurdle, up from our Triple-A affiliate the previous September. He'd already won Minor League Player of the Year in Omaha that year, and he was a tremendous natural hitter. Good size—he was 6-3, 195—and a *beautiful* swing. When he was with us, Clint Hurdle tore the cover off the ball.

He was ready for a major-league job. We sent him to play winter ball in Venezuela to stay sharp, and at the age of twenty he hit 18 homers, a winter-league record. The following spring, 1978, he made the cover of *Sports Illustrated* as a coming star. Everybody in baseball was talking him up. I wrote him in as my starting first baseman.

But a bad wind was blowing. Clint Hurdle, for some mysterious reason, suddenly couldn't catch a pop fly. I saw this happening and alarm bells went off. I went straight to Joe Burke, told him to send Hurdle back to Omaha, and said that when the kid straightened himself out, we'd bring him back.

You see what's coming. Clint was a homegrown talent, a tomato-cheeked kid the Royals wanted to be a star, and Burke didn't want to hear it. *"How can you say that?"* he said at the top of his voice. *"How can you say that?"* He ran me out of there like bad news. And from that day on, I knew that as soon as I didn't win the division, I was going to get fired.

I obliged 'em. After one more division title in '78, we finished second, a whole three games back in '79. It was the first time I hadn't won the division for them. They called me after the season and canned my ass. More controversy.

I have nothing against Clint. He's a good person, from a fine family, and his stock really showed as the years went by. After he'd hung on with the Mets and Reds for a few years, I acquired him for the Cardinals in 1986. He became a valuable veteran off the bench for me, even did some catching. Now he's the hitting coach of the Colorado Rockies. That's a hell of a job: They're *always* going to hit in that place. He earned it. But *damn*—he's like Garry Templeton. Clint Hurdle had Hall of Fame talent.

Before he died, Joe Burke told me I'd been right. He even thanked me. It seemed so obvious after the fact. And today, twenty years later, even though I'm still the

Having a ball (or two) as a Senator on Opening Day 1957. Both balls were autographed by President Dwight D. Eisenhower, who was mighty kind to drop by, pay us a visit, and see us lose.

Here I am in 1962 making the most important play in baseball: busting up a double play. I was a Baltimore Oriole at the time; that's Pete Runnels of the Red Sox hurrying his throw. Mission accomplished.

I liked to play hard-nosed, and that kept me in the major leagues. But after a collision with a foul ball in 1961, my nose had to be hammered back into place.

I was the damnedest third-base coach for the Mets in 1966. I used a little Stengel knowhow, some White Rat daring, and a lot of body language to bring runners like Ron Hunt in safely.

Here I am as manager of the Texas Rangers in 1973. We finished 37 games behind, but we were turning things around when our owner, Bob Short, canned me in September.

Three of the better ballplayers I've had the privilege of knowing: Roger Maris—my best buddy and the greatest player not in the Hall of Fame—with my son David in September 1961, as Roger closed in on Babe Ruth's home-run record.

Ozzie Smith, the Wizard of Oz, one of the greatest shortstops of all time, here performing his trademark somersault maneuver; and Jack Clark, who jump-started my Cardinals offense for three years until the organization screwed up and fumbled him away in 1987.

Fishing is no different from baseball. Bring the right equipment to the right pond, and you're going to reel in a winner.

Times were usually good in Kansas City. I got to manage George Brett, take the Royals to three division titles, and help set five straight attendance records. That's a lot to smile about.

Pete Rose and I at the Kansas City Baseball Writers' Dinner in 1978: Pete's a tough sonofagun who's had to learn some things the hard way. But you'll see him reinstated to the game someday.

In St. Louis, Gussie Busch made me both manager and general manager. It was a job full of accountability. If we didn't win, he'd know who to fire. And I never got fired.

Me and the Cowboy in 1993. The main reason I took the job as Angels' executive VP was my friendship with Gene Autry, one of the finest gentlemen I've known. His death in 1998 was a big loss to us and to the game.

The old Eagle sure knew how to dress for a World Series. Here I am sampling a bit of the company product with Gussie Busch right after we closed out Milwaukee in the 1982 World Series.

I don't remember what I said to Joe West, but he sure got hot under the collar. He'd obviously had enough of the Rat for one night.

Baseball and family. Sometimes it's hard to tell 'em apart. These are two of my grandkids, John and Kirsten Urick, with me at Busch Stadium in 1985.

The White Rat with some big cheese at the All-Star Game in Cincinnati in 1988 (left to right): Vice President George Bush, National League President Bart Giamatti, and Commissioner Peter Ueberroth.

Talkin' baseball with my buddy (and fellow St. Louisan) Bob Costas is always a rip. He's got damn near as many good ideas on the game as I do, which is why I've always said he'd make an outstanding commissioner.

My mentor is gone, but he sure ain't forgotten. This was taken shortly after Casey Stengel's death in 1975, and I still think about the Perfesser all the time.

The Rat in 1996, at age sixty-five.

winningest manager in team history; even though I was the first skipper to get them in the playoffs; even though we broke the attendance record every year I was there; I still ain't in the Royals' Hall of Fame. I guess controversy's in the eye of the beholder.

As a kind of joke, we damn near called this book "The White Stuff." The editors thought it was funny—a play on "The Right Stuff," that book about astronauts, on my nickname, and on the word "stuff," as in pitching. It sounded too much like cocaine to me. But then again, that powder just kept rearing its head in my career. Dealing with it, in the 1980s, was part of any manager's job description. Anybody tells you they saw *that* coming in the game can't be trusted any more than the guys who used the stuff.

At the Pittsburgh drug trials in 1985, Keith Hernandez took the stand as a witness, looked back over his previous few years, and called cocaine "the devil on this earth." He wasn't far wrong. That stuff cast a spell on otherwise normal young people that makes your hair stand on end. *Sports Illustrated* ran a story a couple of years back on the 1980s Mets, and it explained a lot. Hell, I know my ballclubs were good back then, but nobody could touch the Mets in terms of talent. They were the class of baseball. Even I wondered how in the hell we beat their ass as often as we did. Who knows how many games Davey Johnson lost to drug use? How many did I?

Not every guy who got screwed up on drugs was a decent person, but many were. We all knew Darryl Strawberry had off-the-field problems, and I'm glad Darryl seems to have straightened a lot of that stuff out. He's in recovery from colon cancer right now, and I wish him the best. But who would've thought a thoughtful person like Dwight Gooden would get involved up to his nostrils? Davey Johnson and the Mets went out of their way to protect him from the dangers of New

York, but there's only so much you can do for people. To me, the real eye-opener was how Doc kept going back to the stuff, even after his problem got publicized and damn near ended his career. In the mid-eighties, when we had to face Gooden, all I hoped was for my players to make contact a few times. That's how good he was. The fact that he was a journeyman junkballer by age thirty tells you a lot. Hernandez had it right.

It's normally a pleasure to keep the fans up-to-date on your team's happenings, but sometimes there are issues you just can't tell them about. That can cause what they call controversy. Maybe a favorite player gets traded and the fans don't know why. That kind of thing happened all the time in this era. After I sent Hernandez, an ex-MVP and the greatest defensive first baseman ever, to the Mets for two pitchers we never ended up using much, it didn't surprise me a bit when St. Louisans raised hell for years. And Cha-Cha never let me off the hook. He came right into our kitchen and rattled our pans for about four years, burned the Cardinals with a lot of big hits. But he was always surrounded by great, high-priced players in New York, and hell, we all knew Keith had a good bat and was a heck of a player. That didn't shock anybody.

St. Louis fans and media still talk about that "controversial" trade. But it was the Rojas syndrome again: If the fans kept their heads, they'd realize I never made a move without a reason. I might not always be *right*, but I stick to the strategy: You've got to have a plan. There was no question of keeping Keith Hernandez. Meanwhile, his attitude as a player kept deteriorating—right up to one game in Atlanta in 1983 when he took it too far.

We were down by a run. We had the tying run on first, one out in the ninth inning, and Keith came to the plate. The one thing you want to avoid is the double-play to end the ballgame. Well, Keith hit a grounder, a possible DP ball. It should have been close, but he jogged halfway to first, got thrown out to end the game, and laughed his ass off all the way to the bench. And by then, his troubles were so well known around baseball that nobody but the Mets—a last-place team going nowhere—had any interest in him. I got what I could for Keith, and that's that. I never lost sleep over that trade, and I'd make it again tomorrow.

This was all an area of behavior baseball people never dreamed they'd be dealing with. It took a while to pick up on the warning signs. But eventually, you had to realize that in the 1980s, spotting drug users was part of your managing repertoire. And I got good at it, boy. Guys who abuse drugs have to sneak around, so they get accustomed to lying; they're fidgety and won't look you in the eye, even if you're discussing something totally harmless. I had some help, too: I had a friend on my team, Darrell Porter, who'd been through his own drug crisis, conquered it, and knew how serious the situation was. He helped me decode the behavior of problem guys. I'd take him out fishing and say, "Darrell, I think so-and-so might be on drugs"—I wouldn't make him put a name out there—and I could tell from his reaction if I was on the money or not. I got so damn good at it I was right almost 100 percent of the time. Even now, if one of my grandson's friends happens to be a little shady in this area, I can see right through it and say something. I could work Narcotics downtown.

Any good manager or coach adapts to changes in his culture. It's the only way the Casey Stengels, the Scotty Bowmans, or the Don Shulas can succeed as long as they do. And if you had any brains, you worked up a plan to deal with this issue. Mine was simple: If I knew a guy had a problem, I gave him a chance to come forward and let the ballclub help him. That's a guy you can work with, because he's honest with himself and still willing to be honest with you. Lonnie Smith did that in '83 when we gave him the opportunity, and I still respect the hell out of him for it. Lonnie went on the voluntary disabled list and took time off to face whatever was bothering him. But other guys, if you give 'em the same chance, stay in the shadows. That's when you call off the hunt. It's less a chemical problem than it is a trust problem; trust is the glue of any organization, top to bottom, and if a guy won't look you or himself in the eye, he's trouble. Get him off the reservation.

Some guys were in the middle. David Green, the outfielder we got from Milwaukee as part of the Simmons deal in '81, might have been the most talented player of his generation. He had every bit as much ability as Templeton, Strawberry, or Hurdle, but David's troubles with alcohol were a nightmare. We worked with him on it, put him into rehab, got him counseling. He gave it a hell of a try. He swore he was clean.

But good intentions and a quarter will get you a phone call. One day after practice I'm driving home from the ballpark, minding my own business, and I end up a couple of car lengths behind him on the highway. He doesn't see me. I'm watching him like I'd watch anybody in front of me, keeping a safe distance. Pretty soon, here come the beer cans flying out of the car. One right after the other, every five minutes, there goes another can. We drove past the hospital where he did rehab—more cans! Good guy, David, but when they get hooked on this stuff, they turn into con artists. They're conning themselves, and they expect you to swallow their bull too. A lot of managers did.

Most of it's flat out of your hands. Another great young player I got to manage was Leon Durham. The only reason he ever left our organization was that the Cubs demanded him in the Sutter deal in 1981. With his lefthanded swing and power to left-center, I traded him to Wrigley thinking he'd hit 35 to 40 homers a year there. He was a wonderful person, too, so I expected him to be a hell of a citizen for them. Two years later, their clubhouse man pulled me aside. "Your boy is having some problems," he said. I thought he was talking about somebody else. If there was one person I never thought I'd see in trouble with this stuff, it was Leon Durham. Bright fellow, a class individual all the way. Turned out the man was right.

Over the next few years, as Leon declined into a utility-type player, he cleaned up his act. I was impressed with that, so I brought him back to the Cardinals in 1989. He showed a lot of class—started at Triple-A Louisville, worked his way back to the majors, and played great for me as a veteran bench guy. I was ready to give him a contract for the next year. But on one road trip to Chicago, they spot-tested him—they normally check you in the town where you first had trouble; that's where your connections are—and I'll be damned if he didn't come up positive. I could not renew his contract. I'm still disappointed by that.

It took a toll on ballclubs, too. The Mets were the class of the league, talentwise, in the middle eighties, but go back five years and you'll remember a team even better than that. The Montreal Expos of the late 1970s and early 1980s was one of the damnedest lineups I ever saw. They had everything. Gary Carter, one of the best catchers of all time, was behind the plate. Ron LeFlore, Warren Cromartie, Ellis Valentine, and big Andre Dawson gave you speed, depth, and power in the outfield. Tim Raines came up as a second baseman and soon moved to the outfield—a great hitter with deadly speed. Steve Rogers, Bill Gullickson, Scott Sanderson and Jeff Reardon pitched for 'em. Between 1977 and 1982, nobody could touch them for talent. Yet they never won a single pennant.

You always have unknown variables—injuries, weather, bad luck. The Expos had to wait too long for a semicovered stadium, and that cost 'em; they have such awful weather up there that they always had a lot of rainouts in April and May. That creates a lot of doubleheaders in August and September, which taxes a pitching staff. The constant traveling through customs is also very exhausting. But when the drug trials happened in 1985, and Montreal was prominently mentioned, I wasn't surprised. Montreal is the drug capital of the Northern Hemisphere, the easiest baseball town to score in—and I ain't talking runs. Guys who had problems were liable to go into a slump in the Great White North. They'd be there in body, but not in spirit.

We all know more about the subject of drugs today. What happened in the eighties forced baseball people to face reality, and ballplayers learned. They're so much more health-conscious today that very few of them even drink. Random drug testing is legal in the minors now, too, so problem guys tend to get dealt with and cured long before they're ready for the big leagues. Cocaine isn't much of a problem anymore, if at all. But it would be good for the game if the players' union agreed to the kind of random testing we have in force in the minors. What would it hurt? If you're clean, who gives a damn? It would erase all doubts, maybe help a few guys, and sweep out the last dregs of a problem that really hurt the game.

Some baseball problems never change. Personnel choices—trades, drafts, and so on—are always going to yank some people off. After all, my ideas on building the team aren't the same as yours. But I can always tell right off if a guy's going to help me or not. If he can't, I move him. Why screw around?

When I took over baseball operations for the Angels in 1992, mostly as a favor to my old friend Gene Autry, their owner, I made some moves that reminded me of trading Ted Simmons. The fans were wailing, but in the long run, it brought the Angels closer to the title the Autrys wanted. That was my job. I wasn't running for mayor.

First I had to decide what to do with Jim Abbott, our left-handed pitcher who'd just won 18 games. Jim was a great kid, an all-American type. The fans loved his story: He'd been born without a right hand, and he'd licked the challenge. He married an Anaheim girl. He was the kind of kid the Cowboy and his wife, Jackie, wanted to lock up for the long term, and he had a million good reasons to stay with us. But he had two years before free agency, and I always say the longer you wait to build a building or make a deal, the more it's going to cost you. It was time to make something happen—sign him up or cut him loose.

I put a whopping offer on the table: $16 million for four years. It was superstar money—Roger Clemens pay—and Roger'd been around a lot longer than Abbott. If I'd been Jim, I'd have snapped it up. But he and his agent—the ex-Cardinal farmhand, Scott Boras, and one of the toughest negotiators around—turned it down.

Every move is made in some framework. My California mission was to cut payroll from $35 million to $20 million, bring kids through the system, and get the Cowboy's ass in a World Series before he rode Champion into the sunset. The GM has to keep an eye on the future—who's in his walk year? who are my keepers and non-keepers? how long can we pay this or that guy top dollar?—as well as winning today. So when they rejected that deal, I knew I couldn't risk losing him as a free agent. I'd get nothing back. I told Jim, "Son, you realize if you don't take this offer, I'm going to have to trade you." Abbott winced, but he consulted his wife and they stayed the course.

I shipped him to the Yankees for J. T. Snow, the young first baseman, that December. And when word of the deal came out, there was more wailing in Anaheim than the day Bambi's mother died. But I'd do it again.

Fans love certain players, and that's good, but they also don't understand baseball economics. Free-agent deals, agents' demands, payroll limitations—these things force your hand, and you'd better look ahead. I felt bad for Jim. In bouncing from the Yankees to the White Sox and back to the Angels over the next three years, he lost his stuff, and he never made half the money we'd offered him to stay with us. Did his agent help him here?

Andy Benes ended up in the same kind of mess five years later. Benes, a righthanded Cardinals pitcher, loved St. Louis, wanted to raise his five kids there, and got to pitch on the same staff as his brother Alan, a hell of a young righthander. The Cardinals wanted him back: They offered him $32 million on a five-year deal. But Boras, from all reports, had to squeeze out another half million. While he was nickel-and-diming the Cards, the clock ran out on negotiations—literally. Baseball rules said that if he didn't sign with his own team by midnight on December 7, 1997, he couldn't join them until May. Boras came to an agreement forty-five minutes too late. Benes ended up an Arizona Diamondback, going 14–13 for an expansion team, and the deal he got was for $18 million for three years. That ain't pocket change, but neither is the guaranteed millions that went down the toilet. It's beyond me why these clients don't speak up.

I also got massacred in the Los Angeles press after the '92 expansion draft. We left our top relief pitcher, Bryan Harvey, unprotected, and the Florida Marlins grabbed him with their first pick. I couldn't blame 'em: Harvey could throw a split-finger 92, 93 miles an hour, and for a time, boy, he was the equal of a Sutter, a Fingers, of any of the greats I ever saw. And he went right out in their first year and racked up 45 saves. Every save he got, our fans hollered louder. But they didn't know I'd talked to Harvey's doctor, who told me he wasn't going to be able to throw the split-finger much longer because of ligament damage in his arm. He still had $11 million coming on his contract, and without that pitch, Bryan wasn't going to be no multimillion-dollar guy. He lost his stuff inside a year, dropped to 6 saves, and the kid we protected, Troy Percival—we had converted him from a catcher into a closer—is striking out a batter and a half per inning right now and averaging

30 saves a year. Sometimes your acts of treason are really just staying ahead of the curve.

Even my time with the Cardinals, my best-known era, ended up in so-called controversy. I quit in the middle of my last season, 1990. That surprised some people. People still argue why I did it. You hear the craziest rumors: There were schisms in the team, I was fired, there was dissension and backstabbing, it was a plot among the Freemasons. If you knew the real situation, you'd see it like my other so-called controversies: It was nothing in the world but plain common sense.

After Gussie died in 1989, the brewery's interest in baseball had gone down the drain. I don't think Little August, who's running the company today—and doing a damn fine job, I have to say—could ever stand the game. They say he was the one who bounced his dad off the brewery's board of directors, so you know they didn't get along too good; maybe baseball just reminded him of the old guy. I don't know. The change in leadership was like a bad-hop grounder—sudden, rough, and right in your face. Their new way of running things made it impossible to win.

We had ten of our twenty-five guys coming up for free agency. All our most valuable players were on the list: Coleman, McGee, Ozzie, Terry Pendleton, even Pedro Guerrero, the player I got in the Tudor trade with L.A. and the only reliable RBI man I'd had since Jack Clark left. The Cards had been pretty harmonious for a few years, but yesterday doesn't mean a thing in baseball: The cold winds of the modern game were blowing.

Well, that's fine; you deal with it. You get assets for assets. We could've traded 'em for prospects and stayed competitive. The Mets needed a centerfielder and the Pirates needed a third baseman, so we could've dealt McGee and Pendleton and gotten something good in return. And hell, look at Terry: A year later, he led the Braves to the World Series and got named MVP of the league. But the Cardinals were mad at Terry that year;

he had gone into arbitration against them in the off-season and won, and the brewery people *hated* Pendleton for it. After I left the team that year, they wouldn't play him anymore, which wasn't fair, since it was his walk year, and by not playing him the last two or three months they hurt his numbers. It was a horseshit thing to do; Terry Pendleton was a winner, and he deserved better from the Cardinals than he got.

Anheuser-Busch had decided they weren't going to sign *any* of those guys except Ozzie—they'd have axed him, too, if they hadn't known the fans would mutiny—and instead of dealing them, they decided to let 'em all walk as free agents. They wanted the draft picks, which cost a lot less. Even that would have been okay; the Cards had some good prospects coming up, like Ray Lankford and Bernard Gilkey. The thing was, they could have helped me out and didn't. Fred Kuhlmann decided not even to *negotiate* with our free-agent players. He wouldn't even talk to their agents. I said, "Man, at least talk to them; let 'em *think* they might be coming back! That way they have something to play for." But they wouldn't do it. There was never any contract talk the whole year—nothing. Maybe the brewery just wanted to get rid of my ass; I can't tell you that. I know they left it flapping in the wind. Forty percent of my team knew they would not be in Cardinal red the next season.

Why is that important? For our type of ballclub, it was death. We were a team without power; if we were going to win, we had to hit to the right side, play team ball, and sacrifice personal stats—in other words, play Cardinal-style. But if you were up for free agency, and if you knew the club didn't want you, would you shoot the ball to right? Or would you try for your own numbers, for average and homers, and grab the best deal you could for the next year? I know what *I'd* do. In other words, what these guys had to do as individuals would wreck our team. Economics clipped the Cardinals' wings.

It didn't surprise me that nobody gave a damn that year. We played horseshit and got worse. One day on a road trip, I finally called Mary Lou and said, "It don't matter who manages this team. I ain't gonna make myself sick over it anymore." Hell, I *hope* I can use my time better than that. And I did, too: That summer, I became the world's highest-paid fisherman. While the Cards went in the tank, I had a hell of a year.

Ever since Charlie Finley gave me my first coaching job, I've been known as a brash, opinionated guy. People in baseball don't like that. My own bosses would ask me about a ballplayer, then look like they'd seen a ghost when I told them what I thought. I'd say, "Hell, I don't care if you *agree* with me; you asked me a question, and I'm giving you my answer. I ain't going to argue about it!" You only get so much time and so much oxygen in life; I won't waste either one. If people in baseball don't like to hear the truth, that's their problem.

Does that make me controversial? You tell me. Maybe I'm really just the same sonofagun who used to jockey the bench with Dick and Darrell. Baseball's a game, and it's fun, but winning makes it that way. As long as I'm in there, I'm going to do everything I can to end up on top.

The way I do it might leave you laughing. It might leave you throwing a fastball at my head. It doesn't matter to me. Either way, I'll get up, dust off my pants, and dig back in for more. I might find a way to get on base and win us the ballgame.

· 11 ·

The Overlords

Gene Mauch, manager of the Twins, made a statement in the newspaper on August 30, 1977, that I'll never forget. Four teams were bunched at the top of the American League West, including his boys and my Kansas City Royals, who were half a game in front. "Nobody in our division has the horses to pull away from the pack," he said. "It's going down to the wire." He meant it as a positive—you know, *we're in for a hell of a fight, folks*—but what I remember thinking was, "God almighty, what pennant race is he watching?"

We had the stud hosses, all right. The 1977 Royals were by far the best baseball team I ever managed, not to mention the best in the game. We had power with Brett, John Mayberry and Amos Otis. We had speed with Otis and Frank White. We had good defense at every position, strong starters in Leonard, Splittorff, Gura, and Jim Colborn, and a solid bullpen. That team had no weaknesses. And the minute Gene made his comment—*abracadabra*—we started kicking his theory in the ass.

I'll bet fewer than five percent of the people in my game realize it, but that September, we put on the greatest stretch drive in the history of baseball. We started with sixteen straight wins. We lost one when Doc Medich of the A's shut us out, 1–0, the night after a doubleheader—which we played during a lightning storm and flash flood—that kept us all up till three o'clock in the morning. After that, we ran off eight more wins in a row. By the time it was over, we were 24–1 in one stretch in September, had 102 total victories, and took the division by eight games—eighteen ahead of Mr. Mauch's Twins. I didn't read no Gene Mauch quotes after that.

Problem was, the best team in baseball wasn't the one that could win a title. For the second year in a row, George Steinbrenner's Yankees beat us in the fifth game of a five-game playoff and went to the Series. They beat us again the year after that. This was when I figured out the ABC's of building a modern team. Steinbrenner had bought a good map to the new territory, and it showed you the way. Ewing Kauffman hadn't even gone to the store.

In four and a half years in Kansas City, I heard one refrain from the front office: "We're going to do it the right way; we're building through the farm system." Now, on the face of it, that ain't a bad philosophy: Even today, your ballclub has to keep the minor-league system stocked. You have to have good young players and bring 'em along. That's your foundation. That was even truer before 1975, when the Andy Messersmith decision started free agency. Before that time, you had no stars selling themselves to the highest bidder, so if you wanted a superstar, you had to scout him, sign him, and develop him in the minors yourself.

Free agency changed that. Some owners caught on right away; some didn't. To small-market owners, it seemed like the ruination of baseball. They thought the deep-pocket guys like Steinbrenner could just go out, open their wallets, and buy championships now. Kauffman was a small-town guy to the core, and he saw all this as one big plague he didn't plan on catching. In my time with the Royals, if I heard it once, I heard it a million times: "Nobody's ever going to make more money than Brett; no pitcher's getting more than Leonard."

They were true to their word. In all that time, we signed one free agent—Jerry Terrell, a utility infielder, and that was to a $40,000 deal. In the meantime, Steinbrenner was handing millions to the Reggie Jacksons and Catfish Hunters of the world. The Royals became one of the best regular-season ballclubs of the seventies—just good enough to be postseason patsies for the Yankees.

Remember Jack Clark and his boat? You figure out what you need by scoping the territory. Free agency changed the baseball landscape, and to win championships, man, you had to adapt. Good ownership did. And you can pinpoint *my* ideas about building modern baseball teams by looking at what happened those three years we lost to New York.

You get to the playoffs by winning a marathon, the 162-game season, with all its ups and downs. That's the heartbeat of baseball: skills measured over the long haul. But in the modern game, once you get into the postseason, they change the rules on you. You spend six months running your marathon and get in the winner's circle. Then they line you up with the other winners and say, "Okay, boys, for the championship, now we're running a fifty-yard dash." It's apples for the regular season, oranges for the playoffs. That's why you can never tell who's really the best anymore. You don't know what the hell they're measuring!

The reason that's happened, by the way, is that the owners don't love the game as much as they love money. When they started seeing the other sports—like the NBA—making a ton of dough with *their* play-off formats, they just tried to force baseball into the same pattern. Never mind that in basketball, you really *can* tell who's the best team by playing a seven-game series. In baseball, you can't. Too many freak bounces can happen. But what I'm trying to tell you is the Royals' system back then was good for success in the regular season; we just weren't built for that sprint at the end.

Normally we'd beat the Yankees' ass eight out of twelve times during the regular season. A lot of times, we'd face them right after they'd played the Red Sox. We might happen to miss Ron Guidry, the top starter in baseball, in our three- or four-game series. Also, our bullpen was pretty deep, so I could mix-and-match against their hitters real good. That's baseball during the marathon. In the playoffs, they'd run Guidry at us twice in five games. We had no backbreaking starter to go against him. That was the first big difference.

The second was the bullpen. In both the '76 and '77 series, we took them to the fifth and final game. The first year, we went into the ninth inning tied; the second, we led by a run. But both times, they could bring on a great stopper at the end to slam the door—Sparky Lyle, the great lefthander. He was so dominant in '77 he won the Cy Young as a relief pitcher. We couldn't counterpunch, and they put our ass on the canvas.

With free agency, we could have solved the problem. Right after we lost the second time, the Pirates' Goose Gossage went on the market. He was the scariest right-hander in baseball, and we could have had him as our closer for $600,000. It would've made him the highest-paid Royal. I *begged* Ewing Kauffman to sign him; I begged Burke. I begged Kauffman some more. Goose was even a Colorado Springs native, which in baseball geography practically made him an honorary Royal. But again, I heard the same refrain: *No player's gonna make more than Brett, no pitcher's gonna make more than Leonard.* Sometimes I wanted to throttle those guys!

Well, not only did I not get Gossage, I had to watch while the damn Yankees did. George Steinbrenner does everything in his power to win, which I admire the hell out of, and now he had Lyle *and* Gossage. Meanwhile, I had Hungo, Mungo, the Duck, and the Bird, and if *that* ain't going into a duel without a musket, I don't know what is. Al Hrabosky (the Mad Hungarian), Steve Mingori, Marty Pattin (he did a hell of a duck impression), and Doug Bird were smart pitchers, and they served me good during the regular season, but in the playoffs, none of 'em was that one ass-kicking closer who could punch 'em out quick. We never got that guy, and a hell of a ballclub turned into an also-ran.

The thing Kauffman hadn't faced was simple: In any pro sport, if you're serious about winning, you have to take advantage of every avenue available to you. In modern baseball, that means three things: the farm system, the trade route, and free agency. The farm system is your foundation. You seed it, water it, and bring it along. Then, if you have good scouting and player evaluation, you can use trades to supplement what you've built in the farm system. Then there's free agency: There's only one way to use it successfully. You cannot *build* a ballclub out of free agents. That's been proven. But if you have a strong club already, you can use free agency to buy that one star you need to get you over the hump, the guy that will turn an already good team into a champ. The Padres showed that in 1984, when they had a good club that needed a right-handed bat and a veteran leader to get to the next level: Add Steve Garvey, and you kill two birds with one stone, get San Diego's first trip to the World Series, and prove my point to a "T."

Pro sports is competitive today, man. If you want to win, commit to it, because a lot of other clubs are going to. Skip any of the three avenues, and you're going to find you ain't bringing home any titles. If the Royals had figured that out, I might have ten, twelve pennants to my name. I'd still be managing in the City of Fountains.

Ewing Kauffman had a plan, all right, but it didn't fit the modern game. He never really gave us a chance.

I can't tell you how it happened, but from the fly-by-night screwballs in the loud plaid jackets, to some of the greatest captains of American industry, I played, scouted, managed, and slaved for some of the damnedest owners in the history of the game. In what other business could I have worked for one guy who was a pantyhose salesman, another who was a singing cowboy, and a third who ran the most successful beer operation in the history of the world? Some of them couldn't plan their way out of a paper sack, and some knew more about planning than I ever will. But they all gave me an idea of what a baseball owner should be—and shouldn't—if he's trying to build a champion.

The first owner I managed for was Bob Short, who hired me to replace Ted Williams with the Texas Rangers in 1973. When I first got there, a reporter asked me what I thought of the team's chances. I'd looked at that pitching staff, and all I could say was, "This is the worst excuse for a big-league ballclub I ever saw." I was right: I managed my ass off all year, and we still finished thirty-seven games out. On top of that, Arlington Stadium, in the middle of a Texas summer, felt more like a frying pan on a griddle than a ballfield. We were lucky to draw 8,000 fans a game. It was a comedy of errors, and the tone started at the top.

Short was a fast-talking, fast-buck kind of guy—the exact wrong temperament for baseball. He'd made his money in the trucking business. His operations were based in Minneapolis and he'd done pretty well for himself up there. Problem was, empty grandstands day after day weren't what he had in mind when he sprang for a major-league baseball team. He wanted to remedy that, so he swung into action. Matter of fact, he took to hyping the gate like one of those guys wearing the sandwich boards outside the local circus.

Most owners like to promote their team with an occasional Ball Day, where they give out free baseballs, or maybe a Bat Day or a Cap Day. Bob's personal favorite was Pantyhose Night. We'd have them things a couple times a month, boy. He'd load a couple of his trucks with stockings up there in Minnesota, roll 'em down to the Lone Star State and give out a free pair to every woman that came through the turnstiles. Well, that was a hell of a deal! Bleacher seats only cost a dollar and a half, and word got out the stockings were worth three or four bucks a pair. It was—pardon the pun— sheer pandemonium. We'd get thirteen, fourteen thousand fans to the ballpark them nights, and those fans were happier than armadillos on a warm stretch of pavement.

Only problem was, they never turned into baseball fans. They wouldn't stay to watch the game! By the time the National Anthem was played, those folks were on the freeway home. How could you blame them? I mean, once you got your hose, why sit through all that torment?

You could have renamed the owner Short Term for the way his mind worked. That was never more clear than the way he handled the greatest schoolboy lefthander ever to come out of Texas. David Clyde had mowed 'em down in high school, thrown as many no-hitters as anybody in the history of the state. When Short read about him, he didn't just see a great local story; he saw dollar signs. We drafted Clyde number one overall. He graduated in the spring of '73, and when Short was in Houston negotiating with the kid, Bob called and said, "If we give him two starts in the big leagues, he'll sign." I said, "We're in last place, what the hell do I care if we start him?"

I agreed to pitch Clyde two games, then farm him out to the minors, where he could build his arm and confidence over a couple of years. I figured you'd pitch him a little, let him get a few big-leaguers out, then send him home in August. You'd ship him to the instructional league that fall, where he could get good coaching and pitch with guys his age. Next year, 200 innings at Double-A; the year after that, 150 or so at Triple-A. *Then* you bring him up to stay. I don't give a damn how good he is, that's how you develop a young pitcher.

It never happened. In that circus, Clyde was just too good too soon. People started coming to the park, and that lit Short's eyes up. First time out, the kid goes five good innings and gets the win. Second time, he loses 2–1 to the Tigers, but goes six more. He's already my best pitcher, and everybody in town is talking about David Clyde. Suddenly Short figures he invented baseball. I beg him to do what he said and farm the kid out. But he's like P. T. Barnum with a good freak show. Why shut down your best booth?

Before the kid fell apart, you saw a little bit of what he could have done. In his fourth start, he went into Fenway Park and struck out Carlton Fisk, Carl Yastrzemski, and Orlando Cepeda—three future Hall of Famers—*three times each* in six innings. It was something. All-Stars don't do that too damn often. But every young pitcher goes through a period when the hitters start to lay off his curveball. When that happened, Clyde didn't have what it took to adjust. He'd been hanging around with the wrong crowd, a bunch of older guys—hell, the whole *team* was older guys to him—and that didn't help him any. The Rangers never sent him down, he never came out of his tailspin, and inside of two years, David Clyde was nothing but a cautionary tale. He worked a little for the Indians five years later, but that was it. A great young career was over.

So long-term planning is crucial. And so is building an atmosphere of trust. I was director of player development for the Mets from 1966 to 1973, which is something like being the GM of the whole farm system. Every year I did as much one-on-one coaching as I could, drilling everybody on the fundamentals and checking their skills. I combed through the teams at every level to figure out who belonged where, and I moved 'em up and down the ladder accordingly.

I loved that job, but it mostly taught me you can't do it all yourself. You've got to hire good people and trust them. Find them, sign them on, tell 'em what you want 'em to do, and get the hell out of their way. That breeds confidence in the ranks. It encourages independent judgment. If you know how to listen, it expands your own pool of information. Trust is the glue of any good system.

Well, Bob Short told me on September 1 that I was the best manager he'd ever had. Then he found out Billy Martin was available. I saw it coming: A week later—on my son's birthday, no less—he fired my ass. Trust was about as high on his list as foresight. My next owner, Kauffman, had the same basic problem, and that's why he laughed off my reports on his players. He'd bought a team, so suddenly he was Abner Doubleday. That's a sickness a lot of owners get. Once they do, there ain't any cure.

I did have one owner, though, who knew trust like the back of his hand. It made him the world's greatest beer baron. It also changed my career, and it explains why the man they called the Eagle was the best boss I ever had.

The tone was set the first time I ever laid eyes on Gussie Busch. I arrived in St. Louis in June 1980 to talk about the managing job, and I went out to Grant's Farm, the baronial estate with the wild peacocks and llamas all over the place where the whole Busch clan has lived for years. I met with Mr. Busch, his secretary Margaret Snyder (who would later become the fourth Mrs. Busch), and his lawyer, Lou Susman.

It started off simple. They offered me a one-year contract for $100,000. That was less money than I'd made the year the Royals canned me, but that wasn't the problem. It was the length. I said, "Mr. Busch, I understand it's your policy just to offer one-year deals. But I won three straight titles in Kansas City, and the first time I finished second, I was out on my ass. I won 88 games and got fired." If I'd had a crystal ball, I could've added that Tony LaRussa would win the same number for the Cardinals one year and get named Manager of the Year.

"Thanks for the offer," I said, "but I'm not signing any more one-year contracts." I shook his hand, got up and started walking out.

I made it halfway to the door. *"Siddown!"* he barked in that gravelly voice. "The damn players get five-year contracts, you can get a three-year sonofabitch." I signed that day, and like the man said in *Casablanca*, it was the beginning of a beautiful relationship.

Except for the occasional fish story, there was never a dishonest word spoken between me and Gussie Busch. Hell, there wasn't even a diplomatic one. Here I was, the son of a brewery worker in some little country town in Illinois, and he was a world-class aristocrat who'd built up the most successful beer company in history, and from the first day on we were on the same level. I could say the damnedest things to that man. He said, "I'm paying some of my players damn near $700,000 a year, and we're in last place. What the hell's going on down there?" I said, "Chief, we've got a clubhouse full of mean-spirited backstabbers. They ain't going anywhere. We have to clean house and fast." There was a little pause, and then he looked at me and said, "I'll be damned! I think you know what you're talking about." And before you could say hops and barley, I was in.

Gussie was eighty-one when I met him, and he'd run Anheuser-Busch for twenty-some years, so he was a tough old crow. He tested you; he tested *everybody*. But if he saw something in you he liked, he gave you trust. We were both a couple of squareheaded, no-bullshit Midwestern Germans; we loved a good braunschweiger sandwich, a game of cards, and a few cold mugs of the family beverage. From that, and from the way I talked to him, he realized I had what it took to run his baseball team.

I saw the damnedest scenes over there at Grant's Farm. Gussie played as hard as he worked, and it was *something*. I'm telling you, I'd never seen a guy who could drink like Gussie since my days with Casey Stengel. Casey used to want all his players to go out to dinner in pairs. He figured everybody'd buy a round. He'd say, "You gotta go out for two!" That was his motto: "Go out for two." They did—often.

They didn't have a thing on Gussie. I'd wait till fifteen minutes before I wanted to visit, call him up at Grant's Farm, and say, "Draw me up a Michelob, Chief, I'm heading over." He loved that: *"Wunnerful, wunnerful!"* he'd say. Didn't give him time to schedule another meeting. Hell, sometimes he was just getting out of bed. We'd talk baseball, and by two-thirty, boy, I'd have to start looking for the exit. He'd dive into these big gin drinks, schooner sized; he called them bullets. It'd take me two hours to drink one of them things, and he'd put away two or three and just be warming up. "What d'you want? Have another one!" he'd bark. I'd say, "No, I'd better not, Gussie, I've gotta drive over to Illinois tonight and give a speech . . . I gotta shower and shave and put on a suit and tie!" He didn't give a damn. *"Have another one!"* he'd holler. *"Have one for the ditch!"* That was his favorite expression: "Have one for the ditch." What could you say to that? Sonofagun had a stronger will than Stengel.

I'm not advocating ownership by alcohol; I'm just saying, that was Gussie's way, and the fact he shared it with me put us on the same page. As time went on, things got even more open. I learned the ways of an international beer baron, which don't look a whole lot like yours and mine. All the Busches were hunters, including most of that batch of kids and grandkids and cousins they had. Some of them would shoot at the live game they had on the property. But Gussie traveled to do his hunting. He'd gone everywhere in the world where they had big game. And we'd be sitting there in his huge trophy room, with about fifty heads lining the walls like some embalmed exotic zoo, and he'd start reminiscing. "Shot every damn one of 'em myself," he'd say. I must have heard him say that a hundred times.

"Every damn one." Well, according to his safari buddies, they actually pulled the trigger. Gussie never got out of the jeep! But he had the biggest house, so he kept the trophies. Sounds fair to me!

I think he might have had even more kids and grand-kids than he had stuffed Kodiak. There were so many Augusts and Peters and Margarets running around I got dizzy trying to sort 'em all out. In Gussie's later years, the phone would ring there at the estate, and I'd overhear his end of the conversation: *"Really?* Well, tell 'em I'm delighted! *Wunnerful, wunnerful!* Can't wait to talk about it some more!" Then he'd hang up, and I'd ask him, "Who was that?" He'd say, "Hell, *I* don't know— one of the kids." He had no idea who he was talking to! He was a beauty, boy.

Mr. Busch gave me more power than anybody in baseball since Connie Mack. He was the first guy who realized what I had to offer and how to use it to the utmost. Within reason, if I had a need, I could go out and fill it; if a player wouldn't do things the way I said, I could run his ass out of town. That gave me a lot more clout than managers generally get. I didn't have to ask forty people, a dozen lawyers, and eight committees to make a trade: I could go into a room with Gussie, talk to him straight, get a good, firm handshake, and that'd be that. He'd say, "Just tell me what you're doing before it hits the papers." I'd call him up and say, "We're send-ing this guy to the Phillies, and we'll get so-and-so in return." *"Wunnerful, wunnerful,"* he'd say. Half the time he didn't know who the hell I was talking about. Trust— you can't beat it.

It was never that I didn't have limits. Like any good boss, Gussie put a frame around my decisions. He'd give me a budget for the ballclub every November; I took it seriously. I never exceeded that figure or fell short of it by more than $500,000 my whole time there. I was never in the upper 50 percent of the league in salary; when we won the World Series, we ranked nineteenth out of twenty-six in the majors. I never spent much on my bench. Hell, after we won the pennant in '85, I think I got rid of seven out of my twenty-five players the week after the season ended, just to cut payroll.

As we built the team, if I wanted to add a big salary, he asked me to get rid of one at the same time, and that made sense to me. Or if we did talk personnel, he'd give me one choice or the other. When I first got to St. Louis, I told him about my starting pitchers. He wouldn't let me keep both my right-handed starters, Pete Vuckovich and Bob Forsch. He said, "Which one you want?" I liked Forsch's work habits better—Bobby's the only truly sane pitcher I ever managed, and Vuke didn't take good care of his body—so I said, "Hell, let's keep Forschie." We signed him to a five-year contract, and he ended up pitching eight good years for me. We'd have never won without him.

Every time I ever visited Grant's Farm, Gussie'd sum up his philosophy in two words right before I left. He'd look me right in the face and growl, "*Do it*." What made him a great owner was that he gave me the hammer to make it stick. If I'd fallen on my ass, I'd have been canned; I know that. But anybody worth his salt, in baseball or anywhere else, wants that opportunity. I want a chance to build things my way; if I get fired, so be it, but I want to be fired for what *I* did.

As it happened, most of what I did—trades, waiver deals, even a free-agent signing or two—worked out. We traded for McGee, Ozzie, and Clark. We kept our pitching staff stocked. We sent Tudor to the Dodgers for Pedro Guerrero, who replaced Jack as our top RBI man and damn near won a pennant for us in '89. Pedro drove in 117 runs that year with only 17 home runs, and I can't tell you how many RBIs he got with two outs and two strikes on him. I never saw a guy have a year like that! Nobody else could drive in a run, so I don't know why they ever pitched to him. A year after that, we got Tudor back from L.A. for nothing, and he won 12 games. The teams you saw in St. Louis were the ones I wanted to manage, and when that stopped happening, I said, "Thanks for the ten great years." Cardinal fans owe a decade of so-called Whiteyball to a damn good CEO.

Good management begins with trust from the top down, and I had the same feelings about Gene Autry, the Singing Cowboy, that I'd had for Gussie. He was another great American I was lucky enough to meet through baseball.

I first met him in 1961, his first day as an owner in the big leagues. I'd had my nose broken the day before, in Richmond, Virginia, and after they hammered it back in place and released me from the hospital, I came to the game at Memorial Stadium. Gene Autry and Bob Reynolds were brand-new co-owners of the Angels, and their boys beat the Orioles that night for their first win ever. Afterwards, the Cowboy came into the press room smiling, laughing, clapping everybody on the back. He never realized baseball was so easy! He was 1–0 and, as far as he was concerned, world's champ after one game. He should've sold the club and retired. How the hell else are you going to stay undefeated?

I never met an owner who loved baseball more than Gene Autry. He grew up in Oklahoma listening to Cardinal games on the radio, idolizing the Gashouse Gang, following those great forties teams with Slaughter, Musial, Marty Marion, and Harry Walker. Here he'd been a major star in B Westerns, made millions singing *Rudolph the Red-Nosed Reindeer*, made even more when they used the recording for *Sleepless in Seattle*, quadrupled his holdings in real estate, and lived to build his own Autry Museum of Western Heritage—and I still think the thrill of his life was growing up to be drinking buddies with Stan the Man. Gene bought the Angels for the right reason, because he loved the game and wanted to be around it. Nobody deserved the thrill of that first game more than he did.

We really became friends in 1974, when I was an Angels coach. That's when I found out he loved to talk baseball even more than I did. My family was back in Kansas City, so I was the only coach who was out there by himself, and Gene went out of his way to make sure I was entertained. Mary Lou still calls Gene the finest gentleman she's ever met, and I think it started then. He'd buddy up to me for dinner. He'd have me up to the owner's box after games most nights, for drinks and tall tales. He'd pick my brain about the players he had and the people I knew. He was helping me, but he was enjoying the hell out of it, too. He soaked up every detail.

About midseason, he got a little upset when it looked like I might end up going somewhere else: There were rumors Short was getting ready to dangle my old job back in Texas. Gene just upped my pay from a coach's salary to a manager's. He was going to keep his good drinkin' pal. Hell, even after I left the Angels in '75 to take the managing job in Kansas City, he'd call me up every night after the game. "Why the hell are we in a slump?" he'd say. "Tell me what's going on!" Finally I said, "Jeez, Cowboy, why don't you call Dick up? He's your manager." I was talking about Dick Williams. He said, "Goddamn it, Whitey, we never win, why would I want to talk to him? I'm talkin' to you!"

After I quit managing, I was living in my favorite place on the planet, the great Midwest, still working as a Cardinal vice-president—making good money, driving a fine company car, and even getting in a little bass fishing—when Gene and his wife, Jackie, got in touch. I'd already turned down several managing offers, including one that would've paid me $150,000 more than the highest-paid manager was getting, but Jackie kept on calling the house. It ain't easy to get hold of me, but she kept at it. She even went to work on Mary Lou. She'd say, "Everybody tells me Whitey's the only guy that can get the Cowboy to the World Series! And Gene doesn't have a whole lot of time left."

Mary Lou warmed up to the idea. She reminded me how much the Cowboy had helped us early in my career. She kept saying I was too young to mothball a perfectly good brain. My two-plus years in Anaheim showed again how a good team puts one to use.

I took over as the Cowboy's executive VP in 1991, on a lucrative three-year deal, mostly for personal reasons. I just loved the guy. But I was enjoying life out of baseball, so I made sure I worked out every detail in advance. I wouldn't manage, that was Buck Rodgers's job. But I'd be in complete charge of baseball operations: the minor-league system, the hiring and firing of coaches and scouts, the ballclub's trades and drafts. Jackie was running the business end, which was fine by me. She made sure I knew her goal was to slash the payroll from $38 million—roughly equal to $60 million today—to $20 million. She was very protective of her husband's money. Well, it's tough to cut your payroll in half and still get better. Today, you couldn't even do it. But it's the kind of challenge I get a kick out of.

I only wish Gene hadn't faded out of the picture by the time I got there. He was eighty-five then, and he only ran things in the most technical sense. The chain of command was awful muddy there for a while. Danny O'Brien—who is currently in the Texas Rangers organization—had been assistant to the GM in the previous regime, and for some reason I still don't understand, they never told him what my duties were until I'd arrived. He got protective of his job, cut me out of meetings and so on, and fought my authority for two years. It was exactly the kind of crap I thought I'd prevented from happening. My attitude was, if they didn't want my input, the hell with 'em. I didn't need the aggravation. I was getting paid.

However, they were laying out a lot of money for me. I ain't one to waste money—not even somebody else's.

So I formed a plan of my own. I'd help the team and get out of Dodge at the same time.

I've always enjoyed finding good young players and sticking 'em right in the lineup. I did it with Frank White, Herr, Worrell, McGee, and a lot more I could name. Young guys tend to be focused and hungry, and a trial by fire can tell you a lot about what they're made of. They're also affordable. Now that team payrolls rival the gross national product of some Third World countries, it's an even better strategy. You have to know your minor-league talent.

The thing was, ever since I'd gotten to Anaheim, all I'd heard was how horseshit our farm system was. "Cupboard's bare, Rat," everybody said. "Big trouble down there. We got nothing in the pipeline." You can't always believe what you hear. I figured I'd better see for myself.

I hit the road. I saw ballgames in Cedar Rapids. I saw games in Boise. I saw games in Midland, Texas, in Edmonton, Alberta and every place in between. I lost some money on the gambling boats at Davenport, Iowa, and I met stadium attendants, coaches and vendors all up and down our system. It was a hell of a time: Mary Lou and I got to some beautiful towns we hadn't seen in years. But most of all, the ballplayers I saw really flipped my cap.

I'd already been down to the instructional league in September. I saw a kid outfielder nobody'd ever mentioned to me. I went crazy when I saw him swing. He hadn't even played in the A league yet, but his stroke was wonderful. I said, *"God almighty,* he's a good-looking hitter! He can play in the big leagues some day." Pretty soon after I said that, everybody in the organization was yammering about Garret Anderson. He moved along quick. He's a .300 hitter in the majors right now.

Then I went to Triple-A Edmonton. I saw Damion Easley, the infielder; Gary DiSarcina, the shortstop; and Tim Salmon, the powerhitting outfielder, and some other players up there. I said, "*Damn!* These guys are right on the doorstep of being big leaguers, every one of 'em." I'd seen Easley and Salmon at Double-A in Little Rock a couple of years before that, and I'd been *very* impressed with those two—especially Salmon. But again, nobody seemed to agree with me. All the Angels scout said about Tim was, "Hell, Whitey, the guy strikes out 175 times a year." I thought, *The kid's got a swing like that, and you ain't gonna give him a chance to learn the strike zone?* When there's a big upside to a kid, you've got to *spot* it, man! Then you build on it, and the weaknesses might go away. Half the battle is just knowing when it makes sense to be positive. Tim blossomed at Triple-A a year later, and he's been a perennial 30-homer guy in the big leagues since then, the Angels' best player.

You're probably wondering why nobody realized how good these guys were. Well, we did have good baseball people, so I can't really answer that question. You'd be surprised, though, how many scouts, even when they're looking good talent right in the eye, just don't want to stick their necks out. I can't tell you what they're thinking. Maybe they wonder how they'll look if some kid moves up a level and falls on his ass. But if you buy a hundred acres of land and find out there's oil on it, aren't you going to drill? If you won't promote your talent, it's the same thing as not having it. Fear is awful expensive to a ballclub.

Normally, a player's either ready or he ain't. If he looks ready, move him up; give him a chance! If a kid's ready, I speak up. So I pulled Buck Rodgers aside and told him what I'd seen. "You've got five guys in Triple-A that can play in the majors next season and be good players," I said. Buck started laughing at me. "You've got to be kidding, man," he said. "The hell I am," I told him. "We got more prospects than you think! There's a lot of good players here!" The front office all thought I was nuts, but I know what I saw.

I kept on combing through the minors. I saw more good young players. I made notes. I studied our holes—we were weak in starting pitching—and started looking at other organizations, checking out the places they could help us. That got some good deals in motion. I put together an overall plan. By the time O'Brien finally left in '93, we were bringing some of these kids in. DiSarcina became our shortstop. Salmon, Anderson, the centerfielder Jim Edmonds, a catcher named Jorge Fabregas, Easley, and other guys made the big club. We packaged a few other guys for deals.

Within a year, the Angels had cut their payroll to $21 million. By 1995, they led the West most of the year. They stayed in the race till the last day that season and ended up tied with Seattle. The Angels had the bad luck of facing Randy Johnson in a one-game playoff, and there ain't many teams that can beat him. So they lost. But hell, they were in the hunt again. Orange County baseball was back.

When I finally handed the reins over to Billy Bavasi in '94—I'd been grooming him to replace me—he said, "Man, you're leaving at the wrong time! You're the guy who put this together, and it's ready to blossom." I knew it was, but I didn't need any credit. I'd won the World Series, won pennants, done all that stuff; I didn't need to go down the same road again. I just moved back to St. Louis, which I'd planned to do all along, and got back to retirement. I followed the team in the papers like any fan would.

Before I left, I told Bill he'd have a winner for years to come as long as he went outside to get some starting pitching. That was the one weakness we had throughout the organization, and the one he had to address. It was hard for me to do much about it. The ballclub still had the two veteran lefthanders, Mark Langston and Chuck Finley, who were making upper-echelon money on long-term contracts, even though they'd both lost a yard off their fastballs. The Angels were stuck overpaying them.

They were decent veteran pitchers now, but not worth the $7 or $8 million range anymore. That limited what they could do in going after other pitchers. Bill could handle that. I'd done my job. I gave him my recommendation and went home.

He never made those deals, and I think it cost that organization. But overall, I'm happy with how things worked out. Given the payroll we cut, we ended up with a competitive team. We used our baseball sense to make it happen cheap. Bill and his cohorts have handled it pretty well since then, and they've stayed near the top. I only wish that before the Cowboy sold the whole rodeo to Disney, he'd had his chance to ride into the World Series.

A good owner has to love the game, hire good people, and give 'em room. He has to trust others to do their jobs. He has to use every means available to him, and he has to have a long-term plan. Kauffman, Short, Gussie and the Cowboy had different degrees of each.

But the owner who intrigues me is the one everybody dumps on today. He isn't patient. He hired and fired the same manager seven times. He spends half his life using football tactics in baseball, and he meddles his ass off most of the time, even when he's winning. But you know what? I'll be damned if I still wouldn't want to work for George Steinbrenner of the New York Yankees.

George stomped me three times in the 1970s, and he kept piling up more and more talent so he could do it even worse. He got better every year while we stood pat. He still drives the Yankees with his pedal to the metal. He'll send his scouts anywhere to get ballplayers; I don't care if it's Alabama or Australia. He makes $55 million a year in cable rights and spends it. He knows all the rules and uses 'em. He'll sign free agents, he'll make deals, he'll bring people up through the minors. Sure, he's given away some talent, but he's also brought along good kids—Mariano Rivera, Derek Jeter, Bernie Williams—who help him. Hell, when he won it all in '96, his two best players, Rivera and Jeter, were making rookie pay. Sure, his 1998 team won 114 games—an American League record—largely by kicking the hell out of the bad teams; they were 10–0 against Kansas City, a far cry from the late seventies. But he really planned well in putting that team together. George has a short fuse and a Hall of Fame talent for surrounding himself with yes-men, but the one thing you have to say about him is he's always been committed to finishing first. Baseball needs more people like that.

Yankee fans still hate the sonofagun. I remember when they used to chant "Steinbrenner sucks" at the Stadium—or words to that effect. But let's not forget what he did in the seventies: That team had been playing lousy baseball for ten years—call it the Horace Clarke era—and George came in, played by the rules he had, and brought Yankee fans two World Series titles. How can they gripe about that?

He's a lot like me. You're here to be the best, and more owners, players and managers should play it like that. George and I appreciate each other that way. He used to tell people I was "the second-best manager in baseball" and walk off laughing like a hyena; I was second to whoever happened to be on the hot seat in his dugout at that time. But after he beat me in the '76 playoffs, he came in the Royals' clubhouse and told some reporters, "I'll put it this way—the best *manager* didn't win." Guess I was number one for a day. Did *that* ever set Billy Martin off.

One afternoon in Hawaii, George spotted me at an airport and asked me a hell of a question about baseball. "How in the hell can you win with Joe Oquendo playing rightfield," he said, "and I can't win with Dave Winfield?" If you could answer that one, Mr. Steinbrenner might hire you tomorrow. A lot of owners would. You'd know a lot more baseball that they do.

I was never looking for work when George needed somebody, so we never hooked up. And in Joe Torre, he's really got a good manager for that team. But I'll tell you this: I'd handle it different from most people. I would not sign a contract to work for George Steinbrenner. I'd do it on a handshake. That way, I could concentrate on being the second coming of Casey Stengel, and he could do his thing. If he ever interfered, meddled, or got in my face, I'd tell him which skyscraper to jump off of and head back to the strip pits in Missouri. I don't need that kind of bullshit and there're no tyrants on a fishing pond. But you know what's funny? I think even George would get a kick out of that.

If I'd worked for Steinbrenner, it would've set off some sparks in my old stomping grounds in the Bronx, that's for sure. It might even have shed some light on the game. I can't tell you how long we'd have gone before somebody ended up in the East River, but the fun of it might make up for what happened years ago, when Ewing Kauffman did a lot less than George did to bring home a winner.

I remember one thing about George back then: He was right there, laughing and grinning and kicking my tail as hard as he could. He'd do it again if he got the chance. Now that's a guy you can work for.

· 12 ·

Ahead of the Hounds (or: Remember the Elmers)

Sometimes people wonder if a manager thinks about baseball away from the park. I can't speak for everybody, but I can tell you I never took a game home with me—except once. After Mr. Denkinger's call at first base in '85, we did have a family chat around the kitchen table. Fairly gloomy one, as a matter of fact. Otherwise, by the time I got home from Royals Stadium or Busch, that night's ballgame was over with and I was on to the next thing. Why worry about it?

My family tried to oblige me, but that didn't always wash. One night, I'd brought in a relief pitcher late in the game, he gave up a long home run, and we lost by a run. When I got back to the house an hour later, Mary Lou's dad, my father-in-law Elmer Sinn, was sitting with her in the living room. They were talking in low tones, like two mourners at a funeral, obviously doing a post-mortem on the game. Elmer's a great guy—retired furnace and air-conditioning man, a big baseball fan—but he's got his opinions about the National Pastime, boy, and if he couldn't let 'em out right then, he was going to bust like an overheated duct. Before I could even squeeze past him and get to the kitchen, he got in front of me, put his hands on his hips and said, "Just tell me—

what in the hell'd you bring *that* guy in for?"

I didn't feel much like a rhubarb, but I stopped and looked him in the eye. "Elmer," I said, "were you at the game tonight?"

"You're goddamn right I was!" he said, jabbing a finger at me.

"Well," I said, "why didn't you come down, stick your head in the dugout and tell me the next guy was gonna hit a three-run homer? If you'd done that, I'd have never brought him in in the first place!" And I went in the kitchen and had myself a sandwich.

Just about every baseball fan has played the sport at one time or another, and that's the way it ought to be. It's why they think they know as much as the manager. That's the American way, and it's the beauty of the game. When fans come to the ballpark, damn it, every last one of 'em is a manager. I may not have been dying to have a dustup with Elmer the second I walked in the door after a tough loss, but if the day ever came when he felt he *didn't* know better than me, and didn't *care* who the hell I brought in or when, this game would be in deep trouble.

I hate to have to tell you this, but we're already halfway there. Second-guessing the manager may be as basic to the National Pastime as the foul lines and the fences, but the owners have even yanked *that* out of a lot of the fans' bill of rights. And in the long run, that can only be bad for the game.

Let's go back a ways for the best example. Twenty-six years ago, the NFL was surging in popularity and baseball was in the doldrums. The American League owners decided they had to do something to grab fans by the collar. As usual, they decided that meant more run production. More runs, more runs—they wanted more runs. So they said, "Hell, the pitcher can't hit; why make the fans sit through that? Let nine batters hit, not eight." From then on, no AL pitcher had to bat. The designated hitter was born.

Did they reach their short-term goal? Hell, yes. The average American League club scores eight-tenths of a run per game more than the average National League team. Maybe that doesn't sound like much, but in baseball, you multiply things out. There's 162 games a season; that's 100 or so runs per team every year. It adds up! That's a sea change in offense, in defense, in economics. It shifts the whole flavor of the sport.

But was it a *good* change? You and I could sit here all day and argue about that. We know what John Hart, the Cleveland Indians' GM, thinks: He said the only good thing about a pitcher coming to bat is it gives the fans a chance to get up and go to the bathroom. Now, that's a hell of a statement to make! A lot of people in his league agree, and they're entitled to their opinions. But that won't stop me from asking a question: The owners slid into home on that one—getting more offense—but what got lost in the cloud of dust?

In baseball, in business, or in working in the yard, if you want to make a change, think it through first. Why do you want to do it? What are the consequences going to be? What'll you gain and what'll you lose? Ask all those questions, and if you still think it's a good idea, *do it*. If you haven't, you're just shooting first, aiming later. And when there's holes in the living-room wall, you've got no one to blame but yourself.

Well, nobody thought through the DH beforehand, and it's too late to do it now. That was typical of the owners, who have got to be dumber about their own business than any group of people I've ever seen. The real issue isn't offense, defense, or how many bulbs are flashing on the JumboTron. Its whether the Lords have enough brains not to kick away the best parts of the sport like a one-hop grounder. And the scouting report ain't good.

But we're all grownups here. We've had the DH for twenty-six years now. Let's at least look *backward* and give it some thought. Has it been good for baseball or hasn't it? Should we keep it or not? For the good of the game, let's think about it, make a decision, and plan. It's about time somebody did.

Now, the Elmer scenario happens in either league: You're always going to change pitchers, and you'll always be second-guessed for it. But the DH really reduces the strategy a good fan enjoys. Let's say I'm managing in the National League, and I'm considering a pitching change. I have to *think*. I don't just yank a guy when his arm is tired; I don't just leave him in when he's going good. Half my concern is weighing offense against defense. If Andujar is pitching, we're down by two, and he comes up to bat with runners on base, I'm thinking, "Do I pinch-hit for him now, maybe get us a base hit, and lose him for the game? Or do I keep him in, take a chance on his ugly bat, and keep him out on the mound?" You're sorting more factors than the Diamondbacks have uniforms. How good's he throwing? How good is my bench guy hitting? Is there time to score later on, or is this our last shot?

To a real fan, that's interesting. Any move is a trade-off. It's also as public as an airport, and every Elmer Sinn in creation is thinking along with me. Maybe my move works and I look like a genius; Elmer sees that. Maybe it blows up. Then he *knows* he's smarter than me. Well, that's what you want! It gives him something to brag about to his buddies. It keeps him coming back to the ballpark. It keeps him talking about the game in the dark days of February. It's the dimension that turns a game into a pastime.

On the other hand, take an American League example. Say Terry Collins, the Angels' manager, has a one-run lead over the Mariners in the eighth. Well, he's got Gregg Jefferies, or whoever his DH happens to be that day, batting for the pitcher no matter what. He doesn't have to worry about that. So he brings in his best damn reliever, Troy Percival, to finish the game. That's it! No tradeoffs. Now, if Elmer's at that game, and Edgar Martinez doubles down the line and beats Collins, all Elmer can say is, "Well, he brought in his best; he got beat with his best." He shrugs and goes back to sleep. Humpty Dumpty could manage in the American League. There's nothing to manage!

There's other reasons the DH ain't as fun to watch. Any good fan knows that baseball has many parts, that the real player helps himself by doing a lot of little things. Greg Maddux wins games with his fielding, just like Bob Gibson used to do. And if a pitcher can hit, shouldn't that give him a leg up, too? Bob Forsch won the Silver Slugger award for the National League's best-hitting pitcher four times. Think that helped the Cards? Danny Cox couldn't have hit me if I ran across home plate, but when I asked him to sacrifice, to bunt, to play "butcher-boy" to the right side, he knew how to do it. That's part of being a professional, a Bob Gibson-, a Warren Spahn-type player. The DH punishes the good athletes—the Forsches, the Seavers, the Orel Hershisers, the Gibsons, who know a base hit helps the team win and learn how to get one. The good fan appreciates it.

It's also part of history. Catfish Hunter was a hell of a batsman back in his heyday in the seventies. The year before the DH started, he had 36 hits. You don't do that by accident. The most any pitcher ever had was Wes Farrell's 52 for the Red Sox in 1935. Catfish had a good chance to tie that record someday. Yet after 1972, he never came to the plate again. He spent his whole career in the American League, and fans still don't know if he could have done it.

The DH changes other basics. Let's look at one of today's designated hitters, Chili Davis of the Yankees. Now, Chili's a good hitter and a decent person. I ain't arguing with that. But if you put him in the field, he ought to have to wear a helmet; that's how bad he is. For 100 years, managers had to face up to this problem: If a guy's got a good bat and no glove, where do you put him? They used to hide the donkeys in leftfield or at first base and manage around 'em. You had to think about it, boy: What if he drives in three today but gives away four? Is he worth the risk? Are you losing more than you gain? A good ballplayer does everything well, and he should get rewarded; if he can't, he ought to pay a price. The DH gives you something for nothing— Chili's bat but not his glove. That ain't the way the game was made.

Hell, I remember in 1979 when Don Baylor was voted American League MVP. How in the world can a DH be the best in the league? He never puts on a glove! You have to pay other people to go out on the field and make outs for him. *He* sure as hell ain't doing it. When they first started the DH rule, half the reason they did it was to keep the old, crippled guys working for a couple more years—the Harmon Killebrews and Orlando Cepedas. They could still hit like hell but couldn't run across the dugout to get a drink from the water fountain. It takes the balance out of the game.

It also kills a lot more strategy I could talk about. In the National League, you make double-switches; that adds brainwork. Let's say you're Tony LaRussa, the Cards' manager, and Donovan Osborne is tiring a little. It's late in the game, and you're down by two. You need a run soon or it's over. So you look ahead, and you realize Osborne's due to bat next inning. Well, you take him out right now and bring in Lance Painter. You substitute for your left fielder, Ron Gant, at the same time. You bring McGee in for him. Willie's got a better bat than Painter, so you bat *him* in the pitcher's spot, which allows him to bat in the next inning! That gets you a shot of offense when you need it. Painter can bat later, and you can worry about that when the time comes. It's just one more thing in your bag of tricks.

In the National League, you're thinking. You teach your pitchers to sacrifice bunt. You balance your batting order. You use your bench. You play for a run at a time.

The good fan can take the time to learn about these things. He gets rewarded for paying attention. The owners never thought all this through back in 1973, and they still don't realize the half of what I'm saying, but the DH takes all of it away. The AL manager sits, waits and watches. So do the fans in the stands. What's so great about that?

Baseball owners seem to think fans are so damn dumb they'll only stay awake for powerball, for the big-blow game. The facts dispute that. If that was the case, the American League would outdraw the National, but just check the attendance figures! The National League has always been the better draw, even since the DH began. In fact, till four years ago, NL attendance was measured in turnstile count (the number actually in the seats), and the AL reported tickets *sold*. Even by that comparison, the National League has kicked them in the ass year after year. The owners just don't know the fans. The DH doesn't draw anybody.

So even in the owners' favorite language, money, the designated hitter is a loser. In fact, it makes you scratch your head. For the past twenty years, the owners have been crying poverty: "We can't make any money in this business!" "We're all going bankrupt!" "The players are stealing us blind!" They sound like a bunch of scared old ladies clutching their handbags. You and I will never know if all that's true, since owners haven't exactly rushed to open their books, and when they have, you've gotten such a mishmash of parking, concessions, and figures from subsidiary companies it makes your head spin. It's a big shell game, and they're doing the sleight-of-hand.

Let's you and I use our common sense. Here these people are crying financial hardship. They were crying about it back when payrolls were $20 to $25 million a year and superstars were getting $2 million. Today, the national TV money is about half what it was then, yet they're giving the Gary Sheffields, Albert Belles, and

Mike Piazzas of the world $55 million, $60 million, $90 million deals. Where's all that money coming from? Somebody's lying.

The DH makes the smell even worse. If money's such a problem, why would an owner volunteer to pay nine offensive players instead of eight? That's in *addition* to the pitcher, who you're paying whether he bats or not. Do fans know the average DH makes a salary that's above the average? When the median was still below $2 million a year, in the early nineties, the average DH was getting $500,000 more. Between '95 and '97, our man Chili was raking in between $3 million and $4.5 million in the Angels' and Royals' batters' box. All that for a guy who never goes on the field! You're spending more and getting less. You have run inflation and monetary inflation. That's good for the game?

There are great ballplayers in the American League, don't get me wrong. I'm sure they'd like to play some real baseball if they had the chance, and they'd be damn good at it. It's just that the American League is a joke. I'd like to see some of those AL managing geniuses come to the National League, boy. You'd get a hernia from laughing at that. In the World Series, they don't know which end is up! The thing I really want to stress is this: Here's an idea that costs you strategy and fan involvement. It doesn't help attendance. It's more expensive; it's less cost effective. It gains runs, but it costs you a lot more. Why do we have it? All I'm saying is, do what the owners didn't: Think about it.

Really, the fact we have the DH isn't even my gripe. It's basically still baseball. Whichever way we go, the most important thing is to get the rules the same in both leagues. You can't have interleague play that makes any sense without that. But what really fries my bacon is the way they flushed all those things down the drain without having the first idea they did it.

Here's a rule of thumb for you: Know your product and have a little foresight, or the little things are going to vanish from your business. Then it'll be too late. And that's when you'll figure it out: They weren't such little things after all.

In my career, I learned to hit the curve. I learned to wave runners home, bullshit with the writers, and handle a pitching staff. I hammered out contracts, hollered at agents, and balanced big-league budgets. That's why I can take a team apart and put it back together and do a damn good job of it. I've learned the nuts and bolts of baseball.

But the average baseball owner—well, he's not like me. He's made millions, but he did it in some other game. Maybe he knows banking or pharmaceuticals. Maybe he can build ships, sell beer, or write software. But what he *doesn't* know is baseball is different from any other industry. He doesn't know a baseball asset is unique.

He doesn't know what a pitcher's arm is worth, how to take care of it, or how it depreciates. He doesn't know how quick he has to keep turning over his roster. He can't tell you how much a young shortstop is worth or how you maximize his value. As sure as I'm sitting here, the biggest problem in my profession is that the guys running it *don't understand the business end of baseball*. That's the real reason their short-term plans, like the DH, end up in the long-term swamp.

Just look at the way owners build their organizations today. Big-league clubs own fewer farm teams than they ever did before, especially at the rookie-league level. That's a major change from when I was coming up. They're trying to save money. "We spend so much for major leaguers, how in the hell can we afford that many minor-league clubs?" That's the thinking. Sounds sensible, right? That's what they think, anyway.

Well, they're full of it. The fact is, with big-league salaries what they are, it makes more sense than ever to own minor-league teams. It used to cost about $80,000 a year to run a rookie-league club, including salaries, bats, balls, and travel. Say it's $100,000 now. If you have eighteen guys playing every day at that level, and good coaches to teach them, you might develop two guys who go on to play in the majors. Well, a full-fledged big-leaguer costs you $5 million a year now. Was that hundred grand a waste or an investment? Your payoff might not come for five years, and when it does come, you might not be able to open your books, point to one column and say, "See, here's where it happened." But in my business, that's how you build your asset base. Start early before your costs go haywire. Save at the front end. It's called being smart.

Owners don't understand that kind of thinking. It's hard to put a dollar-and-cents value on the care, growth, and feeding of ballplayers. It's even harder to explain it to a guy who got rich in some other field. Let's say you're Bud Selig, who was the Brewers' principal owner before he was named commissioner in '98. You made your money selling Chevrolets in Wisconsin. In that business, you might've made thirty cents on the dollar for your money: Lay out a dollar, make $1.30. That's one kind of math. Well, in baseball, it may look like you're only making a nickel on the dollar. Maybe you've got yourself a twenty-year-old pitcher in Double-A who throws 94 mph, but he's just figuring out how to bust the hitters inside. That's a growth asset. How do you quantify it? It might be worth millions down the line, but it ain't like a shipment of Camaros: You can't drive it up on the lot and count it. The problem is, owners want to ledger their baseball assets the way they do sedans or bottles of beer.

When I was with the Mets and later with the Cardinals, I pitched an idea that would have been good for either organization. I said they ought to spend $5 million, as a franchise, to build a dormitory near St. Petersburg, Florida, where both clubs had spring training. It would sleep 150 minor leaguers. They could feed the players right, get them out of the motels, keep them off the streets, and have better surveillance over them. Maybe out of the 200 guys they had in spring camp, two would turn out to be major leaguers who wouldn't have done so otherwise. Maybe the plan kept them from becoming drug addicts; maybe it made them bigger and stronger by putting them on some diet other than McRibs and Coke. For a $5 million outlay, they'd have ended up with two players worth $20 million. That's really how you have to look at it.

If you do end up with a prospect you like, the rules are on your side: You've got him tied up for nine years. You can keep him for three before you put him on your big-league roster; then you own him for six more. Have faith in your system and your baseball judgment. With good coaching, teaching, and a little bit of luck, it's going to happen. You're rolling the dice a little, but in the end—if you're good—it's a damn safe bet.

Just try explaining that to a baseball owner. I did. I approached the Wall Street money guys who ran the Mets with this exact plan, and they just about laughed me out of their office building. I took the same idea to Anheuser-Busch later on, and they wanted to see a guaranteed 18 percent return for every dollar they'd lay out. That's what they always looked for in an investment. "We aren't in the hotel business," they said. I told them they ought to be. In baseball, you can't look at it their way! They were using the wrong model, and that's the reason they flushed away a whole lot of assets they never knew they had.

It happened again with the Cards in the mid-1980s. Lee Thomas was my farm director—he later became general manager of the Phillies—and the two of us knew of a region that was really ripe for baseball. We asked the brewery to put a farm club in the Midwest League in Springfield, Illinois, about 100 miles northeast of St. Louis. We couldn't prove they'd get that 18 percent back, though, so we had to fight them tooth and nail for months to get the franchise fee. Finally, we did: They put up $18,000 and got themselves a team. Three years ago, they sold it. The price tag: $1.5 million. I wish I'd put up that eighteen grand.

So when fans want to know why owners make rotten decisions, they can look to their business philsophy. But you can't overestimate the ego-trip factor, either. That takes bad judgment and makes it worse.

These guys might have made millions in their lives, but very few of them have seen their names in the paper before they buy a baseball team. Suddenly they're on TV; they get the best tables in restaurants. They're the talk of the town. Everybody's interested in their opinion. None of them knows a squeeze play from a share of stock, but they think they're Branch Rickey all of a sudden. You try to tell them something from your experience, and it's "piss on you, buddy; we're doing this my way." A lot of 'em have to learn the hard way.

One owner I hear is a good man is Drayton McLane, the Wal-Mart executive who bought the Houston Astros in the early nineties. But he stuck his foot in it right away. First thing he said when he got the team was, "We're gonna spend. We're gonna have a $39 million payroll." That was high at the time—equivalent to about $62 million today. But that was his plan: Nail down a good team for the fans. First thing he did was sign two veteran pitchers, Doug Drabek and Greg Swindell, to big-money contracts. That looked good in the papers, and I'm sure it made him feel pretty special.

Problem is, he hadn't looked into the basics of his business. He didn't take the time to realize that his $39 million payroll included four players who were up for arbitration at the end of that year. Those guys—Steve Finley, Ken Caminiti, Jeff Bagwell, and Craig Biggio— were all making about $250,000, and they also happened to be his four best players. Anybody familiar with arbitration at all could tell you that next year was going to be a lot different. But when each of those guys jumped to something like $2.2 million at the end of the year, McLane went into shock. In a span of a couple of months, his payroll jumped a good $7.5 million. He could've seen it coming and made allowances, but from everything I hear, the whole thing caught him by surprise! If you're running a SuperCenter, that's like leaving your dry goods out in a rainstorm. I don't think Sam Walton would have liked it too much.

He had to take drastic action, and that meant a blockbuster deal. McLane's gaffe, and nothing else, triggered the twelve-player trade with San Diego in December 1995 that changed the balance of power in the NL West. McLane had his consultant, Tal Smith, call his son Randy Smith, the young Padres' GM, to work out a trade. So it happened: Finley, Caminiti, and their mammoth salaries went to San Diego. Derek Bell and some cheaper guys came to Houston. It was the biggest trade in baseball in thirty-seven years! The Astros kept Bagwell and Biggio, cornerstone guys, but Caminiti tore the cover off the ball, fielded great, and became Most Valuable Player in 1996. He and Finley turned San Diego into a contender. Every year, more and more baseball history gets written by gaffes and screwups, not by baseball judgment.

How could an otherwise smart man mess up *that* bad? You tell me. All I can tell you is, it happens every day. The owner buys the team, and within six months, it's, "I'm buying this and that; if you don't like it, get a new job." Then it's, "My God, this guy's paid salary is going from a quarter of a million dollars to $3 million? Our payroll went from $35 million to $44 million in two months? How the hell did that happen?" So you tell him, "Well, we lost two arbitration cases in February, we settled with three other guys who were eligible, and such-and-such a player was re-upped." You explain that because of salary arbitration and other stuff, a major-league payroll today grows 18 percent every year even if you don't change a face on your ballclub. Here you're teaching him Baseball 101, and the final exam's already come and gone.

The same insanity changed my career. Once Mr. Busch had faded from the picture in St. Louis, Anheuser-Busch had a pretty peculiar way of doing baseball business, too—a beer seller's way. I could see it coming, it was dumber than hell, and before they knew what hit them, it cost 'em all millions. It cost all of St. Louis the outstanding team we'd built. And the whole thing could've been prevented.

Back in the middle eighties, Jack Clark was our most important guy. Most people considered Ozzie our most valuable asset, and there's no doubt he was a wonderful baseball player. But we also had Jose Oquendo, a hell of a defensive shortstop who had a career on-base percentage of about .380. He could have filled in fine for Ozzie if, God forbid, we'd ever lost him. But in that big mausoleum of a ballpark, we had a stable of singles hitters. Jack Clark was the only guy who could drive the ball. His bat was what turned our track team into a big-league offense.

The comparison between Ozzie and Jack even caused a feud on the ballclub. Jack's wife, a very nice lady, always thought her husband contributed just as much or more to our success as Ozzie, and that he was never rewarded fairly, the way Ozzie always was. I'm not so sure she was wrong. With Jack in the lineup for three years, we won two pennants. The one year we didn't win, Jack was hurt in June and never played again. His final season with the Cardinals, in 1987, we went to Game 7 of the World Series and drew 3 million people, about the same number who bought tickets to watch Mark McGwire chase Maris's record in 1998. And the team had raised ticket prices a dollar the year before, so that meant a $3 million windfall right there. All Jack was asking for to stay with the team was $1.8 million a year. That would've been a bargain.

So you'd think if you understood baseball.

Right after the World Series ended, I pulled Jack aside and said, "I want you to call me before you leave town. We'll drive out to Grant's Farm, we'll have a beer with Gussie, and we'll get you signed." It would've been simple. He agreed to. I still don't know why in the hell he didn't. All I know is, I was in Colorado skiing that winter, and picked up the *Rocky Mountain News* one morning—it was January 2, 1988—and saw the headline: CARDS' CLARK SIGNS WITH YANKEES. I had two immediate thoughts. First, "God almighty, how in the world can you let go of the one guy who's making you rich?" And second, "There went my offense." Here we owned the goose that laid the golden egg, and we chased his ass off the farm over a sack of feed! Before I even put the paper down, I knew it was the end of an era.

What the hell happened? I don't know for sure because I wasn't there. But I do know that by this time, Fred Kuhlmann and Lou Susman, attorneys for the brewery, were calling the shots, and they didn't understand baseball. From what I heard, they hardballed Clark from the start in his negotiations. Here was a free agent we needed to keep, and in the first five minutes they apparently told him he was "a one-dimensional ballplayer." Clark came up as a third baseman, and he still had great hands at first base, a lot better than people thought, so that was a load of crap. But I don't give a damn if it's football, hockey, or jai alai, when you're negotiating with a free agent, you have to blow a little smoke up his ass first. Tell him how good he is; lay the money out there! Criticize him *after* he signs. It's different from an arbitration hearing, where you've already got the player under contract and all you're figuring out is how much to pay him. But I guess they wanted to be the tough guys.

I believe Jack's agent had already decided to serve up a big free agent to George Steinbrenner, and that didn't help much. Jack shouldn't have listened to that bullshit. St. Louis was the place for him, not New York or Boston or the other towns where he ended up playing. He fit our scheme perfectly, and we fit him. But I'm sure that got things off on the wrong foot. Jack's such a bull-headed sonofagun, when he heard that "one-dimensional" stuff, I'm sure he went ballistic. It would have been good business for the Cards to do Jack Clark right; instead, they took a shotgun to their own cleats. So-called Whiteyball was never the same.

After all that happened, the brewery and Dal Maxvill, our GM, knew they had to do something to appease the fans, and fast. That's when we saw the brewery's genius in action. They went out and signed a right-handed power hitter who'd been in the National League nine years and hit *one* home run at Busch Stadium. Bob Horner had been a 30-dinger guy for the Braves, but that was in their old Launching Pad ballpark, and it didn't take a genius to see that Busch, with its deep power alleys and humid air, was too big for him. They made the deal anyway. Well, they thought Jack was expensive, but panic is a lot worse. They gave Horner $2 million—more money than Clark ever asked for!

It's funny. Bob was a nice guy, but how many runs does that get you? I had a nickname for him: I called him "Buddha." He was a little on the portly side and spent a lot of quality time slouched in his chair in the clubhouse. And I'll never forget Opening Day in 1988, when the contrast with Jack really hit home.

I had a rule that everybody took infield before the game, but I didn't see Horner out at first base, so I went in the clubhouse to find him. There he sat, in one of his deep trances. I said, "Hey, Bob, what the hell you doing? You're supposed to be taking infield!" He looks up at me, blinks like an old frog on a lily pad and says, "I'm tired." A hundred and sixty-two games left to play, and the man is gassed!

Horner hit 3 home runs that year and spent 102 games on the trainer's table. I don't know what the problem was. Maybe he was doing some beechwood aging. Thank you, Anheuser-Busch.

Expansion, realignment, the expanded playoffs—the newspapers will tell you these are bold maneuvers, acts of progress, good for the game of baseball. But the same guys who gave away Jack Clark and stripped the '95 Astros are the ones bringing you the "big changes." They're really nothing more than today's scramble to fix yesterday's screwup. That's how the game of baseball is run.

The so-called big story of 1997 was interleague play. AL and NL teams would face each other during the regular season for the first time in the 125-year history of baseball. And to hear the owners tell it, it was the Second Coming of the Golden Age. It would promote rivalries, with the Mets playing the Yankees, the Cubs facing the White Sox, and so on. It would jazz up fan interest. It would do this and that. It was visionary, boy.

All I saw was a novelty that was going to wear off fast. Sure, there were bigger crowds in four or five ballparks the first couple of times. But I had to laugh. That first weekend in Pittsburgh, attendance really jumped. The Pirates had just sent Jeff King and Jay Bell to Kansas City in the off-season, and who should come to town that weekend but the guys in Royal blue? The fans wanted to see how they looked in their new pajamas! For a minute I wondered how far ahead they'd planned those trades.

As with all gimmicks, the shot wore off quick. Two years later, the "magic" has subsided. Who gives a damn about the Marlins and Devil Rays playing in July? Florida's a nice state, but you're going to drive across it for that?

Just like the DH, interleague play is a bad idea for a lot of reasons. For one thing, the travel is ridiculous. But I really oppose it because it's unfair. American League East teams only play National League East teams; AL

Central teams only play NL Central teams. Right now, the AL East is the best division in baseball, with the big-dollar Yankees, Red Sox, Orioles and Blue Jays blowing the little guys out. On the other hand, the AL Central—with the Tigers, White Sox, Twins and Royals—is glorified Triple-A baseball. So, the New York Mets' twenty-four interleague games are tough; the St. Louis Cardinals' are easy. Yet if both teams end up with eighty-eight wins, the record says they're tied. The Cards might even go the the playoffs while the Mets stay home. You talk about unfair!

As dumb as it is, the funniest thing about interleague play is that they never really planned it out in the first place. They didn't hatch the idea to better the game. They weren't thinking of the good of baseball. They did it to drum up some cash. And they did it, like they do almost everything, to form the last link in a long chain of screwups.

To see how the whole thing really happened, you have to go back about six years, to the early nineties, when the first domino tipped over. At that time, baseball was talking about expanding into the Phoenix and Tampa Bay areas. Money and politics, not baseball, were driving the whole deal. The people of St. Petersburg, Florida, had damn near gotten the Chicago. White Sox to come there. They'd gotten a domed stadium financed, built and ready, but baseball jilted them at the last second. The Sox stayed in Illinois, and the state of Florida was plenty red-assed about it.

The state looked into suing the game, and their strategy scared the hell out of everybody. It was simple: Challenge baseball's antitrust exemption. That exemption, which is based on legal grounds everybody admits are pretty shaky, is the basis for the game's survival. It basically says that major league baseball can enjoy a monopoly on the game. The last thing baseball wants is to see it challenged in court. They were afraid of that. And the dominoes started falling.

The commissioner's office was still empty then, which was a disgrace to the game. And they didn't want to fill it. They were looking for a new guy the way O. J. Simpson searches for his "real killer." But *this* kicked 'em into action, boy. They suddenly wanted to give the job to the Democratic Party senator from Maine, George Mitchell. Nobody knew what his ideas were or if he'd have made a good commissioner or not, but if the exemption got challenged, they'd have themselves a guy with buddies on Capitol Hill. Same old strategy: Pull the trigger today, aim tomorrow, clean up the mess next week.

It never happened, but something else did. That same problem was behind baseball's decision to expand by two more teams. Sure, the Diamondbacks and Devil Rays paid $130 million each in franchise fees. Sure, the owners love revenue like a junkie loves drugs. But they really gave those teams to Tampa Bay and Phoenix to avoid getting sued. The cart was hauling the horse again. They'd sort out the details later.

Well, when you do it that way, you always wake up in a whole new fix. Suddenly they had other problems. You're adding two teams? Okay. Where you going to put 'em? What leagues do they go in? Those are questions you'd probably think out ahead of time. I know I would. But the owners ain't you and me. First they awarded the franchises, *then* they thought about where to put 'em. And that got them in a mathematical bind they didn't see coming.

There were twenty-eight big-league ballclubs at the time—two leagues of fourteen teams each, even numbers all around. In baseball, even numbers are necessary for the schedule: Every team plays 162 games and plays basically every day; every game requires two teams. But the owners' first "plan" was to think, *Hell, let's put one new team in each league!* That would be fair, right? Problem is, it leaves you with two fifteen-team leagues. You can't have fifteen-team leagues any more than you can have three teams playing a game, yet here were the owners, heads of the industry, thinking about it.

Well, somebody finally did some math and saw they had a problem. So they wriggled and wormed some more. They figured it out: If you pool all thirty teams together, you have an *even number*. You could have the two leagues play each other. You could squirm out of your Chinese handcuffs. And you could say, "Hey, look at this fan-friendly innovation we came up with! We sure care about this game." And so, in June 1997, the owners reversed a century of big-league tradition for the sole purpose of slapping a patch over their own backsides.

As always, a little planning could have prevented all this. You could have put both teams in one league or the other, leaving you with fourteen in one league, sixteen in the other. You could have committed to adding two *more* teams in 2000, giving you thirty-two total. That's the number we still ought to aim at. The product's already so watered-down, two more teams won't hurt anything, and with thirty-two, you could set up a schedule that makes sense. But who looks that far down the road?

Problems of alignment and geography made their plan unworkable anyway, so *then* they had to realign. They had to beg one AL team to jump to the National. How's that for planning? The Brewers did it, but when you hear how warm and fuzzy it is that Milwaukee is finally a National League city again—returning at last to its twelve-year home in the NL after a mere twenty-eight years in the AL—just remember that was never a plan. It was just one more toxic-waste cleanup on the owners' farm.

Interleague play is just one more stroll on that property. What owners really like to do is go up to the barn, open the gate, and let out the horse. Then, all of a sudden, it's, "Good God, that monster needs a saddle!" By the time they've gone to town and found some lassos,

Old Paint's up in the mountains looking for a mate.

    If that's progress, I'm the Lone Ranger.

Remember Ewing Kauffman, the savior of Kansas City? He wasn't going to ruin baseball. He wouldn't spend a dime on free agents. Well, eight years after I got fired, he sold his pharmaceuticals company, Marion Labs, to Merrill-Dow for $500 million. The shoe was on the other foot. He finally went after that relief pitcher: He signed Mark Davis, a Padre lefthander, for $14 million. He gave David Cone a $9 million signing bonus. The man lost his mind. He made George Steinbrenner look like Jack Benny. The same guy who used to say "We're doing it the right way" now said, "Screw it! I made all this money, and the government ain't getting a dime." He didn't care what it did to baseball.

    The owners are still shooting themselves in the foot, hopping down the road and bleeding all over the place. Here it is a quarter of a century later, and we *still* haven't made up our minds on the DH, among other things. It's the longest one-year experiment in history! And all *that* means is we haven't decided what kind of Pastime we want.

    I can tell you right now how to solve the DH problem. First, announce if you're going to phase it out three years ahead of time. That gives the Chilis, the Harold Baineses, and the Cecil Fielders time to prepare. Then round up every guy who's managed in both major leagues since 1973 and let them vote. They've seen the game from both sides. I can't tell you how Sparky Anderson, Dick Williams, Tony LaRussa, or Bobby Cox would go; I can't say which way Lou Piniella, Billy Virdon, or Jack McKeon would vote. But at least you'd get the rules the same in both leagues. You'd know the decision was made fairly, by people who give a damn what's best for the game. And you know what? That way, you'd have a game every Elmer Sinn in the world would be happy to watch.

The best way to keep this game interesting for the people who love it is to do what good baseball people always have done. Pitcher or manager, owner or league president, know the game, pick your goals, and make a decision. You'd better stay ahead of the hounds. If you don't, you'll be like a Little Leaguer facing Nolan Ryan. You're going to get smoked.

That's truer now than it's ever been. From the field level on up, you've got to know baseball. You've got to look down the road. You've got to have a plan.

That's too important to leave to people like the owners. Let's work up our own.

Part Three

Minds over Money

· 13 ·
The Capital Game

My brother Butzy is funny. He's two years younger than me—he retired not too long ago—and he's always been a whole lot different. I'm brash and noisy; he likes the background. I got out of New Athens and saw the whole world, from Yankee Stadium to the Glockenspiels in Munich; he only went away for his Army days in the fifties. I've got Mary Lou, three grown kids, and eight grandkids; Butz never married. But family makes room for all kinds, and I'm sure glad he lives nearby. He lives in the little house he, my older brother Herman, and I all grew up in, forty minutes from where I am now, and I get over to see him all the time.

Butz has a hell of a sense of humor. His kitchen clock's got a sign on it: "I never drink till 5." Then you do a double-take and see it's fives all around the dial. He's mad about pigs, too. He's got pig clocks, pig calendars, pig paintings, pig boot scrapers, pig Christmas lights strung up year 'round, even half a porcelain pig sticking ass-first out of the living-room wall. Anybody in town goes on a holiday, they bring Butz back some kind of pig. He's famous! I even gave him a live pig once—a Vietnamese pot-bellied fella. Came over a week later and found the two of 'em in the living room, watching a movie and sharing a bowl of popcorn. First he'd take a bite, then *he'd* take a bite.

But a taste for porkers isn't his only quirk. One day I was talking to Butz about a rainy spell we'd been having, and he turned his head to point out the window. I saw a lump on the back of his neck the size of a Little League baseball. I couldn't believe it! I said, "Butz, what the hell is *that*?"

He felt it and gave me a sheepish look. "*Waalll*," he said—he talks in one of those old German accents—"it's probably just an ingrown *hairrr*."

"Who told you that?"

"The *barr*ber," he said.

I turned his head and looked again. That bulb was huge! I said, "You'd better get your ass to the doctor!" I wasn't letting him off the hook.

I'm glad I didn't. Thirty-nine radiation treatments later, even though Butz had lost his taste buds, the physicians at Barnes Hospital had busted up a malignant tumor. They kept him out of an early grave.

Southern Illinois Germans don't like to make a fuss, and that includes going to the men in the white coats. My dad was like that—never had one checkup in his life. He also died at age forty-eight. Who knows what the hell was wrong with him? They think they're being self-reliant as hell, but if you ask me, it's a form of cowardice. I get checkups once a year no matter what. If something's wrong, man, I want to know about it; I can get it fixed that way. Otherwise, I'll end up like Butz and his pals—relying for everything on a real nice fella with a bottle of Brut and a pair of scissors.

Well, my townsfolk aren't unusual. They don't want to look things in the eye; they're afraid of change. How different are the geniuses running the National Pastime? Ewing Kauffman didn't want my diagnosis, so he tossed me out of his office. Cardinal fans hollered when I came to town and busted up *their* tumor. And what about these owners telling us the game is back now, better than ever? Nineteen ninety-eight did have some home-run fun, but the game still has a lump on its neck. Pretend it's an ingrown follicle, you might as well start measuring for a pine box.

In this chapter, I'll focus on money, the owners' favorite subject. It's gotten so huge in this game that it's damn near out of control, and that's changed the climate of the sport—including how it's played. That's one big problem area. There's others, too. Our rules on the field inhibit certain styles of play that the fans love. That hurts. The game has also lost its fairness, which is like saying they've decided they're going to play hockey on grass. And the Lords still don't understand the game well enough to market it right. All that's got to be addressed. In the next few chapters, I'll lay out a plan of treatment, and if the patient wants to listen, fine. If not, the hell with him!

That pot-bellied porker I gave Butzy grew up to weigh 300 pounds; he ain't eating any more Jiffy Pop. Matter of fact, we moved him out to a farm where he can roam around and eat all the feed he likes. And his pal Butz is doing good. He loves his retirement. He keeps track of everybody in the family and all the local gossip. He tells me who's pitching good in Little League, who's gotten out of the hospital, who's given up golf or needs a visit in the nursing home. I drive over now and then to fix the mower or check on the lawn, but mostly I'll just sit with Butz over a cup of coffee. He always keeps me up-to-date.

I'm gladder than hell he still can. There's never been anybody like him, and once he's gone, there never will be again. I hope my game's smart enough to listen to the doctor, too. Let the barber cut hair.

One of the standards for good home run hitting was always 30 homers a year. If you hit 30, you were a power hitter. You were for real. Nineteen ninety-six was the year that all changed.

It was the year of the big bang. Brady Anderson of Baltimore, who'd never hit 22 in his life, cracked 50. I saw more checked-swing, opposite-field fly balls clear the wall than I ever saw in my most awful nightmare.

More homers were hit than ever before—4,962 altogether—including new seasonal records in each league,
with 2,742 in the AL and 2,220 in the NL. And not five
or ten or fifteen ballplayers, but *forty-two* hit 30 or more
dingers. Last year, in '98, the trend continued. Four guys
had 30 by the All-Star break. Thirty-three ended up with
30 or more by the end of the season. The exclusive club
is handing out memberships on the street.

There's no doubt that's been exciting for a lot of fans.
When Sosa and McGwire were dueling down to the end
in '98, I got a kick out of it, too. But in the middle of
all this hysteria, I can't help asking myself something:
Who in the world is going to *pay* all them home-run
hitters?

Is this all some kind of owners' conspiracy to lure the
fans back? I do know the ball is jacked up. I've given
it my own bounce test, and it comes back up like a super
ball. Who knows where that decision is made? Did some
higher-up order the smaller strike zone, the shorter
power alleys in the new ballparks, and the rag-arm,
Double-A pitchers we're seeing? You can't get three
owners to agree on what drinks to serve at a meeting,
so I doubt it was some kind of plot. But if it had been,
at least I'd know somebody was acting with intent.

The fans high-five each other as the baseballs fly out,
but they forget that everything on the field has its cor-
ollary in money. And in the midst of the uproar, nobody's doing any economic reckoning. They'd better
start quick.

Let's look at the homers first. Thirty doesn't mean a
thing now; feed Humpty Dumpty some creatine and he'll
hit that many. The real problem is, those homers are less
important than they used to be. Add up the number of
runs a team scores in a year; then figure out what percentage of that number the 30 homers accounted for. It's
a lot lower than it was twenty or even ten years back.
The *value* of 30—to winning games, pennants, and baseball fans—has declined. And I mean sharply.

But even though that 30-homer guy is giving you less than he used to, he's still getting paid like he's a superstar. Times have changed, but our economics haven't. We're getting less bang for more bucks. That's called *inflation*, it's rising faster than earned-run averages, and unless somebody finds a way to rein it in, the more the homers fly out, the worse problems we're going to have.

I'll give you an example. In 1996, the Texas Rangers' shortstop was Kevin Elster. When he was with the Mets in the 1980s, Kevin Elster couldn't hit twenty flyballs to the warning track. Suddenly, in '96, he hits 24 over the wall (and throws in 99 RBIs for laughs). Well, give the guy credit: Yeah, the ball's jacked-up, but he still must have had to work hard, gain some bulk, and hone his swing to make that happen. Yet something is out of whack when a guy like Elster wakes up one day as the second coming of Ernie Banks.

Now look what would happen if that took place again. How about Fernando Tatis, the Cardinals' young third baseman? They got him in a trade with Texas in 1998. He hit 8 home runs that year. What if he suddenly pulled an Elster, became an iron-pumping fool, and went deep 30 times in '99?

Now: Would that help the team? The Cards hit more home runs, 210, last year than they ever did in their history. That's double what we used to hit in a good year. Mr. McGwire hit 70 alone. They led the National League in homers and drew 3.2 million fans. Yet they finished third in a weak division, 6½ games out of a wild-card spot, and were out of the race by July. If they don't get depth for their bullpen and stop striking out with people on base, thirty home runs more ain't going to add a thing.

Except payroll. Mr. Tatis is going to look around baseball. He'll see another young third baseman, Scott Rolen of the Phillies, who hit 31 homers in *his* second year. He'll see Rolen's got a $10 million contract over four years. Pretty soon he'll get similar money. Put him alongside Gant, Ray Lankford, McGwire, and (if he's still there) Brian Jordan, all of 'em already in the 25-plus category, and you've got *five* guys with bigtime power numbers. Your team won't climb in the standings, but it will in costs. And they're already at $54 million.

This isn't just an ownership problem. When Drew Baur and Bill DeWitt, the Cards' owners, have to come up with more money than ever just to field their team, you know what's going to happen: Joe Sixpack will be on his feet cheering the latest 500-foot home run, spilling his popcorn and Cokes and beer, and while he isn't paying attention, they'll be reaching into his pockets. Somebody's got to pay for all that excitement.

I used to sit in on owners' conversations when I worked in the front office, and I can tell you exactly how they go. They've noticed the mess they're in. They panic. Somebody says, "We need more revenue." Somebody else says, "Let's raise the price a dollar. They won't care. They won't even notice." I'm ashamed to tell you that people in my profession talk that way all the time.

Well, maybe the fans *don't* notice it right away. But eighty-one home games a year, boy; a dollar for a ticket here, a dollar for parking there, a dollar for a beer, a program, a hot dog—it adds up. Before you know it, you're forking over twenty or thirty dollars a ticket; a dad is paying $150 to take his family to the ballgame. As far as pro sports go, it's still the best deal in town, but old Joe's eventually going to realize he's paying more and more for less and less, and he isn't going to like it. We're going to cross his line.

From everything you read, you'd think we were in the fan-friendliest era of all time. Owners want you to forget the strike. They want your business again. They're giving you bells and whistles and gimmicks. You've got interleague play, you've got wild-card playoff teams, you've got realigned divisions. You're sitting in friendlier ballparks that have real grass. You've got the DH. You've got it all.

But there's one thing you're *not* getting: good old-fashioned fiscal responsibility. Think about it. Do we *want* this many moonshots? What's the price tag? Is it worth it? If not, do we go back? Do we do it by raising the mound, using a deader ball, staying on the umps till they call the strike zone again? These things factor in, but there's *no plan*. It's just like a McGwire home run: Swing hard, make a *crack*. Who knows where it's going to come down?

Let's try *this* gimmick: using our brains. Let's bring baseball's costs and values into the line. Let's think through what kind of game we want. Let's not be secretive, stupid or willy-nilly about it. God almighty, we've tried everything else.

The fans are paying enough as it is. Let's give them something in return. Wouldn't *that* shock everybody?

I go back to the days of traveling by train. My first years as a player, we only went as far west as the Mississippi, so it made sense to ride the rails. We'd play double-headers on Sunday, get Monday off, and hop the Super Chief to the next town. In the coaches and the sleepers, we'd deal cards for six, seven hours on end. We'd bullshit, tell stories, ride till two or three o'clock in the morning. It gave us a feel for each other as teammates, and it was a great chance to pass along what we knew about the other pitchers, the other hitters, about the game.

Well, by 1957, we were hopping on planes for two road trips a year. The year after that, all our travel was by air. We all took United charters then. You'd get on board; two hours later, you were looking out a hotel window. Talk about speeding things up! That changed the whole way of baseball.

Travel was only part of it. It's tough to get across today just how incredibly chintzy the owners were, how bad and brutal and unfair to the players they were. If you wanted a ball to autograph, they took it out of your pay. If you ate on the plane, they took it out of your meal money. If you wanted to leave six passes at the window, you'd better prove to them that four were for members of your family; if not, you paid for those, too. Hell, I remember Opening Day in Washington in 1956, when Calvin Griffith, the owner, charged our *wives* to get into the ballpark. When I got claimed on waivers by the A's, I was supposed to get rail fare and $300 to move my family from Washington, D.C., to Kansas City. I got the cash, but I'm still waiting for the rail transportation. What could I do? The union wasn't strong enough then.

Fast-forward about forty years. The 1998 Baltimore Orioles, who finished 35 games behind the Yankees, 13 games behind the wild-card team, and 4 games below .500, had a payroll of $75 million. Half the clubs had payrolls of $50 million or more. Now throw in the luxury tax the owners stuck up their own butts in the new labor agreement they signed in '96 and by the year 2001, it's going to cost you $85 or $90 million a year to operate a major-league ballclub. The Calvin Griffiths, God love 'em, are dead and buried, and those old trains ain't running anymore.

What happened in between was baseball history, and I saw it from a ringside seat.

The express train started rolling when Marvin Miller, the first president of the players' union, came along in the seventies. For baseball players it was like the coming of Jesus Christ. Marvin was a smart, smart man; if the owners had had any sense, they'd have made him commissioner. Marvin saw all the legal and financial implications of what the owners were doing. He explained labor rights to the players. He gave them tools to negotiate their fair market value. He knew the laws of supply and demand: He realized if *every* player became a free agent at once, that would flood the market and keep prices down, so he only had a few guys become available each year. That drove salaries sky high. When I saw where he was taking all this, I told everybody who'd listen we would see a $20 million-a-year ballplayer in my lifetime. They laughed themselves Dodger blue, but it doesn't seem so funny anymore.

The first million-dollar ballplayer was my own first baseman, John Mayberry. My GM with the Royals, Joe Burke, knew less baseball than the guys I fished with, but on the financial side, he was savvy. He started the first long-term player contracts. In 1976, he gave Mayberry a five year, $200,000-a-year deal. The genius of it was, John only got half of that each year; the other hundred grand was deferred, interest-free. Well, that made John a rich sonofagun, but it also gave the Royals half a million to invest over the life of that contract. If I'm the Royals, and I put that money in the bank or deposit it in funds, I can make a hell of a lot of that million dollars back. John never saw a dime of the money *his* money was making, but for a while there, he was the richest ever to play baseball.

Then things moved like a bullet train. By the time I took over the Cardinals four years later, baseball had its first million-dollar-*a-year* player, the Pirates' Dave Parker. After we won the World Series in '82, I figured Ozzie's glove was worth that much all by itself, so I gave him $3.1 million over three years. That made him the first million-dollar *infielder* in the history of baseball. My colleagues wanted to fit me with cement spikes, but by the time that contract was up, I wasn't hearing a whimper. We won again with him in '85, and I made him one of three players in the $2 million-a-year club. The others were Mike Schmidt of the Phillies and Gary Carter of the Mets, two other future Hall of Famers. Not bad company for a .243 hitter.

That standard went fast. So-called owner collusion put the brakes on the whole thing for a short time in 1987— thanks to Peter Ueberroth, the commissioner, they finally worked together for a while—but once that all got settled, next thing you know, Kirby Puckett of the Twins became the first $3 million man. Then the Cowboy rode in with his saddlebags full of money and threw $16.5 million at Mark Langston, the Expos' lefty, for a five-year deal. By 1990, boy, if you made $2 million, you weren't a star, you were a peon. In the span of a year, Kirby sank from number one to number fifty-nine.

Crazy as it sounded, it was mostly fine by me. You have to put it in perspective: When Barry Bonds signed for $7 million-plus a year with the Giants in '92 and Junior Griffey got similar money from Seattle, you were talking about guys who help you win titles. Very few players can do that. Besides, baseball was just catching up to the rest of the world. If Oprah can haul in $45 million, Bill Cosby can rake in $90 million, and Michael Jordan can pull down $100 million a year, why shouldn't the top major-league leftfielder get the same? If Roberto Alomar is the best second baseman in the world, why shouldn't he make $6 or $7 million? Who's to gripe at Mike Piazza for turning down an $81 million offer from the Dodgers if he can get more from the Mets or some other team? Not me.

Piazza did end up with the Mets, which surprised me. If I were Mike, I'd have signed with the Rockies. He's got 22 homers in 32 career games at that place! You talk about setting the home-run record and making some money. With his power to all fields, he might have topped McGwire easily at Coors Field. Not only that, he wouldn't have to worry about throwing people out, because nobody steals there. But that $91 million he got from New York? That's the American free market at work. They do call it the National Pastime, don't they?

So it isn't the money I object to. It's that when the stakes get this high, you have to have a plan for managing it. You have to use your brains! Our industry has no means of regulating its costs and doesn't seem interested in learning.

Do you know that when we won the world's championship in 1982, we did it on less than a $10 million payroll? That's less than Albert Belle makes today. It's less than Greg Maddux makes pitching every fifth day. If your payroll isn't at least $45 million today, you have no chance. And even at forty-five, you'd better get lucky with a couple of rookies. And yet the rules we have for our finances haven't changed at all since the day Bruce Sutter closed out the Brewers and won me a World Series.

It's the money driving the train, not us. We'd better get behind the wheel.

I already told you Griffey and Bonds are worth $7 million or more a year. If you didn't know baseball, you might think a guy who's half as good—say a Glenallen Hill or a Charlie Hayes—is worth half as much money. You'd be wrong. Their talents aren't complete; they can't do enough to make a difference in your team's fortunes. You could replace them with a lot of guys from the minors or other ballclubs and not lose anything. In other words, even though they're good athletes compared to the general population, their skills aren't at a premium at the major-league level. Yet we're paying them like they were—$3.5 or $4 million a year. Look at what the Red Sox did last off-season, signing Jose Offerman for four years at $28 million. Drew Baur, the Cardinals' owner, said it best: "They just paid over 6 million dollars a year for a guy who can't catch the ball." It's more bad math! We've let top-end salaries drive the cost of mediocrity through the roof. That's killing baseball.

To stop this from happening, you would have needed leadership with brains, clear thinking, and principles. Yet look at the captains of our industry. Ewing Kauffman had his "philosophy" of building through the farm system, but when he fell into those Marion Labs millions, he didn't want Uncle Sam to get it. Overnight, he turned into the biggest spender of all time. And they're just as greedy and self-centered now. Last year, the

Cardinals wanted J. D. Drew so bad they couldn't see straight; he the number-five pick in the '98 draft, and they gave him $7 million before he ever swung a bat in the pros.

Now, J. D. looks like a hell of a player. He's had success in college, in the minors, and even in his first month in the big leagues, in which he hit four homers and stayed above .300. If that continues, the Cardinals have made a hell of a deal. But that deal wasn't just a signing; it was a precedent. Where we used to pay the number-one pick in the country less than a half million to sign, now the number-one pick, free-agent wise, is getting $10 million. We used to spend a total of $2.5 million to $3 million on scouting and development per year—on player procurement, put it that way—and now we're spending that much or more on just our first two draft picks, guys who have never played a damn inning in the minors! Just because a guy can hit a baseball in college with an aluminum bat doesn't mean he's gonna hit with a wooden bat. Just because a pitcher can throw his so-so curve outside in college and get people out doesn't mean he can do it in the majors; he's going to have to bust the ball inside, bust the bat. We don't know if these guys will be any good, and we're paying them all that money. Very few top draft picks turn out to be as good as Drew, yet from this point on, every number-one pick in creation is going to ask for at least that much. It'll keep going up—more money, less value. Do you think Walt Jocketty and the Cardinal owners gave Thought One to that? That's the way owners have always been.

You could talk about a hundred owners this way, but nobody compares to Jerry Reinsdorf, the White Sox boss. Here's the biggest antilabor hawk of all time, the guy who spent years lecturing Jackie Autry and the other owners on financial restraint. He *wanted* to force a strike and he *wanted* to cancel a World Series, if only just to break the players' backs. He got his way in '94 and put the game on a respirator. Yet the second the thing was settled, who was there backing the Brinks truck up to Albert Belle's house? Reinsdorf gave him so much money it bent the whole salary structure out of whack. He needed a big-name draw. He didn't want his division rivals, the Indians, to keep Belle. He wanted what he wanted, and screw the rest of it.

As a matter of fact, Ebenezer Scrooge got so damned excited he forgot how to count. The top salary at the time, in 1996, was $8 million. Reinsdorf skipped right past nine and ten and went straight to $11 million a year! That was the biggest fast-forward in the history of the salary spiral. The average Joe's eyes might start glazing over once that many zeroes start flying around—you know, "Once you're past $5 million, what's the difference?"—but this is still planet Earth, and three million's three million. It matters a lot.

You can't call it an intelligence problem. Here's the owner who built the Chicago Bulls. That didn't happen by accident. He was also smart enough to keep Michael Jordan in the fold even when Number Twenty-three wanted to quit and play baseball. Instead of fighting him, Reinsdorf *paid* Jordan to hit the diamond. He paid Michael his full basketball salary to play in the White Sox system, which Reinsdorf also owned. Not only did the money roll in during spring training—the $2 million Jordan Baseball Show—but if Jordan ever unretired back into basketball, he'd still be Bulls' property. Three more NBA titles later, Jerry looks like a pretty sharp tack.

Why do those smarts disappear when it comes to baseball? When Jerry got Belle, we know it screwed the game. Was it even good for Jerry Reinsdorf? Does a slugger with personal problems and holes in his game merit that kind of money? You have to get twenty-seven outs a game to win. How's his defense? How's his arm, his running? Off the field, will his PR kick you in the ass? For $55 million over five years, you need to be getting a guy who'll transform your organization. Is

Belle that guy? I can't say, because I haven't seen him play much, but did Jerry take all those factors into account? Does any owner?

As for principles, you can forget it; even when they're forced to be honest, the owners don't know how. In 1987, commissioner Peter Ueberroth—a very accomplished man—ordered the owners to open their books for the good of baseball. We were supposed to see where the game stood financially. Even then, all you got was disinformation. August Busch III, who took over Anheuser-Busch when he kicked Gussie, his own dad, off the corporate board, owned the Cardinals then. He was always claiming the team was the only subsidiary losing money, when I knew damn well we were doing great. As general manager, I knew how much we were paying in salaries, and I saw how big the crowds were every day. Who knows how the figures got juggled? It all depends on how you count.

I'll take it a step further: Not only were the Cards making him money, but they actually turned Anheuser-Busch around. When they first bought the ballclub in 1953, they couldn't sell 25 million cases of beer a year. They never sold 50 million till after I got there. By the time I left, they were selling 90 million a year. So don't tell me they didn't get a lot of great free advertising, with all those neon A-B letters and eagles flying around the stadium. Miller gets the same kick from sponsoring the Brewers today, and Coors does with the Rockies. Baseball teams generate a lot of value you can't put in black and white, and the owners take full advantage.

That problem's worse today. With so many media outlets owning baseball teams, the shell-game accounting is easier than ever. When Fox, a global TV network, owns the Los Angeles Dodgers; when Turner Broadcasting owns the Atlanta Braves; when Disney owns the Angels and the Tribune owns the Cubbies, think about it: On top of the value those clubs already have, now they're *programming*, too. They generate ratings like any good TV show. They make cable deals possible. When they're on the air, they save the owners millions for whatever programming they'd otherwise be subsidizing. That's a lot of value, but don't expect to see it anywhere in black and white.

You can't trust them to be honest. Just think what owners have been telling us for the past ten years. In 1991, the national TV contract with CBS, which was for $1 billion over four years, paid every team $14 to $15 million a year. The top players were making $3 million a year, and the highest payroll, Oakland's, was at $36 million. Fay Vincent, the commissioner, went on TV and announced that twenty-two of the twenty-six big-league ballclubs were still losing money. And today, with a smaller national TV contract ($975 million for five years) that only pays each club $12 million a year, the best players are making three times as much as they were; average payrolls have doubled. The Orioles alone have gone from $15 million to $75 million a year! Yet sensible businesspeople still stand in line to pay $150 million to $300 million for these teams. Think there's anything they ain't telling us?

On the field and off it, trust is the glue of baseball. Yet the players can't trust the owners, the owners don't trust the players, and the owners can't trust each other. And, in the middle of all this mess, now the fans don't trust either one of 'em.

Maybe Marvin Miller was just too damn smart. Maybe everything has just mushroomed too fast. But there's nobody steering this runaway train.

If I woke up one day commissioner of baseball and had to call an owners' meeting, I'd go to the head of the table and say, "All right; we've heard enough about money. Today, we're talking about the game. We ain't mentioning dollars and cents." Boy, you talk about shocking people.

I used to go to owners' meetings for Gussie Busch,

and it's the same today: The only thing they ever talked about was money. *How can we raise more revenue? How can we get more money?* That's why we have an extra tier in the playoffs now; that's why we have inter-league play—more revenue. It's why we have the DH, thirty teams, and everything else we have in the game. More revenue, more revenue! It's junkies panting after crack.

Think about it a minute—and this couldn't be more important. The owners can talk about revenue all they want; they can *make* all the revenue they want. But what you never hear these people say is the most basic fact in baseball today: It makes no sense to discuss revenue, because under the rules we have in place now, any extra revenue you make gets sucked up by players' salaries within two years. That's right: No matter how much money you make, it gets absorbed right back into the players' salaries. It's a simple mathematical equation: The more you make, the more you pay. It's a zero-sum game.

There's plenty of revenue in baseball. We just don't know how to handle it. The system in place right now guarantees the owners can't keep what they get. They're nothing but gerbils on a treadmill.

Well, any rodent is smart enough to get off the wheel and sniff around once in a while. Maybe he can tell that wheel ain't spinning right. Maybe he needs a rest. So he stops. But the owners don't do that. They figure if they're running hard, they're getting somewhere. So they run harder. The wheel spins faster. But the only sensible thing to do is crawl out of the cage and take the whole thing apart. The system has to be changed.

Baseball fans are big on numbers. Sixty-one was huge for almost forty years; 367, 714, 190, and now 70—each one tells a story. Well, here's the most important one you never heard of: 18. That ain't a uniform number or a win total, and you won't find it in the record books. It's an economic percentage. Right now, with the rules we have, that's the percent by which any ballclub's payroll will grow from one year to the next *if you never make a change in your roster.*

That's been the rule of thumb for ten years now: Payroll grows by 18 percent a year. If you're a GM or an owner, keep that figure in mind or you're going to end up in the soup.

There's a few reasons for that figure. Seniority is a big part of salary now: A fourth-year outfielder with a .300 average will make such-and-such; a fifth-year guy gets more. More time in, more money. Players sign more long-term contracts now, so you can get locked into a salary spiral. With union rules, agents, and salary structures the way they are, you can forget about cutting a guy's pay even if he's total horseshit. So that keeps climbing. The single biggest factor in this ever-mushrooming system, though, is a right the owners gave the players in 1973.

Maybe it seemed innocent at the time, like a good bargaining chip to put on the table. But it's backfired so bad, the whole works has gone haywire. It's the biggest single reason for the 18 percent figure, and it's screwing up baseball.

I'm talking about salary arbitration.

Here's how it works. A team and a player are negotiating, and they reach an impasse. Let's say it's two years from now, and Brant Brown, the centerfielder, is still with the Cubbies, and he's talking contract with Ed Lynch, the Chicago GM. They're miles apart: Let's say Brown wants $3 million; Lynch offers $500,000. Well, by the rules the owners agreed to, Brown would be eligible, as a third-year player, to have an arbitration hearing. A third party, usually a judge, is brought in to mediate the situation.

Well, what Judge Jones knows about baseball usually wouldn't fit on a Topps card. Once I was at an arbitration hearing for one of my pitchers. He was a very good middle-relief guy, and the Cardinals had made him a generous offer, but the judge sided with the player. After the hearing was over, His Honor pulled me aside in the hallway. You know what he said? "What's a save?" This was the guy with final say!

But let's get back to Mr. Brown's hearing. He would then submit the figure he wants to get; the Cubs would submit the figure they want to pay. The judge would listen to arguments from both sides. And instead of averaging the two, or finding some middle ground, his or her job is to pick either Brown's figure or the team's. One or the other; that's it. That's the amount Brown would get.

Sounds fair, right? That must be what the owners thought when they granted this right, but it's played out very differently. When you look at the real results we've gotten, you see that arbitration always favors the player, and to a disproportionate extent. It *always* hurts the ballclub. And it's got to be thrown out.

Let me explain why.

In this situation, Brown has nothing to lose. The rules place no limit on what he can ask. He might get a sympathetic arbitrator and get his amount chosen, so what the hell? He might as well go for the moon. Let's say Brant's played his three years, and in that time he's averaged .290, stolen 20 bases a year, and driven in 200 runs. Not bad production. But he's only played three years, so that hurts his value. Half a million, maybe $600,000 sounds good to me. Instead, he might think, "Hey—Ray Lankford hit .288 for the Cardinals and stole 27 bases, and *he* made $5 million. Why not ask for $4.5 million? What the hell, I might get it." So he and his agent might submit that number.

They'd have Lynch over more of a barrel than you realize. There's no limit on how *low* Ed can go, either; that's true. But he's got to be careful. Here's a young, attractive player with promise. Lynch wants to keep him around a while. Maybe he doesn't want to make the kid mad. However, Ed's got a budget he's planning. A sudden jump to a $4.5 million salary for a fourth-year player would be disaster. He *has* to offer a figure he knows the arbitrator won't laugh at. And he doesn't know Judge Jones or what tickles his funny bone. He's got to make sure his offer is seen as reasonable, or he's screwed.

So instead of offering what he believes the player is worth—$600,000 or so—he would have to offer much *more* than that just to stave off the high-end risk. He'd take a deep breath and offer $2 million. *That's* the amount Judge Jones will pick. The ballclub "wins."

The problem is, it really loses. In arbitration, the rule of thumb is simple: *Even when the ballclub wins, it loses.* Price has jumped quicker than value. It's the main reason costs are out of proportion with merit. It's the biggest cause of rocketing salaries and lunatic budgets. It happens because agents know the system. Realizing the ballclub will have to up the stakes, they always go in at least a million dollars high. People don't understand this about baseball today, but it's the prime way in which the agents are running—and ruining—baseball.

Now I was a player, and I was always known as a player's manager. But a "right" that helps individual players and agents so much it cripples the industry— that ain't a right, it's a problem.

Hell, a ballclub's got to stay in operation. When I ran the Cardinals, Mr. Busch gave me a budget in November for the following year. I worked my ass off to stay within it, and I always came within half a million dollars. That's how you run a business, I don't care if it's a bait shop or a baseball team. But how can you stay within your budget when you know that arbitration hearings are going to happen in February, and the $1 million salary you counted on suddenly turns into $4 million? What if you've got three guys like that, and your $38 million budget jumps to $45 million? I'm all for players' rights, but you can't run a business that way; the stakes are high, yet you can't plan! In the end, that money's going to come straight out of the fans' pockets.

Here's something else most people don't realize: Arbitration ain't even good for the players. Sure, it's good in the short term for the Brant Brown who strikes it rich, but for the rank-and-file player, it's a curse. Arbitration leaves the good, veteran bench player—the guy you need to build a good ballclub—out in the cold. Why? Well, let's say you're John Schuerholz, the Braves' GM, and one of your guys—Keith Lockhart, your second baseman—comes up for arbitration. He's valuable to your team, partly because he's a four-year veteran. He's an intelligent, versatile guy; he knows the game, and he doesn't make mistakes. But GMs are wary now; ball clubs realize they can bring along a Triple-A kid to play for the big-league minimum and get a lot of the same things out of him, but not risk getting locked into a $2.5 million commitment to a player who ain't a bona fide star. They might even get lucky and get more.

So what would you do? You don't want to get stuck, so maybe you decide, far in advance, you aren't going to *offer* Keith Lockhart arbitration. Maybe you release him. And he'd sign with another ballclub as a free agent, maybe for $350,000 and change. Who knows? As a veteran, he deserves better than that.

It's an illusion that arbitration "helps the players." It's like a lot of things Donald Fehr, the current union president, and his buddies do now: It only helps a certain *echelon* of players, the stars. The rest of 'em are hung out to dry, and that ain't fair.

Arbitration is very, very harmful to the game of baseball, and we'll never get anywhere solving our problems till we get rid of it. The problem is, the union is so strong now that the game can't just eliminate it. You've got to make a swap: *Hey, boys, we'll give you this right if you give up that one.* It's all you can do! The day's not too far off when a couple of teams will go belly up—the Twins and the Royals get my vote—and that's going to cost the union fifty major-league jobs. The players will listen then. But till that happens, they've got the hammer, so if you want to help the game right now, you've got to be ready to deal. And you've got to make it sweet.

Bobby Costas told me a story not too long ago. Bob's a bright guy with as many good ideas as anybody I've met, which is why I always thought he'd make a good commissioner. Still do. He came up with a perfect example. He pulled Marvin Miller aside fifteen years ago and said, "Marvin, the players have always told us, 'We just want what every other worker wants: freedom to see what the market is.' So what would happen if the owners called your bluff? What if they offered you increased free agency—say, free agency after four years instead of after six—in return for the end of arbitration? They'd be offering you more freedom, which is what you say you want." Marvin had a lot of power, of course—him against the owners was like Joe Louis boxing Elmer Fudd—but he looked at Bob and said, "That would've been tough to turn down. It would've been consistent with what the players were asking for."

Or you could try what I call Arbitration II. If you're a player, the first time you apply for arbitration, you could get a 200 percent raise, tops; the second time, you'd get 100 percent, the third time, 50 percent. Put a ceiling on it! That way, if a three-year player filed who was making $200,000, the most he could make the next year would be $600,000. The next time, it'd be $1.2 million. The time after that, $1.5 million. So in the "walk" year of his contract, you'd be negotiating with him from a base of $1.5 million, not the $3 or $4 million you are today. You couldn't force that setup on the players, but you might be able to trade something for it— like doing something similar to what Bobby suggests, giving free agency after four years instead of six—in the next labor agreement in 2001.

You can work out the details however you like. I can't tell you if this plan would be perfect. But there are things you can do if you give it some thought. There are ways you can get that 18 percent problem under control if you try. Problem is, nobody's seeing the big picture. Nobody's even looking at it.

Come to think of it, the owners would have to get smart, learn the game, and show a little bit of foresight to do that. That's like asking Willie McGee to lay off that curveball in the dirt. I guess stranger things have happened.

When I was talking with John Harrington, the Red Sox owner, about taking the Boston managing job, the strike was still on. After damn near eight months of that, John was squirming in his seat, boy. He was feeling the heat. I remember him saying, "Whitey, we want to bring this to an end." I asked him why. "The media are really making us look bad," he said. "We're taking a hit in the press!"

Well, if *that* didn't belong in the "no-shit" category. When they decided to shut down baseball and cancel the World Series for the first time in ninety years, did they think they were going to be media darlings? Hadn't they been reading the papers for the last eight months? After all that criticism, why should they care? I said, "John, why do you give a damn? After all this mess, you ain't giving in over that, are you?"

Three weeks didn't go by before the work stoppage ended. The main force behind it was U.S. District Judge Sonia Sotomayor's ruling in a New York court. She thought the owners had engaged in unfair labor practice, and she ordered reinstatement of the main provisions of the old collective bargaining agreement. Well, the owners had nearly burned the whole thing to the ground, they'd suffered $800 million in operating losses over three years, and they'd done it because they saw the system we had in place wasn't working. If things were so bad they had to do all that, they should have stuck it out. They could have appealed. They could have kept bargaining, forced a lockout, used replacement players, shut the whole thing down. They'd made an opportunity. Let the players try and play without any teams, boy!

But the owners lose time and again because they don't stick together; they don't agree on anything as a group. Not only did they cave, they agreed to the same damn conditions they said made baseball unworkable in the first place. Back to arbitration for five years. Back to 18 percent. Back to the old, bad math. Back on the treadmill, fellas. Here they'd finally gone to the wall to make a stand, and part of the reason they surrendered was they couldn't stand the bad press! I never saw such a goddamn waste in my life.

Even the "concessions" they got were a joke. For one thing, they agreed to minimal revenue sharing in the form of a luxury tax. Any team with a payroll higher than $51 million would take 9 percent of the whole payroll and kick it into a common fund for the have-not teams. *That* was a hell of an idea. By 2001, when the agreement expires, *three-fourths* of the teams will exceed $51 million. That isn't a luxury tax; it's a tax on the masses! Never mind that the owners could have come up with that plan on their own in a meeting and never dragged the players into it at all! In other words, for what they got, *there never had to be a strike at all*.

Well, to put it in Butzy terms, the owners saw the lump on their neck, went to the doctor, and got the full workup, all the tests. They set up the surgery appointment and paid the bill. And when it came time for the operation, they had something else to do. Now they're walking around with a shit-eating grin telling everybody they're fine. It ain't a question of if; when's the cancer going to spread?

I'd rather think of it like managing. It's late in the game. You're on the road, ahead by a run. Your pitcher's getting gassed. He walks the leadoff batter. He walks the second guy. The crowd's on its feet. They're roaring so loud you can hardly hear yourself think. The heart of the order is coming up.

That doesn't bother the owners. They think they've got the game won. They don't even have anybody warming up in the pen.

· 14 ·
The Great Divide

Sometimes the damnedest guy can make a good scout.

When I took over the Angels, I already knew world-wide player acquisition was the wave of the future. It was obvious the United States had run out of talent to stock the twenty-six major-league rosters, and with expansion sure to come, the problem was only going to get worse. I sat down with Jackie Autry one day and talked her into setting money aside for a scouting operation in Central America, especially in the Dominican Republic. That's the only place in the world where kids still play ball the way we did when I was growing up—six, seven hours a day, all over the country, and with the joy of fellas who can't think of a thing in the world they'd rather be doing.

I knew the ballclub that tapped that pipeline was going to get ahead. We even got a nice little ballpark built there—Gene Autry Stadium—for the purpose. And as soon as I could, I got my favorite Dominican on the phone: the good old Goombah himself, Joaquin Andujar. He hadn't pitched in about three years by then, but I knew he lived in a beautiful house he'd built down there in Santo Domingo, and that he'd been giving money out the blowhole to youth baseball in the area. I thought he might want to get back into the action. So I said, "Hey, Joaquin! Get out of the city for a while. Leave Santo Domingo and Maracaibo to the other ballclubs. How'd you like to go up in the hills and the jungles and find me some ballplayers?" He just laughed and said those two favorite words he always said: "Okay, Whitey!" We had ourselves a scout.

I'll never forget the time I flew down there to see what he had come up with. He did his job, all right. He drove me to a ballfield not far from his house, and he'd lined up a bunch of kids, mostly teenagers, for a workout. A lot were skinny and wiry, hopping around barefoot or in sneakers, sharing gloves because they didn't have one of their own. But I watched those kids throw and take some cuts at the plate, and I'm telling you, he'd found himself some ballplayers. Some of 'em weren't even fifteen yet, and most had no polish at all, but that bunch had more tools than a True Value store. Every last one of them was an athlete.

Joaquin always loved giving Whitey a hand. He was busting his buttons like a proud daddy. And the only real way he'd ever had to get himself across was by pitching, so I wasn't surprised to see old Goombah drift out to the rubber himself before too long. First he starts tossing to get warm. Then he decides to throw BP. Before you can say Felipe Alou, he's buzzing it around the plate. Half these kids ain't ever swung with anything but a stalk of sugar cane, and suddenly here they are looking out at an ex-big leaguer with a 90-mph fastball, a bug-eyed grin, and foam flying out of his mouth. Joaquin Andujar is the only scout in history to strike out every one of his own prospects.

By five o'clock, they were all dragging their asses. I had no idea if they could hit or not! I was laughing. And Goombah figured he'd had himself a hell of a day. He just handed me the ball, smiled, and said, "Still got my good stuff, Whitey!"

Well, whatever I thought of Joaquin as a scout, there's one main reason we couldn't have kept him: The Angels didn't have the money. Even the younger prospects were signing for half million-dollar bonuses by that time, and we weren't any superstation juggernaut. We weren't even a medium-budget deal. Not too long after that, Jackie chopped worldwide scouting from the Angel budget like palm trees from a rain forest, and we left that zone of the tropics for the big-market Dodgers, Blue Jays, Yankees, and Braves to slice up. They're still plundering down there, and half the teams in the big leagues can't afford to do the same. The Pittsburghs, Kansas Citys, and Minnesotas are left on the sidelines.

This is one of the most important trends in baseball, though once again, I never see it written about. You haven't seen the full effects of it yet—it hasn't been happening long enough—but you will before too long. Worldwide scouting is only one aspect of the great divide that ruins baseball today. And something's got to be done.

You can't separate any of baseball's problems from the others. Disparity is a huge one, maybe the biggest, but it's got a lot of causes. You can't talk about it without branching into other issues. If we look at a few, they'll come back together in the end. Just the way baseball might, if we ever used our brains.

In spite of all the bullshit flying around my profession, I think every reasonable person would agree that two things are important in a healthy baseball industry. First, the teams should be competitive with each other. After all, good games are what we sell. And second, baseball should be about who plays the best, not who's got the most money. There will always be areas of life that tell us the rich are the best. Who needs another one? The Pastime, like the country, is supposed to be about who does things right.

I'm not one of those old-timers who sits in his rocking chair moaning that everything was better in the old days. First, you couldn't get me in a rocker if you held a gun to my head, but second, in a lot of ways, it didn't used to be better. The fact is, though, we've crossed into an area where there's a rich and a poor in baseball, where the rich teams live in a palace and the poor ones are confined to the slums. Under the current rules, the rich will keep winning and getting fatter if they have any brains at all, and the have-nots will have even less and less hope. Let me ask you something: If you were a Kansas City Royals fan, and you knew your team had no chance of winning, would you go to the ballgame? Baseball has gotten like some crazy banana republic, where if you're born in the wrong class, you're screwed no matter what you do.

Four main factors, all of them new to baseball in the past twenty-five years, keep the tyranny of the rich people in place. The first is a changed TV landscape. The second is the system we have for player procurement. The last two are a changed agenda in the players' union and the rule differences between the American and National leagues.

As the new millennium gets closer, many of my game's most fundamental issues are still up in the air. Interleague play, the designated-hitter problem, union issues, a labor agreement that expires in 2001, and styles of play on the field all are parts of the bigger picture. Pull them apart, juggle 'em a little bit, and put 'em back together again in a new and different way, and you have a chance to handle some of the worst problems—including the most dangerous one, the gap between the big-fish teams and the little minnows that makes the game so unfair that it's hard for a lot of good fans to watch.

1. TELEVISION

TV is more than just a medium that transmits games into the living rooms of couch potatoes everywhere. Television means money, money means power, and power has a direct effect on how well the different teams can compete on the field. And the TV situation is a whole different ballgame now than it was just 10 years back. The explosion of TV money in some places has shifted the competitive balance too much. Regulate the flow of that money even a little, and you'll stabilize competition. That's another way of saying you'll improve our product.

Unlike other sports, baseball's appeal isn't national; it's mainly regional. In football you've got fans from California to Maine who'll sit with their beer and their bowl of Cheetos and watch any NFL teams—the Bengals, the Giants, the Jaguars—slug it out for three hours. In baseball, there's always been more of a local flavor, and that's one of the strengths we can build on. There's something about the proximity of Chicago and St. Louis that makes Cub-Cardinal games special—and that was true long before McGwire and Sosa ever came to the Midwest. East Coast fans think the game begins and ends with their Yankees, Mets, and Red Sox. But this also means those fans aren't going to spend three hours watching the Mariners play Texas too often.

The reasons for that aren't easy to explain, but one thing it means is you're never going to get the kind of big-dollar, national network TV contract that the NFL or the NBA get. You're not even going to get the kind of contract baseball had with NBC back in the eighties, when Bob Costas and Tony Kubek broadcast the *Saturday Game of the Week* across the country. With ESPN and the different superstations going full tilt all the time, there's ballgames on the air from all corners all season long, so even the national games you do get don't have that exclusive feel about them anymore. No, times have changed. Most of the TV money you're going to get for baseball is going to come from local contracts—the ones ballclubs set up with the local cable and broadcast companies.

Problem is, those contracts vary tremendously in size from one city to the next. The most important factor in determining TV revenue is the size of the market: The bigger the region, the more TV money you tend to haul in. At the highest end, you've got Steinbrenner's New York Yankees, who have their $486 million, twelve-year cable TV deal with Cablevision Systems Corporation, which owns the Madison Square Garden network. That puts more than $40 million a year in the Yankees' coffers, which is bigger than the payrolls of about half of the teams in the major leagues. Last year alone, that money accounted for a third of the team's total revenues—$12 million more than George made selling tickets to Yankee Stadium. That contract is coming to an end in 2000, and by that time, George will be raking in $55 million a year on it. I don't think I have to explain all the competitive advantages that gives Steinbrenner, and he's using them to the hilt.

He's not the only one. Baseball's long history of rich, greedy, selfish owners used to getting their way is alive and well. Right now, Steinbrenner, the Rockies' Jerry McMorris, the Diamondbacks' Jerry Colangelo, and Peter Angelos of the Orioles, among other people, are doing just fine, thanks, and in their view, baseball teams are independent companies, each one operating by its own rules and not beholden to anybody. That way, every owner is free to get as fat as he wants on TV revenue—as well as whatever gate receipts he can drum up in his own ballyard—and the hell with everybody else. I still don't know why San Diego and the Giants voted to allow Rupert Murdoch and Fox to buy the Dodgers for $311 million: He's got a global TV network, and he's not going to stop spending on that team till he's got a $100 million payroll and he's buried everybody else. Then you've got Ted Turner's Atlanta Braves, who are nothing more than one of the many programming alternatives—right alongside *Andy of Mayberry* and those Burt Reynolds shoot-'em-ups—on his wealthy, worldwide Superstation. The Cubs have their Tribune and WTBS superstation money. And so on.

At the other extreme, you've got the Padres and the Royals, who don't even have a cable TV deal. The last

I heard, the Royals were getting less than $3 million a year in TV revenue. Milwaukee and Montreal are in the same kind of fix, each of them pulling in less than $8 million a year. As recently as 1994, the Rockies—who do a hell of a gate anyway—made only $3 million in television money, or about what one starting ballplayer earns per year. Those bigger clubs have the Al Davis, Oakland Raider mentality that says, "Hey, we're free agents," and you can't blame 'em. The problem is, if these so-called independent companies don't have other independent companies to play against, they haven't got a product. What we really sell isn't Dodger Blue or the Yankee pinstripes or the Minnesota Twins, but the competition between them. The more one-sided that competition gets, the worse our product is. And in the end, if there aren't any Kansas City Royals to stomp on, how are you going to make money stomping them?

Maybe the worst part of all this, and what we have to guard against, is that these factors give some teams a big advantage—in scouting, in signing players, in hiring talent—that does not derive from baseball. Geographic and economic coincidence should have nothing to do with deciding champions on the field. It should be about who plays the best, who has the most savvy. But today, those coincidences are bigger factors than ever. Everybody says 1998 was the greatest year ever in baseball, but how good was it in Minnesota, in Kansas City, and in Pittsburgh, where it didn't matter how well their players played? Those fans have less hope than they ever did, and that makes the last few seasons some of the worst.

When Duke Snider or Willie McGee went back for a flyball, or Juan Marichal or Jesse Orosco bore down on a hitter, there was suspense. The fans cared about what happened. The more they realize money has taken precedence over how the players perform, the less they're going to give a damn what happens on the field. Baseball has to find a way to close the gap in TV money.

2. FOREIGN-BORN TALENT

The Joaquin story tells you about another important trend. It has to do with how teams procure foreign-born talent, and it gives the money-bags teams a great place to spend all that extra cash they have in the vault.

Baseball has expanded way too fast for the good of competition. When I was managing, you really never had a starting pitcher whose ERA was still higher than 5.00 after the first of September. Look at the papers now: You have whole pitching staffs higher than that. Two or three guys in every rotation are above 6.00! I hear people ask, "God almighty, where's the pitching today?" There's a simple answer: There ain't any, at least not in this country. Many factors have caused this problem, and other problems, on the field, but the most important is supply and demand: There are fewer kids playing baseball in the United States today. It's too expensive for too many school districts; a lot of fans and parents and potential players think the games take too long; there are too many competing activities now. To compound that problem, there are more teams than ever at the big-league level, way too many for us to fill. This ain't calculus. We don't have the talent in the United States to stock thirty big-league teams.

That means if a ballclub wants to improve, it has to look someplace else: It's why worldwide scouting is so critical now. Go down to the Dominican Republic now. That's the number-one place for baseball. Check out the fifteen-, sixteen-, seventeen-year-old leagues; you see arms the way you used to see them here in the 1940s. Everybody's firing the ball; everybody can throw.

That's the way it's getting to be in Australia, which has become quite a hotbed for baseball. All our clubs have contacts there now. They don't have professional leagues Down Under, just amateur leagues. They have a whole lot of older guys playing with the younger ones there—twenty-seven-, twenty-eight-year-olds that nobody'll touch—but now they're getting more eighteen-year-olds coming along, and they're pretty good players. It's about the quality of the high school leagues here. Our teams all know who the blue-chip prospects are.

Baseball is new in Korea, but the players are enthusiastic. They'll come up with some pitchers; they're getting bigger and stronger. In Japan, the pitching is outstanding. The average pitcher there is better than our average big-league pitcher now. The problem is, it's so regimented over there, the players don't seem to have much fun. It's like a job to them. And for a long time, their players wouldn't come over here because they all get lifetime jobs after they retire with whatever company owns the team. A Hideo Nomo gives that up when he comes over here—but he makes so much money in the big leagues today, what difference does it make?

Cuba's always been a power, and it's starting to open up. With all these sources becoming available, if a big-league ballclub wants to stay in the hunt for championships, it's got to find a way to tap those markets. It's that simple.

As usual in baseball, the big trend is already in place before there's any system to deal with it. We're behind the curve. Our main problem is with our free-agent draft. Baseball instituted the draft in 1965 to give everybody a fair chance in the player-procurement area. But baseball never anticipated this worldwide talent hunt. The rules say that the free-agent draft can only govern American-born and Canadian-born ballplayers; all the rest are, in effect, unrestricted free agents, available to the highest bidder. Anybody with enough yen, rubles, or pesos can sign them players. Obviously, that means wealthy ballclubs like the Yankees and the Dodgers can swoop in with planes full of cash and head back home with even more good talent for their rosters. The small fish, the Minnesotas and Pittsburghs, get left out in the cold. And once again, we get closer and closer to a day where money, not performance on the field or judgment in the front office, is the determining factor in our competition. It's even more of a cash-for-championships deal.

I've said before, you haven't even seen the ballplayers George Steinbrenner's got locked up right now; they're in the pipeline, and in five or six years, his lineup's going to look like a Hall of Fame version of the United Nations. Look at what happened with Orlando "El Duque" Hernandez, the great Cuban pitcher who climbed on a rickety boat and sailed for the United States. He didn't seek asylum in America, since that would have placed him under the rules of the draft; instead, his agent rushed him off to Costa Rica, and Steinbrenner swooped in and snapped him up, handed him the ball, and made him part of the best starting rotation in the American League. The year before, when the Marlins were still spending money, they did the same damn thing with his brother, Livan Hernandez, who ended up MVP of the World Series. These guys are already helping to decide championships, and in a few years, that's going to be even more of a trend. How can a team like the Cincinnati Reds or the Milwaukee Brewers compete with that?

The only have-not team that's defied this trend has been the Montreal Expos. Their manager, Felipe Alou, has outstanding personal contacts down in the Dominican, and that does counteract the fact that they can't go down there and hand over million-dollar bonuses to sixteen-year-olds. There's a lot of loyalty to Alou, and that's helped Montreal. But that ain't going to last long, and even if it did, the Expos aren't going to have the money to keep those players around for more than a couple of years. They're going to lose 'em to the Dodgers and the Orioles and the Indians and have to start from scratch.

Without any official restrictions in place, the big-dollar clubs can drop those big bonuses on as many players as they want to. You think Rupert Murdoch or Ted Turner is going to feel that? They don't give a damn. And in the meantime, they leave nothing behind for the smaller clubs. The balance of power swings further and further away from the ballclubs in the lesser markets.

3. CHANGES IN THE UNION

Personally, I can't complain about the players' association and what it's accomplished. The work Marvin Miller and his followers did has brought me and my family the kind of prosperity I could never have imagined when I first started traveling the country in a baseball uniform. I didn't just stay around and scrape by like a lot of good ballplayers used to do; I ended up well-to-do and now have the pension of a retired CEO. There's no doubt it was fair for the union to make it economically feasible for professional ballplayers to play the game, stay in it, and make it a livelihood.

But there comes a point where a union can get too strong for its own good and for the industry's. Today, the union delves into areas it doesn't even belong in. That's distorted things in the wrong direction; it upsets the balance we need. And worse than that, Donald Fehr, the union president, and his boys have gotten so drunk with the high-end money in baseball, they've forgotten the union's original mission, which was to serve the rank-and-file guy. The money the big stars get is so huge now, the union has turned into a tool for big-time agents like Dennis (Go-Go) Gilbert and Scott Boras, guys who have a lot invested in getting the highest salaries they can for a handful of guys, never mind the rest of them. The union ought to be stabilizing the industry for the good of all players, but it spins salaries out of control and widens the have/have-not gap by spending its time on the high-end guys.

First of all, I don't see why the union should have anything to say about player procurement. How the owners acquire their players in the first place and negotiate with them isn't the union's business; their job is to protect the interests of players who are already pros, who are already union members. Fehr and his federation don't see it like that. Fehr works too closely with the agents, who spend half their time pumping up contracts for amateurs like J. D. Drew and Travis Lee. Drew, who was a college star at Florida State, ended up with $7 million in guaranteed money before he ever stepped in a professional batter's box. Lee got even more than that from the Arizona Diamondbacks. That doesn't help the union's interests or the game; it undercuts both.

Why? Well, never mind the fact that college success in baseball doesn't predict big-league success; the skill levels are too diverse, the bats are made of different materials, and many an aspiring big-leaguer will never develop the techniques he's going to need till some point later in his life. And those guys aren't even union members yet! This kind of signing also screws up a salary structure that's already so far out of whack it's harmful to baseball. But most important, having the clubs pay a rookie that kind of money undermines something the union fought for years to establish: the connection between seniority and pay. Mark McGwire and other pros got snippy with Drew and his agent, Mr. Boras, because they were making demands that mocked the years veterans have put in. But Fehr and the agents don't care about that. The whole deal makes the Pastime even more of a money game.

Fehr really does only work for the superstars now. He supports salary arbitration, which favors the top-end player and screws the run-of-the-mill veteran. Well, when Fehr gets hot and bothered on behalf of untested guys like Drew and Lee, it's obvious the people he sees as his other real clients are the agents. Who else benefits?

It sure as hell ain't the Minnesota Twins of the world, who drafted Lee first in 1996 but lost him in a bureaucratic screwup. When they failed to tender him an offer within a certain time limit, they lost him; hell, I can't explain why they didn't send him a ten-dollar contract just to meet the requirement: "Here, Travis; here's an offer." But they couldn't have met his and Boras's demands anyway. It certainly ain't the Phillies, who had to watch while Drew sat out a whole year asking for more money than they could afford to pay him. It sure ain't baseball, which saw those two go to a couple of pretty well-heeled teams, as usual, not to struggling teams that need all the young talent they can get. But two more moneymen rang the big cash register. They ought to rewrite that song: It's root, root, root for the agents.

Agents have no incentive to help the sport; their interest is in taking as much from it as possible. I've already told you how their ignorance stresses a lot of meaningless statistics that hurt the way the game is played. They also practice a form of collusion that's far worse than anything the owners ever got caught doing. It isn't collusion in black and white, and you'll never see them paying a $280 million fine for it like the owners had to, but it's collusion nevertheless, and it does more than anything else to ruin the industry.

I've been watching the process for years, and here's how I think it works: The agents somehow agree on who the number-one available free agent is going to be. Usually it's not a tough call: If a Jose Canseco–, Roger Clemens–, Barry Bonds–type superstar happens to be available that offseason, he's the guy. Now, until that number–one player signs his contract, no agent will negotiate with any general manager in relation to any other, lesser player. They won't even talk to you; they won't tell you what they want. Let's say I'm running the Angels; and say Tim Salmon has just hit 50 homers for me, and he's the top free agent out there. And let's say I'm also trying to sign Garret Anderson, who's just hit 25 home runs. Well, Anderson's agent will not even get into a conversation with me about Anderson until Salmon has signed his contract. That's because he would want to use Salmon's new salary—say it's $48 million over six years—as his base. He's going to work off that.

All this has nothing to do with baseball, with baseball value or achievement, yet it's driving up prices. It's every bit as unfair as the so-called owner collusion of '87, when they decided amongst themselves not to bid on free agents. It's ruining baseball, and there's very little you can do to stop it.

Agents are really a rogue element in baseball, and they seem capable of hook-sliding around any kind of regulation. One area like this is the way they hook up with college stars now. The NCAA explicitly prohibits any college player from signing with an agent. That makes the player a pro—and therefore ineligible. But a lot of the agents don't back off. Instead, they call themselves "financial advisors," worm themselves in with the player's family, sign up with them in that capacity, and go about their business. When the player signs, the "financial advisor" is in on the ground floor, and he gets rich.

They even manage to work some of the game's institutions for personal gain. Take the free-agent draft. It was instituted in the sixties to promote parity, giving the weaker teams top crack at the best talent and so on. That worked a lot better when there were fewer teams; with thirty, nobody gets enough selections to make much of a difference. So big damn deal. But the draft accomplishes one thing today: It puts money in the agents' pockets. The scouts out there create numerical rankings for all the prospects: This guys the number-one guy, that guy's number five, the other guy's number fifteen and so on. Well, those numbers become a yardstick. They help the big-time agents put price tags on these unproven guys, and it leverages their salaries even higher. In other words, when scouts turn in their reports now, they're scouting for the agents.

I don't know if you could get rid of the draft now, but if you could, it would be good for baseball. It isn't accomplishing what it was designed to do, and they've already exploited this system to jack the No. 1 guy's bonus up to a ridiculous, and dangerous, level. Soon the top guy's going to be asking for $15 and $20 million, and we're going to be stuck with that and never be able to look back. Baseball needs to recognize that trend and put a stop to it, or the spiral's going to keep climbing, widening the gap between rich and poor.

4. GETTING THE RULES THE SAME

The American League adopted the DH rule in 1973 as a one-year experiment. In the National, the pitcher still bats. This difference makes competition between the two leagues a farce, including the World Series, but it also has labor and management repercussions. As long as the rules are different, so are the teams' roster needs. That affects the number of available jobs; that affects players' livelihoods. It also screws up any real chance we have to take baseball apart and put it back together again in a sensible, systematic way.

I could go on for pages about how that works, but here's one important fact: The current roster size for a big-league team is twenty-five. That means twenty-five jobs per team and 750 jobs in the big leagues, so those become important numbers to the union. They're also important to managers: They need to have the resources to make good moves. But I've managed and won in both the American League and the National League, and I can tell you right now that when the designated hitter is used, I do not need a twenty-five-man roster. I don't have to pinch-hit for my pitcher in the fifth inning when I'm behind, so I don't need a tenth pitcher. With the DH, I just don't need those extra people to pinch-hit and fill in, because I just don't have to make those moves in a ballgame. I don't need a third catcher, I don't need a sixth outfielder, I don't need a fifth infielder. I can manage a ballclub with twenty-three guys and not have a problem.

Now, keep that in mind. It's going to give us leverage and some options when we want to reassemble the pieces in a way that's good for the game. Some of those changes will equalize competition, reduce the cash-for-championships problem, and return good thinking, good scouting, and good planning to the National Pastime.

To be honest with you, I don't think we've ever had a time in baseball where all the teams were in perfect balance. When I was playing, you even had one big-league club (the Kansas City A's) that was basically a farm team for another big-league club (Casey's Yankees); a guy would come up through the A's system, develop into a big leaguer, and the New Yorkers would send Kansas City a wad of bills and snap him up. I was on that shuttle myself, even if it was in the wrong direction.

But it was simpler times then: Baseball was able to straighten all that out. New York was too good, so the game took measures to break up that team and the stranglehold it had on talent. One way they did it could teach us a lot today. I'm talking about bonus rules.

Bonus rules were simple and made a hell of a lot of sense. In a nutshell, they said that if a team spent more than x number of dollars to sign a ballplayer, that player was required to stay on the club's major-league roster for two years. When the rule started, that figure was $25,000; if you gave a guy more than a twenty-five grand bonus, and you didn't put him on your twenty-five-man roster the following year, or if you tried to send him out later, he automatically went on waivers. The worst team got first crack at him, and that worked its way up to the best team. Anybody who wanted to could claim him for the $25,000.

So in other words, if I was George Weiss, the Yankee GM at the time, and I found a good prospect, and I handed him a $40,000 bonus, I'd better be damn serious about it. I couldn't just bury him in Kansas City, the way the Yankees did with Moose Skowron, and control his contract for years on end. No, he was going to be a

Yankee, for better or worse, batting and fielding and drawing a Yankee salary.

Now, what are the effects of that? The rule didn't limit the number of bonus boys I could sign; I could go out and get ten if I wanted. I could get fifteen. But if I did, I had to pay the price. If I'm trying to win a pennant, I only want to carry so many raw youngsters on the roster, or I ain't going to stay in the hunt for long. I want veterans, proven guys out there. The better a chance I had, the fewer of these guys I'd want to carry on the big roster. So it was self-regulating. I'd be careful just to sign one or two, and that would leave more young talent available for the lesser ballclubs. It worked great.

There's a few reasons bonus rules would serve us great right now. Let's say you're Kevin McClatchy, and you've just bought the Pittsburgh Pirates, and you want to keep them in town. Well, you know from the beginning you're not going to get the same kind of revenue as George Steinbrenner, or as the owners of the Mets or the Dodgers. That's the way it is in baseball, and you aren't going to change it, so once you're in, don't start crying about it. People don't understand: It's pointless to try to keep the rich guys from having more money than you. They're going to have it, and that's it. So don't whine. And it ain't going to help you to try to fool the fans with gimmicks, either. That'll only get you so far.

But there is something you *can* do: You can go about it in reverse. You can't keep the rich guys from having money, but you can find ways to keep them from *spending* it. That's the only way to do it. And the best way I can think of is to go back to some form of bonus rules.

Obviously, you'd adjust the figures to suit modern economics. You'd make it $450,000 now, or half a million: Give a guy over 500 grand, you have to keep him on your major-league roster for two years. And you pay him the whole thing the first year, too. Don't let the teams string it out like they do in football, slipping some of it to the family or stacking the back end. If you went in this direction, there wouldn't *be* a number-one draftee, a number-ten draftee, or a number-thirty draftee. The agents would finally have to figure out on their own what each player is really worth. We wouldn't be doing their scouting for them the way we are now.

The system still gives the Steinbrenners an edge. He can give his prospect $2 million if he wants; he can give him $5 million or $10 million or a share in the World Trade Center. You'll still be able to outbid other teams for the top guys. But if you're after a pennant, you aren't going to want to carry more than a couple of those guys. That creates a natural ceiling. The way things are now, Ted Turner or Steinbrenner or Murdoch can go to Latin America and sign every damn ballplayer he finds, but with bonus rules, there will be players left over for the lesser clubs. Instead of Steinbrenner getting ten prospects and the Twins none, both teams might get two. That's fair! You'd level the playing field, and it wouldn't cost you a thing.

When I say owners never discuss the game itself anymore, this is the kind of idea I'm talking about: not a way of scoring fast cash, but something that can substantially help the game. It really isn't that hard if you give it some thought. That's what I've done. Other baseball people—like my former bosses, Hank Peters and Bing Devine—do the same thing. These guys have the knowhow and the savvy to understand what's worked in the past and how to adapt it to the present. But has anybody asked 'em? Not to my knowledge.

Bonus rules are the best solution to the biggest problem in baseball, yet nobody writes about it; I've never heard it mentioned. Nobody's talking about the real issues. It's crazy.

So is the way baseball divvies up its TV money. You can always learn from other sports, and football has shown one thing: Total revenue sharing is a lousy idea. Totally collective economics don't work in sports. In the NFL, you have owners guaranteed huge revenue even if their teams never throw a pass. Our ex-St. Louis owner has been so mediocre for so long, it almost seems he wants it that way. The NFL rewards people for being lazy and stupid. So that's out.

But God almighty, it can go too far the other way. You can't have one team raking in $55 million and another getting nothing! Baseball's going right in the tank in some fine cities if we don't change the rules on this score, so it's in all the owners' interests to take a deep breath, think a little, and come up with a modified plan to share local TV money for the good of everybody.

Baseball should decide on a number that every team, up to that number, puts into a common pot. I don't give a damn what the number is; let's say it's $20 million. So let's say George Steinbrenner makes his $55 million from cable this year. He throws his $20 million in the kitty. He still keeps $35 million! Let's say the Mets and Blue Jays each get $35 million a year; they kick in their $20 million, too, so they keep $15 million. That's good money! If you can't make headway with $15 million, you've got your head up your ass anyway.

Now let's go to the lower rung of teams. Let's say the Pirates, Twins, and Expos get $6 million a year each in TV revenue. That's less than the $20 million, so they each put *all* that money in. If the Royals and the Brewers are getting $3 million a year, they put it all in. Okay? Then you add up the total from all thirty teams. There's your common kitty.

Now. Baseball takes that kitty and divides it up 30 ways. Maybe it averages to $10 million a team. Every team gets that $10 million back. So Steinbrenner ends up with $45 million—a fat bag of change. The Mets and Blue Jays end up with $25 million each, which ought to help those teams tremendously. Most important, the Royals, the Pirates, the Twins and the Expos will each get their $10 million, so they actually have something to work with. Juggle the figures however you want, but if you follow a plan like this, you'd close the gap a little bit.

Now, here's where you start putting the pieces together. Add in the bonus rules, which limit adventurism by the rich teams. Now you've got a situation where good baseball sense can get rewarded again. If everybody's got some money, and if everybody's got a fighting chance, it'll be the team that scouts the best, that coaches the best, that plays the best, that wins. Brains, judgment, initiative, and good scouting will be back in the thick of it. And so will baseball.

If it were up to me, I'd abolish the free-agent draft altogether. It's not doing a thing to equalize talent, it's costing us money instead of saving it, and it's illegal to begin with. I'd let bonus rules dictate the procurement of amateur talent. The system would run itself. We'd be done with scouting for the agents, with putting price tags on guys who haven't played. But even if you kept the draft, bonus rules would leave more players available to more teams. It would bring some sanity back.

You'd have to find some way of putting these changes in effect, and nowadays, that's never easy. That means dickering with the union. Here's where those other variables come into play. You look at the big picture, look further down the road than the end of your nose, set up a plan, and create global change, not more goddamn gimmicks.

Let's look at expansion first. If baseball was going to expand, it should never have wasted its breath adding a team to each league. It shouldn't have been trapped into begging Milwaukee to change leagues. It should have added both new teams to one league—I don't give a damn which one—and planned ahead a couple of years. Start with thirty teams (sixteen in one league, fourteen in the other) the first year, then two years later, have your plan ready to go to thirty-two.

Now you've got options. You can have two sixteen-team leagues. You can have four divisions of four teams each. You can weight the schedule toward play within those divisions. You can get rid of the wildcard idea, have a single champ for each division, and get rid of interleague play if you want to. You'll have $400 million in new franchise fees and a lot of options for improving the game. First, you can settle the DH mess. Let's say you use it in both leagues for that two-year span. That way, you can cut the roster size for every team from twenty-five to twenty-three. Now. When you make that cut, you free up two players from each club, or sixty altogether. Those players are already in the major leagues. You can use them to stock your two expansion teams, so when you expand again, you aren't diluting the talent pool. But it's still a big boost to those players. Why? Well, when you add two new ballclubs, you take sixteen guys who are benchwarmers and make them starting players. They'll be making starters' salaries. Now you have thirty designated hitters (not just fourteen or sixteen) employed for two years. And at the end of that time, having given it a good look, you can get all those managers together who have worked in the AL and the NL since 1973. You can have them vote on it. That would be the final word on the DH. And either way they vote, we would keep bonus rules and go back to twenty-five-man player rosters at that time.

I'm not saying all this is going to happen; I'm not saying there ain't problems with some of it. I am saying there's things you can do if you look these things in the eye and talk about them. Take all the variables and work 'em together. Blend the DH, the TV-revenue issue, player-acquisition rules, and expansion, and you can make better use of the resources you've got.

On the field and off the field, I'll take brains over bucks any day of the week. That's the way of the game.

Mr. Andujar was never too big on thinking ahead, but in a fastball pitcher's case, that won't always set you back. If I'm the manager, I can do some of his thinking for him; on the mound, a guy with some fire in his eye can take you a long way. Turn him into a scout, he'll probably turn up a few other guys like him. That's what you want.

But not everybody sees it the way I do. Goombah did take it a little far. He knew I liked him, so he'd go over the other Angel people's heads sometimes. He'd get my permission for this or that without consulting other people. Then the spur-of-the-moment trips started. He was scouting all over Central America, boy. His zeal didn't impress the Angels' brass quite as much as it did me, and finally, even his old Papa couldn't bail him out. I haven't seen my friend Joaquin since.

I tried talking to Goombah before it was too late, but I guess he was just having too good a time. He loved the hell out of being a scout. I just hope baseball decides to look down the road a ways farther than he did—and stops whiffing every one of its own best prospects.

· 15 ·
Fair Game

Back when he was still coaching the Bears, Mike Ditka got it right. He said the Hubert H. Humphrey Metrodome was a hell of a place to rollerskate but a horseshit one to play football. And it was *designed* for football. If it's bad for Mike's game, you know it's got to be worse for mine. When my Cardinals played the Twins in the World Series, I found out how true that was.

The 1987 Cards were the damnedest team I ever managed. Two of my best pitchers, Tudor and Cox, went down with freak accidents early in the season, costing them four months' worth of starts between them. It was the year of the jacked-up ball, and we had only one power threat, Clark, and *he* twisted an ankle on September 7 and never played again. Somehow, we led the majors in runs through August 1. When we got our pitchers back, suddenly we couldn't hit to save our lives, but Tudor and Coxie and Forschie pitched like hell and kept us in the hunt. We strung together 95 wins and took the National League East by 3—even though none of our pitchers won as many as 12 games. That will never be done again.

We drew Roger Craig and the Giants in the playoffs, and, without Clark, we really had to improvise. That team was a bunch of wiseguys. They came into St. Louis for the first two games and called it a "cow town." Every homer Jeffrey Leonard hit, he did his asinine slow run around the bases with his one wing flapping. Will Clark, who must have never learned to play right at Mississippi State, slid into Ozzie with his spikes up. We split the first two at Busch, then went to San Francisco, where we fell behind by four runs in Game 3.

Well, I shot all the dice in the sixth inning. I used my whole bench and had 'em running. We squibbed a bunch of chink hits, and you should have seen the fun: They were chucking the ball all over the field like the Keystone Kops. We beat their asses by a run, Cox and Tudor shut 'em down back at home, and the big, bad Giants still can't figure out why they didn't make it to the Fall Classic.

But then we got to our final stop, the Homerdome, where baseball met bad science fiction. With that Hefty bag for a rightfield wall, that lunar-surface AstroTurf, and a ceiling that looked like the bottom of a UFO coming in for a landing, you felt like you were about to play America's game in a biodome on Mars. Come to think of it, some of the games *did* seem to defy gravity.

I still call it the NBA World Series, and not just because the games were high-scoring. In basketball, the home team has a big edge. That was the first Series ever played where the home team won every game. We did fine in the three at Busch Stadium, but up there, all hell broke loose.

It was like nothing I ever saw. The ball and the roof are the same color, so every popup is a flight to the Bermuda Triangle. There's 55,000 fans in one room, all of 'em waving hankies and hollering so loud you can't hear the ball hit the bat. You lose all your bearings as a ballplayer, and three or four games aren't enough to get them back. AL teams only go there a few times a year, so it's unfair for them; we might as well have been playing with earplugs and a blindfold.

Well, stats bear out what I'm saying. At the time our Series began, the Twins had won 62 percent of their home games since the dome was built. On the road, they'd only won 44! That year alone, the Twins lost 52 of 81 away games for a .358 percentage—rotten even for a mediocre team. But they kicked such hell out of everyone at home (56–25) that they snuck in the playoffs under the rules we had and got a crack at winning it all. In the '91 Series, the Atlanta Braves couldn't win a game up there, either. The Twins are the only team ever to win two World Series without ever winning a game on the road.

The World Series ought to show off the best of baseball, but in '87 and '91, it was like a lot of things in the game today—unfair, silly, and very poor at representing what's most interesting about the sport. In the end, when the hankies stopped waving and the uniforms were folded and put away, the fans had no more idea who was good and who wasn't than if they'd gone to a craps game and rolled a fistful of dice.

Baseball deserves better, and so do the people who pay to see it.

Baseball isn't a colossal spectacle, like football. It's no razzle-dazzle, run-and-gun show like the NBA. It ain't GameBoy or rollerblading or an Armageddon film. Well, Ozzie never swung like Mark McGwire, but they're both going to end up in Cooperstown, right? Baseball has different strengths. If it's going to flourish, it has to remember those and play them up.

With their 154-game and 162-game championship seasons, baseball teams have always been tested over a long haul. If you had a weakness, it came out. Baseball was the only sport that had every team play the same schedule: When I was a player, the Yanks faced the Senators, the Indians, and the Tigers twenty-two times each; the A's and every other AL team did the same. National League, same thing. Baseball was a controlled experiment, which is the fairest way of comparing the teams. Up till 1969, when we added division play, it was the only game that hadn't watered down the playoffs.

There was one champ in each league. If you were the best, you made the Series—period.

What baseball always had on the other sports was *fairness*. For a century, baseball was the fairest game. That's called *integrity*, and it's what fans come to our game to see.

Unfortunately, changes over the last thirty years have pissed that quality right down the tubes. The scores go higher and higher, but each year the games mean less and less. If the Marlins can finish 9 games back of Atlanta and still make the playoffs and win it all, why should I care if they get swept in some series in June? If the Twins can finish barely above .500 with the fifth-best record in the league and still end up on top, what did those six months of baseball I just watched amount to? If a club can be horseshit in the long term and good in the short term, and become champs, is that baseball?

The so-called purists love to go on about "tradition." Tradition isn't just about pinstripes, sleeveless uniform tops, or ivy-covered fences. Hell, I'm still the only guy on record as saying they ought to raze Wrigley Field out of respect for the sport. The real tradition to uphold is fairness.

Fairness is a good yardstick for a lot of issues. Let's start with interleague play. Regular-season play between the leagues has made a little bit of dough in the short term. But look closer and you'll see it's just one more poke in the eye to fairness, and that's why it belongs in the trash bin.

Interleague play, at least the way we have it now, offends the purists because it fouls up the "mystique" of separate leagues. But the product is already so watered down, who cares which team is playing which? The real problem with interleague play is that it gives some teams advantages that have nothing to do with baseball.

The first one has to do with the rules. You can't have sensible competition between the leagues if the rules aren't the same in both. I hate to be a broken record on this, but if nobody else wants to point out the obvious, I will: Playing with the DH in one league and not the other sets up two different sports. It's messed up the last twenty-five World Series, and it still gives off a bad odor. Interleague play during the regular season only makes the problem worse.

Let's look at an example. Say the Indians get to the Fall Classic. They've won 110 games over six months to get there. And Charles Nagy, their number-one pitcher, has never had to swing a bat in any games. He's forgotten *how*. That's all right, because those are the rules he plays under. But in the World Series, it's different. Let's say the Indians are playing Atlanta. Down in Georgia, Nagy has to bat. Now, whether you like the DH rule or hate it, that championship can come down to whether Nagy can do something nobody's asked him to do all season. That taints the competition. Whichever way we go, we've got to make the rules the same.

Interleague play is also a logistical nightmare. It's worse than anybody could ever imagine who ain't a player. When I first heard the game was considering it, the first thing I said was, "They ought to make the damn owners get on the airplane and travel with the teams to all those cities." Interleague play gives you even more six-day trips to three different cities. Getaway days are a disaster. Now you've got even more tired ballplayers, and that's bad for the fans.

Interleague play is unfair in other ways. One of the equalizing factors in baseball is the schedule: The fairer the schedule, the fairer the results. Interleague play mangles the schedule and makes it less fair.

Here's an example I've already touched on. Under the current rules, if I'm a National League East team, I play all my interleague games against AL East teams. I never see any AL Central or AL West clubs, and some divisions just happen to be better than others. The Mets are in the NL East, so their thirteen interleague games are against AL East teams. The AL East is the best division in baseball. The Mets face powerhouses like the Yankees, the Red Sox and the Orioles, and pitchers like David Wells, David Cone, Pedro Martinez, and Mike Mussina. But the Cubs, NL Central guys, face a division that's got one major-league team. Nothing against the Twins, the White Sox, the Royals, and the Tigers, but there's a reason Cleveland had a .549 record and still finished nine games in front in '98. Those teams couldn't put a big-league staff together if you pooled 'em into one roster. Comparing the Cubs' and the Mets' interleague games is crazy, and it's a disparity that's got nothing to do with baseball.

Yet under the wild-card system, you have to. In 1998, they were both fighting for the wild-card spot. The Cubs and Giants wound up 89–73 and the Mets 88–74. Now, how can you say the Cubs' 89 wins, with all those weak teams on their schedule, are better than the Mets' 88? You can't! It ain't fair.

Here's another problem, and I've never heard anybody mention it. Because we have so many teams now, you can only *play* about thirteen interleague games. You have to play every team in your corresponding division, and that means you're going to play certain teams only two or three times each. That ain't fair, either.

You've got to play a team six times a year for it to mean a damn thing. A big part of baseball is getting to know your opponent, figuring ways to exploit his holes and so forth. Two or three games is such a small sample, it leaves the games up to chance. If the Cards beat the Detroit Tigers two times in a two-game set, what does it mean? You're just as liable to be talking about chink hits, bad hops, cold weather, or rain as you are good play. In baseball, big samples make it a game of skill. Little ones make it a crapshoot.

Finally, interleague play goes counter to the way a baseball team is put together. Each team has to have four or five starting pitchers. That includes a number-one guy, the ace of your staff. If you're the Braves, you've got three more good starters, but nowadays, you're lucky if you've even got a good number-two guy. The quality drops off from there, and sometimes it's like falling off a cliff.

Now, that means that if you're going to test a baseball team fairly, you have to face its number-one and number-two guys *and* the pitchers further down the ladder. That tells you what that team's strengths are. But interleague play doesn't allow that to happen. Let's say I'm Jim Riggleman's Cubs and I'm facing the Twins three games this year. I may never hit against their number-one guy, Brad Radke. Radke's a hell of a pitcher; he won 20 games for a terrible team in '97 and 12 more last year. But my division rivals, like the Cards, Pirates, and Brewers, might *get* Radke. Not all three-game series against the Minnesota Twins are created equal, so you can't compare one to the other.

How could you fix that? Well, you could schedule *more* games against each team you play. But there's only so many games to go around. And if you can't play a team a certain number of times a year, you shouldn't play 'em at all.

Interleague play is just one more short-term payoff that screws up the long-term picture. Owners will tell you, "This system is as fair to one team as it is another." I've got a two-word answer to that: bull*shit*. Here the novelty's already worn off, and we're stuck with the fact they threw a hundred years of tradition over the side without giving a thought to fairness.

Think about what you're doing, or today's brilliant idea is just a turd you've got to scrape out of your cleats tomorrow. Interleague play is about as good for baseball as Bob Short was for David Clyde, and for the game's sake, I hope it lasts about as long.

By the time baseball expanded to include the Angels and the new Senators in 1961, and then the Mets and Houston Colt .45s (later the Astros) in 1962, you had ten ballclubs in each league. That's a lot of baseball teams competing for one title. It's also a lot of teams out of the race by July—and a lot of fans in a coma by August. Well, in '69, we expanded again, adding the Expos, Padres, Royals, and Seattle Pilots. We broke each league into two divisions. That created four pennant races, kept more teams in the hunt, and gave everybody a chance to do a little bit better at the box office.

It also opened a can of worms. The '87 Series showed that it's unfair to play for a title in a hall of mirrors. It also showed how easy it is for mediocre teams to get that far in the first place. Our system today allows lesser clubs to claim they're champs. That cheapens baseball, and once again, it hurts the fairness basic to the game.

Baseball's going to have division play? Fine. There's good reasons for it. But you've got to be sure to have a schedule that will keep it fair. And if you're going to go to division play—I don't give a damn if it's four divisions, like it was from '69 through 1994, or six, like there are today—you cannot retain the equal-schedule concept. You cannot have every team play the exact same schedule, the way they did for years and years. To keep fairness in play, if you've got divisions, you've got to go to an *unbalanced* schedule. Each team has to play more games *inside its division* than it does anywhere else. I'll tell you why.

In 1987, the Twins played the exact same schedule as the Yankees, the Angels, the Red Sox, and every other team in the American League. They ended up 85–77. But by an accident of geography, it so happened they were in a division with six other teams that did worse. Mathematically, their .525 winning percentage gave them the best record in that group, but *four* teams in the East Division—the Tigers, Jays, Brewers, and Yankees—did better under the same conditions. In other words, Minnesota was not the best team in the American League. They were not the second-best team. They weren't even the third-best or fourth-best team. The Minnesota Twins were the fifth-best out of fourteen teams in the American League in 1987. And they won the World Series.

There's a lot of shoddy thinking in my game, from the top on down, and if you don't use your brain, you can get sucked up in it. A casual fan might say, "Hey, the Twins did what they had to do to win their division. They didn't *have* to beat the Eastern teams." But he's not thinking right when he says that. The balanced schedule is designed specifically to measure all teams head to head, against each other. In the end, you should judge by that standard—all teams against all teams, rewarded or punished for how they did. Well, by that yardstick, the Twins finished in the middle of the pack. But geography, not wins and losses, slides in and decides everything. It's apples for six months, oranges at the end. That kills fairness.

Think about this, now. You want to have two teams play each other for the pennant? Fine. If everyone plays the same schedule, it makes more sense just to line everybody up at the end, regardless of division, see who finished where, and take the two teams with the best records. Then let *them* play each other. That way, the two best teams, as decided by your baseball competition, are in. In '87, the Tigers would've played Toronto, the Twins would've been playing golf, and you'd have some idea right now who the best teams were that year.

Or let's say you still want to have four playoff teams in each league. Why screw around with wild-card stuff? Those teams didn't win a thing. Just take the four best: one, two, three, four. Do it like they used to in the minor leagues: one plays four, two plays three, and you go from there.

Again, baseball owners will argue: "You'd lose pennant races that way!" Well, in the National League in 1998, every second-place team was so far out there was no competition for first. The Cubs finished 12½ behind Houston, the Mets 18 behind Atlanta, and the Giants 9½ behind San Diego. Yet the fans in those cities could stay excited because the wild card was still undecided. So the thinking goes. But if each of them had been playing for fourth place overall, you'd have had the same thing! The Cubbies would have taken fourth with their ninety wins, just ahead of the Giants (eighty-nine) and Mets (eighty-eight). Everybody would have been in it till the end. Don't tell *me* you'd lose pennant races.

Now, all that's true if you're going to stick with a balanced schedule. But if you decide you *have* to go to division play—and there are good reasons for doing that—you have to do it differently: You have to have separate schedules for each division. Make things different in each division, in a competitive sense. That way, divisional play will really mean something. If you don't, divisional play is just a mirage, and so is any division championship.

What you do is unbalance the schedule. Have the Twins play more games in their own division than against the others. A *lot* more. Under this system, the '87 Twins would have played many more games against the Royals, A's, and Angels than against Baltimore, Boston, or the Yankees. You'd have had distinct, parallel seasons within each division, each one with integrity. The teams would get to *know* each other; they'd play head to head down the stretch for their own pennant. You'd have real pennant races. You'd have more weekend home-and-home series, the way the Cards used to have with the Cubs every year. That's good for excitement, for color, for the local economies. And if you ended up first—even if you *were* only 85–77—you'd really be *champion* of something. You'd *deserve* to play another first-place team for a title.

With a little basic math, we could set it up that way, easy. Right now, we've got so-called divisional play, but each team only plays fifty-five games inside its own division. That's barely a third of its games! Look at the Cardinals. They play the other NL Central teams—the Cubs, the Reds, the Brewers, the Pirates, and the Astros—eleven times apiece. They play the other divisions' teams—like the Phillies and Mets in the East, and the Dodgers in the West—nine times apiece. You don't have to be Einstein to see that's hardly any difference. It's sure as hell not enough of one to establish a division race.

Let's change that; let's give it some meaning. We really ought to have the Cards play 100 games in the Central, but let's not give anybody a heart attack; let's just start with ninety. There are five other teams in the division, so that's eighteen against each one. That's a good sampling. You'd have those teams training their brains on each other, picking each other apart, trying to get the best matchups. You'd have the Cards and the Astros developing a history, the way the Cards have done with Chicago. You'd have a *division*. Then you'd have ten teams left—the ones outside the division. You'd play each of them seven times. That's ninety plus seventy, or 160 games. Now you've got yourself a schedule.

I'm not saying these are the only figures you can use. There are other possibilities. But let's talk about it. Let's throw some ideas out there! At least you're trying to preserve what's good about the game that way. You're on your way back to fairness and integrity, not random chance. And you might just give the fans a playoff they can get interested in.

This wild-card setup is something. I was laughing myself bowlegged in 1995 when the Colorado Rockies, in their second year of life up in my old stomping grounds, finished a game behind the Dodgers and snuck into a playoff spot. Everybody and his bat-boy was jabbering about it: "It's the first time in history an expansion team has made the playoffs in its second year!" "It's a great achievement!" "It's never been done before!" God almighty! After I'd stopped busting a gut, I did what I always do: I explained how that thinking was one more pile of Rocky Mountain oysters.

Now, I do respect the way they built that franchise. Bob Gebhard, their GM, is a fine baseball man. I even offered him the job as Cardinals' pitching coach at one time, though he went someplace else. But to come up with *that* as a story angle is so crazy it makes you shake your head. The damn press—they'll write anything.

First of all, expansion teams aren't *expansion* teams anymore. No team with a $35 million payroll is really an expansion team. Times have changed; in the old days, when the rules for player acquisition were a hell of a lot stricter, an expansion team was a bunch of ragamuffins, old guys hanging on by their knuckleballs, and skinny, goofball rookies who hadn't been around the block yet. Those were the only guys baseball made available to you in the draft, so that was what you dealt with. It took years and a lot of baseball knowhow to make a roadster out of that scrap metal. By the time it was up and running, it operated pretty good.

Today, the new teams have big, corporate bankrolls. They have more freedom. First of all, you have free agency now, which you did not during the first waves of expansion. The Arizona Diamondbacks did a lot of wheeling and dealing right around their first expansion draft, and they ended up signing free agents like Jay Bell. He'd just had a career year with the Royals, with 24 homers and 92 RBIs, and was already established as a Gold Glover at shortstop, and they handed him $6.8 million a year for five years. Then they traded for Matt Williams, the third baseman, and signed him for five at $9.5 million a year. So you're starting out in a $375 million ballpark, a $32 million payroll in your first year, and $81 million committed to the left side of your infield. If you want to make me laugh, compare that team to the 1961 Angels or the '62 Mets.

The second thing is, you don't have to *win* anything to make the playoffs now. Everybody was jacked up about the Rockies, but they were a second-place team in a horseshit division. Hell, if there'd been a wild-card setup in 1971, the Royals would have made the playoffs in their third year; they finished second to Oakland. Were the Rockies better than the 1962 Los Angeles Angels, who had Dean Chance, Bo Belinsky and Ken McBride on the mound? Bill Rigney managed his backside off, Leon Wagner hit 37 homers and drove in 107 runs, and Lee Thomas, who was later my Cardinals' farm director, had 104 RBIs. In *their* second year, in the junkyard era of expansion, they were first in the AL on July 4, went down to the last month in contention and ended up within striking distance of one of the great teams of all time, Roger and Mickey's Yankees. All that happened with Colorado was the rules had changed. Let's not get too much Rocky Mountain fever.

The worst thing is, baseball's fairest test is the regular season. We play 2,430 games a year—by far the biggest part of our product. In a short series, any fluke thing can happen, but over a whole season, the best team always wins. The breaks and bad hops even out, the depth of your pitching gets tested, your weak players get exposed. In the end, the standings have meaning, and they're fair, but the wild card undermines it all.

Look at what happened two years ago. The Atlanta Braves kicked the Florida Marlins' ass by 9 games in the regular season. That should have sent the Fish back out to sea, but they got in anyway. Atlanta had to beat them in a short playoff to get into the Series, and we all know what happened: The lesser team took advantage. The Braves had played so good for so long they deserved a reward, but they got exposed to the randomness of a very short series. And got sent packing.

You want to have the wild card? Okay, keep it, but bring it into line with what baseball's about. If you're going to let a second-place team in, penalize them. Reward teams for finishing first. That protects the regular season, and it promotes the excellence we want.

I can think of a few ways of doing that.

One way is to change the playoff format, which just

isn't working. I'll give an example. In the '96 AL regular season, the Indians ran away with the Central by 14½ games and had 99 wins, the most in baseball. They drew the Baltimore Orioles, who won the wild card by finishing second in the East. Well, Cleveland was 11 full games better than Baltimore, but what did it get 'em? Home-field advantage (three home games) in a five-game series. That's really no advantage at all! It's not nearly enough, given how much better they'd proved themselves to be that year.

Now, if I'm the only team left that did not win a division, I should expect to get punished. I should have to play the best team in the league first, but that doesn't always happen. If I finish second in my division, as Florida did in '97, and the number-one team in the league happens to be in my division, too, I don't play them. Why not? The Marlins should've faced the Braves (who won 101 games) first, but because of geography alone, they got San Francisco. The Giants not only were 11 games worse than Atlanta, but also were 2 games worse than the Marlins! The schedule did not punish Floria's mediocrity, the Marlins swept the Giants, and they ended up world champs.

Other ideas have been tossed around. You could exaggerate homefield advantage, giving the first-place team even more home games—say, four out of five in a five-game set. You could even decide that the first-place team has to win fewer games to advance—say, only two in a five-game series (or three out of seven). But however you do it, you have to create incentive to finish first.

Besides the wild-card problem, there's one more unfair aspect of the playoffs today: We have too many off-days. You don't have so many days off during the year; why should you have 'em in the postseason? With plane travel today, you don't need to take a whole day off!

Here's why it's unfair: The playoffs should be a test of what got you there, and you always win your division by using your fourth and fifth starters. The regular season is a test of depth. But in a seven-game series now, we play two, get an off-day, play three more and get another off-day. That's too much chance for a manager to rest his top pitchers. He can get by with only three starters, the way I did in '85, against the Dodgers and the Twins. He can even get away with two! That's basically what Tom Kelly, the Twins' skipper, did against us in the '87 Series. All he really had was Frank Viola and Bert Blyleven. That's one reason they finished in the middle of the pack, with a 4.63 team ERA. But with our format, he could hide that weakness. It never made a difference.

Whatever system we have, we should set things up so they reward quality and reward finishing first. Maybe your favorite team won't win that way. Maybe mine won't. But at least if they lose, we'll know it happened fair, square, and for the best.

The season is like the glacial age now—longer than ever and frigid at the end. With the extra tier of playoffs they added in '95, you have to win eleven postseason games to be World Series champs. Add that to the 162-game season, and you're looking at seven full months. And naturally, nobody planned how to do *that* right. We're going to have crucial postseason games in the snow. *That's* when the owners will decide it's a crisis and start a rush on shovels.

The Metrodome problem could have been solved ahead of time, but here it is, twelve years later, and nobody's faced up to the unfairness of some home teams' advantage. And the Homerdome isn't the only problem park. When baseball has a pennant winner in Wrigley Field, in Fenway, or in a few other places, you're going to see more World Series that aren't a true test of the game.

I've already mentioned Wrigley in Chicago. On the wrong day, a pop fly hits the airstream and comes down in southern Wisconsin. The winds at Candlestick, the

Giants' park in San Francisco, create a huge home-field advantage: Maybe Barry Bonds and his buddies can look at all the flying hot-dog wrappers and tell where the ball's coming down, but the visitors can't. Fenway, with that lunatic Monster in left, turns cans of corn into trouble, and try learning *those* bounces in a couple of days. Quaint as those ballparks are, for visiting teams—especially from the other league—they just aren't fair.

The most extreme home-field advantage has to be Coors Field, the Rockies' park in Denver. If they used their advantage smart, they could run amok in this game. In their first few years, they did, too. But if some poor American League club went there for the World Series, all bets would be off. It's like a more scenic Metrodome: Conditions are so warped you can barely call it baseball.

Denver is a wonderful sports town, and Denverites are great fans. Mary Lou and I kept an off-season home there for fifteen years, and we still ski there every winter. For their sake, I hope the Rockies win it all someday. That doesn't change the facts. Far more homers are hit and runs scored in Denver than anywhere else. I learned about the thin air in 1955, when I played centerfield for the Bears in the American Association. I'd see a line shot come right at me off a guy's bat, charge in the way you would on any sinking line drive, and end up watching that sumbuck carry over my head, keep rising, and go over the wall. It hasn't changed. Coors is extremely deep in the alleys—390 to left-center, 375 to right-center—but if you hit it on the trademark, you're going to launch it into some purple mountains' majesty. Everything in the air is a thrill.

"Carry" doesn't explain all the runs. The infield is grass, but it's still the fastest in baseball—faster than the Busch AstroTurf ever was. It's like lightning, and it's hell on fielders! But more than anything, the thin air affects pitching. Very few people realize how much—even the players.

When Denver got a team, I kept hearing people say,

"Damn, they better get some breaking-ball pitchers and keep that ball down!" Everybody thought that'd keep the ball in the park. They had it backwards. You cannot be a breaking-ball pitcher in Colorado and survive. The reason is the air: There isn't enough of it for a curve to work. It doesn't break sharply; it rolls. That's all the difference in the world! Ask Darryl Kile; he found out in a hurry. He's a breaking-ball pitcher, and he won twenty games for Houston in '97, signed with the Rockies as a free agent, and ended up losing seventeen with a 5.20 ERA one year later. Same thing happened to Billy Swift, the ex-Giants' pitcher, before him. You cannot be that type of pitcher in Colorado and win.

Why is that important? Eighty-five percent of guys who throw baseballs have mediocre fastballs—average fastballs, average sliders, and sinkers. Then you have 10 percent that have above-average fastballs, and 5 percent who have the junk to survive with below-average stuff. But 85 percent of 'em are mostly the same. They can win if their control is good, because their breaking ball will allow them to change speeds and make their other stuff look better. Just watch the visiting pitchers, even good ones like Maddux and Tom Glavine, early in the game, thinking their breaking ball is going to snap off. Hell, it does at the twenty-nine other ballparks on planet Earth! But here, it won't do what it's told. I have to laugh: I think Tom Candiotti, the knuckleball pitcher, moved to the A's and the American League just so he wouldn't have to throw there anymore!

That's the main reason you have Rockies who hit seventy or eighty points higher in Colorado than anyplace else. They know damn well they don't have to look for the curveball. That ball's going to come in straight, and the Dante Bichettes and Vinny Castillas are going to knock the piss out of it! Goes out nice and straight, too. Look at the stats: In home runs alone, I'd say it's about three to two—three homers at Coors are equal to about two anyplace else. It's a different game.

So for the vast majority of pitchers, you've got almost no hope at Colorado. What you've got to have is that 92-mph sinkerball, a spitball that dives, a hard, heavy ball that stays down and makes 'em hit it back up. That kind of guy might be able to win. But he's got to have the stuff for that, and very few do.

I say, let 'em play their eighty-one home games there. Let their hitters sit on all them wounded-duck curveballs. Let the fans buy their 3.4 million tickets a year and holler their lungs out. And let Jerry McMorris, the owner, figure out how he's going to pay all those forty home-run hitters who wouldn't hit twenty-five anyplace else.

But God help the American League club that goes in, sight unseen, and has to play three or four World Series games. It's like asking them to win on the moon.

This is probably just me talking, and the old-school contingent will think I've finally blown a gasket. This will probably never happen, but ballparks like Coors Field and the Homerdome convince me of the biggest step we need to take in baseball. For the sake of fairness, we ought to play every World Series at one neutral site. Seven games, one place, no travel. Same place every year.

The purists say it would take too much away from the teams' hometowns. It'd take away the charm of one league playing for all the marbles in the other league's stadiums. However, some of these places guarantee that the field, not the players, will decide some championships. A neutral-site World Series would bring back fairness and give us a chance to make the World Series what it ought to be: the number-one spectacle in American sports.

Now hear me out. Let's say baseball picks a nice Central Time Zone city, one without a big-league team; preferably in the South, for purposes of climate. Nashville, Tennessee is a hell of a bet. They've got hotels there for the Grand Ole Opry. It's centrally located with good access; it's a hub city for American Airlines. The climate is fairly warm. Let's say we go to the people in Nashville, and we tell them we want 100 acres of land twenty miles outside town. We'd have every damn club owner kick in $15 or $20 million—that's about $600 million—and we'd build a big, beautiful, 80,000-seat baseball-only ballpark in the old-style tradition the fans love in Baltimore, Cleveland, and Texas. We'd give it a retractable roof so that no games can be rained out, snowed out, or stormed out. We'd plant real grass; we'd put up plenty of parking next door. You think the city leaders wouldn't give baseball that land? You'd have the damnedest, one-of-a-kind, baseball venue in the history of the world.

Now: Every year, during a given, single week, you'd have an uninterrupted, eight-day World Series extravaganza. You'd play it Sunday to Sunday, every game in prime time at a reasonable hour, one game a day. Play four, take Thursday off if you want to, and finish up with a bang on Friday, Saturday, Sunday. You wouldn't need travel days. Everybody plays by the same rules, same park, same atmospheric conditions, same bounces off the walls. Eight days in a row in prime time, the World Series. You'd have the world's attention! You'd stir up more interest than the Super Bowl. And you'd have something worthy of that red-white-and-blue bunting we strap up every October.

Baseball has got to come up with some *ideas*, boy, and this is the right ticket.

Traditionalists will spew their Cracker Jacks. "What about the flavor of the home parks?" "What about the local economies that would be hurt?" But like with most good ideas, the more squawking you hear, the better your idea's going to be.

First, you'd gain so much in fairness it would outweigh any sentimental loss. The neutral-site Series would make so many memories of its own, it would develop its own tradition. And there's other advantages. The TV network could come down in advance, set up its cameras, and keep 'em in place through the whole deal. With no travel days, the managers would have to use all five starters. What about your economic critics? Well, the World Series does generate good revenue in the home towns, but before they started division play, each city was only guaranteed between two and four Series games. Today, with the five-game miniplayoff and the seven-game LCS, you've got at least three and up to seven guaranteed postseason games before you even make it to the final round. The home cities haven't lost a dime! And you'd set it up so that everybody who's got season tickets in the participating towns gets first crack at seats. If a guy's had four for the Cardinals, and they make the Series, he gets to buy four. He'll see St. Louis play the World Series in Nashville, Tennessee.

Now what would you do with that place the other fifty-one weeks of the year? Here's how you turn your sinkhole into a gold mine.

People are living longer than ever. And every sono-fagun that retires at sixty-five gets a new set of golf clubs. He can't hit the ball from here to that wall over there, and it takes him six hours to play eighteen holes, but he's out there hacking away. But today, people are living so *much* longer, they survive past golf. At eighty, they can't hit the links anymore, they can't fish, they can't swim, they can't go skiing. There's millions of people like this. And they've got money, time, and the gaming spirit.

Where do they all go? What do they do?

The answer is bingo.

Have you been on a cruise lately? Mary Lou and I go a couple of times a year, and you've never seen anything like it. Everybody in the world eighty years old and older is on them boats, and they all show up at ten in the morning in the bingo hall. They buy their cards, they sit there, they keep their eyes on the cubes in the steel cages. They watch for bingo! Sometimes they win, sometimes they lose, but they keep coming back. They spend their money on bingo!

Now, what I'd do is, I'd take this baseball facility, and I'd set it up for bingo. I'd call the damn thing "Baseball-Bingo City." I'd make it the world's largest animated bingo hall. You could let the customers play up to ten sheets. I don't give a damn how many nights of the year you'd want to do it, but you'd have it open to the public. Ten dollars a game, ten games a night; $100 is the most they could lose. I can see it now, the announcer at the loudspeaker, the giant letters flashing on the JumboTron: *B-4! Bingo!* It's all they'd have to do—watch for bingo. If you announced, "We're gonna have a world's bingo championship here on December 10," do you think you wouldn't get 90,000 people there, all of 'em eighty-five or ninety years old, to play bingo? They'd come just to show everybody they're still on this side of the grass.

There's a whole graying economy out there, and I'm telling you, if baseball was smart, we could tap it. People don't realize what bingo can do for you! People who read this are going to say, "Old Whitey's finally crackin' up." But the first guy who tries it is gonna make more money than Don King.

I'd go one step further if I was baseball. I would build an interactive museum; I would build housing, I would build hotels, and I would own the whole deal. I would have a fixed rate for rooms year round, for World Series time and the rest of the year. I'd *control* all that. You could put fantasy camps there, keep the old-time fans coming. You might have the All-Star Game, the Olympics, even the College World Series there someday. You talk about revenue! You'd have the damnedest baseball paradise you ever saw.

There's more competition than ever for the sports dollar. There's NCAA March Madness. There's the Super Bowl. There's the NBA Finals, NASCAR, the golfing boom, the Stanley Cup. Well, baseball's the National Pastime. It's a game of little plays, but if the other guy's throwing you rag-arm slop, why not go up there thinking grand slam?

Let's have an idea. Let's set a precedent. Let's put all the pieces together. Baseball can be number one.

I still don't know how you win at the Metrodome, and I'm not sure I want to know. I do know one week isn't enough for a baseball team to figure it out. The Cardinals could've played there till Easter and never won a game.

I have given some thought to Coors Field, though. I know I could put together one hell of a ballclub there. Give me about three years, and I don't know if I'd ever lose.

It's like anything else in baseball: You've got to work with what you've got. The Rockies started off their franchise great. Good baseball people. They drafted well, made good hires, spent their money right, got the right hitters for those conditions. But I don't know what they're thinking now. Last year, the Rockies even lost their home-field edge. They were a losing team at Coors! They're a worse team than they were when they first started.

I don't know if they're too good at thinking big up there. Without a plan, you aren't going to win in Denver. I'll tell you what mine would be.

First, you've got to keep those big hitters you've got—the Bichettes, Castillas, and Larry Walkers. They'll keep doing well there. Keep signing them. But then, you've got to realize something: You ain't going to sign any free-agent pitchers. Especially after what happened to Kile, no pitcher will come there on his own, and if he did, he'd be so goddamn dumb you wouldn't want him anywhere near your team.

No, in Colorado, you've got to grow your pitching staff. You've got to draft your pitchers and start working with them young. You've got to not only teach them how to pitch, but you've got to teach them how to pitch in Colorado.

To win at Coors Field, you've got to throw hard, spot your fastball, have a heavy sinkerball. If you've got that ninety-plus sinker or split-finger, and you can control it, like Mike Scott used to do with the Astros or Kevin Brown does today, and you can mix it with that plus-fastball, you've got a chance. If you get behind the hitters once in a while, you can buzz one up high and get 'em out upstairs with a good heater. How many have the stuff to do it? Not many. And you can't teach stuff. You *can* teach how to change speeds, but I've told you that don't matter in Denver.

That means one thing: You've got to teach 'em how to cheat.

I'd make Gaylord Perry my pitching coordinator. Hell, he went to the Hall of Fame with K-Y jelly all over him; why can't other guys? I'd teach those kids the spitball, the mudball, the shine ball. I'd show them how to use grease and vaseline—anything to make it dive and sink and get people out. I'd show 'em how to scuff it, cut it, make it drop and do tricks. Then I'd do what Don Sutton did. He was pitching in Chicago one day and they caught him decorating the ball. He was going to be suspended, but he said, "Hey, you want to kick me out of baseball? Fine; I'll take you to court." That changed their tune. He never missed a start! Now that's a good legal precedent for my staff. I would teach my pitchers to think that way at a young age.

Now, don't get me wrong; I'm not encouraging young people to break rules. What I'm saying is, if it's your livelihood, you're trying to feed your family, and they set it up so you can't win, what choice do you have? The way the rules are now, they've taken so much away from the pitchers, and that ballpark just takes it across the line.

Well, my Cardinals lost a World Series that wasn't fair. Teams make the playoffs now that don't belong.

The schedule's less fair than it used to be. We've gone a long ways down the wrong road.

Before managers start having to teach illegal means in a shower of spit, let's use our heads and straighten things out. Hell, it's the National Pastime. You shouldn't have to cheat to make it fair.

· 16 ·
Rules of the Game

A few of my ex-players have tried comebacks lately. I mentioned Willie McGee returning to St. Louis and playing like hell off the bench. Two summers back, there was some talk of Ozzie returning, either for the Cards or the Giants, though I knew it was just one of those half-assed press rumors. But Vince Coleman, one of the greatest base stealers of all time with his 752 career thefts, really did try to come back with the Cardinals last year. Through his friendship with Willie, Vince got invited—at age thirty-six and after eight years of bouncing around with the Mets, Kansas City, Seattle, Cincinnati, Detroit, and everybody else with a major-league cap—to try out for Mr. LaRussa's Redbirds. Gave it a hell of a shot, too; Vince hit .335 in spring training, one of the best marks in camp.

He didn't make the cut. Like most managers now, Tony was looking for some pop off the bench and went with another guy. When Vince finally headed home to Arizona, he sounded awful disgruntled. He told the St. Louis papers he could still play, but said "Everybody's looking for the big boppers. The stolen base is a lost art. I need Whitey back here. Where's Whitey?"

Well, Vince and I are still friends; he knows where to find me. He was really asking a bigger question about baseball, and a damn good one. Whatever happened to the style we used to have just ten years ago, the one where it was possible for a Vince Coleman to electrify a crowd with his arrogance and speed? What happened to the stolen base, to the running game? You don't have the kleptomaniacs you used to, and where you do, they're not the focus of an offense. Baseball forgets that fans love a go-to-hell running attack just as much as all the dented scoreboards—maybe even more.

Baseball has remained pretty much the same in terms of rules for the past seventy years. There have been different ways of *playing*—the lively-ball era, the arrival of Babe Ruth, the coming of the relief specialist—but during my lifetime, there haven't been any major rules changes (except the DH). That's good for continuity and tradition. But a few adjustments could do a hell of a lot to energize it, to give the fans a whole range of approaches. And we wouldn't have to sacrifice a thing.

It's always been hard to run. Even when my Cards were running everybody ragged in the 1980s, some silly-ass rules hindered our style for no good reason I could ever figure out. I'm sure none of the Lords of Baseball could tell you what they are, but the Cards had to dodge them every day, like so many half-assed tags in a rundown. If some of those rules were changed, we'd be turning more of our speedsters loose to wreak havoc, jangle the pitchers and catchers, and cause the kind of movement fans have loved since way before any of us was ever born.

With all the sit-on-your-ass games today, it's hard to believe how much we used to stir things up with our speed. I remember one game up in Montreal. Coleman led off with a single, and their starting pitcher, a guy named Dave Palmer, got so paranoid about Vince's lead, he threw to the bag not once, not twice, but *nineteen times* in a row. That's how anxious he was. I used to tell my pitchers, "If you've got a horseshit move to first, don't use it! Why show 'em what you can't do?" Palmer didn't see it that way, and I think it just got Coleman's motor running. By the time Palmer came to the plate, Vince was covered neck to kneecaps in Canada dirt.

Still, first pitch, he was off and running and into second in a cloud of dust. They couldn't stop him!

Even on the road, the fans loved it. Coleman, Lonnie, Willie—they'd get on base, and the ballpark would buzz like a beehive in a spray of water. But for no reason I could see, there were rules and standards in place that impeded that style. They're just more ways that baseball takes the game away from the fans. I thought it was bad for baseball then, and the rules still haven't changed.

I'll give you an example. It used to tick me off royally the way first-base umpires positioned themselves. Imagine a straight line from the pitching rubber to first base, then extend it thirty feet beyond the bag toward the stands. Well, tradition says the ump plants himself right on that line. I don't know why, and I've never heard an umpire explain it, but I know he can call plays at first base from any number of spots in that area. It doesn't have to be that spot! So there's no positive reason for it. That positioning is like a muddy track for the running game.

Why? Well, when you lead off as aggressively as Coleman, one goal is to force a bad throw. That pitcher and first baseman had better be on the same wavelength, or that ball caroms into no-man's-land and the rabbit race is on. In other words, if David Palmer bounces one in the dirt, he's going to pay a price. Which is *fair*. It's also a fair reward for a daring lead. But what happens? There's our friend, the stationary man in blue, right in the line of the throw. He's a human backstop. The ball hits him—thwock!—and drops dead as a bunt. It sets up for the first baseman to grab.

That can have a big impact on the game. I did a little research that year, over a two-week period, and found that other teams threw to first base fifty-seven times a game against us. That's a bushel, and with that many, there are going to be some bad apples. In that same period, *nine* wild throws got away from the first baseman but hit the umpire. On at least three, we'd have scored or gone into third standing up. That's three runs we earned but didn't get, on a team that needed every run.

Baseball's laziness about this kind of problem has always dumbfounded me. Every manager goes to the winter meetings, and that year I said, "Why don't we bring the umpires in and *talk* about this? Why not call in the whole crew, the supervisor and all the umpires, and let them talk and let us talk? Why do they have to stand *there*, in the line of that pickoff?" It never happened. Maybe nobody wanted to help Whitey and the Cardinals, but this kind of thing would help *baseball* more than any single manager. But you can never get people together in this game to talk about what happens on the field. Those umps are still in the same damn place and they're *still* getting hit. Check it out sometime!

Here's another one for you. You probably took geometry in high school. What's the first thing they teach you? Rule number one: The shortest distance between two points is a straight line. Have you ever thought about the restraining-line rule? I'm talking about that forty-five-foot-long box, the one you see along the outside of the first-base line. What's it for? Well, according to the rules, if you hit an infield chopper or you're trying to beat out a bunt, you're supposed to stay inside that box, outside the restraining line, to the *right* of what would be a straight line to first base. Now you tell me: If you're hauling ass to get there the quickest you can, are *you* going to step to the side and take the scenic route? That hinders a team that likes speed. You want to be able to lay down that bunt and beat out those choppers! The restraining line is bullshit, as we all saw when Tino Martinez hit Travis Fryman with a throw in the ALCS in '98, and the umpires actually said that Fryman was *entitled* to be in fair territory to get to the bag. Still, I didn't hear anyone raise the simplest way to settle the issue: Get rid of the damn rule!

The other needless rule that used to burn my ass was the balk rule to third base. Some of the pitchers we faced figured this out, and you really have to give them credit: They found a loophole in the rulebook that worked against our speed. It was clever, but for the life of me, I still can't see what purpose that rule serves.

The basic balk rule, which governs first base, goes like this: If you're the pitcher, and there's a runner at first base, and you step toward first with the ball as if you're going to throw there, you *must* follow through with that throw. That way, you can't just fake whenever the hell you want and keep Coleman or Rickey Henderson or Eric Young diving back time after time. It's a good rule; it makes things fair for a runner trying to get a lead. If the pitcher violates that rule—if he makes a move but *doesn't* throw—it's a balk: Vince, Rickey, or Eric goes down to second.

Well, for some reason, that rule says first base is the *only* base you have to throw to that way. You can fake to second and not throw; you can fake to third and not throw. I have no idea why. Some clubs figured out a way to exploit the rule. And once again, it hampers the running game.

Let's say Coleman's on third and McGee's on first. Let's say the pitcher is a righthander—Doc Gooden. And let's say he's afraid, as he ought to be, that we're going to double-steal on him. In other words, we're going to send Willie to second on the pitch, draw a throw there, and in the middle of the commotion, have Vince sprint for home. With speedsters like them, it's a real threat.

So Doc reaches into his black bag for some preventive medicine. He comes to his stretch position, but he slides off the rubber and steps toward third, as if he's going to throw over toward Vince. And McGee, at first base, sees that move and takes off running for second. Well, under the rules, Gooden doesn't *have* to go ahead and throw to third. It can be an empty fake. He can wheel around and catch Willie in a rundown, or he can spin and go to second and nail him there. That play can make the pitcher look like a jackass if he screws it up, because the third-base runner is going to trot home with a run. But check it out—it really works sometimes.

You can argue all you want that McGee ought to learn how to play that right, that he ought to resist that fake and not fall into the trap. But if the rule serves no purpose in the first place, why should he have to? It would be better for the game if the balk rule was the same for all bases. The pitcher and the defense would have to adjust and be on *their* toes. Just one more tweak that would open up the running game and give the fans something they love to see.

Speed's only one thing we'd be smart to add. A few shifts in the rules could raise the level of fairness, too, especially in the postseason, where some strange idiosyncrasies get in the way of picking the right champion.

I'd just been fired in Texas in '73 when my old pal and nemesis, Mr. Charles O. Finley, pulled a World Series stunt for Oakland that would affect my managing career. I always felt sorry for Dick Williams, his manager: Finley might have been the most intrusive owner of all time. I don't know how Dick could stand it, because he was a strong-minded man, and Charlie knew as much baseball as Williams knew about Finley's mascot mules. Anyway, during the Series that year against my other ex-team, the Mets—the A's beat them in seven games—the Oakland second baseman, Mike Andrews, booted away a groundball and a game.

Well, Finley was so damn hot about it he wanted to ship Andrews to Siberia. Since the rules wouldn't allow that, he decided he'd just bounce the guy off the team right then and there. In the middle of the World Series, he had his team doctor sign a certificate saying Mike Andrews was injured! Oh, he was injured, all right: He had bad hands, that was his injury. Finley managed to get his ass off the roster, replace him with Manny Trillo, and get away with one of the great World Series cheats of all time.

For a few days, anyway. At that time, the commissioner had the power to act in the best interests of the game without too much interference. Bowie Kuhn *hated* Finley and had no patience with that bull. He ordered Andrews reinstated, and Mike played again in the Series. Then Bowie fined Finley, and in the off-season, he instituted a new rule: No matter what happened, you could not replace a player on a World Series roster once it was turned in. If a guy got hurt, you played a man short.

Well, it's a dumb hunter that uses a shotgun on a June bug. Bowie solved that problem, but he caused bigger ones. The object lesson came in my last two World Series.

The goddamnedest things would happen to my players just before the postseason. It started in '85, when my offensive catalyst for that year—Mr. Coleman again— was warming up before game four against the Dodgers. He didn't see the automated mechanical tarp rise out of the ground and start rolling toward the field, and he let it run up his calf. Vince thought it was going to pull his leg out at the ball joint. The whole accident strained his leg so bad we thought it might be broken. He had to miss the rest of the playoffs, and we didn't know if he'd make the Series or not.

After a couple of days, the doctors told me he'd be able to play, so I wasn't too worried about it. I put him on my twenty-four-man World Series roster, which was due Monday at midnight. Then Vince went for an MRI exam Tuesday morning—right before he was to travel to Kansas City—and I'll be damned if they didn't find a fracture. His year was over. I knew before the World Series ever started that Vince Coleman would not be able to play. Yet because of the Finley rule, I was not allowed to replace Vince Coleman on my roster.

Not only did the country miss out on the real Runnin' Redbirds—one reason we only got fourteen runs in seven games—but I had to play the World Series with twenty-three guys instead of twenty-four. That screwed my ability to get good matchups against Dick Howser, it kept Tito Landrum out of my lineup, and it gave the country a less competitive World Series. Fair, huh?

The same damn thing happened in '87. Jack Clark was on his way to one of the greatest offensive years in Cardinal history when he sprained his ankle on September 7. It was a Tuesday; the doctors said, "He'll be back Friday." When I saw the size of that knot, I said, "You mean Good Friday, right?" Which is exactly what happened, because Jack didn't take the field again till the following year—on Good Friday, 1988—as he started his brief Yankees career.

Well, we got a double whammy. Clark was leading the league in slugging, and he already had thirty-seven homers and 106 RBIs at the time. Terry Pendleton, my third baseman, had twelve homers and ninety-six RBIs that year. Those two accounted for 25 percent of our runs batted in and half our home runs in 1987. But Pendleton went down during the playoffs against the Giants. So we played the World Series without our two best hitters.

But the worst thing was the roster rule. The doctors had said Clark *might* be able to play, so I had to put him on my roster. But halfway through the Series, when it was clear he wasn't going to play, I couldn't replace him with Curtis Ford or any other player from our system. We ate that roster spot, I was outmanned by one player, and we fell behind the eight-ball, all because of that one dumb rule.

Since that time, I've talked with baseball people many times about this. They all agreed at the time it was unfair, and it's unfair now. But nothing's changed! Once a guy is on your roster for any postseason round, you still cannot replace him for that round. Well, when you have an injury in baseball—I don't care if you're in Johnson City, Modesto, or the big leagues—you replace that player with someone else from your organization. In a playoff, you shouldn't be allowed to replace a starting pitcher after the fourth game, because he ain't going to pitch again anyway, and that'd be a good way for a manager to cheat and get an extra arm. But other than that, it would be fairer if the manager could make a replacement. Why haven't they changed the rule?

It probably isn't 10 percent of the people in baseball who even remember who played in the 1985 World Series. After all, it was just two Missouri teams; a lot of the national media just pulled out and went home. They missed one of the greatest Series ever, but one thing that made it hard to forget was how it pointed up two more screwed-up rules that ought to be changed.

First of all, people still talk about Game 6—the Denkinger fiasco. Obviously, I think we should have won it in that game. I cannot understand why people in baseball don't see the importance of *some* form of instant replay. I would never advocate replays during the regular season; the umps generally do fine, and when they do screw up, it's part of the game to react in the right way and overcome it. But like I've said, in the regular season, you've got time to make things right. In the World Series, the key thing is getting the call correct. There's no coming back from some bad calls.

Why I ended up the guinea pig for so many of these controversies, I have no idea, but we *do* need some kind of replay for the postseason to prevent the major gaffes. You'd have to limit the number of appeals a manager could ask for, or some of those guys would have us all gathered around a video screen for nine innings on end. You'd get one per game, maybe, or a certain number per series. But when the stakes are so high, you have to have recourse for the flagrantly unfair call.

Fans still think game six was the turning point in that Series, but if you followed it closely, you know the night that really turned it around was game three in St. Louis—which pointed up another problem.

We'd gone into Kansas City for the opening two games, beat their ass both times, and come back home in what looked like a hell of a position to put the Royals away in four. But something awful strange happened. An American League umpire was behind the plate that night. And a couple of strong righthanders were on the mound: Joaquin for us, Bret Saberhagen for Kansas City. Both were throwing good, but what screwed that game up was that those two pitchers had different strike zones. Not mildly different, not different by a couple of inches; we're talking about different time zones. Saberhagen's zone that night was twenty-two by twenty-two inches; Joaquin's was about six by six. If you don't believe it, I'll show you the tape!

Saberhagen pitched good that night, that's true. But hell, I could have struck people out with *that* strike zone. And Joaquin had an awful lot of pitches on the black that were called balls early in the game. By the time he found the zone the ump was calling, the Royals were sitting on the middle of the plate. Whatever came through there, they hammered senseless. Instead of being up three games to none at home, we had ourselves a street fight, and everything came out different.

Now, how does something like that happen? It's simple human nature. Let me tell you what I think was going on: After the first two games, everybody—the players, the press, and even the umpires—piles into their buses, cars, and planes and heads the 250 miles east down I-70. And the three AL umps are sharing a car or flying together, see, talking about what's going on. And maybe the subject comes up: "Hey, the American League team's down 2–0, we're going to the NL park. Our league's getting embarrassed." If it happens, it's more subconscious than anything, but they aren't any different from players, writers, or anybody else: They feel an allegiance to their league; if you'd umped in that league all year, and gotten to know all the players up close, and didn't know anybody in the other league, wouldn't you? Maybe they just don't want their league to look foolish.

Now, I'm not saying these guys were crooked. I'm saying they're human. Maybe they ended up calling the strike zone they *wanted* to see. It sure looked to me like Saberhagen got a hell of a lot more than Andujar got. I might do the same thing if I was them! But here's the key question I don't hear anybody asking: *Why the hell are there American League and National League umps in the first place?* Why don't umps work in both leagues all year, so you get rid of the attachment that creates the *possibility* of bias? Why not just eliminate it from the beginning?

To be fair, there really did used to be a cultural difference between the two leagues' umpires. Equipment differences caused it: The AL guys wore those bulky, outside-the-jacket chest protectors, which meant they couldn't bend over very far to get a good look at the low strikes. That's why the AL strike zone was consistently a little higher. Today, that's changed; umps can put the protectors wherever they want to, so there's no difference anymore. And that means there's no reason to have separate umpiring crews from the NL and the AL.

Umpires ought to all work under the commissioner's office, for Major League Baseball, not for the league presidents. We should rotate each crew through both leagues equally. Expose each ump to every player, manager, and coach in the big leagues during the season. You could even do it geographically: Have some crews do mostly Western time-zone games, whatever the league; others stay mostly in the Central, the rest in the East. You'd save on travel and wear-and-tear. And you'd eliminate any question of bias when World Series time rolled around.

It's no surprise that nobody in baseball seems interested in the on-field game. Look at the top three executives—Bud Selig, who's an owner to the core, and the two league presidents, Leonard Coleman in the National League and Gene Budig in the American. All three are decent human beings, but don't you think it matters that not one of them has ever pulled on a pair of stirrups? How should they know you can better the game by re-examining the rules?

They don't seem to know a basic law of business: The best way to sell more is to make the product better. Or maybe they just don't know the product.

Change a few rules and you can make the game fairer. Change a few others and you can bring back the running game. But baseball is also a game of balance. There's tension between offense and defense. There's tension between pitcher and hitter. There's tension between the batter and the fielders. The more these opposites are kept in motion, in balance, the more interesting the game. But the game has lost a lot of its balance in the past ten years. A few rule changes could bring that back, too.

To me, a perfect ballgame is a 5–4 or maybe a 6–5 game. It's a closely fought game that's gone down to the wire. There's been enough offense to keep your attention; there's been enough defense and pitching to challenge the offense. There's balance. But check out the box scores now. How many 11–10 games do you see? Offense is interesting, but when the game is *all* offense, what the hell is there to cheer about? The offense has just gotten too big; the scores have gotten too wacky. We've got to get the balance back.

Let's be realistic, though. A lot of the offense is just evolution, and we ain't evolving back. Fans seem to like the closeness and the intimacy of the little ballparks, like Camden Yards and Jacobs Field, and they're cash cows, so you aren't going to see *their* fences moved back. Nobody knows who juiced up the baseball, so how can you say that's going to stop? No, those trends are here to stay, for a while anyway. And so is the biggest one: horseshit pitching.

The pitching problem—as in, there *ain't* any—may

be harder to reverse than any of the others. It's part of society. Like I've said, kids don't have much initiative now. Go for a drive some day after school's out, over to a park or a playground or just through some neighborhoods. See how many kids you see out on their own, just playing catch or getting up a game of Indian ball or throw-it-and-hit-it. I don't care if you're talking about Central Park in New York, the streets of San Francisco, or schoolyards in the Midwest: They're not there. Kids are so used to the grown-ups organizing things, it doesn't occur to them to shake out the cobwebs themselves. If there aren't pro-looking uniforms, five coaches for every kid, and perfect foul lines, it doesn't count! And maybe their folks are so scared those kids might end up on the back of a milk carton, they don't let them wander off unsupervised. All I know is, they're not pitching enough. They aren't building up their arms.

Politics have hurt baseball, too. Now that school boards have to spend equally on boys' and girls' sports, it's cheaper for them to field a single track team than it is to outfit a girls' baseball team and a boys' baseball team. So you have fewer kids learning the craft of pitching. When they *do* play, they're going against aluminum bats in high school and college, so they aren't learning to bust the hitters on the fists and break their bats the way you have to in the pros. They're throwing dipsy-doodle stuff, spinning the ball, dancing around the outside edge. When I traveled the country as a scout, I used to see three or four no-hitters a week; now, if you see one kid who throws 90 miles an hour, every scout goes apeshit. Nobody wants to throw hard! I don't see that changing for a while.

Too many factors work against pitching and defense today, and they've worked their way into the big-league game. They make it less interesting to watch. But if you changed a few sensible things in the rules, you could get the balance back, too. Here are six ideas.

1. THE HILL

Baseball history is like a pendulum: It's swung back and forth between offense and defense over the years, and the game has always made adjustments. You had the dead-ball era, pre-1920, when Frank Baker used to win home run crowns with a dozen a year. Then came the lively ball and Babe Ruth, who hit 54 one year, then 60, and changed the whole thing. When Bob Gibson had his 1.12 ERA and Drysdale, Marichal, and Denny McLain handcuffed the hitters throughout baseball in 1968, the commissioner saw *that* lack of balance as bad for the game and shaved four inches off the mound. Well, nobody objected to that; it gave the hitters a break, and it brought the balance back again.

It's funny, though, when you think about it. The game has changed its rules now and again, but they've rarely done it in the direction of pitching and defense. They've added livelier balls a few times. They outlawed trick pitches in the 1920s and decided to put new, more visible balls in play more often. They did the number on the mound in 1969, and the new aluminum bats in college have just about killed inside pitching. But for the good of the game, why don't we try a rule that gives the pitchers a break?

Why not start with the mound again? Let's move it higher. Get it back up to fifteen inches. A lot of the pitchers are bigger and taller than ever; look at Randy Johnson, who's 6-10 with the wingspan of an albatross. It'd look like his pitches were coming out of the sky! As a hitter, you'd have less of a chance to tee off; the higher mound gives you a less flat angle to come at the ball, which makes it harder to hit that round ball "square." But hitters would still have a fair chance, all things considered, and the game would even out. We'd get a little balance back.

2. FILL IN THE HOLES

Back when my Cards were still wrangling with the Mets every year, everybody used to wonder how in the hell their third baseman suddenly turned into Mickey Mantle and went deep thirty-six times in 1987. I'll answer it in one word: *cork*. Illegally drill out a hollow center in your bat and fill it illegally with the stuff, and you get yourself a little better speed through the hitting zone. We commandeered one of his bats back then, hustled it into our clubhouse, and put it under the knife, and the surgery was a success: It wasn't no premium-grade ash from stem to stern, I'll tell you that.

Players are still stuffing their bats with that crap. Albert Belle was busted for it in '96—as if he needs the help—and a year later, they even caught a Dodgers' rookie, Wilton Guerrero, with contraband flying out the end. Because there's no mechanism for checking, I think the practice is a hell of a lot more widespread than anybody admits. It's an obviously unfair and illegal edge that the hitters don't need, and you can take two easy steps to eliminate it.

First, the rule book says a manager can have an opponent's bat checked once a game. That's a terrible rule. It means you can't appeal in the first inning. Why? Well, what if you try it and you're proven wrong? They're going to know you can't check again that game. And everybody on that club's bench is going to hightail it to the clubhouse and break out his corked bat. Give the manager two chances to appeal per game, or three. That'll take care of that.

Second, it'd be simple to set up X-ray machines in every ballpark. Make it like those security scanners at the airport, or the beepers at the grocery score. Have a guard sitting there in the dugout, scanning the damn bats. Every time you go up there—*beep!*—you're in or you're not. The technology's easy, it'd take no time at all, and you'd be evening out the odds a little more. Players will always cheat however they can get away with it, so don't let 'em.

3. SATURATION POINT

I talked about spitballs in Denver. As long as it doesn't hurt the game, I can't blame a guy for cheating to win; that's really part of baseball, and anyone who's been around the game knows it always has been. Look at Gaylord Perry: He won 300 games, and he was a damn pharmacy out there with all his unguents and lotions all over his uniform and cap and body and God knows where else. Sonofagun *belongs* in the Hall of Fame. He was the best there ever was at his craft!

The thing is, instead of forcing guys to cheat, I'd go a step simpler: I'd legalize the spitter across the board. I'd teach it as a real pitch. For somebody that knows how to throw one, it's a good weapon. Why shouldn't he be rewarded for that?

I don't think three people in baseball could tell you why the spitter's illegal. To begin with, it was banned for safety reasons; Carl Mays had hit Ray Chapman, the Indians' shortstop, in the head with a pitch and killed him in 1920, and baseball wanted to keep it from happening again. That's understandable. But in those days, batters didn't wear helmets like they do now! A "shine ball" won't hurt anybody any more than a good split-finger will. It's as safe as any other ball.

Beyond protection, there's no good reason the spitter's got to be illegal. It's a skill pitch, a tough one to learn, and it takes a lot of practice—just like any pitch. And it's a lot harder to catch a guy throwing one today anyway. Bruce Sutter developed the split-finger pitch only twenty or so years ago, and if you throw that thing right, you really can't tell it from a spitball in the first place. That's good camouflage for the spitball pitcher. A guy throws a wet one now, the umps and the other team just think it's a Sutter Special.

And finally, just look at the law. After Don Sutton threatened legal action over the spitball and they backed down, what argument does baseball have? Hell, if the game has conceded you can't legally prevent it, why not just *make* it legal?

The only thing I'd do is give it a different name; "spitball" is a little nasty. The shine ball was nice. How about dewball or perfume ball? Make it sound a little more socially acceptable, teach it to the kids, and let it fly.

4. SOFT-SERVE

People talk about the jacked-up ball, but how many realize that when they juiced the baseball, they also changed the cover? In the old days, the horsehide of the ball was stitched right onto the inner part, and it was only the seams that held that skin in place. In the areas between the seams, there was no glue holding the skin down tight. That created some "give," some wiggle. A good pitcher could work a ball, find the soft places, and make it move around. Today, the cover is glued down, too. The whole thing's hard as a rock. There's fewer ways for a pitcher to get movement. Why not get rid of the glue?

5. IN THE ZONE

Two years ago, when Wade Boggs was still a Yankee, I was catching the late West Coast ballgame on my satellite dish, New York against Seattle. It was late in the game, ninth inning, with the Yanks down 7–6. Two outs, two runners on base, and they're trying to even the score. Well, Lou Piniella, the Mariners' manager, does what he ought to: He makes a move, bringing in his young lefthanded relief pitcher.

The kid works him to a 2–2 count. And he brings the next one right down the pipe—*middle of the plate*—pecker high. If you were writing a textbook and trying to find a picture of a strike, that'd be it. Boggs takes the pitch, it's called *ball three*, and he hits the next ball out of the park for a three-run homer.

I can't tell you why the umpires haven't been calling strikes the last few years. I'm sure it's happened gradually, the shrinking of the strike zone. I *can* tell you that up to about a year and a half ago, the zone that big-league umpires were calling had almost no overlap whatsoever with the strike zone that's defined in the rule book. It's supposed to be twenty-two inches by twenty-two, from the top of the letters to the top of the knees. They got to where they were calling it twelve by twelve, and if a pitch came in above the belt, it was a ball. But I *never* saw a call this bad at such a crucial time. The Yanks won, 9–7, and I'm not exaggerating when I say that that call decided the ballgame.

I don't know how or why this change happened. One theory says the hitters are so big now, they're calling strikes the only place where the studs can't handle 'em—low and away. But that ain't fair; a strike should be a hittable pitch, or it shouldn't be a strike. Whatever the thinking is, if any, it's been unfair to pitchers, it's elevated scoring, and it's changed the whole game of baseball.

First of all, pitchers end up giving walks that shouldn't be walks. Their best pitches get turned against them. The hitters get to narrow the zone they're sitting on, and wait for one right down the middle. There are many more deep counts—3–2, 2–2—which makes the games longer and tires out the pitchers still more. This change has swung the pendulum toward offense more unfairly than any other, and it might be the easiest to fix, if baseball wanted to.

The public outcry against the small strike zone has had some effect. I really see some umpires making an effort to enlarge it. I don't think they should go about it the way Eric Gregg did in the '97 NLCS: He just added a foot to either side of the plate, and he punched out a lot of good hitters that way. To their credit, the Marlin pitchers, especially Livan Hernandez in the crucial fifth game, figured this out and worked it to death, right down to the last strike of the last strikeout of the game. That ball had to be fourteen inches outside, yet Gregg punched out Fred McGriff. That was the end. You don't have to overcorrect; you don't have to take *balls* and call them strikes. What you need to do is get the umpires to enlarge the zone up and down, not side to side; get them to call that *high* strike. That's where the trouble is.

However baseball wants to do it, they should get together with the umpires and make it clear they want the strike zone bigger. Hell, make the batters go up there thinking, "If it's close, if it's an inch or two off the plate, I've gotta swing at it." It'd speed up the pace; it'd add to offense. And it wouldn't call for a single change in the rules. This has to be done.

6. TAKE 'EM TO SCHOOL

We've heard a lot the last few years about umpires' attitudes: They're too confrontational, they pick fights with the players, they try to show everybody up. That's true up to a point. Fans don't come to a ballgame to see the umpires. But what you don't hear as often is how flat-out bad the umpiring is. Everybody knows we've got a watered-down product on the field, but we also have a major shortage of big-league umpires.

When I was first coming up, the umpires' talent base had not been diluted yet. There were only eight teams in each league; only three umps, not the current four, worked all but the most important games. And at that time, you might have *argued* with an umpire, but you hardly ever questioned his calls. That's how good they were. Today, with more teams, games, and umpires per crew, you have more spots than you have good umps.

On top of that, umpiring is a much cushier job than it used to be: Whereas they used to work straight through from spring training till October, big-league umpires get a vacation each month now. That means that at any given time, there are a hell of a lot of *replacement* umpires out there, too. So one problem is, we don't have guys who *can* call the right strike zone. They don't know how. And that makes it harder for pitchers to do their job right.

One thing I don't understand is why more ex-ballplayers, guys who get released, don't take up umpiring. We spend too much time trying to make bakers or butchers into umpires. It doesn't work! Baseball players know the strike zone; they've made their living in it. They know the game and know how to bring common sense to it. I know from my own days refereeing basketball—I reffed high school, college, and ABA games—that no matter what sport you're talking about, *common sense prevails.*

We ought to take more ex-players, possibly ones who have their college degree, ones who are intelligent and patient, who are good teachers, and pay them good money to go into the rookie leagues and start a new career. Hell, it's a great job today! It'd be good for everybody and good for the game of baseball.

When I talked about Vince's comeback effort, I wasn't second-guessing Tony LaRussa. Hell, as a manager, I was always climbing on Vince to diversify. He could have made more money that way. After his great rookie year, he couldn't get you that two-out RBI as often, which you look for in a good leadoff hitter. He never did learn to take a walk, hike up his on-base percentage, or hit the breaking ball too well. He wasn't the nimblest outfielder, either, so we couldn't play him in center; and left, where we finally moved him, is more a spot where you look for more offensive production—RBIs, home runs, gappers.

In spite of all that publicity you heard about the firecracker—when he threw that cherry bomb in the parking lot at Dodger Stadium—I loved Vince Coleman and still do. I have it on good authority that that whole thing was blown way out of proportion. I know he's a fine athlete, a guy who takes great care of himself, and a good family man. In the end, when I finally quit the Cardinals, he was one of the first guys to call and say thanks for everything I'd done for him. A class move, given some of the tiffs we used to have.

It's too bad there weren't more ways Vince could help you off the bench. At its best, baseball's a game of balance—speed and power, offense and defense, pitching and hitting. It's Mark McGwire *and* Rickey Henderson.

As much as I got a kick out of Vince, I mostly just loved the electricity. In the best of worlds, there'd be room for him, too. And we'd all be on the edge of our seats.

· 17 ·
The Commish

Back in the 1980s, my Cards and I had a dust-up with a certain umpire. The sonofagun didn't only blow a call behind home plate, he made a game's worth of horseshit calls, and it escalated as the innings went on. I didn't know *what* he was up to. Sometime in the eighth or ninth—this was in early June—I stormed onto the field, got in his face, and chewed his ass redder than it's probably ever been chewed before or since.

It happens in baseball. Players have bad days, umps have bad days. You're not always going to like each other, either. But if you're professional, you go out there, say your piece, leave it on the field, and head back to the dugout. You both get on with your jobs.

That's what I tried to do, but this guy had other ideas.

For the next two months, every damn time I hooked up with his crew, we got the most one-sided officiating you ever saw—bad calls at second, dead-wrong foul-line rulings, shrunken strike zones. It kept getting worse! They had it in for us, no doubt about it. Well, everybody knows umpiring is subjective, so you don't want to bitch about it too much, but when you're getting *screwed*, man, you're getting screwed. And you can't let *that* go on.

It finally came to a head one day. This ump and I had such a donnybrook that he ran me off, sent a report to the commissioner's office, and got me fined a few hundred bucks. It felt like a big setup job. Naturally I appealed, in hopes of straightening the whole mess out. The next time we were in New York, I stopped by the baseball offices on Park Avenue to talk with the National League president.

I didn't know what to expect of Bart Giamatti. I knew he'd been president of Yale and had a hell of a brain. I knew he loved baseball as much as anybody and could talk about it like it was Homer's *Odyssey*. I knew he weighed too much and worked too hard and barely took care of himself. What I didn't know was if he knew which end of the bat to hold and which to hit with. I found out soon enough.

He was taking long draws on a cigarette when I got there. He looked like he hadn't slept since the All-Star break, and the eggplants under his eyes made him look older than he really was. The ump's report was in a folder on his desk. He slid it across to me. "I'm not supposed to show you this," he said, "but I thought you ought to know what you're dealing with." So I snatched it up and started to read.

I was glad he'd stepped around the rules. That goddamn report was farther-fetched than a Stephen King novel, and almost as scary. I never saw such a pack of lies in my life! I couldn't believe what I was reading. The ump must have figured I'd never see the thing, because he accused me of two things—cursing him and trying to stall the ballgame—that I absolutely did not do. He got the whole thing wrong. I'll say this for the guy: It was as fair as his calls behind the plate.

When I finished, I looked up, and Giamatti was tugging his goatee, studying me as if I was one of his classic books. His eyes were twinkling a little through the smoke. "What do you think?" he said.

"This is the biggest pack of horseshit I ever read," I said, and I tossed it on his desk.

"Horseshit, eh? You dispute the gentleman's account?"

"Half of it's made up. This never happened; that never

happened." I told him point by point what each of the distortions were.

Like I've said, I always tell the truth. But very few people are able to sniff out a whopper when they hear one and when they hear the straight facts, it just makes them mad. So I didn't expect much—maybe some arguments that had nothing to do with anything and then a half-assed ruling that wasn't fair to anybody. Most of the time, that's the way it goes.

Bart was different. We didn't argue; he didn't interrogate me. He looked me in the eye, smiled, and gave me an answer: "Whitey," he said, "that's about what I expected you were going to say. I believe you. Case closed." And he slid the folder back into the drawer of his desk.

I don't know how he understood it so clearly, but I do know the man was as good as his word: From that day on, the schedule was changed, and the St. Louis Cardinals did not cross paths with that umpiring crew again. We ended up winning the pennant that year, but that's not the point; the important thing was, it all happened fair and square, which it wouldn't have if Giamatti hadn't stepped in and acted the way he did. Give me a level chance and I'm a happy Rat.

I've known five commissioners in my life, including the current one, Mr. Bud Selig. I've read about all the rest of 'em, from good old Judge Kenesaw Mountain Landis, who was a hell of a tough guy and saved the game after the Black Sox scandal, to Happy Chandler, Ford Frick, and General Eckert (who wouldn't have known a strike if he was behind the plate and it came down central at 80 miles an hour). Not all commissioners have known a damn thing about the game. Some were outstanding; others were weaker than bad beer in a mug full of ice. But would any of 'em ruled like Giamatti? I doubt it.

I asked him later on why he took my word, and the way he answered told me all I need to know about the kind of leadership we're always going to need: "Whitey, I've got good friends around the game," he said. "People I trust. They all tell me you're a man of your word. You tell the truth. I don't need to know any more than that." Simple, strong and, if you ask me, right on the money.

You might say that's kind of an arbitrary way to rule, but people of honor recognize each other. I really believe that. It takes a little bit of wisdom or insight or whatever you want to call it. It takes a good man to know a true thing from a lie and to act on it, and it takes a smart one to favor fairness over the black-and-white rules. Trust was the law of the land for Bart Giamatti, and who can you say that about in the game today?

Baseball threw heaters and curves at Giamatti in his short time in office. Steinbrenner's shenanigans and the Pete Rose gambling disaster were enough for a lifetime. But he always seemed to see the spin on the ball, stay back, and hit it on the sweet spot with a level stroke. It was a terrible day for baseball when that heart attack killed him. If he'd have lived, we'd have a different game today—a better one, I think. He'd have taught us a few things about this Pastime of ours.

The Red Sox ain't won a World Series since they traded the Babe. The Cubs haven't even been *in* one since 1945. Those are some streaks. But they've got nothing on baseball, which supposedly couldn't find a chief executive for six and a half years. I never heard of a slump like that.

It's the owners who hire and employ the commissioner, and there were all kinds of rumors about who they *wanted* to get. For a time, like I said, it was Senator George Mitchell of Maine. Then I heard it was President Bill Clinton, who they were going to get after he left office. Some of it was nuts. I heard my name mentioned, the way it used to be quite a bit when I was still managing, and a few others even *more* unlikely. The truth of the situation is, they didn't really want a commissioner, so they ended up with the next best thing: They hired their good buddy, a guy they all know, and the person they wanted from the beginning, Bud Selig.

Now, I don't mean to knock Bud. I like him; he's a good person. When I worked for the Autrys and he was still interim commissioner, I used to sit in the press box with him, and I'd fire baseball ideas at him like a pitcher in batting practice, and he'd just hang in there as long as I wanted and keep on swinging. Nice guy, and there's no doubt he loves the game of baseball. And let's face it: How many guys sell enough Chevys in their lifetime to purchase a major-league ballclub? You can't be a dim bulb and do that.

The thing is, Bud is an owners' guy. No, check that: He's an *owner*. He ran the Brewers for years, so that's his type of thinking, and let's face it—putting the team in a trust with your daughter running the operation don't exactly take it out of the family. But back when I was in the game, I used to read Bud's public statements, or hear them on TV, and I'll tell you right now that if I hadn't known who said those things, I couldn't have told you if it was Bud, Jerry Reinsdorf, or Jackie Autry talking. It was the same stuff, almost word-for-word, out of all their mouths, day after day, like a bunch of broken records. Unless he changes some, Bud won't ever challenge the owners on anything important. But stranger things have happened.

I see Bud a little bit like the way I saw Neil Allen when I got him for the Cardinals. I'd rather have had Bruce Sutter as my closer, but he'd gone to Atlanta; it was over, so why cry about it? I didn't feel perfect about Neil, but he was the best I had, so I handed him the ball and hoped for the best.

Well, commissioners are a little like closers. They may all have a different "out" pitch—like Dan Quisenberry's submarine sinker, as opposed to Gossage's fastball—but good ones have certain qualities you can't do without. A good commissioner always loves the game of baseball. He *knows* the game. He's honest; he has integrity. If somebody pulls his chain or says something asinine in a meeting—and that happens all the time—he'll call them on it and tell them, straight to their face, what he really thinks. It comes back to his knowing in his heart what the game's about, what's good for the game, and how he wants to get it there.

But baseball goes through cycles. And that's why the profile of the job *has* changed over the years.

When I first got to the big leagues, the commissioner was the rock. Or if I want to use a bigger word, I'd say he was an absolute ruler. He had that clause in his contract about "acting in the best interests of baseball." Whatever he took that to mean in any situation, he had the hammer to act on that basis. Nothing stopped him from doing that. You couldn't sue him if you didn't like his ruling; you couldn't threaten him. If you ran a big-league ballclub or played in the big leagues, you signed a statement to that effect: The commissioner's word was final. He was the *boss*, man. And somebody's got to be! Somebody's got to make the final decisions. That's *still* the way we ought to run things.

Over time, I saw commissioners use that power for better and for worse. When I think about it, Bowie Kuhn's really a good example of both. On the surface, Bowie seemed like a pretty good guy, but you'd be pretty hard-pressed to say his rulings were good for the game. He's the guy who became the model of the too-strong commissioner that all the owners still hate and fear. That happened in the early seventies, when there was a work stoppage one year in spring training that Bowie stepped in and put an end to. You don't hear it talked about much, but that move still reverberates through baseball.

It was an owners' lockout, though they didn't use that word at the time. There was a labor dispute, and Kuhn thought a stoppage would be bad for the game. So he just defied the owners and ordered the players onto the field. And the players did come back, and the owners had to pay 'em. And that was that. Well, I wouldn't be collecting my handsome pension today if Bowie hadn't done that—and neither would a lot of other ex-players and managers—because that move did more than anything to solidify the players' union into a force. It banded 'em together. And they eventually became one of the strongest labor unions in the history of the United States.

The owners are still hot about it. Looking back, they think that if Bowie hadn't stepped in and done what he did, they could have broken the union. And they would have saved themselves all the spiraling salaries and all the labor unrest that's gone on since then and never stopped. They might be right. Maybe they could have forced the issue and broken the union before it got too strong.

The worst thing about Bowie, though, was he just plain had his likes and his dislikes, and he let it affect his job. When he had a decision to make, he liked to rule in favor of his buddies, especially the Dodgers' O'Malley family and John McMullen, who owned the Astros at the time. They were Kuhn's crew. On the other hand, he disliked Gussie Busch, the Cardinals organization, the Cincinnati Reds, and Charlie O. Finley of the Oakland A's. They weren't in his circle. He didn't like *any* of those folks, but he *loathed* Finley.

Well, after he'd won himself a few World Series, Charlie decided he'd raffle off his stable of thoroughbreds, the Oakland A's, in 1976, trying to get something for his players before they left him as free agents. He had Rollie Fingers and Joe Rudi sold to the Red Sox for $1 million apiece and Vida Blue to the Yankees for $1.5 million. He was stripping down his car and selling it off for parts. And Kuhn, acting in "the best interests of baseball," stepped in and squashed the whole deal. I guess he thought Charlie Finley was acting in the best interests of Charlie Finley.

Well, maybe he was right and maybe he was wrong, but how could you tell? Bowie had hated Finley so long you had no idea if he was thinking about fairness. And if Bart Giamatti were still around today, you could ask him: a CEO has got to be fair—to *everybody*.

I do think an owner should be able to sell off his players. They are his assets, after all. Why shouldn't you be able to sell off your assets? And where are you going to sell them if not to other professional baseball teams? The thing is, it should be done fairly, in an orderly way. Any player being sold outright should be offered to the last-place team first. Then you'd work your way up. If the first twenty-eight or twenty-nine teams didn't want you, then okay; George Steinbrenner could have you. It wouldn't be an open bidding war, because then the rich would just get richer, and that ain't good for the game.

Well, Bowie wasn't fair. My second year with the Cardinals showed that. We won the 1981 National League East by 3½ games. We had a hell of a year! Yet because of Bowie Kuhn, that was the only year in history when you could actually finish in first place and not get into the playoffs. Now that's great logic. It was unfair, which, like I've said, is the worst thing you can be in baseball. And the reasons behind it were personal.

That was the year of the fifty-four-day midseason strike, and baseball decided to change the rules in midstream. Just to cover their bases, they decided halfway through the season to break it into two halves. The first-half winner in each division would play against the second-half winner to decide the pennant. Now, nobody had ever heard of half-seasons in big-league baseball; it's crazy to do it that way. That didn't matter. Whoever happened to be in first place at the time of the strike was declared first-half champion. In our division, that was Philadelphia. The Phillies were crowned winners of a race they didn't even realize they were in.

Now, in the second half of the schedule—the part played after the strike was over—it so happened that the

Cardinals had thirty-one road games scheduled and only twenty games at home. You talk about a disadvantage! We still played good, and we *still* ended up just a half-game back of Montreal for the second half. You know why that was? Baseball stuck to its original schedule, and it so happened that we had one less game than the Expos did. We never got a chance to make up that game! I mean, they *stole* it from us. So overall, we had two good halves. They added up to the best whole-year record in the division—by 3½ games. But because we didn't win either half, our asses were out on the golf course. The same thing happened, by the way, to the Reds in the NL West, and I'm just as mad about it on *their* behalf.

Well, I always thought one reason behind all this was a longstanding feud between Gussie and Kuhn. I don't know why Gussie and his lawyer, Lou Susman, hated Bowie so much; I can't tell you that. I do know they were trying to get him fired. Susman was just the kind of guy who never seemed happy unless he was trying to get *somebody* canned, so in a way, when I first got to the Cardinals, I was happy he had his sights on the commissioner. That way he wouldn't come after me! By the time he got done with Bowie, I'd been so successful in St. Louis I knew he wouldn't touch me.

But in '81, I think Bowie saw a chance to get even by starting that split-season gobbledygook. He stuck it right in and broke it off. And you know what's worse? That year, in spite of the fact that Tommy Lasorda, the O'Malleys, and the Dodger organization did not even win the NL West for the year, they went on to win the World Series. What kind of world's champion is that? You talk about asterisks; there's where you need an asterisk.

Peter Ueberroth, the next commissioner, was a brilliant man who used his clout a lot better than Bowie. He'd just run the Los Angeles Summer Olympics and made a lot of money for everybody, so he knew about tight ships. He realized it made no sense to take the job if he couldn't rule for the good of the game. And to him, that meant one thing: prevailing on the damn owners to act completely against their nature, get together, and put a lid on their spending. Hell, somebody had to.

He got hammered for it, but I really don't blame Ueberroth for the so-called collusion case of 1987. We should always have *that* kind of unfairness. Ueberroth got the owners together to refuse to offer any free-agent deals for that year. It's their money; they can decide not to spend their money, can't they? It was about damn time they acted as a unified group for a change, not as separate agents out to screw each other. Yes, the Basic Agreement forbids members of either side to act "in concert," but that's a pretty fine line, and if you think you can't sidestep it, you ain't thinking. *I* could have done it. To me, the only thing the owners did wrong was to decide they weren't going to offer any free agents *any* contracts. Detroit offered Kirk Gibson a $13.5 million long-term deal; I wish somebody else would have offered him $13 million. I wish somebody else had offered him $11 million. "Here, Kirk; here's $10 million. You don't like Detroit? Come with me; play in L.A." How are they going to call that collusion? That's an offer! All those teams have to say is, "Hell, that's what we figure he's worth!" That's all they had to do.

They could've saved themselves a lot of trouble that way, but how many things can you ask owners to do right in a row? They ended up having to shell out $280 million in restitution later on, and that helped some ballplayers out—Jack Clark, for one—but at least you have to say Ueberroth went down trying to run things like a real businessman would.

Barring some miracle, you couldn't do that today. I have asserted this before, but every owner acts in his own interest; screw how it affects everybody. They all *know* that now. You could not dispute that after you saw what Jerry Reinsdorf did—handing $55 million to Albert Belle after he'd been the hard-shell preacher of fiscal restraint all them years. It'll be a wonder if they ever agree on anything anymore.

That's a terrible way to run things. If you're the Cincinnati Reds and want to ban facial hair and colored shoes, it's easier if *everybody* does it. If you're the Diamondbacks or the Astros and you want to get rid of farm systems, or fake turf, or only use free agents, it works better, and it's fair, and you can make it happen, if *everybody does it together.* Try something alone, and you end up in the recycler. Baseball has to have a strong commissioner, the way Ueberroth tried to be, to get everybody more or less on the same page, or the game ain't going anywhere. In spite of the gains you probably think we've made, it might not even stay alive.

And the commissioner is even weaker than you think. To see why, just look at football. Do you think the rest of the sports world didn't notice when Al Davis kicked the NFL's ass in court? He wanted to move his team; they said no. He said *screw you, I'm doing it anyway,* and every owner ended up forking over $7 million in legal fees. He took the commissioner, Pete Rozelle, and his successor, Paul Tagliabue, and left their caps spinning on their heads. I'm sure Don Sutton had that kind of precedent in mind when he threatened to sue baseball over the issue of allegedly defacing the ball. It's a fact of life: The commissioner has to worry about getting sued.

So the climate's different today. Kuhn was able to put the kibosh on Finley, but who was there to do the same to Wayne Huizenga, the Florida owner, who dismantled the Marlins right after they won the '97 World Series? It was just what Charlie had tried to do, but worse. There's never been anything like it. Here's a guy who spent $154 million in one year, proved you can buy a World Series, then decided even a world's championship team couldn't make money in South Florida. Well, hell, I could have told him that: With all that rain down there in the summertime, Miami's always been a terrible place to play baseball and a bad big-league market. But does he have to sell everybody off and melt the team down? The thing is, our leadership is so feeble, whether it's good for baseball or not doesn't even enter the conversation.

Today's commissioner should have ideas and vision, but that won't be enough anymore. With salaries and costs so high, and with all the money TV can bring in, and with all the complexities of media-mogul ownership, he'll have to know how to handle the media, negotiate deals, and walk through the minefield of modern corporations. He'll have to know Fehr and the union; he'll have to have the owners' trust. People will have to like him. Most of all, because his official powers are so limited, he'll have to be a persuasive person. He'll have to be a salesman, a good bullshit artist. Nothing else says they have to listen to what he says.

Is Bud Selig that guy? I can't tell you. People used to ask if I would want the job, but my personality's too brash, I talk too straight, I don't like politicking, and I would never trade the Midwest for life in New York City, especially with a toothless job. I like what I'm doing now, and besides, if I ever need the money, I can go back to managing again. I've always thought Bob Costas, with his knowledge and love of baseball, his foresight, and his savvy with the media, would be the best candidate you'd find. He's also trusted by every faction in the game, from the players on up. Bob said from the start he wasn't interested, though, so it was never an issue. And besides, how big a pay cut can one person take?

So the owners settled on Mr. Selig, the quail they were really hunting all along. Is he trusted enough in baseball? Do the owners even listen to him? Will he take a stand like Giamatti could? Can he talk anybody into anything? I guess we'll find out soon.

The one thing I can say is he's willing to ask questions. Right after Bud was named full commissioner last year, the day before he moved his stuff into his new office there in Brewers country, I happened to be in Milwaukee for an umpiring camp Bruce Froemming was running. Bud found out I was in town, gave me a call, and invited me over. When I arrived, he had this long list of questions and ideas he wanted to go through, and he wanted my response to each one. I heard him out and gave him my opinions, and he sure took a hell of a lot of notes; whether he'll use what I said, I can't tell you, but at least he's smart enough to ask people who've been down there on the field. That's important.

In the end, Bud's the only guy we've got, so what the hell? Let's give him the ball and see what he's got. He might fare a little better than Neil Allen did for me.

Well, I'm not the commissioner and I'm never going to be, and Bud didn't ask for *my* list. But you know I have a few opinions of my own.

As an ex-player, scout, coach, manager, and GM, I've looked at the game from as many angles as anybody who ever walked the planet, and God knows I've given it a lot of thought. I watch games, I talk to people, I read, I stay in touch. I find all these problems interesting. I've thought about what good commissioners have done, about what one should do now. If Bud wants to use some of these ideas, fine—no charge.

If I were commissioner, I'd look into six areas where I could help give the game back to the people who own it—the fans. Some are large, some are small, and they cover a lot of ground. But here's what I'd suggest to Bud.

1. SHAQ ATTACK

I've got four grandsons who play baseball. One's a real good player, a high-school junior who pitches and plays first base in Blue Springs, a Kansas City suburb. He doesn't have a plus fastball yet—you never know when a pitcher's going to get his velocity—but he can get people out, and that's what you look for. So the scouts are interested. But I'll make a bet with you: I'll bet he's the only one of my grandsons who knows who Ken Griffey Jr. is. And yet the amazing thing is, if you got all four of 'em in a room and asked who's heard of Shaquille O'Neal, they'd all jump up and down and holler, "Shaq! Shaq!" To them, he's the man—or at least one of them. And that's typical.

O'Neal, the center for the Lakers, is still raw material. He's never won an NBA title and may never do it. Hakeem Olajuwon handed him his ass in the NBA Finals, and he *still* ain't learned to sink a free throw. Griffey, on the other hand, is a five-tool superstar who's been around the National Pastime for a long time, has won home-run titles and speaks well for our game. Now *you* answer the question: Why in the hell do these kids know Shaquille O'Neal and not Junior Griffey? The answer is marketing. Baseball's marketing is terrible, at a time when it's more important than ever.

Baseball is like any form of entertainment. If it's going to do well, people have to know about the stars who play it. Mark McGwire, the modern Babe, isn't the only guy we can get in the public eye. The game's got a lot of attractive young players: Alex Rodriguez of the Mariners, Mike Piazza of the Mets, Griffey, Barry Bonds, Chipper Jones, Juan Gonzalez of the Rangers, and a lot more. Garciaparra on the Red Sox; Sammy Sosa. The list goes on. It's really a *good* time for star players in this game.

But let's face it: Baseball's been a public-relations nightmare. Maybe it's because the club owners resent the damn players so much and don't *want* to support them; I don't know. But the stars need a national profile. The game is targeting younger audiences, and that's important to do, but is it doing that right? Remember that 1997 ad campaign on TV? "*Baseball. If you don't like it, move to Norway.*" What the hell does that mean? You can't think of something *in* the game to feature? Baseball's a game that invites people in. If I don't like the game yet, is some rude message going to grab me? Hell, after I heard that, if I'd had a little time, I might have got on a plane, flown to Oslo, and not come back.

For good marketing models, look to two other big sports. Football is naturally telegenic. Bert Bell, the NFL commissioner in the fifties, and later on Pete Rozelle, played that up great. It's what made their league. Check out the job David Stern's done as NBA commissioner; look at how *they've* promoted. Pro basketball players are the greatest athletes in the world, with Michael Jordan at the top of that list, and those Lakers–Celtics rivalries were wonderful, but *marketing* put that league over the top. They lose Magic Johnson and Larry Bird, Jordan leaves to play baseball, and all of a sudden, all we hear is *Shaq!* Shaq drinking Pepsi, Shaq in videos, Shaq dunking basketballs like Godzilla. Then it's Penny Hardaway, Grant Hill. Think that's an accident?

Well, where are the Mike Piazza ads? *Try Mike Piazza Pizza from Pizza Hut!* Where's the Chipper Jones potato-chip ads? *Chipper eats Pringles!* How come Mark McGwire only has that one little Big Mac section in the upper deck at Busch Stadium when he should be smiling down from the Golden Arches? I hear he's negotiating with McDonald's now, but that's just a natural. How many fans know Greg Maddux's off-the-field personality, or Randy Johnson's, or Larry Walker's? Those kind of endorsements would make the players some money, but it's bigger than that: They'd also publicize the sport. Hell, I'll bet you more people know Ironhead Heyward, a second-string NFL running back, for soaping up in that Zest commercial than realize Tony Gwynn has won seven batting titles—*seven!*—in San Diego. Let's use TV, be funny, show off the players that matter, promote the game.

2. THE LITTLE SCREEN

Two games are better on TV than they are in person: football and golf. With football, unless I'm right on the fifty-yard line, twenty rows up, I can see more of what's going on right in my living room without having to go out in a big crowd and freeze, than I can in person. Golf was the dullest dishwater on television fifteen years ago, but it's wonderful now: They don't have the lulls, they've got cameras all over, they shoot you back and forth, they rerun a great putt or a nice shot if you miss it, and now they even throw a bone to all of us hackers by showing it on replay when Tiger Woods or Mark O'Meara skulls one into the lake. Now that's a good time!

Baseball hasn't adapted that way. It's really not a good TV sport to begin with. Cameras *are* situated better than they used to be, but you still don't get a feel for the whole event. The best place to watch baseball in person is between the first-base dugout and the third-base dugout, because that's where you can hear the pitcher, hear the ball smacking the catcher's mitt, get a good sense of the game. TV hasn't found a way to capture that yet.

The announcers don't help. Baseball's a simple game, but it's got to be a mystery to some fans because of the commentary. A few announcers are fine, and I *know* it's a tough job, but God almighty! Some of these guys ought to have five marbles in their mouths so you can't understand what they're saying. If they're not trying to prove how much inside stuff they know, they're flat-out cheering for the home team, and either way, the viewer never learns a thing about what's really going on. You hear so much about *signs* you want to scream! Signs don't mean a thing. I can tell you from experience, half the guys can't remember what signal they're supposed to be looking at. And when a guy really does screw up, the home announcers won't comment. "Looks like he got a bad jump on the ball!" they'll say. *Say* it: "So-and-so got a terrible jump!" Explain why. I wish they'd make me an announcer, boy; I'd say it: "So-and-so ain't hit a cutoff man in five years!" If the outfielder throws to the wrong guy and the runner goes to second, that eliminates the double play. That's important in a baseball game. But they never comment on things like that.

I enjoyed the hell out of Harry Caray, but he was another guy I had to *translate* sometimes. *We're only two games out of fourth place*—that meant they were last in a horseshit division! If it was 80 percent chance of rain, Harry would have called it a one in five chance of sunshine. That's just the way he was. I actually prefer his son, Skip, who does play-by-play for the Atlanta Braves. They're so different you can't believe they come from the same family. I managed ten years in St. Louis, and Skip is so low-key I don't think he came down on the field one time to shoot the bull in all those years. Just keep to himself, stuck to his business. On the air, his humor is dry and his delivery is calm, but when he and Don Sutton talk, they know what they're saying. Pay attention and you'll really learn what's happening on the field. Tom Paciorek and Ken Harrelson, the White Sox announcers, are like that, too. They've got a good comedy act on the air, sure, but they'll also tell you what's going on in a game, good or bad. Listen to them sometime. There's not too many like that.

Maybe you can't do much about announcers; I don't know. I *do* know you can't change the fact that people ain't going to sit inside for three and a half hours on Saturday afternoon to watch baseball anymore. There's too many other things to do now. But a commissioner could do some things to shorten games. He could order a return to the true strike zone, which would force hitters to be more aggressive and reduce the long counts. He could penalize the showboating that goes on with a lot of the hitters, stepping out of the box and dusting themselves off and so on, which takes up too much of everybody's time for no reason. That used to be self-regulating: The Bob Gibsons and Don Drysdales would just throw the old rib-cage fastball, knock the hitter on his ass three times his next time up. That'd be the end of that. But modern pitchers don't do that; it's really changed. So *that* adds time.

Bud might even reconsider a change baseball made that not many fans know about—the length of time between innings. Those breaks used to be sixty seconds long during the regular season, but baseball expanded them to two minutes each to make room for TV commercials. If you were ever sitting in the stands and cussed out a ballplayer because you didn't see him sprinting like Carl Lewis out to his position, remember: It ain't laziness you're seeing. Why should a guy hightail it out to centerfield, then stand there for two minutes while they run another Gatorade ad? Ozzie used to sit in the dugout an extra minute just so he wouldn't end up standing around out there, but how many guys put that much thought in it? I never hear this mentioned, but baseball tacked seventeen minutes onto each game without ever throwing a pitch. Maybe the fans would watch more often and watch longer if the whole deal didn't take so much time.

Shortening games would call for some trade-offs. You're cutting into some profits. The owners won't tell you this, but the fact is, they *love* longer games. They sell more beer and hot dogs that way. Have you noticed there are more long rain delays now? It used to be that if the game didn't start on time, an ump had two hours to decide whether to cancel it. In '97, we started having *three*-hour delays. Now, that's unfair to fans. Some of them—a lot of them—have driven 200-plus miles, like Peorians who come see the Cardinals, or Wichitans who love to watch the Royals. Those folks have to change their plans, sit around forever to figure out whether to cash it in, and maybe get back home at 4:30 in the morning. That ain't right! The owners only notice that *people keep drinking* those three hours. Well, you need a commissioner to put it straight: If it's bad for our fans, it's bad for the game. We've got to give it back to the fans!

3. WINTER BLUNDERLAND

Before the days of ESPN, Headline News, and round-the-clock, wall-to-wall, year-round coverage, it used to seem like a hell of a long time between the end of the World Series and the opening of spring camp. Those were long, cold months for baseball fans, a long time to sit on your hands. But baseball wanted to stay in the headlines, remind everybody the season was just around the corner, and spark a few season-ticket renewals. So what did they do? All the general managers, owners, and managers got together for a week in some warm, toasty place—Phoenix, Palm Springs, St. Petersburg—to talk to reporters, make a few trades, shoot the shit, and have themselves a hell of a good time. And the winter meetings were born.

Well, in case you haven't noticed, times have changed. A week doesn't go by in the off-season where you don't have some free-agent signing, agent whining, or ballclub threatening to move if it can't get a brand-new ballpark. It all makes the papers; the fans can't get away from it. There's more than enough baseball to choke a Clydesdale. Why in the hell do we need winter meetings?

Maybe it's to facilitate trades? Well. Let's say Walt Jocketty, the Cards' GM, is on his way to the hotel hot tub there in Scottsdale, and he runs into Bill Bavasi, the Angels' GM, who's got his bag full of Pings and is headed to the first fairway. They're both probably in pretty festive moods, and Bill knows he needs a lefty reliever and before you can say Bo Belinsky, maybe Lance Painter's on his way to Anaheim to wear that crazy new Angels logo with the sprouting wings. It *can* work like that. But admit it: We're in the age of technology. The world is smaller. You can't pick up the phone and call? You can't use that fax machine on your desk? You could do that business better from your own office. Why do you need meetings?

What's more, the way they schedule winter meetings wipes out even that purpose. Arbitration hearings didn't exist at the time of the first winter meetings. Now they do, and they're held in January. Well, that's the single most important off-season month now: That's when those cases get settled. So prior to the first week of February, Ed Lynch might not know if he's going to be paying his leftfielder $500,000 or $4 million. If it's the second figure, he might have to deal the guy. He doesn't know his salary structure or his needs. He doesn't know what he's got and what he ain't got. He doesn't know a thing yet! Why do we have winter meetings in December?

Winter meetings are asinine. They cost baseball a lot of time, money, and energy. Let's face it: They're an excuse for everybody to drink martinis, slap backs, and get out on the golf course. Let's use our resources right. Let's dump the winter meetings altogether. Or if you can't part with them, hold 'em after the Super Bowl, in the first week of February, when general managers know what's going on. That way, God forbid, there might be a point to it.

4. THE SHRUNKEN APPLE

Today, the two league offices and the commissioner's office are in the same building in New York, one floor apart. People act like that's an edict sent down from Abner Doubleday in heaven.

Before Bowie Kuhn, a New York lawyer, put his offices in New York, there was no real link between baseball's front offices and the so-called Big Apple. Warren Giles, the National League president, used to be in Cincinnati; Will Harris, an American League president, had his office in Chicago. The commissioner's office, when Ford Frick was the boss, was in Chicago. Happy Chandler had his in Louisville, Kentucky. Think about it: Now that we've got teams on both coasts, geography says offices in Chicago, Kansas City, St. Louis, or Milwaukee make the most sense. You're only two hours from the West Coast, one from the East. That way, the game might even recall that most of its fans, and a lot of its history, are out there across the fruited plains, not in some office building on Park Avenue in Manhattan.

If you saw Ken Burns's TV documentary, *Baseball*, on PBS, you saw this prejudice in spades. There were college professors up the backside, boy, but how many ballplayers did they talk to? And from that movie, you'd have thought the game was played on the East Coast alone. Bullshit! Baseball is America's game, not just a private party between the Yankees and the Red Sox. You're going to tell me you're making a movie about baseball, and you're not even going to include an interview with Stan Musical? He's one of the greats of all time, man—alive and well! Yet who was doing the talking? Seemed like it was eighteen hours of talking heads from Harvard. Are you kidding me?

I don't really care about it, but that movie just tells you something. As far as our leadership goes, who says you have to have offices in New York? Who says all three offices have to be in the same building? How often do you think you need to have the commissioner and the American League and the National League presidents in the same room? New Year's Eve day, before they all go out and get happy?

If a Bud Selig, or any other commissioner or league president, wants to keep his offices in New York, fine. He should be able to, but he should not *have* to. And Selig has opened an office, or a branch of the commissioner's office, in Milwaukee. Good for Bud. Let's not do things just because we've *been* doing them. Our headquarters should mirror the game itself.

5. A NEW OLD GUARD

Among the people who argue baseball issues, there's a false comparison set up today. You're either a purist or you're a progressive. If you're a *purist* (sometimes they say "traditionalist"), that means you want to stick to all the old ways. You're backward, an old-timer, you hate progress. If you're a *progressive*, though, you're *for* change. You're modern, you want to jazz things up, you want to take it into a new era. You don't want to be stuck in the mud.

Well, that's a bullshit comparison. Those are your only two options? If you've been around, if you have experience, and you really do believe that certain things worked better in the past, you're written off as a crank. Well, here's some news for you: Some things *did* work better in the past. You're going to let all that experience go to waste? Sometimes you have to look backward to go forward, right? If you don't understand that, you've got as much sense as a resin bag.

There just aren't enough people in baseball today who *know* baseball. There aren't enough who've played the game, managed it, been on the inside. Look at the league presidents: Dr. Gene Budig and Leonard Coleman are both gentlemen, but neither has played baseball. Bud's a good guy, but he's not a career baseball man. One reason you never hear about things like bonus rules is that not many people know they ever happened. How the hell would they? They haven't been around long enough. That gives you one less option to pick from, you miss out, and it just goes from there.

Major League Baseball should have a planning committee, a group of four or five guys who have been in the game, who've played, managed, been general managers, and who know what worked twenty or twenty-five years ago. I'd be glad to serve on that, as long as I didn't have to move out of St. Louis. So might a Bing Devine, my former boss with the Mets, who's been a

GM with the Cardinals and the Mets and a creative, intelligent baseball man for fifty-some years—and who was scouting for the Phillies right up until last season, at age eighty-one. Hank Peters might, too; he's the former GM who built the Oakland A's dynasties and kept clubs like the Orioles and Indians viable when they were running on a shoestring. Hank never had a big payroll, so he doesn't get the notice he would have if he'd had more money to work with, but he's got a wealth of knowledge. A Joe DiMaggio, a Sparky Anderson, or a Yogi Berra might be interested. Why not ask them? They'd make up an advisory board, and it would meet monthly, discuss what's happening on the field, come up with ideas to better the rules and the game, and present them to the union and the owners in regular joint meetings. How could you lose?

There's a lot of good knowledge out there, and right now, we're flushing it down the can. Let's use all we've got.

6. Office Affairs

If I were Bud Selig, I'd streamline operations in three ways. First of all, it's costly and cumbersome to have two league presidents; you don't need that anymore. I'd take the league presidents and make them assistants to the commissioner. Second, I would establish a written set of guidelines for the commissioner's job itself, and I'd try to get that officially approved. As far as I know, the commissioner's powers aren't even written down anywhere; nobody knows what they are! I'd work up a clear set of duties and powers of the officer so they could be passed along from one commissioner to the next in an orderly way. And finally, while I would not try to give the commissioner absolute power—that's not a good idea—I *would* restore that clause that says players and teams can't sue him over his rulings. Let everybody agree: He's the boss, we trust him to make the calls, and his decisions are final. Let's let our problems get solved from inside the game.

Even when Giamatti was around, the boss's job was pretty ill-defined. He took it on himself to define it, though. The man did what he thought was right for the game. Not for him, not for the owners, not for the agents, but for the game. We don't have anybody with the power to do that now. Nobody has that job. Nobody even *thinks* in those terms in Major League Baseball. How's that for a way to run an industry?

And Bart had personal authority.

There was one owner Giamatti ticked off more than he did anybody else. That was George Steinbrenner. Like I've told you, I do really like George. Hell, every time I won something as a manager, the first guy who'd send me a telegram would be the guy they call The Boss. But he does throw his weight around like a runner in a home-plate collision, and he doesn't want the catcher to have any rights. That kind of stuff isn't always good for baseball.

Giamatti wasn't afraid to block George and protect the plate. He called him on the carpet, he tested George, he didn't just roll over or look the other way. That showed everybody in baseball something. He was willing to treat everybody, rich or poor, in the exact same way. In other words, he was fair. Now that we've got big sharks and little minnows all swimming in the same pond, we need a leader like that more than ever, a guy who is willing to keep everyone healthy and playing by the same rules. That's harder to get than you think in a CEO, and if it doesn't come down from the top, it won't happen at all.

How many people ever have to handle a situation as tough as the one Bart had with Pete Rose? Here was the Hit King, the guy who had more base knocks than anybody in the history of this sport. And here you had a new commissioner, a guy who had been a college professor, a teacher. You might not have thought Bart stood a chance. A lot of people would have been intimidated.

Giamatti wasn't. What happened with Pete really bothered him. We'll never know what was said in those meetings or what was agreed to. Only three people really know: Fay Vincent, the commissioner after Bart, knows, but he ain't saying. Pete knows, and he'll never tell. Giamatti *can't*. So you and I are never going to know.

But whatever it is, to Giamatti, the welfare of the sport was the overriding factor. He loved that more than anything, so he took a real stand. He even said he believed Rose bet on baseball. And he made it clear what that meant: Charlie Hustle was out. Banished from the game. Pete even ended up playing on a prison softball team. He's a proud, proud man, and a tough one, but I'm sure that took some of the wind out of his sails. I'm sure he realizes he did some things that were wrong.

Bart died only eight days after announcing his ruling. Maybe it was the stress of that situation that pushed him into an early grave. Maybe it was the fact he worked those long hours, smoked like a chimney, and never took care of himself. But it tells you he gave a damn. No matter whose cleats he stepped on, Bart Giamatti was going to act in the best interests of baseball, come hell or high water. Now *that's* a powerful commissioner.

· 18 ·
Last of the Ninth (Cycles)

In the year it's taken to write this book, a lot has happened in the game. Things change day to day, week to week, and month to month. Just like the scores on the scoreboard, the home-run totals, and the top player salaries we have, the stakes in baseball keep rising. I want to talk about that.

They're calling 1998 "The Year That Saved Baseball." I hear that everywhere: "The National Pastime is back," says one writer. "Our troubles are over!" says another. And it does seem like the strike of '94, which ticked off millions of fans—including me—is a lot further behind us. There's never been anything like the '98 home-run derby, where Sammy Sosa and Mark McGwire were first chasing my old friend Roger, and then, at the end, chasing only each other. When McGwire was at 62 homers near the end, and Sammy was at 58, everybody thought it was over, but then Sosa came back to tie it for a day, and Mac had to respond. That added some zing to it. Everybody was jacked up about the balls flying out of the yard, and it was a tonic for the game.

That was true throughout baseball. Wherever the Cards or Cubs played, attendance jumped. Thanks to Mark and his 70 home runs, the Cardinals—a team that was never in the race—sold 3.2 million tickets. With their payroll at about $50 million, they would have lost a lot of money otherwise, so he really saved that franchise. Those two were on the cover of every magazine, smiling and hugging and having a hell of a time, and it was all done in an atmosphere of respect for the game. Across the country, people were talking baseball—and for the first time in a long while, not too many were cursing when they did it.

Still, was it The Year That Saved Baseball? Let's think about that.

To put it in a bigger perspective, let's look at the players. When I think back to the first big-league game I ever saw, I can still see Stan Musial at Sportsman's Park, and when he went 4 for 5—and hit the ball hard on his only out—I'd never seen anything like that. It was a thing of beauty. As one of the great batsmen ever, Stan still only got a base hit about one time in three, but from that day on, every time I saw Stan Musial bat, I *expected* him to get a hit. It kept you on the edge of your seat. That's how good he was. Later on, I felt the same way about Ted Williams; when he got in the batter's box, you always thought he was going to get a base hit. That's good for the game, good for the fans.

No doubt about it, Sammy Sosa had a hell of a year in '98. I always knew Roger's mark was going to fall soon, and I figured somebody would hit 70 not too far in the future. But if you'd asked me before last year who was likely to do it, Sammy wouldn't have made my top ten. Even from his days with the Texas Rangers, he's had superstar ability, but he always swung at anything you'd throw him. That's the beauty of baseball: You think you've seen it all, then something happens that really knocks the birds off your bat.

But McGwire is something different. As a power hitter, I'd put him in the category of the all-time greats. It don't matter to me if the ball's jacked up and the pitching's watered down; 70 is 70, man. They're talking about naming a St. Louis highway after him. And the way he came down to the last weekend with 66, then hit *four more* in the last two days? Don't tell me he didn't have his eye on that nice, round number.

Does the average fan have any idea how hard it is to go to the plate intending to hit a home run, then actually do it? I don't think so. It's tough! That's what Mark did—all that weekend, all that year, right to the last weekend. Talk about focus! That was something. He's like Stan and Ted, but with the home run. Every time he goes to the plate, I actually expect to see Mark McGwire hit one out. Think about what that does to the fans.

It's tough to compare Mark as a hitter to the Mantles, the Mayses, and the others. I think he's the strongest man who ever played the game. He's right to say baseball's a twelve-month job now; like most guys, he does weight training year round, so he's got that incredible power going. But he's a selective hitter, too; look at his 162 walks, a National League record. And on some of them 155 strikeouts, he deliberately let the pitches go right down central because he was looking for the pitch he wanted. He goes up there with a plan.

You can get Mark McGwire out. The top number-one guys—the Schillings, the Randy Johnsons—know the holes in his swing, and they normally stick the bat up his ass. He'll go 0 for 4 against them. I'm not saying he doesn't solve them once in a while—he does—but he's vulnerable to the high strike when the umpires do call it, which admittedly ain't often today. The Seavers, Gibsons, and Koufaxes would have gotten him out, too—but hell, they got out the great hitters in their day; that's the way it goes with the best. All the great sluggers, like McGwire, have always feasted on that second-level pitching, that 87 mph fastball that ain't quite top-notch. There's a lot more pitchers like that today, sure, but does anybody take them to outer space like Mark does? Unlike Roger, the so-called flash in the pan who really was never a home-run hitter to begin with, Mark is a bona fide slugger and always has been, right from his rookie year, and that was long before he ever heard of andro or creatine. Anyone who can hit 50 a year for three straight years would have done it in any era.

Still, I have to say, I don't get all that excited about the home run. I'd rather see an intelligent, well-played game and watch a winning team. I didn't go down to Busch all year, not even for the record-tying homer, not even when ESPN asked me to show up and interview McGwire myself. Home runs help if you've set your offense up right, but this year showed you something I've always said: Big power numbers don't necessarily help you win. We scored damn near 700 runs some years with the Cardinals and didn't hit much more than 70 as a team, and we won pennants. It all depends how they come and when they come.

The Cards finished nineteen games out; how exciting is *that* to a real fan? The Cubs squeaked past the Giants for the wild card, then got swept by Atlanta in three; all of Sosa's heroics didn't get his team within twelve games of a division title. And meanwhile, the other big story of the year was the New York Yankees setting the American League record with 114 wins, winning the World Series, and dominating baseball in one of the best single-season performances of all time. And not one of their players hit 30 home runs.

No, a team can't win just by hitting home runs. There's more to the game than that—a lot more. And baseball can't, either. Ninety-eight was a hell of a year, for sure. But did all those homers mean baseball is really back? Let's look at that.

First of all, we have six divisions in the major leagues now. In 1998, how many pennant races did we have? One. Anaheim and Texas were tied going into the final week. The Cubs, Giants and Mets battled for the National League wild card, too. But outside of that, the other five division winners—Atlanta, San Diego, Houston, the Yankees, and Cleveland—ended up in first place by an average of fourteen games. The American League wild card, the Red Sox, finished twenty-two games behind the Yankees and a comfortable four ahead of the next-best team, Toronto. We have thirty ballclubs in the majors; twenty-three of them finished nine games or more out of first place. There were no races; there was no competition. That's a joke.

Now let's go outside the big-time markets. The game doesn't begin and end in those places. Ask the good baseball fans in Oakland, Pittsburgh, Minnesota, Kansas City, Montreal, Cincinnati, and Milwaukee if *they* thought this was the greatest year ever in baseball. Out of those teams, the nearest one to first place was 14½ games out. Not one of them had a chance from the beginning, and their fans knew it. What's more, they'll have no chance next year or the year after that; they'll never make the postseason again if the rules don't change. Why would anybody buy a ticket? And we ain't even talking about Tampa Bay and Florida, both of which finished fifty-plus games behind! We're supposed to have revenue-sharing in baseball now, but everybody knows that's just spit in the wind. The gap is wider than ever, and it keeps on widening.

There's also a yawning superstar gap. The average small-city team can't even afford one marquee player. Go ahead; name a superstar on the A's, the Pirates, the Royals, the Brewers, or the Twins. Hell, name a regular! Matt Stairs of Oakland can hit, and Ben Grieve is a good young player, but they sure as hell aren't household names. Neither is Johnny Damon, Todd Walker, or Bobby Higginson. If they ever *become* household names, they'll be wearing somebody else's colors when they do. If you can't compete on the field, you at least need one guy who's good for the gate. Until the rules change, a third of our clubs can't even afford that.

Here's something else you don't read: Across the country, fewer people are watching Major League Baseball than they were a few years back. Sure, there's excitement in the big markets. Yankee fans are stirred up;

why shouldn't they be? They can kick the hell out of all those bad teams. Look at what they did to the Royals— trounced them ten times in ten games. That's a far cry from the old days when my Royals teams fought Billy Martin's Yanks tooth-and-nail in the playoffs. But in 1998, attendance in fifteen cities—half the major-league towns—dropped from the year before. Don't those fans deserve a team they can root for? And about 2,000 fewer fans attended the average game in '98 than came to the ballgames in '94, right before the strike happened. Even worse, a marquee World Series—maybe the best Yankee club of all time, in a matchup against a pretty good un- derdog—couldn't keep TV ratings from falling 16 per- cent from the year before. That's unbelievable! And the year before that, when it was Cleveland versus Florida, it wasn't exactly a programmer's dream.

Sure, we had a lot of fans watching the home-run chase. But are they baseball fans, or do they just like the noise and the spectacle? Are they going to be around next year, or the year after that, when there ain't any chase? Or what if there is one; will they be as worked up about it as the first time around? Maybe they don't have world-class attention spans; and we all know this isn't going to happen all the time. Will the shot wear off? Baseball's not a quick-fix game, it's a long-term one. Will they stay around for the marathon?

Now, I wouldn't want to be on the mound trying to get Mark McGwire out. Sometimes you think those guys need a screen out there for protection, he hits 'em so hard. But that's not half as scary as thinking about what all this homermania might be doing to the health of my profession itself. It's been exciting, hell yes, for a year; I don't know if I'd trade the excitement. But you can't give in to this automatic idea that the home run will save baseball, the way it did in the Babe Ruth era.

The stakes are higher now. Our decisions are more expensive. And we might just have a situation on our hands where the exact thing the owners see as baseball's salvation is dooming it to long-term disaster.

If you trace the history of baseball, you see movement in cycles. First you have an era of big offense; then the pitchers and defense catch up till the pendulum swings back. Gashouse Gang–style "little ball," with steals and sacrifices and taking the extra base, takes over for a while; then the home-run game returns. Even in a single ballgame, the players go from offense to defense and back, and the hitter's job is to get on base, touch them all, and end up right where he started. The more you progress, the more you see the things you've seen before. That's the way of the game.

But the last quarter-century, that's changed; baseball history hasn't gone in cycles, it's just been one can of worms after another.

First you had free agency, salary arbitration, and the skyrocketing salaries all that created. Thanks to Marvin Miller, pay for ballplayers rose faster in a shorter time than it ever did in any American industry. It hasn't stopped yet. We've still got arbitration. Free agency keeps mushrooming. John Mayberry's million-dollar deal won't buy you a middle reliever—not even a right-handed one. You had Puckett with $3 million a year; then Jose Canseco topping $4 million; Roger Clemens topping $5 million; and Bonds, Griffey, and Belle pushing it past six, eight, and $11 million a year, all in the span of six years. The curve keeps climbing. Pedro Martinez got $12.5 million a year from the Red Sox before '98; Piazza signed with the Mets for $13 million a year last offseason. It'll just keep going up. Before my clock runs out, somebody will get that $20 million I predicted twenty years back. And nothing and nobody has acted to stop this rising curve or even slow it down.

Why? Here's the thinking in baseball: "Hell, maybe this ain't good for the game, but if I don't give Joe Blow this much, somebody else is going to. Here's the money, bud." They make the offer. Then you have more cans of worms; the next big free agent uses that figure to negotiate from. Costs keep spiraling, the rich keep getting richer, and the average fan gets left further behind. The same, as I've said, is happening with our draft choices. First the Diamondbacks pay Travis Lee $10 million before he—or they!—ever played a game. Last year's top pick, Pat Burrell of the Phillies, got a five-year contract with a guaranteed $8 million. Next time, it'll be higher. That's something you don't hear about The Year That Saved Baseball, and yet it's as important as any home run records will ever be.

And look at the game itself, the way it's played. Now that the home run is king, it just feeds on itself. Everybody wants a new ballpark for luxury boxes; every one of them has the smaller, home run-friendly dimensions of a Camden Yards. There are only one or two ballparks of any size anymore, and they're disappearing fast. So we see more checked-swing, opposite-field, pop-fly home runs than ever. My friend Bob Costas says it's hard to make that home-run call today: "It's a routine fly ball . . . No, it's going back . . . It's outta here!" They're flying out so often. And the thing is, the more home runs get hit, the less each one is worth—but the more home runs somebody hits, the more you have to pay him. Ain't that a kick? You might be wondering why one club can't be different and build a bigger ballpark, with a team to match. Why can't one or two clubs feature pitching and defense and manufacture runs the way we did with the Cardinals? Well, it's built right into the architecture: You only have eighty-one home games, and in every other ballpark on the planet, they'd home run you to death. No, that ain't going to work. You have to adapt.

So the more balls fly out, the more it costs; the more it costs, the less chance the small fish have. Only fourteen teams had payrolls of less than $44 million last year, and all of them finished below .500. A payroll of $50 million-plus doesn't guarantee you a good year—just look at the Baltimore Orioles—but a payroll of less than $44 million is a sure ticket to failure. That's going to get worse. Like I've said before, we're going to lose some teams.

Things can't go on the way they have been. Something has to change, and we're better off using our brains and making the changes now than waiting for the bubble to burst on its own. That's why ideas like bonus rules are so important. With bonus rules, you'd create a situation where the owners would have to regulate their own costs in a sensible way. They could pay all they wanted to in bonuses, but they'd pay a price for it—a steep price—on the field and on the roster. Would George Steinbrenner want more than a couple of raw rookies on his club for two years? Don't bet on it. He wants to win right now, so he'd leave some young talent for the other teams. Then you'd have some control, some balance back in baseball. You'd go back to the cycles, not the cans of worms. You might save the game.

We're lucky the home run chase happened. It was good for the game—for a year. And Mark McGwire is a deserving champion. You want to talk about cycles? How about the way he talked up Roger Maris all year, studied him, and kept his struggles in mind? What about the way Mark shared his moment of triumph with the Maris family? When he hit numbers sixty-one and sixty-two in St. Louis, he didn't have to go over and embrace Roger's boys, but he did, and they fell in love with Mark McGwire that day. It eased some of the suffering they've felt. Their dad didn't have it like McGwire; the whole country was rooting against him, pulling for him to fall on his ass, and it never accepted Roger Maris as a hero, not then or ever. Thirty-seven years later, all of America was pulling for McGwire to do it. That makes a hell of a difference! So when he took all that popularity and used it to include Pat and the boys, that really brought it full circle for them. And it did for me, too.

Now let me ask you something: If Mike Piazza is worth $91 million for seven years, what's a guy like

Mark McGwire worth? People all over North America pay good money just to watch him hit. The Pittsburgh Pirates played at home one Thursday and drew 9,000; the Cards came to town Friday, and they drew 35,000. That happened all year, from Milwaukee to Montreal, and it sure as hell wasn't about seeing the Cardinals' juggernaut. In dollar value, Mark McGwire might even be bigger than the game right now. And how did baseball get so lucky? He's a good guy, a humble person, a man with his feet on the ground. He loves his family, he likes St. Louis. He gives $1 million a year to help abused kids. But more than anything, he really appreciates that without baseball, he would never have had the chance to do what he did. He didn't have to use his accomplishment to honor the game he plays, but he did. How many owners can say anything like that?

If they could, they might act different. They might realize that a home run record ain't going to save baseball all by itself. They might see that a long-ball barrage comes with a price tag, and they might think like grownups about how to fit that price into their budget. They might use this good season to enrich the game. But they see Mark's feat like a cure-all. They're letting him, and those home runs, do all the work. And they're letting a great achievement turn into one more can of worms.

Where's it going to end? I don't know. When McGwire hits a homer, where does it come down? Over the wall and out of sight. Great year or not in 1998, right now, unless we make some real changes, that's where baseball is headed.

You ought to see that picture of me and Casey down in the den. It's been on the wall ever since Mary Lou and I moved into this house ten years ago, and I still show it off when people come to call. He and I are both on that motorcycle. He's gripping the handlebars with a crazed look on his face, like he always got when he was having a hell of a time, and I'm on the seat behind, laughing. If you were on the back of his bike, boy, you got a lot wind in your face; that's the way he was. I'd think the Honda corporation would love to get their hands on it, but the bidding would have to start awfully high. It reminds me of the greatest baseball man I ever knew, how lucky I was to know him. And it reminds me of those cycles in the game.

I think about where mine will end. I never thought I'd manage in the big leagues—I always aimed to be a player—let alone win 1,281 games and go to three World Series, all right here in my adopted home state of Missouri. Which was also Casey's home state. But the Perfesser might have known. Why else did he spend so much time teaching me the game?

Whenever I'm out, I run into people who ask me the same question: When are you managing again? I read the papers around here, and people still write letters to the *Post-Dispatch* saying they want me back in the Cardinals' dugout. They remember the '80s fondly. God, they loved those teams. I do appreciate it, but it's a little embarrassing. I try to stay away from that stuff. St. Louis has a manager, and I sure as hell ain't after Tony's job.

I don't miss the travel, the two- and three-day stops, and the hassles with agents, that's for sure. But I do miss managing; I miss the games. There's nothing like using what you know, angling for an edge, forcing the other guy's hand. I probably miss the strategy more than most: I forced the action so much, I really managed both teams most of the time. See what his weaknesses are, get into his bench early, strip 'em clean. That's the fun of it.

I could still do it. I've got the energy. I get checkups every year, and I'm in excellent shape for my age. I've even got great kidneys for an old man. My mind is good. I still handle people the same way I always did. Talk to them straight, and if you do that, I don't give a damn how old you are or how much money they're making, it can work. If they respect your knowledge of the game, and you treat 'em like men, if you tell 'em the truth, you can handle baseball players or anybody else. It's about people more than anything. I could do it tomorrow, and I could put some of these other skippers in the food line by July. I still think about it.

I would never campaign for a job, but I've had a lot of offers; I get calls all the time. The Royals offered me their managing position a few years ago, but the details weren't right. I've said no to the Cubs—hell, you can't fish in the daytime in the summer there!—and the Red Sox twice. The first time was right after I left the Cardinals; this last time, in 1996, I declined because Dan Duquette, their GM, couldn't assure me they were going to sign Roger Clemens, their number-one starter. Even though they had a hell of a hitting club, without Clemens I figured they were only about the twelfth-best team in that league. That's what I told Dan. Hell, you can spend a third of the money they offered me and still finish twelfth! Little did I know they were going to go out and get Pedro Martinez; I'd have thought twice if I'd known that, boy! But you can't worry about it. You go with what you know, make your call, and move on.

The thing is, I really do love my retirement. I get to do what I want when I want, and at my age, I feel like I've earned that. I'm happy in the Midwest; I'm not an East Coast or a West Coast kind of guy. I love the four seasons, and the hunting, the fishing, and the friendships are better for me right here than they are anywhere else in the country. My brother, my hometown pinochle buddies, my barber, and my kids and grandkids are all pretty close by. The last couple of years, I've even gotten to like that purple dinosaur, Barney, a little bit. My youngest grandson, Alec, is a big fan, and I'm a hell of a big fan of his. So I've got lots of reasons to stay right where I am.

But if the situation were right—if it was a contending team that had a chance to win, if they paid me more money than anybody else, and if it was a team in the

Midwest or at least one that has a rich baseball tradition—I'd think about signing on for the short term. I would not stick an owner with a long-term deal at my age. That wouldn't be right.

I think of my career like I do a ballgame: You make the moves you know you should make; if they don't work out, hell, that's out of your hands. Just remember, a manager can lose ballgames by not being prepared, but no manager ever won a baseball game. A good manager does everything he can to put his right people in the right situations, where his players have their best chance of succeeding. He thinks, he plans, he knows his personnel and the other team's. He looks ahead. He creates the most favorable situation for his team to win. But it's the players who go out and get the hits, who throw strikes, and run the bases. If I do everything in my power as manager and still lose, I can look myself in the mirror when it's all over. I've done my job; I can sleep at night. And I can tell you I never lost a ballgame through my managing.

If I never managed another game, I'd be happier than hell at how everything's worked out. It's been a wonderful career. We've made great friends. We've seen the country. I've had the chance to manage both big-league teams in my home state, and I took them to the post-season six times. How many managers can say that? My teams were successful, drew millions of fans, and kicked up a hell of a ruckus some years. I can't complain about how it's all turned out.

In my game, though, you do want to be seen as the best, and that means the Hall of Fame. I won't lie to you; I'd like to get in. I know I did well enough to get close. I retired pretty early. If I'd taken that Red Sox job, or another one, and just stayed in the dugout another few years, I might have won two-thousand games easy. That seems to be a standard they look at. So does winning two World Series; I only won one, and I still think that one damn call—my friend Mr. Denkinger finally retired last year, by the way—might keep me out. But if I had a chance to take over a team that was close and maybe get near the winner's circle again, if I could go after that second one, it might be worth my while. I'd really have to think about it.

But you can't worry about it too much. Getting in can be a political thing. Hell, Roger Maris belongs in, but he never played that ass-kissing game. I don't have time for that stuff, either. I wouldn't do anything he didn't do. But the bigger problem I have is how we decide who gets to go in. I still think we don't know what we really value in the game of baseball.

One of the most unjust things that ever happened in this game was in 1947. That year Ted Williams hit .343, with 32 homers and 114 RBIs. He also drew 162 walks, for an on-base average of .499 to go along with his .634 slugging percentage. You couldn't say he was a shoo-in for the MVP, as Mr. DiMaggio had a heck of a year too, but do you know Ted lost in the balloting by one point? The writers choose the MVP by listing their top ten players for the year; a certain number of points are given for each ranking, then they add up all the totals to determine the winner.

Do you know what happened? One writer—I think it was a New York guy—looked at Ted Williams' season in 1947, and *did not list him in his top ten players* for that year. It cost Ted the MVP. Williams was a prickly guy, of course; not everybody liked him. But what's that got to do with it? That vote was personal, boy. A writer who pulls that kind of crap ought to be shot. Or if not quite that, he should at least forfeit his right to ever vote again. If he's a professional, that's malpractice of the worst kind. But that's the way things happen in baseball.

Roger Maris and the Hall of Fame—it's the same thing. He should be in, but he rubbed people the wrong way. Hack Wilson, who drank too much, had one of the greatest years in the history of baseball; he had 190 RBIs in 1930—a record that's stood for damn near seventy years and might never fall. Think about that. The man had 55 RBIs in one month! Hack died a nonmember in 1948, and he didn't get elected till 1979. Well, you say, he didn't play long enough? He didn't have enough good years? Does that mean it's longevity we're looking for? If so, that explains how Don Sutton made it in 1998. He won 324 games over twenty-three seasons in the big leagues and only won twenty games one time. He pitched strong year after year. So how does it explain Koufax? Sandy had only six good years out of twelve. A few were some of the best pitching years ever, but he only won 165 games, and *that* ain't longevity. For the position players, is it all-around play? Then Maris belongs in—and Ralph Kiner, who is in, doesn't. Ralph could hit home runs, and he was a slugger for the Pirates, but he couldn't run, he couldn't throw, he couldn't play the outfield worth a damn. What exactly are we measuring? Personality? Manners? The number of championships? Whether you played for the Dodgers or Yankees? If you can explain it to me, go ahead.

I could say the same about managers. Danny Murtaugh and Dick Williams both won two World Series; they're two of the best of all time. Why ain't they in? Danny was with the Pittsburgh Pirates his whole career, won 1,115 games, and had a better winning percentage (.540) than some guys in the Hall. Dick was a winner with three very different ballclubs, the late '60s Red Sox, the world champion A's of the '70s, and the late-'70s Montreal Expos. And Tommy Lasorda? He hadn't been retired long enough to paint his house when they waved him through the doors. Now, Tommy was a good manager and an outstanding ambassador for the game. He won 1,699 games and stayed with it for twenty years. But are wins the main factor? When Tommy got named, the first thing you heard was people saying, "Well, there's managers who won more games that aren't in." What does that prove? Your win total only tells you one thing: How long you were around. I'll bet those same guys *lost* more than Tommy did, too. Connie Mack managed for fifty-three years and won more games (3,776) than anybody in history. But he *lost* 1,000 more, too (4,025). What's your percentage when you're in there? That's the question.

My record puts me in the ballpark. I can't take sole credit for it, but my teams set more attendance records than any manager's in baseball: ten in fifteen years. That stimulated the game in Missouri. I'm the only man ever named Manager of the Year and Executive of the Year in the same season (1982). My teams played in three World Series; we won one, and the damnedest things happened in the others. You might be able to measure success the best by division titles—that's winning over the long haul—and I won six division titles in my fifteen years; Tommy won the same number in twenty. If they hadn't taken ours away in '81, I'd have had more than he did. Tommy won two World Series, too, but in his first, '81, his club didn't even win the NL West on the way there. Don't get me wrong; Tom is deserving. I'm just saying we need to look at every case for what it is and give some thought to what we're looking for.

If this fly ball dies on the warning track, I'm not going to gripe. I did things the way I thought was right. I never lied to a player. I made a million friends; I saw every town from Atlanta to Yakima, got to know some great Americans—some of whom you've even heard of—and enjoyed every minute along the way. While I stayed in the game, it was always a hell of a good ride, and when it stopped being fun, I left. I'm still having the time of my life. Can every guy in the Hall say that?

One who could was Casey Stengel. I thought of him a little bit when I saw what the Yankees did last year. That was one of the greatest teams I ever saw. And the Yankees have had a few, that's for sure.

The '98 Yanks weren't no Murderer's Row. Their everyday lineup was pretty ordinary. I like some of their players fine, but they ain't going to keep you awake at night the way Casey's clubs did. New York spent more than anybody in history on their bench players this year—Chili Davis, Darryl Strawberry, Chad Curtis, Tim Raines—but nobody ever equalled the depth Casey had with Mize, Slaughter, Tommy Henrich, Hank Bauer, and that bunch he could run out at you. But both those teams had depth. They could wear you down in the late innings.

Like I've said, the more some things change, the more they stay the same in baseball. You could not win in 1948 without good pitching, and you can't win without it today. The strength of Joe Torre's team last year wasn't power hitting, stolen bases, homers or two-out RBIs; it was their pitching. I used to have to bat against Early Wynn, Bob Lemon, Ray Narleski, Mike Garcia, and Don Mossi in Cleveland, and I've seen some wonderful staffs—like the one we built in the sixties with the Mets—but I don't know if there was ever a pitching staff as strong, one through ten, as the New York Yankees of 1998.

You had five good starters in David Cone, Andy Pettitte, David Wells, Orlando (El Duque) Hernandez, and Hideki Irabu. That's two good lefthanded starters and three good righties, each of them with different speeds, looks, and strengths. With that starting pitching alone, they're like the Atlanta Braves: You know you're going to have a chance to win the game every single day. You're never overmatched. In today's game, watered down as it is, that's rare.

How deep was the staff? Irabu, who won 13 games and had a hell of a year, never worked in the World Series. Never threw a pitch! More than that, their bullpen was deep. Strong middle relief from both sides. The top closer in the game, Mariano Rivera, with his 36 saves, to come in and shut the door. You had six pitchers with ten or more victories. That's something. Casey won ten World Series in twelve years, and he never had a pitching staff that strong, deep, or dominant. But what I'm saying is, what wins you games in baseball—and maybe even makes you the greatest of all time—ain't always what makes the headlines. The Yankees proved that again.

Even their manager, Mr. Torre, did a hell of a job. He ain't exactly "tra-la-la" like the Perfesser was, but he's the right man for that ballclub. He's a native New Yorker. Very steady person. Has his players ready in the right situations. Most of all, as Joe will tell you himself, he knows how to stay out of the way and let them do their jobs. That's a big part of the game.

So once again, in 1998—The Year That Saved Baseball—you end up coming back to the Yankees. That's where it all started for me, and where you always begin and end when you talk about the game. The mystique and the history are there, the power of the name alone, the team of Ruth, Gehrig, DiMaggio, Yogi, Mantle, and Maris. It's always had value. Generally, that name has stood for playing the game right. It still does. And when I think of all that's happening in baseball right now, I wonder what the greatest manager of all time, their best manager ever, would think.

I don't know for sure. In all the years I knew Casey, I never heard him talk about the off-the-field aspects of baseball. He was a nuts-and-bolts guy. I know he'd have loved McGwire in that lineup, maybe batting between Maris and Mantle. He'd have realized Mark can field his position and is a student of the game. I think those long homers would've made his jaw drop—he'd have to make up some new words to describe 'em—but he'd still be the only guy you ever met calling the greatest slugger in baseball "doctor." He never could remember anybody's name.

What about where the game is headed? Could a Casey Stengel still relate to the players? Would he still enjoy it as much? It's a hell of a question.

I do remember how in the old days, forty-some years ago, Hank Bauer and me and our buddies would go out after a long day of spring training with Casey. We'd get us a few tasty beverages, get ourselves all worked up and make some noise, and we'd end up making our way back to the ballfield in the middle of the night. That was kind of my stage.

I'd take the boys right around the bases, pointing and gesturing and standing over 'em just the way Casey had done that day. I'm a hell of a mimic—you don't have to twist my arm to give you my Gussie Busch, Gene Autry, or Stan Musial—and I'd do the old guy's gruff voice, wave my arms, and talk just the way he did. I'd go through what he'd said exactly that day, in exactly his tone of voice, in his exact words. Most of these guys couldn't understand Casey in the first place, and when they heard that doubletalk come right out of my mouth at two in the morning, I'd leave 'em rolling in the basepaths. I think Casey knew I could imitate him—stuff like that gets around a clubhouse—but if he did, he never said a thing.

Well, I see Hank and a lot of the other ex-Yankees at Roger's golf tournament every year. It's in Fargo, Roger's hometown, every July. This year, as a matter of fact, I was telling everybody that Mark McGwire would break Roger's record by Labor Day. Nobody thought he could keep up the pace he was setting, but I said, "Hey, McGwire can go into a slump and still break it, because he's capable of hitting ten in a week." He tied it September 7, then broke it the next night, so I was off by a day. Not bad.

But anyway, every year, like clockwork, I walk into the cocktail lounge at the Fargo Holiday Inn, and there's Hank, laughing that laugh of his, and the first words out of his mouth are, "Hey, Whitey! Give us a little Stengel!" And the show starts, just like it did forty years ago.

And what I end up saying is some of the stuff he

always said: "Now, Mr. Lopez, he has some pretty good pitchers over there in Cleveland, and they're gonna win him some games. But we've got Mr. Ford and Mr. Raschi and Mr. Lopat over here, and they're gonna win us some games, and I'm gonna teach you how to pick the ball up off this wall," and so on and so forth. His words just come right out. And in my mind's eye, I see those kids in rookie camp, gathered around Casey and listening. And I'm one of them. I'm cocky, but I'm nervous, I'm soaking it all in. Hell, man, I ain't stupid. I want to wear the Yankee pinstripes. The greatest uniform on earth.

Then I try to picture Casey doing the same thing today, with the young guys we have now. Is it really the same? I see him surrounded by first-round draft picks, bonus babies with millions in the bank—kids who get their money and fame whether they ever learn a single thing or not—and what are they doing? They're clowning around, socking each other on the arm, goofing off. They're thinking about the home runs they're going to hit and all the money they're going to make. And suddenly Stengelese—the best language for baseball anyone ever invented—starts to sound like gobbledygook.

Then I remember: In the strangest times, it's the best people among us who look like fools. That's where the hope is. I think about the guy who drank all those writers under the table, who had the bird under his hat, who knew the sport from top to bottom and taught it to me one little bit at a time but never, ever forgot it was a game.

And I see him at one of the newfangled ballparks— like Coors in Denver, Ted Turner Field in Atlanta, the Jake in Cleveland. And something funny happens.

He's standing at second and gazing up at the VideoTron, smiling and scratching his head. He's never seen a scoreboard like that. He looks around and marvels at the size of the place. He sees the picnic areas where we used to have bullpens, and later on, he heads to the concession stands. He orders up some tacos, some sushi, and a bottle of Guinness stout. "Hey Herzog," he hollers through a mouthful of food. "Try some of this! Best grub you ever ate!"

Then I see him at Bank One Ballpark, the spanking-new Diamondbacks field, with that sliding roof, computerized amenities, and swimming pool they have behind the fence. A lot of the big stars are there—Griffey, McGwire, Chipper Jones—gathered in the outfield. And Casey's hitting fungoes off that swimming-pool wall, teaching 'em the bounces.

Even Albert Belle's there, leaning on his corked bat and scowling. "Hey, Doctor," Casey says to Albert, poking him in the collarbone. "Ever seen *that* kinda fence before?" And he hits another one. Even Albert cracks a smile.

McGwire is laughing out loud, and so is Griffey, and the other guys are, too. They're ballplayers, and they're listening to the master talk their game. And you know what? They're having the time of their lives.

• Index •

382